Walking on Fences

A Girl's Life on the Marolt Ranch in Aspen

Vicki Marolt Buchanan

Copyright © 2023 by Vicki Marolt Buchanan

All rights reserved. Except as permitted under US Copyright Act of 1976, no part of this publication may be reproduced, distributed, or stored in a database or retrieval system without the prior written permission of the author.

ISBN: 979-8-9871403-0-7

Library of Congress Control Number: 2022920772

Vicki Marolt Buchanan
19201 Sonoma Highway, No. 243
Sonoma, CA 95476
vickimarolt@gmail.com

Cover Design and Formatting: Word-2-Kindle

Photo Credits

Cover Photo: Betty Marolt

Back Cover: Original Photograph for the Postcard in the Prologue
Copyright © Robert C. Bishop Photography LLC

Dedicated to Mom, Dad, Keith, Judy, Peggy, and the family and friends who shared our ranch and our home beyond the shadow of Aspen Mountain.

Chapters

Prologue - A Day on the Ranch vii
Part I – People and Places 1
   Family Background 2
   The Setting – The Homestead 31
      Entrance to Aspen 32
      Our House 36
      The Outbuildings 53
      Water 67
   The Characters 72
Part II – Life Before School 101
   On the Ranch 102
   Going to Town 114
   Across the River 134
Part III – Grade School 145
   After the Midland 146
      New People – New Friends 147
      Pent-up Demand – Remodeling, Jeeps, and Furniture 155
   The Seasons 172
      Fall 173
      Christmas 186
      Winter 204
      Spring 224
      Summer 239
   Transition Year 284
Part IV – The Next Six Years 305
   Only Child 306

  High School 322
    The Start – Freshman Year 323
    The Pinnacle - Sophomore Year 336
    Upper Classman 356
  Summer of 1967 372
Part V – Home and Away 387
  The Aftermath 388
  Gone But Not Forgotten 406
Epilog 417

Prologue

A Day on the Ranch

Prologue

A Day on the Ranch

Shortly after I joined an Aspen group on Facebook, I ran across the R.C. Bishop postcard shown below. In the foreground are the Meadows, the old racetrack, and a corner of the tent for the music school. In the background is the then recently cut Thunderbowl run on Aspen Highlands. The Highlands opened in 1958, so this photo could have been very close to that year.

Copyright © Robert C. Bishop Photography LLC

In the dead center of this photo, there is a discernible triangle formed by the Castle Creek Road, Highway 82, and Castle Creek itself. The triangle is the center of our ranch and includes the big field, the cottonwoods along the Marolt Ditch, our house, our barns, and the big building we called the granary. We also owned some property on the east side of Castle Creek and most of the sloping property on the west and south of the Castle Creek Road.

When I saw this photo, I felt a profound longing for I knew I was there. On that day, if it were possible to have enough magnification and resolution, one would see Patty, our horse, and Nipper, our dog. Dad is near the granary sharpening and replacing a couple of blades on the hay mower. He has just finished mowing a section of hay in the big field – the section lying flat in the photo. Mom is hanging laundry. In this photo, I am a microscopic dot lying on the granary bridge.

I am almost nine. My long brown hair is in two braids, and I am wearing clean "play clothes." I have on a pair of hand-me-down boy jeans with rolled cuffs, a short-sleeved pink cotton shirt with a permanent mustard stain below the collar, dingy formerly white, but clean, socks, and brown leather shoes with a strap across the instep.

It is mid-day, the sun is high, and dinner is over. We call the noontime meal dinner because, as part of the ranching tradition, this is the biggest meal of the day. The evening meal is supper. Dinner fuels the day's work.

For dinner, we had roast beef, mashed potatoes, green beans from the garden, and a tossed salad of leaf lettuce – also from the garden – dressed with homemade French vinaigrette dressing. I always made it fresh in a Mason jar with half oil, half vinegar, salt, pepper, dry mustard, a bit of sugar, and some paprika. My sister Peggy made a cake. Cream puffs were for Sundays.

Except for dessert and the salad dressing, Mom cooked the meal. To tease her, Dad used to say, "If I built your mother a kitchen counter 40 feet long, she would mess it up making a cheese sandwich."

As always, there were lots of dishes, because we have no dishwasher, there were dishes and glasses and many pots and pans. By now, they are all done. My sisters and I cleaned up. Peggy and Judy are teenagers six and eight years older than me. While Peggy washed and I dried the dishes, Judy swept and mopped the floor. The double sink is below a window. It has a view of our yard and a stand of cottonwoods beyond the fence. The west side of Aspen Mountain fills the background of the large picture window. The kitchen was designed on purpose to incorporate this view. When we remodeled the kitchen, Mom said, "If I have to stand here and do dishes, I might as well have something nice to look at."

Before dinner, our uncles, Steve and Ted, left the daily gathering in our kitchen and are now at their own homes. Because Steve and Ted are no longer actively involved in ranching, they drop by most weekday mornings for coffee and conversation. These get-togethers are shorter and more sporadic in the summer because Dad is still running his portion of the ranch on the south side of Highway 82.

Although Steve lives in town, he has what he calls "the pasture" off Owl Creek Road. He checks on his cattle grazing on the property and does chores. During the mornings, when they are not at the pasture, Polly, Steve's wife, doesn't like "Stevie" being underfoot. She sends him to our house.

Steve and Polly have no children. Ted never married and recently sold his ranch. His ranch, west of the Castle Creek Road, belonged to my grandfather and was the family homestead. We call it the old ranch. When Ted sold the old ranch, Dad gave him a lot across Castle Creek upon which Ted built a small house.

I'm not sure what Ted does when he goes home. He reads a lot. He is the middle of making an iron spiral staircase extending from his lower driveway to an upper deck.

Earlier this morning, Dad sat on a kitchen chair between the table and the west-facing kitchen window where he rested his right elbow on the sill. Mom busied herself around the kitchen. Ted leaned in his usual spot in the corner between the kitchen cabinets and the back porch door jam. He was wearing his hearing aid, which is on a band spanning the bald spot on the top of his head and resting behind his ears. It had a small wire leading to a transistor radio looking device in the breast pocket of his western-style work shirt. As he stood, he continually fidgeted, adjusting a dial on the device. He said sometimes it buzzed, and he changed the volume to stop the buzzing.

Steve hunkered down with his back against the narrow wall between the interior back porch door and the refrigerator alcove. This wall is the place where he always "sits" and from which he tends to pontificate.

While sitting in this spot, Steve rolled his cigarettes. He took out a small can of tobacco from his overalls and tapped some onto one of his Zig-Zag cigarette papers, and using one hand, rolled it, and licked it closed. As he smoked, the ashes grew and grew until he knocked them into his large, calloused hand and put them into the rolled-up cuff of his bibbed overalls. When he left our house this morning, as he entered the driveway, he rolled down his pant cuffs and let the ashes disappear in the breeze.

Mom and Dad also smoke, but they used an ashtray that was overflowing on the kitchen table. Dad used to roll cigarettes, but he and Mom now buy Winstons. They buy Winston cigarettes because they own R.J. Reynolds stock. Ted owns the same stock, but he never smoked, and even having a stake in the company does not motivate him to buy cigarettes.

This morning they talked, as usual, about the stock market or politics. It seems they disagreed on politics because I heard Steve use his assertive lecturing tone. I wouldn't be surprised if this is when Ted turns down the volume on his hearing aid. I think Mom and Dad are Democrats because I cast my pretend ballot in the Weekly Reader presidential election for Adlai Stevenson. I suspect I followed my parents' lead.

Another reoccurring subject is the stock market. The stock market is where the brothers put much of their money after they sold portions of the Midland Ranch a few years ago. Today, I overheard an argument about which was better – General Motors or Ford. They agreed that American Can and Kern County Land and Cattle were good investments.

I am now lying on my stomach on the bridge to the granary below – the granary bridge. It crosses the Marolt Ditch, which at this spot, varies from three to five feet wide and one to two feet deep. Dad built the granary bridge in the late 40s, replacing two railroad ties. It has a wooden deck attached to floor beams between two concrete abutments. The bridge is eight feet long, four feet wide, and a foot above the water. It used to be outside the yard – now it is inside.

I lay on this bridge often when I feel like daydreaming or when I am kind of bored or when I write. I am rarely bored on the ranch. When I'm at school, I dream about all the things I would do if I were home. I could decorate one of the playhouses. I could clean out a section of the granary. I could work on my 4-H sewing project. I could read or write. I could paint or draw. I could get Patty and go for a ride. I could throw balls for Nipper to chase and hide. I could even practice the piano; now, that is desperation.

I can't watch television because we don't get good television reception. Most of the time, the TV set our Denver relatives gave us picks up soundless shadows in the snow. Some of the town folk, including my uncle, Albert, are working on bringing in television from Grand Junction. The channel works from time to time when we turn the antennas just so. Regardless, in the middle of the day, with no friends around, I don't mind just lying on the granary bridge.

The granary bridge goes from the south lawn to the trail leading down to the granary. The granary is a large building we use for storing grain, but it also houses Dad's workshop and a storage area. It is one of the remaining buildings from a massive mining facility, known as the Lixiviation Works, that once existed on this property. The granary is on a level about fifteen feet below our house.

The granary sits near the edge of a steep riverbank descending to Castle Creek in the canyon below. The western portion of Aspen Mountain, the part with the angled sedimentary outcroppings visible from town and the ranch, is across the river. It looms above this bridge. From my viewpoint, Aspen Mountain is close enough and big enough to blot out half the sky when I look in that direction.

In the mining days, what I call Aspen Mountain was West Aspen Mountain. Some people now call it Shadow Mountain. I never use that name. When I have to distinguish it from the middle part of Aspen Mountain with the ski runs, I sometimes refer to the central portion as Ajax. Newcomers gave it this name because of the Ajax Mine on that part of the mountain.

The steep trail descending to the granary starts at the gate at the end of the granary bridge. Mom talks about one winter day when she filled two buckets of skim milk from the milk separator and gingerly headed to the granary to feed the chickens that roosted inside. She slipped and fell, losing the milk and gashing her leg. She sat in the puddle of milk, in the snow, and sobbed. Mom says she felt like the woman who wrote *The Egg and I*.

The hillside from the bridge to the granary has no trees near the bridge. On the south side, are a few red dogwood bushes leading to some willows and cottonwood trees further south along the ditch. North of the granary path, the hillside is mostly covered with soccer ball sized boulders, wild Oregon grapes, and a few small cactus plants. I built my Log Cabin village on this hillside earlier in the summer. My village had roads and bridges and fences made of small stones cemented together by silt from the ditch. The houses were Log Cabin maple syrup cans.

I wanted to emulate the Log Cabin village my brother, Keith, made further up the ditch a few years ago. He not only built a village;

he gave it a complete water system he engineered using connecting beer cans stretched far enough up the ditch to drain into the small waterways surrounding his town. Not surprisingly, Keith is now attending the University of Colorado to become a civil engineer. Although my village was also on a ditch bank, I could only supply water one bucket at a time.

As I said, the granary bridge is in our yard. That was not always the case. Last summer, Mom and Dad decided to build a wooden fence and included the ditch in the yard. When they decided to bring the ditch inside the yard, I guess they were pretty sure I was old enough not to drown.

The new fence also enclosed a grove of serviceberry bushes and a large boulder in the southeastern corner of the lawn. Before it was made of wood, the fence was one made of utilitarian diamond-mesh wire hanging on mismatched posts.

Keith, who is thirteen years older than me, was responsible for building the new fence. He had access to heavy equipment because he worked for Jim Hayes every summer in Jim's earthmoving business. With Dad's input, Keith surveyed the site, made the measurements, ordered the redwood, and did the work during his summer breaks from college and while in the army reserves. He dug the postholes himself. Dad helped only to coax out a few of the boulders with the help of a friend who knew how to use some strategically placed dynamite. As Dad says, "They don't call it the Rocky Mountains for nothing."

This particular fence has one-by-six boards screwed to the top of the posts and is stable enough and strong enough for balancing. It surrounds the entire quarter-acre yard and is painted white. Everyone takes part in the annual ritual of scraping and repainting sections of the white fence. As with the Golden Gate Bridge, it is a job that is never done. In the meantime, it is a perfect fence for one of my favorite activities – fence walking.

Because the ditch borders the east and north edges of the yard, the fence crosses the ditch in two places. The area on the southeast entrance of the ditch is a little tricky because the serviceberry bushes and willows overhang the fence. They need trimming to do unobstructed fence walking. The crossing in the northwest corner of the yard is high and over rapidly flowing water. It is the most challenging section of the fence and the only part that scares me.

Before Keith replaced the old wire fence, the vegetable garden was in the southwest corner of the yard. Dad plowed it under when bindweed took over. The garden is now across the ditch and the granary road on the north side of the house. A wire mesh fence surrounds it to prevent our horses and cattle, when they are allowed to graze in the area, from trampling the vegetables.

The garden is near the ditch on purpose. Dad built a metal diversion box, so the garden is irrigated with water flowing down the neat rows. The small ditch also irrigates the several-acre scrub triangle between the main road to our house and two roads leading to the granary. In the spring, wildflowers like lupine, Indian paintbrush, and alpine sunflowers cover the upper half of the scrub area. The diversion box is next to a pipe that leads directly to the Red Butte Cemetery about a mile away. They use this water for the lawn surrounding the graves.

The garden is large – twenty-five by thirty-five feet. Each spring, Dad brings up manure to mix with the soil. Dad's manure pile, which sits behind the red cow barn, is his version of composting. By all accounts, it is some of the best gardening manure ever – fluffy and dry. Mom and her sister, Pearl, and their brother, Riley, use it for their prized sweet peas.

Ray Akin, who lives across the river at the base of Aspen Mountain, trades raspberries for manure. He has a large raspberry patch in his back yard and supplies several local stores. One of my summer chores is going with Mom to pick raspberries. Pick one – eat one. We did that a few days ago. When we came home, we had raspberries and cream, and later Mom made a raspberry pie.

Our garden has green beans, peas, spinach, green onions, carrots, beets, new potatoes, cabbage, cauliflower, and lots of leaf and head lettuce. From time to time, Mom tried to grow other crops. Neither corn nor tomatoes matured soon enough to yield much of a harvest before the first frost. Birds ate the strawberries. To prevent the carnage, Dad built wooden planter boxes with chicken wire covers. Although that stopped the birds, the strawberry beds only lasted a few years. I suspect opening and closing the large lids to get a few berries ended up being more trouble than it was worth. Dad removed the covers and attached them to the back of the house as trellises for Mom's sweet peas.

I helped plant the garden this spring. We set out the rows with strings and used the grubbing hoe to make troughs for the water. Everything we planted came from Burpee Seeds except the onions, potatoes, cauliflower, and cabbage that came from starts. Mom got the cabbage starts for a penny from Mrs. Zelnick, who lives in the east end of town.

After the lettuce started in June, the garden bounty was the focus of our meals. Once or twice daily, we go to the garden, get the vegetables, and rinse off some of the dirt from the root vegetables in the ditch before rinsing and cleaning them in the kitchen sink. One of our favorite side dishes is what Mom calls Mulligan stew. I don't think this is traditional Mulligan stew. Her version is baby carrots, peas, and pearl onions in a white sauce.

During the day, I often go to the garden for a quick carrot or pea snack. Nipper loves to catch and eat the peapods I drop in the ditch.

For a short time before the wooden fence was complete and the ditch was still on the outside of the yard, the garden bridge was a single large plank. It was over the part of the ditch with a steeper incline and "rapids." It was the future site of the scary fence-walking spot. Mom used to be terrified of that route to the garden because the plank was only about a foot and a half wide and bounced over the quickly moving water. Sometimes she went out of her way to use the culvert and backtrack to her garden.

Her fear was worse when she came "face to face" with Bambi, my black-faced lamb. He stood like Billy Goat Gruff in the middle of the plank. She would shout for him to "scoot," but that only encouraged him to stand his ground. I had to come to get him. Bambi liked to butt people behind the knees, especially anyone precariously balancing on a plank over the ditch.

Bambi no longer lives on the ranch. Every year we get orphan, bummer lambs from the Gerbaz ranch and raise them for the summer. Judy and Peggy raise theirs for their 4-H livestock projects. I raise mine for fun. When the lambs arrived, we fed them warm milk in brown beer bottles with nipples. When Bambi was no longer a lamb, I returned him to the Gerbaz ranch to join the rest of the flock. My sister's lambs were auctioned and sold after the 4-H show. I choose to believe Bambi is living a long and happy life cavorting with other lambs and sheep on the Watson Divide above the Gerbaz Ranch.

As soon as the fence was changed to include the ditch, Dad made a wider garden bridge on the north side of the house leading to the garden. He put together two long three-inch by fifteen-inch planks. It sits less than a foot above the water. The bridge is now on a direct path from the front door of our house and the garden.

It's only technically the "front door" because of the architectural styling. It is a fancy door with beveled glass windows atop a stone porch and a foyer with a curved arch inside the door. However, we never use it as an entrance to the house. That's because the front door is on the north, snowy, side of the house. It is far from the parking area. There is no sidewalk leading to this porch. Instead, everyone enters our home through the back door. It is on the west side of the house at the end of a concrete sidewalk leading from the driveway. An enclosed room we call the back porch connects directly to the kitchen. We use the front door for access to the garden, and in the summer with a screen door, it provides a cross breeze in the house.

The ditch runs along the east and north sides of the yard. There is an apple tree outside the fence at the northeast corner of the yard. The white blossoms on the tree are beautiful, but the apples are bland. Dad says the tree probably grew from the apple core of a store-bought apple not native to this climate. I suspect someone working on the ditch left it.

The inside of the ditch, from the granary bridge through the curve, is rimmed with lilac bushes. They are mostly the French varieties with large, aromatic flowers. There are two Persian lilacs that Mom accidentally purchased to fill in for two of the French lilacs that did not make it through one winter. Their blossoms are smaller, and they do not have nearly as much aroma. This summer, the lilac bushes are about five feet high.

They finished blooming a couple of weeks ago. That's too bad. They smelled so good and filled vases throughout the house. Mom used them to decorate family gravesites at Red Butte Cemetery even though it was too late for Decoration Day. Because of the lilacs, the granary bridge is not completely visible from the back of the house. It seems private – perfect for hiding when we play kick-the-can.

The water under the granary bridge is deep and dark and moves slowly. There is tall grass on the bank and a silt-like mud below the surface. It is a perfect place for minnows to spawn. On another day, I would amuse myself for hours catching minnows to see if I could break the record of the 48 minnows I caught one particularly good day last summer. Catching minnows involves wading along the edge of the bank and reaching down and scooping them into cupped hands and temporarily putting them in a Mason jar. It must be at the right time of day – not too bright but not too shadowy. Mid-morning is the best time to catch minnows.

I love to look at them. Minnows are perfect miniature trout, less than an inch long– transparent silver with rainbow stripes or brown spots. I can see their skeletons and internal organs and their tiny beating hearts. Although I always let them go, it is rare to see an adult trout in the ditch. That doesn't keep me from putting a worm on a fishing line attached to a willow branch and dangling it for hours off the bridge. I have never caught a fish in the ditch. I don't think I have ever caught a fish period.

On the other hand, Dad catches lots of fish. After most of his work is done, or sometimes before he starts, Dad goes over the bank behind the barns and drops down the steep hill through the bushes into the Castle Creek riverbed. We own the land under Castle Creek from the south end of the ranch to Highway 82. Most of it is in a steep canyon.

Dad is a fly fisherman. I'm not sure if he ties his flies in that tiny vice on the workbench in the basement or if he buys them. Dad keeps them in a small leather book with felt pages to which a variety of flies are attached and organized in some fashion. He knows the exact time of day, the right sun, the right fly, and the precise holes in which to use them. Sometimes he goes with my brother Keith, but mostly goes by himself and rarely shares his secret fishing spots. When he goes over the hill, he wears the irrigating waders so he can go into the pools of the river. I know it can be kind of dangerous with the deep holes and the fast-moving water, and it makes me nervous when he goes over the hill.

On the other hand, I can understand how much Dad enjoys these times. I'm sure there is something meditative about the process – flicking the line, reeling it in, the dappled light in the canyon through the cottonwood trees. The world is blocked out except for the sound of the rushing river and a sliver of blue sky. Years from now, when I see the posters for *A River Runs Through It*, I think that could be Dad standing on a rock in the middle of Castle Creek.

When Dad goes fishing, after a couple of hours, he returns with his wicker creel filled with freshly cleaned ten to twelve-inch rainbow or German brown trout. He'll rinse the creel with the hose and hang it on the end of the clothesline pole to dry. I like the smell. So does my cat.

Sometimes for supper or breakfast, Mom dredges the trout in flour and fries them in bacon grease. We peel pinkish flesh from the bones. Although I am not much of a fish person, I like trout. Each time she serves trout, Mom warns us to watch for stray bones. She says that some little child somewhere was not careful with his fish bones, and one caught in their throat, and they either died or, if they survived, they were never quite the same.

Besides wading and catching minnows in the ditch in our yard, my friends, cousins, and I "swim" from the granary bridge to the garden bridge. The water in the ditch is cold – very cold – but "swimming" is not swimming at all. It involves getting in the water, which varies from a foot or two feet deep, lying on our stomachs at the granary bridge, and walking downstream on our hands with our bodies and legs floating behind. The goal is to "swim" from the granary bridge, behind the lilacs, through a willow stand, and end at the garden bridge – a breathtaking feat. It is not at all fun, even if we pretend it is when showing off to friends or out of town relatives. It is horrible. There is no way I will ever do this without an audience. On the other hand, tubing for the mile or so on the ditch above our yard is fun. It does not involve exposing as much skin to the cold water.

So, on this day, at the moment R.C. Bishop snapped this photograph, I am lying on the bridge on my stomach, resting my head on my left arm and looking downstream at the slow-moving water. My right arm is dangling over the edge of the bridge. I am poking a stick into the surface of the water to form a wishbone wake. The sky and those few wispy clouds in the photograph reflect on the dark mirrored surface.

Today I am dreaming about how someday I will write a book about how much I love my life and my family and my friends and how glad I am to live on this ranch, in this house just beyond the shadow of Aspen Mountain.

Part I

People and Places

Family Background

Family Background

The Marolts

Michael Marolt, my father, was one of twelve children. His parents were Frank Marolt and Francesca "Frances" Rupert. Their children in descending ages were Mary, Pauline, Frank Jr., Angelina "Elsie," Rudolph "Rudy," William "Bill," Louis, Dorothy, Stephen "Steve," Michael "Mike," Rosaline "Rose," and Theodore "Ted."

Frank was from Marolče Ribnica Slovenia – a lovely mountainous area reminiscent of Colorado. He was raised as the oldest son on his father's farm, along with eight siblings. As a young man, because he was from that region Slovenia, he obtained a Keiser and Koening license. That license allowed him to sell chestnuts at St. Stephens Cathedral in Vienna. At one point, Frank tried to join the army. They rejected him either for his physical condition or because of his age. He decided to come to the United States as had his siblings Anton, John, and Helen before him.

Before coming to the United States in 1887, Frank lived in Graz, Austria. He made his way to Cleveland, Ohio, which was a primary destination for those arriving from Frank's region of Europe. After staying in Cleveland for a short time, he and Anton Kastelic headed west. When they left Ohio, they said, "Good-bye, Cleveland. We're going to America."

Frank and Anton walked, stopping here and there to earn money for food and other necessities. They landed in Leadville, Colorado. Frank worked for a while as a miner but later began working in a saloon and boarding house for another Slovenian, Matt Mautz. The saloon and boarding house were in Stringtown, a Slovenian enclave on the west side of Leadville. Matt and Frank eventually owned the property together.

In the meantime, in 1893, Frances Rupert, who was from Ig near Ljubljana, Slovenia, came to the United States. Her sister, Mary, who was married to Matt Mautz, and her sister Rose were already in Leadville. Once in Leadville, Frances met Frank. They married and, over the next years, had the first of their twelve children, Mary, Pauline, Frank Jr., Elsie, and Rudy.

During this time, Matt, who was quite an entrepreneur, and Mary moved across the mountains to Aspen, Colorado, where Matt opened another saloon and boarding house at 700 East Cooper Street. Matt paid $220 for the Aspen property. He then sold the Stringtown saloon to Frank.

In 1900, Matt was on the move again – this time to Salida, Colorado. Frank purchased the Aspen saloon from Matt and moved his family to Aspen. He named the saloon the Frank Marolt Bar.

Although no longer in the same town, the Mautz and Marolt families remained close. Over the years, they sponsored each other's children at their confirmations. The cousins traveled across the mountains, and the families got together often.

The Frank Marolt Bar, the boarding house, and the attached home covered the lot from street to alley. The boarding house was above the bar, and the family lived in a two-story addition in the back. Frances cooked and cleaned for the boarders and her growing family. Between 1902 and 1914, Frank and Frances had seven more children – Bill, Louis, Dorothy, Steve, Mike, Rose, and Ted.

From time to time, Frances sponsored Slovenian women to come to the United States to help in the boarding house. The women ended up marrying local men, and they and their families became part of the Aspen community. Frank and Frances paid for the women's weddings and acted as their sponsors. Frances often made the wedding dress. Some of their married names were Garrish, Zupancis, Skufca, Gregorich, and Oblak.

One of Frances's Slovenian boarders, who was working at the Montezuma Mine, came stumbling into the boarding house, covered in blood, and asking for help. As it turns out, the boarder stabbed and killed another Slovenian man in a fight in another saloon.

Such fights and murders were not uncommon on Cooper Street. The boarder was arrested at the boarding house. It is unknown whether he was charged or convicted of murder. The evening was even more memorable because it was the night before my uncle Steve was born.

The family raised sheep and milk cows on the back and side of the building. Although the front and side of the saloon part of the building looked like it was clapboard construction, in reality, much of the front part of the building was a log structure. It was one of only two buildings on the Cooper side of the street. Because of the slumping economy, many of the lots around the buildings were empty.

The family kept their carriage horses at Bill Tagert's livery on Cooper Street west of Spring Street. The older girls, Mary, Pauline, and Elsie helped take care of their younger siblings. Based on numerous photographs, it appears the girls had an active social life and a large circle of friends. They exchanged clothes, talked of fashions, bemoaned their lowly status as Slovenians or Austrians, gossiped about some of the more socially acceptable girls, and took lots of photographs.

When they lived in town, the kids went to the Lincoln School along with the other east end, Slovenian kids. The Marolt boys enjoyed living in town. In the summer, they played on Aspen Mountain and caught trips up the hill with the muleskinners hauling ore from the mines. Sometimes, they got to ride one of the team horses into town. In the winter, they skated on the rivers – especially at Stillwater and the pond at the Newman Mine. If it was cold enough, they helped flood the river below the Cooper Street Bridge and skated there. They used toboggans to sled down the hill on the side of the mountain leading to Monarch Street. Sledding was especially fun in the moonlight.

In 1915, Colorado enacted its form of prohibition – years before the Volstead Act. Frank could not survive operating his business selling soft drinks. Therefore, in 1916, he reverted to his family's roots of farming and bought the Thomas Owens ranch on the outskirts of Aspen. The family moved to the ranch in January of 1917. The school-age kids ranged from Bill, who was 15, to Dad, who was seven. The kids continued to walk to the Lincoln School that winter but transitioned to the "more prestigious" west end Washington School the following year.

The ranch was in the area between Maroon Creek Road, what became the Castle Creek Road, and the base of the mountain south of the property. Shortly after buying the ranch, Frank sold the western half. He thought that part of the property was worthless for farming or ranching. That part now houses the Aspen schools.

The portion of the ranch Frank kept was an elevated area between a line drawn south from the intersection of Castle Creek Road, Maroon Creek Roads, Highway 82, and to the west, until the property sloped down toward Maroon Creek. It is the area west and south of the Prince of Peace Church, which is now known as the Aspen Chapel. It included what is now Meadowood.

On this part of the ranch, there was a small two-story house, a couple of barns, and a few smaller outbuildings. When the family moved to the ranch, the boys slept in makeshift living quarters in what had been one of the barns. It was painted or whitewashed white to look like it was part of the house. The house overlooked the plateau toward town and the Holden Lixiviation Works, a large mining complex across Castle Creek from Aspen.

The family raised cattle and grew hay and potatoes. They had several milk cows and other farm animals, including both saddle and workhorses. In later years, they raised cattle. The family referred to this property as the "old ranch" or the "little ranch." The sisters commented that the move from town to the ranch was good for the boys because it kept them from running around the streets in town and getting into trouble.

As far as the girls were concerned, by the time of the move, Mary, who was 23, was going to school in Greeley to become a teacher, and Elsie, who was 19, was attending Barnes Business College in Denver. When Mary returned from school in the summers, she stayed in a small house she owned. At the same time, her sisters were going to college, Pauline married a handsome local miner named John Ambrose. They also lived in a small house in the east end of town near Mary's home.

Pauline lamented the fact that the Midland Railway was closing, and there would only be one train to and from town, adding to her feeling of isolation. She referred to Aspen as "this Godforsaken town." Mary complained that when the train left town, it was "dull and dead worse, worse every day." In the summer of 1917, Pauline and John had a daughter named Julia. While taking care of her daughter, Pauline took over caring for the two youngest siblings. At that time, Rose was five, and Ted was three.

Sometime in early 1918, Frank Jr. and Elsie, who had now finished business school, left Aspen for California. They went to Crocket to live with their aunt and uncle, Rose and John Smaker. Rose was Frances's sister. Rose and John moved to Crockett from Leadville about the time Frances and Frank moved to Aspen. Frances's sister Mary and her husband, Matt, remained in Salida.

Elsie got a job as a secretary at the C & H Sugar Factory. While in California, she started dating a young man from Oakland named George. All the while, she stayed in touch with her sisters and mother and sent them packages with the newest fashions and shoes from Oakland and San Francisco.

Frank Jr. planned on working as a machinist in one of the many factories, refineries, or shipyards in the bay area. He was unable to find work. Because he was a Catholic, the unions rejected him. At the time, there was a general prejudice against Slovenians because they considered them to be Bohunks, which at the time was a disparaging term for laborers from east-central Europe.

The younger children experienced some discrimination at school or in comments from their peers. While in high school, the older girls commented that they looked pretty good despite being Austrian girls. In later years, some family members fondly identify themselves as Bohunks, embracing that once pejorative term.

Because he could not find work as a machinist, to employ his skills, Frank, Jr. joined the army. For a while, he was stationed at Camp Kearny near San Diego, which was one of the first places in the United States hit with what would become known as the Spanish flu. Fortunately for Frank, the strain at Camp Kearny was relatively mild.

Aspen did not fare as well. In 1918, the flu pandemic hit Aspen. Pauline and her husband, John, became ill. At the time, Mary was teaching school in Craig, Colorado. When her school closed to prevent the spread of the flu, she returned home to help the family.

Everyone in the family experienced the flu in one form or the other. Pauline and John were extremely ill. Dorothy, who was 13, wrote to Elsie, on Pauline's behalf, to thank her for one of her gifts. Dorothy said Pauline could not write because she was too sick. Pauline died on October 25.

Upon returning home, Mary became ill. A doctor gave her a blood transfusion from someone who survived the virus, but she died at the family home within hours of the transfusion.

On November 12, Louis, who was fourteen, died in the hospital. There is little information about him. He was in the middle. He had a sweet, grinning face, which exuded a gentle spirit. He had trouble in school and got mostly failing grades. Louis may have had a learning disability. At the same time, Steve was making high marks.

Louis and Ella Elisha, who was 15, were the youngest victims of the pandemic. Ella died on the same day Pauline died. On that day, according to papers, five people died, and another four were buried.

Frank Jr. was transitioning from Camp Kearney to Illinois, where he was training to be a railroad engineer before deployment to the war front. He heard of Pauline's death soon after it happened. He did not learn Mary and Louis died for many weeks after they were gone. Although he tried desperately to get home, the army was not accommodating.

In the meantime, Elsie came home after Mary and Louis died. She and Rudy both contracted the flu. The doctors told the family neither would survive. Rudy, who was 18, had a temperature of 107. Elsie's fever spiked to 106. She was 21. Both received the last rights of the Catholic Church. Remarkably, both survived, but the illness may have caused Elsie heart problems for the remainder of her life. Others speculated Rudy's mental health suffered because of his high fever.

World War I ended the day after Louis died. Frank Jr. finally made it home in December. Julia, who was a year old, stayed on with her father, who also survived the flu. Together he and the Marolt family raised her as part of the family. She was close to Rose, who was about seven years old.

A grisly detail left out of the history books was that so many people were dying in Aspen from the flu that there were not enough healthy people available to dig graves, especially in the frozen ground. Many people were buried in the Red Butte Cemetery under less than 14 inches of dirt. Over time, a horrible stench drifted from the cemetery. Steve recalled that after he and his brothers bought the Midland Ranch, which was adjacent to the cemetery, he went into the fields near the cemetery and, depending on the wind, might catch a whiff of the horrible smell. The odor hung on for over a decade.

After buying the ranch, Frank tore down the saloon, boarding house, and the residence and used the materials to build a big barn. When he tore down the saloon part of the building, he stored the bar, including the ornate front and back bars in one of the barns. In the 1960s, the Abbey Restaurant on Galena Street used the front bar and back bar. We do not know what happened to them when the restaurant closed. They were not in Jake's Abbey, which was the nightclub below the restaurant.

Frank was a hard worker and a stern father. As a young boy of six or seven, one of Dad's chores was to find the milk cows and bring them home for milking. One day, he went out and could not find them. Instead of coming back empty-handed and incurring his father's wrath, Dad stayed out all night and slept in a ditch. He was chilled and ended up with a cold that developed into pneumonia. The damage done to his lungs caused health problems throughout his life.

Another incident involved Steve. The family ran their cattle up Maroon Creek near Maroon Lake in the summer. Snow came early, and to save the herd from starving, Frank and Steve loaded a sleigh with hay to take to the cattle. Steve was wearing gloves, but they made it difficult for him to control the team. His father made him remove the gloves in the freezing temperatures. Not only were his hands freezing, but they were also getting cut by the reins. Steve claimed it was only the warm blood that kept his hands from freezing. Steve did not forgive his father and had scars on his hands to remind him of his anger.

At some point, Frances suffered a stroke and lost the use of her left arm. For the most part, she was able to manage on her own despite the disability. Dad described how she could cut out and sew shirts for the boys and dresses for the girls using one arm. The children were fond of her and protected her from their father's temper. While he was verbally abusive there is no indication of physical abuse of her or the children. The children referred to their parents and Ma and Papa.

As Dad's siblings grew older, they went their separate ways. All of the children graduated from high school except Bill. He was expelled from grade school, not for doing anything particularly wrong, but for getting in a fight with a school board member's son after that son made fun of Bill for being Slovenian and referred to him with some derogatory term. For his "crime," Bill was never allowed to return to school. Knowing Bill in later years, one would never guess he lacked formal education. Like Frank and Elsie before him, Bill went to California for a while but returned home. While he liked Oakland, he did not care for Crockett, where the relatives lived.

Secondary education was important to the family. Many of the children went to school after high school. Mary went to what would become the University of Northern Colorado in Greeley and became a teacher. Dorothy went to and graduated from what would become Western State College in Gunnison. She hiked over the mountains to get to school. She also became a teacher. Elsie went to Barnes Business College in Denver. Both Elsie and Dorothy married and ended up living in California.

Later, Dad, Rose, and Ted each went to college for a while. Dad went to the University of Colorado in Boulder. Rose went to Colorado College in Colorado Springs for a couple of years and graduated from nursing school at Saint Joseph Hospital in Denver. Ted went to Colorado State University for a couple of years but did not graduate.

In 1926, after Frank Jr. returned to Aspen and Steve graduated from high school, Frank Jr., Rudy, Bill, and Steve bought the Aspen Ranch from the Colorado Midland Railway. They called it the Midland Ranch. The ranch stretched over the plateau between Maroon Creek and Castle Creek and including the area through which the Midland Railroad used to run. At the time they purchased the property, there may have been some access roads, but there was no highway bisecting it. It was open land from the Midland railroad bed to Red Butte. The only property they did not own on the plateau was the 20-acre site of the Holden Lixiviation Works.

Aspen Historical Society, Cooper Family Collection

In 1929, Bill sold his portion of the ranch to Frank Jr., Rudy, and Steve. Bill loved cars and got into debt because of them. The three brothers were concerned Bill's debts would encumber their property, so they paid his debts in exchange for his share of the ranch. At about the same time, Bill married Celia Tekoucich.

The Tekoucichs were a large family that, like the Marolts, was one of the few Slovenian families living on the west end of Aspen. The two families were close.

Although Bill no longer owned a specific share of the ranch, he continued to participate in many of the ranching operations and growing potatoes and raising hogs. For a while, Bill was the one most responsible for making the traditional Slovenian sausages and meat products– klobasa, blood sausage, and headcheese. When he was not working on the ranch, Bill worked in the mines and tended bar at the Red Onion. He held the post as the daytime bartender there for decades. His red Jeep is in many photos of the Red Onion.

At the time my uncles were buying the Midland Ranch, Dad was at the University of Colorado studying engineering. While in Boulder, he worked as a waiter in what was at the time a fancy European styled restaurant – The Sunken Garden. The restaurant had a large fountain called The Sink. In 1929, while Dad was in college, Frances, who was only 58, died. Dad left college and returned home.

When she died, the mortuary was in what later became the Aspen Lumber and Supply on the southeast corner of Mill and Hopkins. Half the building was a mortuary, and the other half was a hardware store. While Frances' body was in the mortuary waiting for the rosary and high Mass, the mortuary caught fire. The presumed cause of the fire was a votive candle coming in contact with a curtain. Frances's body was severely burned, and there was no traditional open casket for the wake. The experience was traumatic for the family. Dad, who was away from home when his mother died, hoped to see her once again before the funeral.

After Frances died, Julia, who was twelve, went to live with her father's brother in Denver until her father remarried. She then lived with her father, his new wife, and her half-brother, Ivan. She remained close to the Aspen family. When Rose moved to Denver, they continued their close relationship.

In 1932, Frank Jr., Rudy, and Steve purchased the Holden Lixiviation Works site from William "Bill" Tagert for one dollar. The lixiviation works complex was built to process low-grade silver ores. At one time, it consisted of a massive four-story building and numerous other buildings. The 27,000 square-foot main building was built on several terraces descending 75 feet to Castle Creek. The terraces were perfect for the operation. They enabled the ore to move through the building with the help of gravity. Chemicals and waste products were deposited in the river. Fortunately for the environment, the plant operated for only two years.

Aspen Historical Society, Masterson Collection

The other significant buildings on the upper terraces included a sampling building which was west of the main building, a salt warehouse south of the sampling building, and an assay office located on an upper level about one hundred and fifty yards to the west. The complex also included two giant smokestacks. One of the smokestacks, closest to the sampling building, was 165 feet tall and was reputed to be the tallest smokestack in Colorado at the time. The other was 65 feet tall. The family referred to them as the big and little chimney.

The Colorado Midland Railway ran next to the buildings where it crossed Castle Creek and headed into town. When Dad was a young boy, he and his friends played "chicken" with the train. They waited for the train to appear in the distance and began running down the trestle toward town. When the train got near, they jumped to a ledge just below the tracks, crouched, and hung on. Remarkably, they all survived without getting run over or falling into the canyon below.

Shortly after the silver crash in 1893, the lixiviation works was put to other uses, but never successfully. The Midland Railway closed its Aspen operation in 1918 and dismantled the Castle Creek trestle in 1920. The largest lixiviation buildings were abandoned. Over the next decades, and especially during the great depression, bankruptcy creditors and people from town and down the valley cannibalized them for wood, windows, and metal. Most of the sandstone foundation remained intact.

A photo taken in 1934 shows the largest building partially dismantled. It certainly is missing its upper story and roof. Another building to the south and east of the big chimney was standing. On the building plans, it is the dry kiln building. All the other miscellaneous buildings over the hillside were gone or almost gone. It is unclear how much of the lixiviation complex was standing when the Marolt brothers bought the property.[1]

The remaining buildings from the lixiviation works became the center of the ranch. The brothers used them for ranching and farming operations. The sampling building included a workshop, a blacksmith shop, and grain storage. Another building, the salt shed, held livestock and tack. The brothers remodeled the assay office into a house.

With the combination of the Midland and the Holden tracts, the brothers also obtained adjudicated water rights in the Aspen Ditch. As part of the adjudication, it was renamed the Marolt Ditch.

The Marolt Ditch originally filled a reservoir on the north side of what would become Highway 82. By the time the brothers bought the property, the reservoir was empty, and the ditch rechanneled for general irrigation. They used the reservoir's depression to build a sizeable earthen potato cellar parallel to the highway.

Potatoes were one of many products from the ranch. The brothers grew Idaho Burbank potatoes. Any potatoes not reaching eight ounces could not sell as firsts. They were given away as seconds or destroyed as culls. Also, the brothers grew a variety of grains and, of course, hay.

The main product of the ranching operations was cattle. The brothers raised cattle on the ranch and on the range. Each fall, one of the brothers, usually Steve, accompanied the cattle on their train trip to Kansas City. The owners traveled with their livestock to assure the cattle were fed, watered, and arrived safely at their destination.

---

[1] The History of the Holden Marolt Site in Aspen Colorado (Wegman-French) indicates the buildings were gone when Bill Tagert bought the property in 1932. This is disputed by the 1934 Aspen Historical Society photograph showing many of the buildings and the highway built after 1930.

During the journey, the cattlemen rode in the drover's caboose, which is sometimes known as a cattleman's car. The car was sparse and had a few benches covered with a thin pad. The cattlemen grabbed food or drinks at the few stops along the way. They returned on passenger trains.

While the brothers were ranching, Rose went to Colorado College and eventually earned her nursing credentials from St. Joseph Hospital in Denver. Although their father was harsh in his interactions with his children, he at least valued education and understood it was not just for boys.

Ted, the youngest in the family, went to Colorado State University. It was remarkable Ted was able to go to college. He was "hard of hearing," probably because of a childhood illness. I assume he had a hearing issue at the time he went to college.

In 1933, while his youngest children were off at college, Frank died of an illness in a hospital in Grand Junction. He died on his birthday and the birthday he shared with Dad. After his father's death, Dad and his best friend, Crocker Brown, traveled to La Jolla, California. Crocker was a nephew of Aspen pioneer, David R.C. Brown. Crocker's father was Harry Brown, who was in charge of most of Aspen's utilities.

Once they got to California, Dad found work as a painter for the Casa de Manana in La Jolla, a hotel overlooking the ocean. The hotel still exists at the same location. Dad reminisced about how beautiful it was in La Jolla. He treasured his early morning walks among the tide pools. He said he would have been perfectly happy to stay there forever.

In the spring of 1936, Rudy succumbed to depression. On the hillside behind the newly remodeled house, he shot himself. None of the family members ever discussed what happened. Whenever Steve mentioned "Rude," he teared-up and went silent. Rudy was the second oldest of the Marolt boys and the intellectual of the family. He had no wife nor children. His features were more angular than his brothers', and he wore wire-rimmed glasses.

With Rudy's death, Frank Jr. and Steve asked Dad to come back to Aspen to help on the ranch. Frank Jr., the oldest brother, and Steve, who was only slightly older than Dad, were running the Midland Ranch by themselves. Dad and Ted inherited the old ranch from their father and were needed to operate it and help on the Midland Ranch. Shortly after Dad left La Jolla, Crocker Brown died in a car accident. I shudder to think if Dad stayed, he may have been with him.

When Dad returned to Colorado, he was in his mid-twenties. He was handsome. As adults, Dad, Steve, and Bill looked similar – no one doubted they were brothers. I suspect Frank Jr. must have looked a lot like them too, but there are only a few photos of him when he was in his early twenties. Ted and Rudy shared similar fine, angular features. Dad had a handsome face with full lips, brown eyes, and dark brown hair. He was about five feet eight inches tall with broad shoulders, narrow hips, and big hands. He was beginning to lose some hair.

His lack of hair was not noticeable because Dad and his brothers, and for that matter, their sisters, had an affinity for hats. The brothers wore work hats and the hats they wore when they dressed up. Mostly they wore hats that were somewhere between a wide-brimmed Fedora and a traditional cowboy hat. The brims of the hats turned up a little if at all and were made of felt or straw. They wore mesh, billed caps while farming. Bill usually wore a tweed flat cap or a newsboy type cap. In photos of Frank Jr. and Rudy, they wore fedora-style hats without a crease in the crown and flat brim. At one time, Steve wore a pith helmet reminiscent of the hats worn by colonial troops in Africa and India. I suspect it was a gift from his wife, Polly, or one of her relatives from the east coast concerned about Steve and the "wild west." Dad's dress hat was always a Stetson, which he cocked over one eye. He kept it in a special box on the side of his bed and took care to shape it exactly the way he wanted.

The Petersons

At the time Frank Marolt was relocating his family to Aspen from Leadville, my mother's family, the Petersons, were already in Aspen.

My great grandparents, Andrew and Matilda Holmstrom, married in Sweden in 1880. Within the year, they immigrated to the United States with their son Carl. Their daughter, Ida, came later. They found their way to Leadville, Colorado, where they had five more children, including my grandmother, Alma. In the late 1800s, the family moved to Aspen and bought a ranch west of Aspen near Brush Creek, which is the site of the current airport. In 1893, three of Alma's older siblings, Adolph, William, and Elin died of diphtheria and scarlet fever.

Alma met Andrew "Riley" Peterson, who was working in the mines. They married at her parent's Brush Creek ranch in 1909. Around that time, Beda, Alma's younger sister, died in childbirth. Her son, William Stapleton, was one of Mom's favorite cousins. His father, William Stapleton Sr., remarried, and many unrelated Stapletons followed.

Mom's other favorite cousin was Ida's daughter, Ida Mae Nelson. Ida Mae was a fiery redhead with a great sense of humor, which she used to downplay her physical infirmity. She contracted polio as a child causing her frame to become stooped and twisted.

Alma and Andrew lived in town in a small four-room Victorian house on the south side of Main Street, a few houses east of Seventh Street. Over the next ten years, they had four children – Adolph, nicknamed "Riley," Opal, my mother, Pearl, and Elmer. Mom used to say if they had had another girl, she would have been named Ruby – another precious gem.

Andrew worked as a miner in a time when mining was a marginal occupation. He moved from mine to mine, but he spent most of the time at the Newman and Durant Mines. When necessary, he went to nearby mining towns. He liked to fish, which was something he shared with Dad in later years. He also spent time in the backroom of Ed Tiedeman's shop on Hyman Street, playing cards with a group of men.

Alma was a housewife doing everything that job entailed. She was a consummate baker and had a huge garden behind the house. Also, she took care of the family finances and kept general ledgers of Andrew's wages and household expenses. She logged income and each expense – from a pair of shoes for Riley, to a dress for her, and to a cube of butter.

Mom had a good childhood. Her best friend, Rachel, lived across Main Street. They played every day and liked dressing-up with Rachel's mother's hats. When Rachel moved away, Mom was devastated.

Mom also was fond of her uncle, Carl, who she called Uncle Charlie. He was a handsome, dapper man with no wife and no children. He lived with his parents, who now lived next door to my grandmother and grandfather. Earlier, my great grandparents sold their Brush Creek ranch to William and Angie Wack.

Uncle Charlie spoiled his nieces and nephews, especially at Christmas. Not only did he bring oranges and nuts, he also made things. He made a doll bed for Mom out of twisted wire to look like a brass bed and painted it light green. The next year he built a matching steamer trunk using tongue and groove wainscoting. The trunk had a curved lid, an inside removable tray, hinges, handles, wheels, and a lock. It was in perfect proportion with the bed, which by that time had a ticking mattress. I still have the trunk.

By 1919, Matilda and Andrew's marriage ended in divorce. Matilda stayed in the small house next to and west of my grandparents' house on Main Street. Andrew moved into a house in Oklahoma Flats, an enclave favored by other Swedish immigrants. Shortly after their parent's divorce, Uncle Charlie died in a second wave of the flu pandemic.

Mom remembered Matilda fondly. She was a "clean freak." She scrubbed the wooden sidewalks until they were silvery white. If she saw a dog relieve himself on a tree, she scrubbed the trunk. Although they were divorced, Matilda made bread and took loaves to Andrew several times a week. He left the bread out until it became rock hard. He claimed that hard bread was the reason he had such beautiful white teeth.

Once a year, Mom and Matilda packed a picnic lunch and hiked to the Aspen Grove cemetery on the east end of town above the Independence Pass Road. Matilda brought flowers from her garden, and they tended the small graves belonging to her young children. The outing took most of a day. The graves were originally marked with wooden markers that deteriorated, and a fire destroyed the burial records. Mom could never find the graves to continue her grandmother's tradition.

In high school, Mom ran around with a group of friends, including Ted Marolt, who was in her class. One time, Mom, Ted, and four others were racing another car loaded with teenagers through town in Frank's newly purchased Buick. The Buick hit a truck in an intersection, braked hard, and rolled over near the *Aspen Times* building. All the occupants were thrown from the car, and, miraculously, no one was severely injured.

Frank was mad. But, by that time, Ted did not face any consequences from his father's wrath. Ted may have fared better than his brothers because of his small size and his hearing problems.

Mom graduated as salutatorian of her class and would have thrived in college. She loved poetry and reading and was a good writer. She was pretty. She was about five feet four inches, slim, but not skinny, and had wavy dishwater blond hair. She had a sweet, dimpled Shirley Temple-type smile. By far, her most striking feature was her eyes. They were blue – really blue. They were the same turquoise color of Paul Newman's eyes. She did, however, have a "birth defect." She was missing the little and ring finger on her left hand. It was a though they simply had never formed because the remaining three fingers on that hand looked normal.

Mom became adept at hiding this imperfection. She hid it in dress pockets or behind aprons. I remember noticing it once when I was a little and asking what happened to her fingers. I do not remember the response, but I understood that I should not mention it again. I never thought about it after that, and although Mom used her left hand, it did not register in my mind as being different. Then one day, when I was in college, I was standing in the kitchen talking to her, she did something with her left hand, and a chill came over me. My face blanched. For the first time in many years, I remembered Mom's hand was different.

After high school, Mom worked for the *Aspen Times* as a society or social reporter. While working, she met a man named Eugene Branson, who was in town working on the water diversion tunnel between Lincoln Creek on Independence Pass and Twin Lakes. According to people who remembered him, he was a handsome man with blondish hair and light eyes. He was quite the charmer. He was from Placerville, California, and was related to the family that founded Branson, Missouri.

Because no one ever talked about such things, it is unknown what exactly happened. Mom ended up pregnant and in Placerville. She either went there with him or traveled on her own only to find out he was married to another woman. Until the child was born, Mom lived with Branson's sister. She named the baby Eugene Keith Branson on his birth certificate. Branson drove Mom and Keith back to Aspen. She never saw or heard from him again.

When Mom returned, she told everyone she married Branson. Newspaper articles refer to her as Mrs. Branson. She then told people that she was divorced – I guess that was better than being an unwed mother. Mom's story was untrue. There are no records of her either marrying or divorcing Branson, although there are records of him being married many times.

When my sister, Judy, told the summer school nuns she wanted to be a nun, one of them told her she could never be a nun because her mother was divorced. Judy did not understand what they were saying. As far as Judy was concerned, Mom and Dad were married. Mom never shed any light on the subject even when asked.

When I was growing up, I had no idea Keith was not Dad's son. It never occurred to me even though he did not look like my sisters or Dad. He was much taller than the rest of us, had wavy, blond hair and blue eyes. We are all brunettes. My sisters have brown eyes. Mine are green. Of course, Keith could have taken his features from the Peterson side of the family. My uncles, Riley and Elmer, were tall, and all of the Petersons have light or blond hair and light eyes.

I assume there was a lot of shame involved in the situation. As time has gone by, I have discovered that Mom's situation was not all that unique, and there were quite a few Aspen couples who had children less than nine months after they were married. Many of them became pillars of the community and had important positions in the Catholic Church.

When Mom returned, Pearl and Elmer were living with my grandparents. Riley was living in Gilman, Colorado, which is now a ghost town near Minturn in Eagle County, Colorado. He was working as a butcher.

To help support Keith, Mom worked for Lettie Lee Brand, who had recently lost her husband. Michael Brand owned and operated the Brand Building in town. Mrs. Brand, as Mom called her, lived in a large Victorian house on the corner of Hallam and Center Streets.

Mrs. Brand was a progressive woman with four young sons. Her youngest son, Larry, was about Keith's age. Mom helped take care of the boys, helped around the house, and helped Mrs. Brand's campaign to become superintendent of the schools in the district. Her duties included door-to-door campaigning from the east end of Aspen to McLain Flats to Woody Creek. While Mom was at work, Pearl and Elmer took care of Keith. That is why Keith was so fond of them.

A Marriage Between the Marolts and the Petersons

During this time, Dad's younger sister, Rose, came back to town from time to time and got together with Mom. Rose was a couple of years older than Mom. Over the years, they formed a friendship. After high school, Mom and Rose went to town and filled lard buckets with beer for ten cents each, made cheese sandwiches, and hiked up the old Castle Creek Road for picnics. Knowing the two of them, they smoked a lot of cigarettes.

Rose thought Mom and her brother, Mike, who was five years older than Mom, would make a good couple. Mom remembered Dad vaguely from when he was in high school. He seemed so much older than her then. She knew him as Ted's older brother. She remembered Dad was handsome, but, like Ted, he was shy.

One day, Rose drove Mom out to the old ranch, where Dad and Ted were living after Dad returned from La Jolla. Ironically, both Mom and Dad had been living in California at the same time. He was in southern California, and she was in northern California. After they visited for a while, Dad drove Mom home.

Mom and Dad hit it off. Every day after Mom finished working for Mrs. Brand, he waited for her in his car down the street. When she got out of work and caught a glimpse of Dad's waiting car, a huge smile crossed her face, and she bounded down the street to see him. He drove her home. I assume they stopped and talked along the way since the two destinations were less than a mile apart.

In the winter of 1940, Mom and Dad drove to Leadville on the back road through Minturn over Tennessee Pass. They stopped in Eagle and got a marriage license. Although Mom was not a Catholic, they arranged for the priest at the Church of Annunciation, a Catholic Church in Leadville, to marry them. The fact they were able to marry in the Catholic Church indicates that Mom's story about being married and divorced from Branson was untrue. She could marry a Catholic in the Catholic Church if she were a repentant, unwed mother; however, a divorced person could never marry in the Catholic Church.

After their wedding, Mom and Dad drove to Denver for a honeymoon. They visited with Rose and one of Dad's favorite cousins, Lou Pozelnik. Lou's mother was Frank's sister, Helen Marolt. After a few days in Denver, Mom and Dad returned to Aspen.

Mom, Dad, and Keith moved into the old ranch house where Dad and Ted were living. The house did not have an interior bath – just a big sink and an outhouse. While continuing to eat with Mom, Dad, and Keith, Ted moved back into the living quarters in the barn.

Dad embraced Keith as if he was his son. Although he tried, Dad never officially adopted Keith. Regardless, Keith was known as Keith Marolt. It is likely they could not locate or obtain consent from Keith's father to relinquish parental rights for adoption. Maybe they did not try that hard because, to them, it made no difference. In Dad's eyes, Keith was his son.

Mom and Dad fixed up the old ranch house. It was a two-story building on a hill and overlooking part of Midland Ranch. Dad hung blue and white, early American wallpaper with sailing ships in the kitchen. He made white painted cabinets and painted the walls. He made a railing for the stairs that he painted white. One day when Mom was canning meat, one of the jars exploded and spattered hot grease all over the wallpaper. Mom was heartbroken and sat on the stairs and sobbed. The one time I remember being in the house, she pointed out the grease stain on the wallpaper above the stove.

In 1940, Frank Jr. died in the new house from complications from drinking. Before Frank died, Steve worried Frank Jr. drank too much and tried to get him to stop. At that time, Steve and Frank Jr. were the sole owners of the Midland Ranch. When it was clear Frank Jr. would not quit, Steve decided it was in his best interest to split the ranch into two parcels.

Judge Shaw, one of the Aspen's leading jurists, warned Steve if something happened to Frank Jr., his widow could cause him a lot of trouble. At Steve's suggestion, Frank Jr. agreed to the split. Steve took the western part of the Midland Ranch on the north side of Highway 82. He also kept the Maroon Creek river bottom, where we later had picnics. Steve did not need a house because he and his wife, Polly, owned a small Victorian in town on West Smuggler. With Dad and Ed Tekoucich's help, they remodeled the house. Ed, who they called Peanuts, was Dad's best friend. He was Celia's brother.

Frank, Jr. took the eastern third of the property north of the highway and all the property to the south including the Holden Tract and the buildings. Steve got more acreage to make up for not having the buildings.

Frank, Jr. and his wife, Elsie Baltizar, lived in the remodeled assay office. Rose lived with them for a while. Frank died in the dining room of the house.

Steve attempted to buy Frank Jr.'s property from Elsie, but as predicted, she refused to talk to him. After a while, she realized no one else was interested in the ranch, and a few months later, she sold Frank Jr's property to Dad for $9,250. Dad borrowed money from Bill Tagert for the purchase. Mom and Dad recounted how every year they borrowed money to pay the interest on the money they borrowed.

After the purchase, the configuration of the Marolt Ranch[2] was as follows:

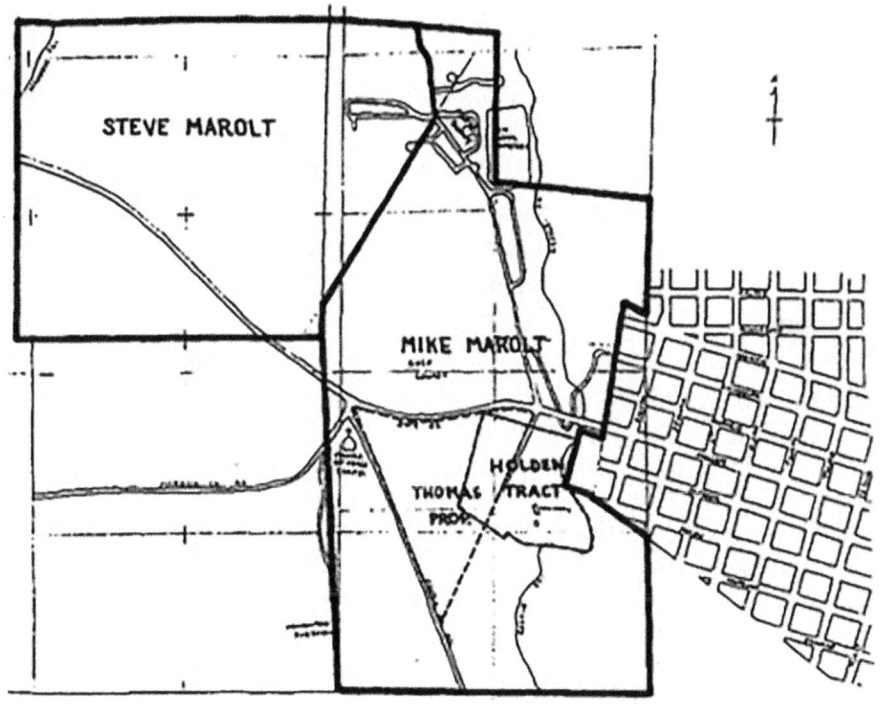

Wegman-French, Lysa "The History of the Holden-Marolt Site in Aspen, Colorado: The Holden Lixiviation Works, Farming and Ranching and the Marolt Ranch 1879 -1986" (October 1990).

After they bought the property, Mom and Dad moved into the house. Ted stayed in one of the extra bedrooms. In its day, it was a lovely house. It had four bedrooms and an indoor bathroom. After Mom and Dad moved into the house, my sister, Judy, was born in February 1941.

Then there was Pearl Harbor, and the United States declared war against Japan, Germany, and Italy. As the country began ramping up for war, the government was looking for training facilities. One of

---

[2] The map shows the Thomas Property and the Prince of Peace Church. These came later and did not exist in 1949. Dad owned all that property at the time. The area below Steve's property and to the left of Mike's property is the location of the old ranch.

their primary objectives was winter and mountain warfare training. They knew a mountain theater would be a big part of the European operations.

One day without notice, a group of high-ranking army officers rolled into the ranch unannounced. They got out of their vehicles and began tramping around inspecting the ranch. They carried maps and made notes. They said little if anything to Dad except that the government was considering the property for military purposes. For several nerve-wracking weeks, Mom and Dad worried the military would take their property. Fortunately, the military decided on Camp Hale, near Leadville. Camp Hale became home for the 10th Mountain Division.

None of Dad's siblings went to war. Neither he nor Ted could go because of physical limitations. Pneumonia, resulting from searching for the milk cows, damaged Dad's lungs, and Ted was deaf. Steve and Bill were too old. Further, they all were exempt because they were ranchers and farmers.

In 1943, shortly after my sister, Peggy, was born, Mom's youngest brother, Elmer, enlisted in the army. Mom vividly remembered the day when he came to our house to say good-bye. He sat at the kitchen table and Judy on his lap. Elmer was wearing a light blue pull-over V-neck sweater. Judy was young but remembered the day because of the emotional toll it took on Mom. Mom said all she could remember was Elmer's blue sweater and wondering if she would ever see him again.

Throughout the war, Elmer and Mom exchanged many letters and packages. After basic training in California, Elmer ended up in Europe. First, he was in England. He was a member of the 893 Tank Destroyer Battalion, which landed on the Normandy beaches shortly after the D-Day invasion. He experienced the Battle of the Bulge in the Ardennes. He was in the group that captured and crossed the Bridge at Remagen over the Rhine.

Elmer was a tank gunner, and because of the noise in the tanks, he suffered severe, permanent hearing loss. When the war in Germany ended, he received orders to go to the Pacific. Thankfully, before the transfer, the war with Japan was over. He received his discharge in December of 1945.

Mom, Dad, and Mom's sister, Pearl, and her husband, Albert Bishop, went to meet Elmer at the train station in Glenwood Springs. As they waited on the platform, Pearl broke out laughing. Mom thought Pearl's laughing was rude and inappropriate for such a solemn event. As it turns out, Mom forgot to take off the price tag from her new hat, and it was hanging down from the back of the hat. I guess Pearl's reaction had little to do with the price tag and a lot to do with letting go of years of pent-up anxiety. When he returned, Elmer worked for years at the *Aspen Times* as a linotype operator.

Other than Elmer, there were only a few soldiers related to our family group. Albert was a merchant marine. Dad's niece and Elsie's daughter, Dorothy Rinker, was a WAVE, and her soon-to-be husband, Chuck Clifton, was a Navy pilot.

George and Leo Tekoucich, two of Celia's brothers, both served. George was in the 10th Mountain Division at Riva Ridge in Italy. Leo was in New Guinea, where he contracted malaria. After he returned, he worked for Dad on the ranch and helped build the cattle barn we called the "red barn." Leo brought the war home with him and, after experiencing what would today be called post-traumatic stress disorder compounded by his illness, committed suicide.

I was born on September 15, 1949 – I assume I was a mistake because, by that time, Mom was 35. At the time, that was old age to have a baby. My birth was complicated. Mom started bleeding over a month before I was due. The doctor determined that she had placenta previa, a condition in which the placenta forms over the vaginal opening. Because of this condition, she went to the Citizens Hospital in Aspen. It was a dark, dismal building on the east side of town near Hunter Creek and much more suited for a horror movie than a place of healing.

Dr. Robert Lewis delivered me via a caesarian section. John Crosby, who also worked as a projectionist at the movie theatre, administered the anesthesia – ether. Mom woke up during the procedure and could feel Dr. Lewis cutting her open. Also, because of the ether, Mom was nauseated and vomited profusely. As a result, some of her stitches tore, and she ended up with what she called a "rupture." It was a hernia that she did not treat surgically for decades. Instead, she wore what she called a "girdle belt" to hold her intestines in place. It was the reason she rarely participated in physical activity when I was a child.

Judy remembered my birth, but not in a good way. She was eight at the time. Earlier that summer, she broke her arm. She and Julia's son, Ronnie, were playing in our horse trailer. They were standing on the front ledge where the horses' heads would be. Ronnie pushed Judy into the trailer. As Judy left for the hospital, Ronnie worried they would shoot her like a horse with a broken leg.

The day Mom went to the hospital, Judy was lobbying for Mom to make her new school clothes. Mom snapped at Judy. Then she "deserted" her for the ten days while Mom and I stayed in the hospital. What made matters worse was that before the hospital visit, Mom did not bother to tell Judy she was having a baby.

Because I was six weeks premature, I weighed slightly less than five pounds. I could come home after I passed the five-pound threshold. Before I came home, Mom bought a baby scale so she could weigh me every day. Dr. Lewis came out frequently to see me and monitor my weight. Within a few days, my weight dropped below five pounds. Dr. Lewis was alarmed. Fortunately, it was a simple mistake. Mom misread Dr. Lewis's handwriting and was using teaspoons of formula instead of tablespoons. After that, I gained weight, although I was smaller than my age group for many years.

At my birth, our immediate family included Keith, who was thirteen, Judy, who was eight, and Peggy, who was six. Besides our immediate family, we had a large extended family. The Marolt and Peterson families were a huge part of our lives. Most of the relatives lived in Aspen, while the remaining family visited often.

The Setting – The Homestead

Entrance to Aspen

I was born in Aspen, Colorado on September 15, 1949. It was a crisp, clear day. A person going to Aspen from Glenwood Springs on that autumn day would cross the Marolt Ranch. At the time, the ranch was over 450 acres. It began at and under the Maroon Creek Bridge and ended on the other side of Castle Creek. After crossing the Maroon Creek Bridge, to the left was an expansive field on a plateau extending from above Maroon Creek east as far as you could see to the ridge above Castle Creek over a mile away.

Red Butte, an angular hill of red rock, rose over a hundred feet out of the plateau's north edge. Other than a grove of cottonwoods near the highway, the land was a patchwork of yellow and green squares of harvested crops and red tilled earth. We referred to this part of the ranch as the Midland named for the former owner, the Colorado Midland Railway. Steve owned the western two thirds and Dad the rest.

On the south side of the highway near the bridge was a shrub-covered, undeveloped knoll. If the traveler could look over this undeveloped land, they would glimpse Pyramid Peak between nearby mountains.

As the person moved toward town, the western side of Aspen Mountain loomed larger and larger. When the highway met the intersection of the Maroon Creek and Castle Creek Roads, the property fanned out on the right into a recently harvested hayfield. Above the field was a sloping brush-covered area extending to a spur of Highland Mountain. Both the field and the sloping land were part of the ranch, as were several acres across Castle Creek at the base of Aspen Mountain. Dad owned this part of the ranch. Other than the cemetery, Dad and Steve owned every square inch of flat land between the rivers.

Aspen Historical Society, Ringle Collection

If the highway continued its trajectory, it would align with the elevated portion of the abandoned Midland railroad bed prominent in the now visible field. After all, most of the highway from Glenwood Springs to Aspen was built on the Midland railroad bed. The Maroon Creek Bridge was built on top of the railroad trestle.

The highway no longer continues straight because the railroad trestle over Castle Creek, unlike the one over Maroon Creek, is gone. It was dismantled years before the highway came into existence.

As built, the highway connected with the existing Castle Creek Bridge north of the railroad bed. Therefore, the highway jogged about 45 degrees to the left and then jogged to the right to align with the Castle Creek Bridge. The town of Aspen was across the bridge.

The elevated railroad bed appeared to go straight into Aspen Mountain. To the left were a stand of cottonwood trees and a cluster of buildings. Although they seemed to be at the base of Aspen Mountain the buildings and trees were on the west side of Castle Creek. They were the heart of the ranch and our home.

The road to our home came directly off Highway 82 just before it crossed the Castle Creek Bridge. To get to our house, a person would turn right, go up a short incline, and cross a cattle guard.

South of the cattle guard, the road split in two. On the left was a meandering road like a well-worn Jeep trail with potholes and dips. The road on the right was wide, straight, and graded. It was the main road to our house.

The main road went south, bordered on the right by a hayfield and fence. After crossing the cattle guard, the road started a noticeable incline for about 20 yards. This incline was a problem in winter if a car tried to make it to our house through unplowed snow.

After the incline, the main road leveled somewhat but continued at an imperceptible slope for about a hundred yards. Brush, jack oaks, and an occasional cottonwood bordered it on the left, and it, eventually, crossed a culvert over the Marolt Ditch. To the left was an open driveway in front of our house and yard. A garage-sized building was straight ahead. The barbed-wire fence, bordering the main road, extended to the Castle Creek Road about a quarter of a mile to the south.

The elevated, scrub-covered railroad bed was south of the buildings. Beyond it was a smaller field bordered on the east by a ridge above Castle Creek, on the south by the Castle Creek Road, and on the west by a fence extension from the main road. This was the "little field." The "big field" was a triangle bounded by the fence extension, the Castle Creek Road, Highway 82, and the main road. The railroad bed bisected the big field creating two smaller triangular fields.

Before the main road reached the culvert, another road branched to the left perpendicular to the main road. It bordered the ditch and cottonwoods north of our house. This road was level for about 100 feet and then declined steeply to a terrace fifteen feet below the house level. Straight ahead was the large building we called the granary. This was the granary road.

Aspen Mountain towered to the southeast across the river. This lower terrace housed several barns and corrals. At the foot of the hill at the edge of the parking area, the granary road met the "well-worn Jeep trail" coming from the cattle guard. This was the lower granary road. The center of the three roads, covered with brush, boulders, and farm equipment, was the scrub triangle.

Our House

Our house sat at the end of the driveway. It was a single-story white clapboard house with a wire fence. There was a young Chinese elm tree next to the front gate and another further down the fence. In the parking area was a cream-colored 1949 Chevrolet and a couple old Jeeps. The listing, garage-sized building to the southwest housed farm equipment.

The house was the center of our life. It was originally the assay and business office for the Holden Lixiviation Works. The assay office was located on the upper plateau far from the other lixiviation buildings to prevent vibrations disrupting the sensitive laboratory equipment. Besides being a laboratory, the building was used as the administrative offices and included a large walk-in safe. The original main entrance to the building was on the east side, facing the other lixiviation buildings.

In 1932 after Frank Jr., Rudy, and Steve bought the 20-acre Holden Tract, they remodeled the assay office into a house. The assay office, not including an attached enclosed porch to the west, was about 50 feet long and 35 feet wide and parallel to the elevated Midland railroad bed. The wooden floor joists rested directly on the ground.

The brothers' first task was to put in a foundation. They removed the back porch, jacked up the building, and installed a two-foot rock foundation under the eastern two-thirds of the building. John Parsons, a well-known stonemason, did the rockwork. The foundation was built with red rocks from Maroon Creek. Mr. Parsons was picky and rejected many of the rocks the brothers provided. He chose only the best ones for the foundation.

Under the western third of the house, the brothers excavated a basement with the help of horses and mules. Red rocks lined the basement walls to the height of the other foundation. The basement was about seven feet deep.

Mr. Parsons also built a foundation on the west end of the house, supporting a new enclosed porch and a rock-lined stairwell leading to the basement. The stairs were concrete, as was the basement floor. We called this addition the back porch.

The stoop leading into the back porch was the stone slab used for the floor of the walk-in safe vault in the assay office. When the rock foundation and basement work were complete, the house was lowered and attached to the new foundation leaving a basement and a generous crawl space under the eastern two-thirds of the house.

Once the structure was in place, the cosmetic work began. It is hard to say which of the brothers was most responsible for the interior. All were excellent craftsmen, but Frank, Jr. was reputed to be the one with the architectural flare. He, Rudy, and Steve planned on living in the new house.

One architectural flourish was adding an addition on the north side with a pitched roof. It had a matching red rock porch with three steps leading to a decorative arched door with beveled glass. This was designed as the formal entrance to the house. There was a foyer in the addition separated from the main house with an arched entryway.

It is unclear why the brothers put the main entrance on the north side a few feet from the ditch. It was not near the driveway. Perhaps they planned on putting in a culvert or a bridge to a driveway to the north. We called this the "front porch," although we never used this as the main entrance to the house. No one ever bothered to build a sidewalk to the unused stone porch.

Inside the northern addition, the brothers built a chimney extending through its roof high above the rest of the house with matching red rocks. On the other side of the wall from the chimney was the living room. Mr. Parsons built a black basalt rock fireplace with a black slate hearth and a mantle five feet above the ground. The rocks for the fireplace came from New Castle, Colorado. Mr. Parsons charged $400.00 for all his work, including foundations, chimneys, and the fireplace.

Clapboard siding covered the house. Decorative shingles were under the eaves and wooden shingles on the roof. Inside, the brothers added lathe and plaster walls and ceilings with decorative arches between the large open dining and living rooms, the entrances to the halls, and the foyer. They installed new double sash windows and new doors ordered from a Universal Builder's Woodwork catalog for the American Sash & Door Company. Maple flooring replaced the plank floors in the living room and dining room.

The kitchen occupied the space in the southwest corner, which initially housed the assay furnace. A chimney extended from the new basement up through the east wall of the kitchen. There the chimney connected to a heating stove in the dining room and a cooking stove in the kitchen. Finally, the brothers added an indoor bathroom on the south side in what may have once been another entrance to the building.

The three brothers moved into the house. After Rudy died and Steve married and moved to town, Frank Jr. and his new wife, Elsie Baltazar, used it as their home.

The Yard

In 1940, when Frank Jr. died, Dad and Mom bought Frank's share of the property from Frank's widow Elsie for $9,250. The purchase included the house. The house sat alone on the edge of the plateau, mostly covered with native grasses and scrub brush. The Marolt Ditch curved around the east and north sides of the house. There was little vegetation near the ditch – a few willows on the bank near the front door and a couple of cottonwoods on the other side.

In January 1941, my sister, Judy, was born. Mom and Dad knew that before she began walking, they needed to fence the yard, so if she wandered off, she would not drown in the ditch. Dad built a fence out of diamond mesh wire. It was inexpensive and readily available as a type of horse or livestock fencing. The fence ran the length of the driveway about 15 feet west of the back door. The back porch part of the house next to the driveway became what we considered the front of the house. The fence continued inside the ditch on the north and east. To the south, the fence created a large garden alcove on the southwest corner.

The fence was not pretty, nor was it meant to be. The posts were mismatched. Some were pieces of lumber; some were railroad ties; others were small tree trunks. It looked as though Dad dug a hole and stuck whatever he could find in it and moved on to the next pole. Because the fence was lightweight wire, it was not necessary to fill the postholes with concrete.

The fence kept kids in and animals out. The wooden gates were leftovers from other people's yards. One gate led to the back porch and another to the granary bridge. A set of double gates in front allowed access for coal delivery.

Mom started landscaping after the fence was complete. The yard was native grasses she mowed with a hand mower. It is hard to say what was below the surface. The house was on an industrial site littered with discarded ore, chemicals, mine tailings, bottles, and clay crucibles. Soil from the basement excavation covered the debris. We have since learned the basement and crawl space are filled with radon gas.

Mom planned a windrow of large trees along the front fence, which was about 120 feet long. She envisioned beautiful trees providing shade and privacy as if the house was an antebellum mansion. She ordered a dozen Chinese Elm saplings. I'm guessing she saw pictures of Chinese elm shade trees in a magazine. Dad planted the elms inside the fence. Mom also ordered a dozen French lilacs she planted on the inside of the northeast curve of the ditch.

After the first winter, only two of the elms survived. Elms may have been great trees back east or in the south but did not hold up to the alpine climate and the heavy snow. One of the surviving trees was by the front gate. The other was on the northwestern corner next to the ditch. Unlike the elms, most of the lilacs made it. Mom accidentally replaced the few dead French lilacs with a Persian variety. The blossoms were not as large and were darker and less fragrant.

Over time, Mom added more and more plants to the yard. There was no master plan. Sometimes someone came back from a trip into the mountains with a cute evergreen. Evergreens were planted along the edge of the fence by the ditch on the north side of the house. Along the southern fence, Mom planted native rose bushes. The western edge of the garden alcove included pink and white spiraea bushes. A lone lilac from a start from Grandma's yard was on the northwest corner of the house. When it died, we regretted not replacing it.

Mom still wanted shade trees. She saw some white willows at a ranch house down the valley. They were big, but not the weeping variety. These trees provided shade, grew fast, and could handle most snowstorms.

Mom got several branches and put them in a bucket filled with water until they sprouted. She planted two willows in front of the garden alcove. Her idea was to have two trees far enough apart to hold a hammock. Both trees grew well for a while, but one broke in a snowstorm and was unsalvageable. The other tree grew as envisioned.

Some of the relatives liked these trees so much they got starts and planted them in their yards. Pearl and Albert had one. So did Steve and Polly. Decades later, my cousin, Max, and his wife, Betty, planted several in their yard.

Inside the House

By the time I was born, the house was in the same configuration the rooms are in today. The west half of the house was a living room, dining room, and kitchen. The kitchen was in the southwest corner west of the dining room. The living room covered the entire area opposite the kitchen and dining room on the northwest corner. The balance of the house had four bedrooms and a bathroom. There were two bedrooms on the north side. The other bedrooms and bathroom were on the south side.

The hall between the bedrooms ended with a built-in linen closet. The linen closet was in what had been the main entrance into the assay office. The hall seemed narrow, probably because the ceilings in the house were twelve feet high.

For my first few years, I slept in a crib in Mom and Dad's room. Their room was in the northeast corner. It had a window on the north and one on the east. I was in the crib long enough to be able to climb in and out on my own. Keith's room was across the hall from Mom and Dad's room. It, too, had two windows. It even had a small walk-in closet cleverly placed behind the linen closet. Until recently, I thought Keith's room was the best in the house, thinking it was the same size as Mom and Dad's room. I now know it was the same size as my room but with two windows. My room was on the south side next to Keith's room.

Because the bedroom ceilings are twelve feet tall, Mom and Dad painted them in dark colors and brought the dark paint down to a line about three feet below the ceiling. This technique was supposed to create the illusion the ceiling was lower, which was a plus in the day. Keith and my room had maroon ceilings and light gray walls. The floors were darkly stained wood planks. My room had linoleum made to look like an Oriental rug tacked on top of the wooden planks. The bedrooms on the cold side of the house had dark blue ceilings and light gray walls. What were they thinking?

All the rooms had double beds and dressers ranging from a simple "modern" blond dresser to an elaborate antique dressing table with curved sides, a lower center for sitting and preening, and an ornate mirror. The dressing table would probably be valuable today. At the time, it was someone else's discarded junk.

When I was too old to stay in a crib in Mom and Dad's room, and I needed a bedroom. Ted moved out. Dad gave him a lot across the river so he could build his own house. Ted rented a room or an apartment in a house owned by Rudy Pecjak until his house was to the stage where he could live there. Ted's apartment was only two blocks from Steve's house.

At the time he moved out, Ted either just sold the old ranch, or the sale was imminent. He sold to Walter and Elizabeth Paepcke, who had moved to Aspen about ten years before and were involved in the Aspen Skiing Company and the Aspen Institute

After Ted left, I got the fancy vanity and the four-poster bed he used. I could stand on the vanity stool and admire myself in the mirror. One of the passed-down stories was that one time when I was four or five, I was playing dress-up with Cherie Gerbaz, who was Judy's age and a close family friend. I had on a bias-cut black slip. Cherie put my hair on my head. I had on some jewelry and red lipstick and rouge. As I stood on the chair before the vanity and turned around, I said to Cherie, "Let's 'tend I'm 21 and can take care of myself."

When Ted used the room, the head of the bed was on the west wall. When it was my room, the head of the bed was on the east wall. The vanity was on the wall next to the hall door. The bed filled most of the room. I used to tie my chenille bedspread to the top of the posts and pretended it was a canopy bed or a covered wagon like the ones in *Wagon Train*. I finished off the decor with stacked wooden crates behind the door for toys and books.

I don't remember much about the dining room except it was bright. It was next to the kitchen. It had a radiator under the south-facing window and was perfect for drying mittens. At one point, the dining room had a heating stove. It was gone soon after I was born. The Marolt brothers used it as a heating source before the coal furnace. It may have been the heat source when Mom and Dad first lived in the house.

By the time I was born, Dad had installed hot water radiators throughout the house. For most of the time I was growing up, there was a spot on the wall where the dining room stove had gone into the shared kitchen chimney. A circular piece of metal covered the hole. Later, Mom strategically placed a picture over the spot to hide the metal plate.

My first memory of the dining room was sitting under the round table, behind the lace tablecloth. I was cutting pictures out of a Sears Roebuck catalog. I cut out the models to use as paper dolls. It was winter because it was light from a reflection of the sun on the snow. At the time, I was about four. I had hair below my chin with soft curls I kept off my face with barrettes. It was pretty. As I sat cutting out pictures, I noticed some of the haircuts on the models. I decided to emulate their styles. I took the scissors and chopped off a chunk of hair above my ear. I went out into the kitchen to show Mom my stylish new hairdo. She was drinking coffee with Riley.

What followed was unexpected. I thought I had done such a good thing. Mom screamed about what I had done to my beautiful curls. She was sobbing. I believe Riley swatted me on my bottom. I retreated to my room. I felt humiliated.

My hair eventually grew back only to survive later horrors of Mom's lack of hairstyling prowess. She cut uneven bangs using Scotch tape as a guide. Then there were brush rollers. She had to cut them out of my hair because they were not meant for long hair and especially not after a night's sleep. Mom tried the rollers at night only once, and it was before a school play or school pictures. She was so upset she sat on the side of the bathtub sobbing as she tried to remove the curlers. I had the feeling she was tempted to hit me with the back of the brush but refrained. Instead, she cut out some of the rollers, leaving odd chunks of hair.

Before the brush rollers, we used metal rollers that left crimps in the curls. Mom finally let me go with braids. I had two braids when I was younger and one down my back when I was older. I stopped having bangs because the Scotch Tape trick never improved. They always slanted in one direction or the other.

The Kitchen

Before the kitchen was remodeled in the fifties, the floor was checkered with large cream and dark green asphalt tiles so dark they looked black. There were two side-by-side windows in the middle of the south wall over the sink. From my perspective, those windows seemed high. They were above a metal sink unit. The unit had one single sink with a built-in drain area on one side and two doors underneath. The doors had black metal handles and pulls. On either side of the sink were matching metal cabinet units. Each cabinet unit had doors above, a flat work area, a couple of drawers, and more cabinets on the bottom.

At one time, when Judy was young, she fell on the corner of one of the metal cabinet doors. She was probably trying to get something in the upper cabinets and severely slashed the inside of her thigh.

There was a new electric stove on the east wall. It replaced the wood stove and a suspended water heater from before the furnace and radiators. Although there was no longer a need to have a wood box for papers and kindling by the stove, it was still next to the stove. The wood box had an opening lid and which, when closed, was a good place to sit. The paint was the same gray and blue colors from the eastern bedrooms. The wood box was still useful as a place for the old newspapers.

As is true today, the refrigerator was in the alcove over the basement stairs on the west wall opposite from the stove. The freezer in the fridge was small – just enough room for a couple of ice cube trays and a carton of ice cream. Our big freezer was a meat locker at Beck & Bishop Food Market. Albert Bishop partially owned Beck & Bishop.

The kitchen table was on the north opposite the kitchen windows. It had a "marbleized" gray top. The corners were slightly rounded and edged in chrome. Two leaves slid out from under the ends and lifted to the level of the rest of the table. The divided drawer in the middle was for flatware. The matching metal chairs had red oilcloth seats and backs. It was the type of furniture found in a diner.

Near the table toward the dining-room door was a tall, narrow built-in cabinet in which there were two fold-down ironing boards – the main board was the size of a regular ironing board, and a little board folded down separately and sat on the big board. The small board was good for pressing sleeves – in particular, puffed sleeves. There was a space in the cabinet for an iron.

A heavy swinging door lead into the dining room. Most of the time, it was open on the dining room side against a small section of the living room wall. On rare occasions, it was closed. The door was probably originally in the assay office and separated the laboratory from the offices. It could open while carrying samples in and out of the laboratory without having to use a handle – just back into it, and it swung open.

My most vivid memory of the old kitchen was the morning after we got our new puppy, Nipper. Our big golden dog, Butch, was hit by a car and killed. Butch was a female and was probably part golden retriever. I have no idea how she got her name.

Butch was making her daily journey from our house to Grandma's house for treats. To get to Grandma's house, she went down the main road, crossed the Castle Creek Bridge, and went up Seventh Street to Main Street. Grandma's house was on the south side of Main Street on the third lot east of the corner. On her way home, someone hit Butch with their car, shoved her off to the side of the road, and left her to die. Dad found her and brought her home, but she did not survive. Dad buried her in a small area north of the yard that became our designated pet cemetery.

The spring after Butch died, Mom, Judy, Peggy, and I, along with Albina Gerbaz and her children, Cherie, and Jimmy, went to Robert Sinclair's house on Owl Creek to see their puppies. Albina was Celia Marolt's sister and one of the Tekoucichs. Cherie was Judy's age, and Jimmy was Peggy's age.

The Sinclairs, who unbeknownst to me at the time were distant cousins, had a litter of puppies, which were either all or mostly border collies. When Dad was in his twenties, his dog, Jigs, was a border collie. Dad raved about Jigs and his cattle-herding abilities and how he leaped up and rode with Dad on the horse. The Marolt brothers had several border collies over the years.

We chose a black puppy with a white chest, paws, and a tip on his tail we named Nipper. Cherie and Jimmy got two puppies. Tip was black and looked a lot like Nipper, and Sandy was yellow and looked like Butch. When Mom and Dad said we were getting a border collie, I only heard the collie part, and for years I wondered why Nipper did not look more like Lassie.

After picking our puppies, we loaded into the back of our car. Judy was in charge and did not let Peggy or me hold Nipper on the way home. She said she needed to keep him safe.

I was not sure at the time how he got his name. For a long time, I thought it was because he nipped at the gloves worn by Teleo "Tee" Caparrella, a water company employee who came to our property to work on the city water pipes near our house. Nipper did not like Tee. Instead of trying to talk to Nipper, Tee kicked him. Tee also wore gloves, which for Nipper, was another bad sign. Nipper tore after him and grabbed and shook his glove. Whenever we saw Tee coming, we put Nipper in the house. Later, I realized someone named him Nipper because of the RCA dog and not a projection of his future interactions with Tee.

The night we brought Nipper home, Dad allowed us to keep him in the kitchen. It was spring and still cold in Aspen. Dad had a funny idea that animals, even pets, should never live in the house, so it was a temporary arrangement. We put Nipper in a bed made with rags in a wooden crate, put it next to the kitchen stove, and went to bed. We closed the swinging door between the kitchen and the dining room.

The next morning everyone was excited to get up and play with the puppy. Nipper was missing. We searched everywhere in the house, in the basement, and outside. I was upset we had lost another dog. Finally, after what seemed like hours and was probably more like fifteen minutes, Mom heard a squeaking noise and found Nipper in a space below the sink nestling in the dishrags.

After that, Nipper slept on the back porch. At that time, the back porch had a sink for washing hands after working on the ranch and before eating. There was an electric milk separator where Mom separated the cream from the skimmed milk. The butter churn was next to the separator.

At the time, we had five milk cows, so Mom used the separator one or two times daily. First, she took off whole milk for family use and then separated the cream from the skim milk. The cleaning process required taking the separator apart. Decades after she stopped the milk operation, Mom said she could still put it together in her mind and used to imagine running through the steps when she was having trouble falling asleep.

The family used some of the cream for desserts and coffee and, of course, homemade ice cream. She gave extra milk, cream, and butter during the War to supplement her parents' ration coupons. In the early years, the ice for the ice cream made in the summer came from a mineshaft on Aspen Mountain above Grandma's house.

Besides the family's use, Mom filled milk cans to sell to dairies. In earlier years, she took the milk cans to the railroad depot. From there, they were transported down the valley to one of the dairies to make into butter. Mom received a credit on her account, and they returned the cans. In later years, she took some the extra cream to the Hoaglund Dairy at the end of Galena Street. Mom used the skim milk to feed her chickens and the pigs. Sometimes there was too much, and she poured it in the ditch.

I do not remember much of the separator operation, although the top bowl made an excellent punch bowl when I had a barn dance when I was in high school. I remember making butter. A couple of times,

I churned it in a crock with a wooden agitator sticking through the hole in the lid. To make butter, we moved the agitator up and down continuously until the butter started separating from the buttermilk. Then suddenly, it seemed, there was a chunk of solid butter.

Mom put the butter in a large wooden bowl she called the butter bowl. She rinsed the solid butter until the water ran clean. Then she kneaded in some salt. For some of our butter, we had a four-cube mold. It was light yellow plastic with four cube-sized chambers. The butter was spread evenly in the mold, and then the bottom of each cube slid open, expelling a perfect cube of butter. We wrapped the cubes in wax paper and stored them in the refrigerator. We had lots of uses for butter.

On the north side of the porch were the concrete stairs and red rock walls leading to the basement. There were two high windows on the north wall as well as a window by the back door. A low wall separated the stairs and the main room. Our visitors' wet coats would be draped over the top to drip on the stairs below. On the stair side of the wall were rows of hooks for coats and hats that hung over the concrete stairs but were not visible from the porch.

The Basement

For some strange reason, I have strong memories of the old basement. It was mostly one large, dark room with red rock walls and a concrete floor. The ceiling was open floor joists. On the north end were two small rooms of equal size covering the width of the main room. The one on the west was the coal room. The door to the room had a frosted glass window that was dirty. When the coal room door was open, there was a wooden dam keeping the coal from spilling into the main room. There was a filthy window high on the west side, leading to a coal chute.

Next to the coal room, also on the north side, was the fruit room. Inside against the north wall were three wooden wine casks with spigots. Above the casks was a small metal door to access the ash trap for the fireplace above. The room smelled like musty wine barrels. Next to the casks was the door to what had once been the safe for the assay office. On the remaining walls were rows and rows of shelves filled with home-canned foods and empty Mason jars. Like the coal room, the fruit room door had a frosted glass window. It was only slightly cleaner. I believe the doors for the coal room and the fruit room were part of the original assay office. They looked like doors from a turn of the century office building.

Mom was responsible for the canning. In late summer, peddlers came to town from down valley – Grand Junction, Oletha, or Fruita. They showed up unannounced in their trucks laden with produce. I looked forward to this time of year. I looked forward to the bushels of Bing cherries. Mom bought bushels of peaches, pears, apricots, cherries, tomatoes, cucumbers, and beets. While the produce was fresh, she stayed up late at night canning before it spoiled. Besides canning the whole fruit and vegetables, she made jams and jellies, applesauce, dill pickles, bread-and-butter pickles, chow-chow pickles, mustard pickles, and chili sauce.

In the center of the basement was the coal furnace Dad installed sometime in the early 40s. At that time, he added hot water radiators to all the rooms in the house. To me, the furnace seemed like it was the size of a locomotive engine. It looked a lot like a locomotive engine. I'm guessing it was more the size of a small car, but it nearly reached the height of the floor joists. The furnace had an automatic stoker filled with coal that fed as needed to keep the furnace burning. The furnace heated the water for the radiators and the hot water used in the kitchen and bathroom.

Until Dad installed the furnace, the only heat in the house was a stove in the kitchen and a wood heating stove in the dining room. They did not use the fireplace in the living room for heat. It was large and drew well. As a result, when the flue was open at night, it sucked what little warm air was in the house out the chimney. During winter, it was so cold at night they filled rubber hot water bottles to keep their beds warm.

Next to the furnace door was a coal bucket that we called the clinker barrel. Clinkers looked like lava rock and were the remains of unburned coal. The clinkers were removed from the furnace with a clawed tool and placed in the clinker barrel to cool. When they were cold, someone took them outside and threw them in a "clinker pile" on the edge of the driveway. They were available if someone got stuck in the driveway in the winter to shovel under their tires. More likely, it was far enough from the house so that any unburned embers did not catch fire.

My sisters had other uses for clinkers. They took a few softball-sized ones and put them in a pan filled with a mixture of saltwater and food coloring and let it evaporate. The clinker grew "hair" the color of the food coloring. Once the first color evaporated, they gently placed them into another color and more hair grew. They became multi-colored pastel stalagmites. The clinker gardens sat in the back reaches of my sisters' dressers, where they could not be bumped and destroyed.

In the corner of the main basement room, next to the fruit room, was the winepress and big wine barrel used to ferment wine. Dad and several Italian ranchers from down the valley shared a truckload of California Zinfandel grapes every year. Sometimes the wine was excellent. Sometimes it was off or "kind of gassy." The finished wine was put in the casks with the spigots on a bench in the fruit room. When they wanted wine, Mom or Dad sent me down to fill up a Mason jar or pitcher.

In this section, between the fruit room and the wine barrel, I set up a little altar with a kneeler. I played priest and gave my Protestant cousins, Gary and Barney, communion hosts made from flattened white bread. The location was convenient because there was plenty of sacramental wine nearby. It never crossed my mind girls were not priests.

The southeast corner of the room was behind the furnace and not visible from the rest of the room. Once, Dad set up a still so he and Edmund Gerbaz, Albina's husband, could make grappa, an Italian brandy made from wine. Once they started the still, they held a vigil next to it for a night or two. The main part of the still was an oval copper tub for the wine. A copper hood with copper tubing welded to the tub for the condensation process. I do not know what they were using as a source of heat. There was a pressure gauge because the still was dangerous. They monitored the gauge regularly and tested the alcohol content of the distilled liquid with an alcohol hydrometer. The brandy was terrible. Dad said it was strong enough to corrode a cup or bend a spoon. I do not know if that's true. The experiment lasted only one season. Later, we used the copper tub for wood next to the fireplace.

Next to where Dad and Edmund set up the still, there was a floor drain and the opening high up in the rock wall to the crawl space. For some reason, I pictured this space when I read *The Cask of Amontillado*. It was very dark and damp in this corner. I am not sure of the water source. Salamanders slithered in and out of the crawlspace, hung on the walls, or huddled in the corner. This corner was dark and creepy.

On the same south side of the cellar and to the right of the stairs as one entered the basement was where Mom had her clothes washer. It was an electric wringer washer that mostly just agitated the water. After the wash cycle, she would put one piece at a time through an electric clothes wringer on top of the tub to squeeze out the moisture. Then the load was rewashed in the agitator with clear water and once again wrung through the wringer. I only remember this washer being in operation for a short time.

In the early fifties, Mom bought a raffle ticket at the Elks and won one of the new, fancy washing machines that washed, spun, and rinsed the clothes in succession. Dad installed it on the back porch next to the milk separator. The back porch at that time was warm because the excess heat from the furnace rose out of the basement. There was no door at the bottom of the stairs.

When it came to drying laundry, Mom hung it outside even in the winter. Initially, there was a line from the back porch toward the driveway. The lines moved on pulleys. Mom could stand on the porch and hang laundry reeling the clothes out and reeling them back as they dried. When the weather was too bad, there were a few lines strung in the basement behind the furnace for emergency drying.

Wooden t-shaped poles later replaced with iron pipes in the yard replaced the original line. The new lines ran parallel to the house. Dad hung a swing for me on the west iron pole. Dad shoveled under the wires in winter so Mom could hang clothes year-round. Often the clothes froze before they were dry. Sometimes the pants could stand on their own for a while.

Standing pants reminds of pant stretchers. When Mom washed nice jeans or slacks, she used pant stretchers. They were aluminum frames that, when inserted in a pair of pants, stretched them, so they did not need pressing and created a crease down the front.

Mom used these forms for Keith's laundry when he first went to college. At the time, kids leaving home for college had a box made of stiff fiberboard in which they put their dirty clothes. They closed the box with straps. There was a window for the mailing address and another for the return address. The cards were switched in the windows, depending on the direction the box was going. What an inefficient procedure. I wondered what Keith did for clothes when he waited for his box.

Finally, in the basement, there was a workbench on the west wall below a window extending from the stairwell to the coal room. The workbench was used for chores and making klobasa, our traditional Slovenian sausage. Dad ground up pork and beef and mixed it in a galvanized metal tub with lots of garlic, salt, and pepper. He put the mixture through the sausage stuffer. Dad ordered the casings and soaked them in salt water until they were pliable. I got to twist a few of the sausages when they came out of the press. Keith wrote the recipe for klobasa with a carpenter's pencil on one of the wooden beams near the furnace.

Dad took the stuffed links to a room under the northeastern corner of the granary for smoking. Originally the smokehouse was in a space created by the flue below the big chimney for the lixiviation works. The smokehouse was moved under the granary when the chimney was gone.

In the corner at the end of the bench near the coal room door was a large industrial sewing machine. Dad used the sewing machine for fixing tack and boots and for hemming irrigating canvases. It was ready and available when needed in an emergency – like a broken bridle or bootstrap. There was a small high window on the west wall above the bench. It matched the window in the coal room.

The window was small and dirty and let in little light. The only lights in the basement were bare bulbs in porcelain fixtures with long pull chains. When Dad hooked the lights to a switch at the bottom of the stairs, it was a big deal. We no longer had to blindly flail at the chains, trying to turn on a light. Just switch them on at the bottom of the stairs.

Also, near this bench was a crock used for making sauerkraut. Mom got the cabbage from Mrs. Zelnick, a local Slovenian woman, and cut it on a wooden cabbage cutter that looked like a large mandolin. After the cabbage fermented in salt water in a large crock, Mom canned and stored it in the fruit room.

One of our very favorite meals was klobasa, sauerkraut, and fried potatoes. We fried the thinly sliced potatoes in our homemade lard until the pan of potatoes had a golden-brown crust and lightly soft center. Dad had the knack for making the potatoes just right.

Although the basement was dark and dingy, except for the creepy salamander corner, I liked being there. Sometimes, I sat at the bottom of the stairs cuddling the big pumpkin-colored blanket I named Suki. I gave her a name after I sewed on button eyes. If I ever did anything wrong, including cutting my hair, I claimed Suki told me to do it. Sitting on the bottom step, smelling the fermenting wine, garlic, and coal, and cuddling Suki, made me feel warm and secure.

The Outbuildings

After the house, the most important building on the ranch was the granary. Like the assay office, it was an original lixiviation building. When Mom and Dad purchased the property, most of the lixiviation buildings were gone. What remained were the two smokestacks, the sampling building, the salt shed, and several small buildings and sheds. Only the tall sandstone foundation, several large footers, and the concrete cooling floor from the main part of the building remained. Timbers and iron bins, vats, tanks, hoppers, chutes, and cables littered the site.

The "sampling building" and the "salt shed" were the hub of the ranch operations. I never knew those were their official names until many years later. We called the sampling building the granary. We called the salt shed the barn. We called the smokestacks the big and little chimneys.

The front of the granary faced west and was about 65 feet wide, 42 feet deep, and was a single story about 14 feet from the floor to the bottom of the interior truss beams. It was another 10 feet to the peak in the roof. Except for the trusses, the entire building was open to the ceiling. The walls of the building were thick vertical boards bolted to the outside of a timber lattice.

The front of the granary had a high porch. The porch was the height of a railroad car for off-loading ore into the sampling building. I did not learn this until long after I no longer played there. The building looks a little like a small train depot. For me, the porch was the right height for feeding the horses oats when they were in the adjoining corral.

The porch, covered by the overhanging roof, spanned the entire width of the building. Three doors opened into the building. The large, heavy wooden doors were each about the size of a single-car garage door. There was one on the north end, one in the middle, and another equal distance from the middle door to the south. When I was growing up, we never used the central door.

There were two sets of stairs leading up to the porch. One set was directly in front of the southernmost door; the other set came up the north end of the porch. On the right of each door was one multi-paned, dirty window.

The porch was packed with equipment. On the north, there was a hammer mill for grinding grain into livestock feed, a large scale with a bed about two by three feet square used to weigh livestock and feed. Near the middle was Dad's homemade welding machine made in part from a truck engine. On the other end of the porch was an air compressor that was handy for filling inner tubes to ride down the ditch or pumping up my bicycle tires. There were lots of pulleys and devices for hoisting equipment on and off the porch.

We used the area under the porch as well. The spaces between the floor joists were open and facing out. Dad stored long pipes and lumber in these spaces. At one time, a pigpen was under the northernmost portion of the porch.

There were several places with openings to access the space under the granary. It was one of those places we were warned to avoid. Dad told us there were huge pits, and if we fell in one, we might not survive. Even if we survived, it might take a long time to find us. Looking under the building convinced me the warnings were accurate. Thus, in all the decades our family owned the ranch, I never crawled under the granary.

The lattice of timbers supported seven huge open beam trusses. The trusses included iron poles were attached by what looked like huge bolts – Queen Rod Trusses. Dad said millwrights, who built the building, learned their trade building ships. He said if the building was turned over, it had the shape of a boat. There was a total of seven trusses, including the two at the ends. Inside, three equal-sized sections corresponded with the spacing of the trusses.

We stored grain in the northernmost section – hence our name for the building – the granary. Dad and Steve raised oats, wheat, and barley. In the fall, Dad set up our threshing machine on the north end of the building. There were two windows on the north side, and it was through these windows that an auger transported the grain into the bins. I remember two bins, but there may have been more.

The day the threshing crew arrived was important. Workers came down the valley and went from ranch to ranch operating threshing machines. On threshing day, Mom and a group of women prepared a meal for the men involved in the operation – several roasts, mounds of mashed potatoes, coleslaw, and pie.

One of the "fun" things to do on threshing day was to stand under the shower of grain coming through the windows. We "swam" in the pools of fluffy fresh grains and itched the rest of the day and sometimes longer. A pile of straw remained outside the granary. We used the straw throughout the year as mulch and to fill and clean the animal pens.

One year in early June, as we returned home from a trip down the valley, when we came to the intersection of the Castle Creek and Maroon Creek Roads, almost simultaneously, Mom and Dad both shouted,

"Oh, my God. The house is on fire."

In the distance, black smoke was coming up from where the house and barns sat behind a grove of cottonwoods. I pressed forward in the back seat as we raced down Highway 82 to our road. As Dad made the turn, he shouted,

"Ah, shit. It's the granary."

It looked as though the north side of the building was on fire.

Dad drove to the house and ran over the hill to the granary. We followed and stood at the edge of the granary bridge, looking over the barns below. The straw pile next to the granary was burning.

By the time we arrived home, the volunteer fire department and local townspeople showed up with a water wagon. At the time, a siren that sounded throughout the town at noon also alerted volunteers there was a fire. The number of blasts indicated the urgency of the situation. The volunteers were spraying water from the truck and desperately looking for a fire "plug." Eventually, they found a hydrant hidden in weeds near the water trough next to the barn. Dad got the tractor and attached ditching equipment. He drove up to the lateral ditch going to the garden and began to dig a channel down the granary road. He ran the new ditch between the straw pile and granary.

Aspen Historical Society, Mary Eshbaugh Hayes Collection

After several hours what remained was a smoldering, steaming blackened pile of straw. Dad used the tractor to drag the pile over the hill. The hill was covered with brick fragments remaining from the now dismantled chimneys and dropped down, ironically, to what had been the cooling floor of the lixiviation works. The cooling floor was the size of two tennis courts and was still in good condition. We tried playing tennis there once but kept losing the balls over the lip of the rock wall below the floor.

That fire was a wake-up call. Spontaneous combustion ignited the fire. The straw pile, which was out in the open, was moist because of the melting snows. The moisture caused a fermentation process that created chemical reactions producing heat at the center of the pile. It finally burst into flames.

Dad never again left a straw pile close to a building. We also became acutely aware the only fire hydrant on the ranch was far away from most of the buildings on the property. There was nothing close to the house. Later, when the city wanted to replace the water lines across our property, one of our demands was they install more hydrants near the house and the barns.

Besides the grain bins in this section of the granary, Dad stored feed in gunnysacks. He made some of the feed by mixing molasses with the grain. He also stacked salt blocks available to take out to the livestock. Some were white, and some were maroon red. One of them contained either vitamins or antibiotics. I'm not sure which were which, but I snuck a lick or two on the blocks. Sometimes there were salty chips and sucked on like candy. I also used to drink vinegar by the glass.

The middle section was mostly for storage and fenced off from the other sections. It had a back door, the size of the front doors, looking over the riverbank and the City of Aspen across the river. Unlike at the front doors, there was no back porch. The door opened five feet above the stinging-nettle-covered ground.

An encounter with a stinging nettle was painful and left raised welts. The only treatment to help cool down the pain was to slather on tons of calamine lotion or a paste of baking soda and water. Between the stinging nettles and the mosquitos, when I wore short-sleeved shirts or shorts, my legs and arms were covered in bright pink patches of dried calamine lotion — followed by scabs—followed by scars.

Relatives stored, or dumped, used furniture such as bed frames, broken dressers missing drawers, tables with warped tops, and trunks full of musty photographs in the fenced-off section.

On the western side of this area, in front of the rarely opened door, Dad set up his blacksmith area. It had a forge and an anvil and sledgehammers. He used it for horseshoeing. He bought the horseshoes in set sizes like "0" or "2" and then customized them to the shape of a particular horse's hooves. He used the forge and anvil to make plowshares, potato diggers, ditch diggers, and branding irons. Dad and Steve tested out their "X-one-eleven" and "U-one-slash" livestock brands on the inside of the southernmost door.

The blacksmith area is the place where Dad welded whatever metal object he was making, from an irrigation diversion box to a lazy Susan for the kitchen to a hard cover for a Jeep. A large metal plate covered the area. I remember sweeping up the little curls of metal and the other spatter left over from one of the processes. In keeping with the metal theme for this area, there was also a pedal-powered grindstone for sharpening axes, knives, and mower blades.

The southern section was the heart of the building. There was a chicken coop in this area for some time. When I was old enough to remember, there still were a few chickens running around, and there was a lot of chicken poop dripping down on the side of the beams. Yes, our chickens could fly, and Dad had to clip a wing to keep them out of the rafters. My encounters with chickens were limited. I found a couple of brown spotted eggs from time to time. I mostly remember Mom's chicken stories.

Dad used this section as his woodworking shop. He was an excellent carpenter and cabinetmaker. It was here that he built the cabinets for our kitchen, Mom's hutch cabinet, my smaller hutch cabinet, and performed cosmetic surgery on our Christmas trees.

A long, thick table sat along the west wall under the window and held several types of vices. On the northwest side were wooden pigeonholes filled with parts. The northeast section was another storage area. Dad later converted it into a workbench with drawers and doors.

There was a radial arm saw near the south wall. It had a conveyor system with rollers leading to and from the saw. I suspect this may have once been a part of a hearse used to slide the casket inside. The sawdust was exhausted into a bin behind the saw. There was another bin on the southeast corner for scrap wood. I built many forts and model boats, which I sailed down the ditch, out of these scraps.

There were windows on this wall partially obscured by a roof for a lean-to attached to the other side. There was also a door leading into the lean-to. For years there was a large orange campaign bumper sticker made from garish orange reflective material. I remember the name began with an "A." It was for either Gordon Allott or Wayne Aspinall; both were prominent politicians at the time. I don't know if Dad was for or against the candidate.

Dad stored tractors and the D2 Caterpillar in this covered area, and it provided shelter for the horses. There were no stairs below the door, so the only access to the area was to jump down or step on the Caterpillar or the tractor parked nearby.

On the east wall of the southern section, in front of the back window, was a wood-burning stove. In the middle of the room were a variety of woodworking power tools on separate stands. There was a router, a plane, a jigsaw, and a drill press. On and under the tables around the perimeter were hand tools and electric tools like Skill saws, grinders, drills, and sanders. The shop seemed dark and oily. I had a desire to clean it. Whether it was clean or oily, Dad performed his magic in this room.

It was from the edge of this section Celia and Bill's youngest son, Billy, decided to build a "chairlift" across the granary. He and several of his friends, Tom Moore, Jerry Morse, and Don Neil Stapleton, worked on it for days. They strung a "cable" from the trusses using rope salvaged from the Aspen Music Festival Tent.

In the fifties, the music tent was made of canvas and looked like an orange and white circus tent. Music programs and other cultural events used the tent. Every year or so, the Music Associates updated or repaired the tent. On one of those occasions, Dad got yards and yards of the white and orange canvas and long pieces of the thick rope used to hoist the tent. He used the canvas for making his irrigating canvases.

After they strung and tied the rope to the trusses, Billy and his friends attached a car they made from lumber scraps and attached it to the rope with a pulley. Besides Billy's friends, Judy, Peggy, Cherie, Jimmy, and I were there to witness the maiden voyage.

Billy, in his white tee-shirt and jeans, got up on a small table balance on one of the large tables. He got onto the chair sitting on the small table. One of the boys stood next to the table, holding the chair in place. The plan was to let the chair go like it was on a zip line. As envisioned, Billy would go from one side of the granary to the other.

When he was ready, Billy said, "Let her go." The chair moved about five feet. Just past the stack of tables, Billy and the chair crashed to the floor.

The boys hurried down from their positions below the trusses. Everyone stood looking at Billy as he sat, dazed, on the floor. His arm was under the chair. Someone came over to help him up. When they removed the chair, it was apparent both bones in his arm were smashed. It looked like there was a step between his wrist and his elbow. Judy ran up to the house and brought back a magazine and some string to wrap the arm in place. They helped him up to the house and called Celia to take him to the hospital.

As he was lying on the couch in the living room, Judy asked if there was anything he wanted. Although he must have been in severe pain, he said he wanted someone to play *Malaguena*, a Percy Faith album, on the Hi-Fi. Billy's biggest problem with his injury was that he was not able to play football that fall. That was the only trip on the granary chair lift.

A couple of years later, Dad "remodeled" his shop, and it was no longer open to the rest of the granary. He put up a partition between the shop and the middle section using creosoted two by fours salvaged from the Castle Creek Bridge. During that remodel, he built the long workbench with doors and drawers on the northeast corner of the room.

He covered the partition with Masonite he got when the army dismantled Camp Hale near Minturn. Steve and Ted used it for their building projects. Dad used it to make cabinets for Judy when she was newly married and living in student housing at the University of Colorado. Student housing was in Quonset huts purchased after the War.

He insulated the wall in his shop with Styrofoam planks from the Aspen Swimming Pool. When the pool was open in the winter, they covered it with the planks to keep in the heat. We stacked them together to use as rafts for the ditch. We only did that a couple of times. They were too long and cumbersome for the ditch in the yard, and they irritated the skin on our knees and fingers.

The Barn

Another important building was the barn. The barn was in the corner of the corral next to the granary. The corral fence had oak railroad tie posts and uniform, lodgepole pine rails. The rails came from the sawmill at Lenado, Colorado. On the outside of the fence, there was a hay crib with stanchion like openings the animals used to access their food.

As far as corrals go, it was a handsome structure - neat and uniform. It had two large gates. One gate was on the north connected to the granary porch and the other connected to the barn. The barn gate accessed a culvert over the Marolt Ditch into the little field. In the western fence next to the steep hill below the house was a small gate to access the tack shed. The southwest corner of the corral was slightly sloped, and trees outside the fence shaded it. Several large boulders were poking out of the dirt. The horses assembled in this area.

The barn was one of the original buildings from the lixiviation works. Its original use was to store salt for the lixiviation process. It was a long building. It may have been a good location for storing salt but was not the best location for a barn. In the winter, there were days when, because of the shadow of Aspen Mountain, it received no direct sun. Dad decided to tear down the eastern three-fifths of the barn to build another barn in a sunny location. He enclosed the remaining part of the building. Like the granary, the barn had truss beams. The remaining building had two in the middle.

Years later, the bottom boards of the barn were rotting because they were sitting directly on the ground. Dad and Keith cut them off and replaced them with a cinderblock foundation. The new concrete floor had a trough to wash the manure and urine out of the building to the riverbank. There were two main parts to the barn. We used the western half to store tack and milk the cows. Dad built stanchions for the cows to stand secured and eat hay while being milked. A small area on the northwest corner was set aside for saddle horse tack. When I was little, the harnesses and collars for the workhorses hung high on the south wall in the milking section.

A few years after the initial renovation, Dad built a hayloft above the milking side between one of the trusses and the outside wall. It had an outer door for loading and unloading hay bales. A ladder on the southern wall provided interior access.

On the eastern half of the barn was one large room with an interior water trough. It was used from time to time to medicate livestock and for the horses and 4-H animals. It had a Dutch door so that livestock could look out over the lower door. I heard the joke about the optimist who received a pile of horse manure for Christmas, and someone asked why he was so happy. The optimist said, "With all this manure, there has to be a pony in here somewhere." I envisioned that happening in this room.

The Red Barn

Dad used the remains of the salt shed to build the red barn in a location north of the granary. Leo Tekoucich, who had recently returned from World War II, helped Dad build it. Leo was Celia and Albina's younger brother.

This barn, which was painted red, was built like the cattle shed with three enclosed sides—the broad open end faced to the south. The eastern third was completely enclosed and was the initial location for milking cows. Like the new barn, it had a concrete floor with a trough and stanchions. It had a loft on the south side with two high windows.

Also, like the barn, it had a Dutch door from the enclosed side to the covered section.

On the east side of the red barn were two sets of gates making a small pen between the side of the barn and a wooden cattle chute leading from the corral. Before the entrance to the cattle chute was a squeeze shoot that closed to hold the cattle in place while they received injections or other medical procedures. The squeeze chute looked like a jail or a torture device. On the other hand, the wooden chute was fun for climbing and jumping. Unfortunately, the sides were too high and steep for fence walking.

There was a large corral on the south side of the red barn that stopped about 40 feet from the granary. This corral was used primarily for cattle. It had a hay crib on the west side and a water trough on the south side. A gate went to an area behind the granary. Dad eventually put in a temporary fence between this corral and the granary so the horses could eat the dreaded stinging nettles. They seemed to like them!

We played around the red barn. We ran up and jumped off the cattle chute and climbed its steep sides. We played in the empty thresher stored behind it. It had a door on the side, and we could climb in and hide. For some reason, I do not remember playing in the enclosed section of the red barn.

The red barn was the site of one of the scariest events on the ranch. Dad was working on the outside near one of the gates next to the enclosed section. Peggy and Judy were bringing in the milk cows through the Dutch doors for milking. One of the cows bumped the door and disturbed a nest of wasps. The wasps started pouring out of the nest like in a cartoon. They attacked Peggy stinging her repeatedly. She was screaming. Dad ran over to rescue her and, in the process, was badly stung. After they got away from the bees, Dad took Peggy up the hill to the house. Mom immediately put her in the bathtub and covered her with a poultice of baking soda.

A few minutes later, she realized Dad was wheezing badly and gasping for breath. She called Doctor Lewis. Unbeknownst to Dad, he was allergic to bee stings and was going into anaphylactic shock. Dr. Lewis arrived in time to give him an epinephrine shot.

Dad came close to dying. From that day forward, he always carried a couple of syringes of epinephrine with him. He kept several in the granary, and there was a syringe in the glove box in the Jeep.

Besides the granary and the barn, there was another sizable building from the lixiviation works that sat on the southern edge of the driveway. It was about the size of a two-car garage, but taller. That building is visible in vintage photographs of the lixiviation works. It had an open area on the north end where a garage door would be, and we used it for storing farm equipment.

In photos, the building appears to be in a different orientation than in historical photographs. I suspect, when the brothers bought the Holden Tract, the building was moved while working on the house. The building looked like it was off kilter. I suspect, like many lixiviation buildings, it did not have a foundation and probably had a dirt floor. In the old photographs, it was next to the Midland Railway tracks and a cattle-loading chute. I don't remember this building, although it was the background of a photo of me when I was one year old. It collapsed under the weight of snow before I turned two.

Cattle Sheds

When I was born, there was a large cattle shed in the big field. It was between the Midland railroad bed and the highway. It is the site of the community garden. Its open side faced south and was shielded from the wind by the elevated railroad bed. The back of the inside had a shelf for feeding grains. I played on it once or twice. The Marolt Ditch, which at this point was wide and shallow, ran behind it.

When it collapsed one winter, Dad built a new shed closer to the house in the little field. It was about half the size of the original cattle shed. Like the big shed, the open side faced south. It sat lengthwise south of the elevated railroad bed just beyond a wire gate to the little field.

At that time, Dorothy Shaw, Judge Shaw's wife, owned the rights to the Midland's right-of-way. She owned many easements and rights-of-way. It is not too long of a stretch to believe she purchased them because of information supplied by her husband. The cattle shed was built on the right-of-way on purpose and separated from the driveway by a wire fence so we could claim adverse possession if we ever got in a fight with Dorothy.

At one point in the sixties, there were rumors one of the government entities wanted to condemn the right-of-way and adjacent property to relocate Highway 82. Had that happened, we would have lost our house and the barns. There was a lot of nervous time fearing that possibility. Eventually, the county and the Colorado Highway Department opted to remodel the current Castle Creek Bridge.

Bale Shed

There was one more important structure added sometime after I was born. Once Dad started baling hay, he needed a place to store the bales out of the weather. The bale shed was about 50 yards south from where the granary road and the main road split. It was parallel to the lower granary road and about twenty yards north of the red barn. The bale shed was a long open, lean-to type building with a sloped roof. It looked like a cattle shed with no closed sides. The front of the shed faced toward the lower granary road. A fence surrounded the entire structure with two gates allowing the hay wagon ingress and egress to put the hay in the covered part of the shed. The fence prevented the horses and cattle from getting to the hay.

The bale shed became a favorite spot for the barn cats and Nipper to keep warm in winter. It was where my friend Ingrid, and I thought it would be a good place to smoke a couple of cigarettes we stole from Mom or Dad. I am surprised we did not set the place on fire. Fortunately, we only did it once.

Although the following map, created over forty years after I was born, it accurately depicts the locations and footprints of most of the buildings and corrals as they existed in 1949.

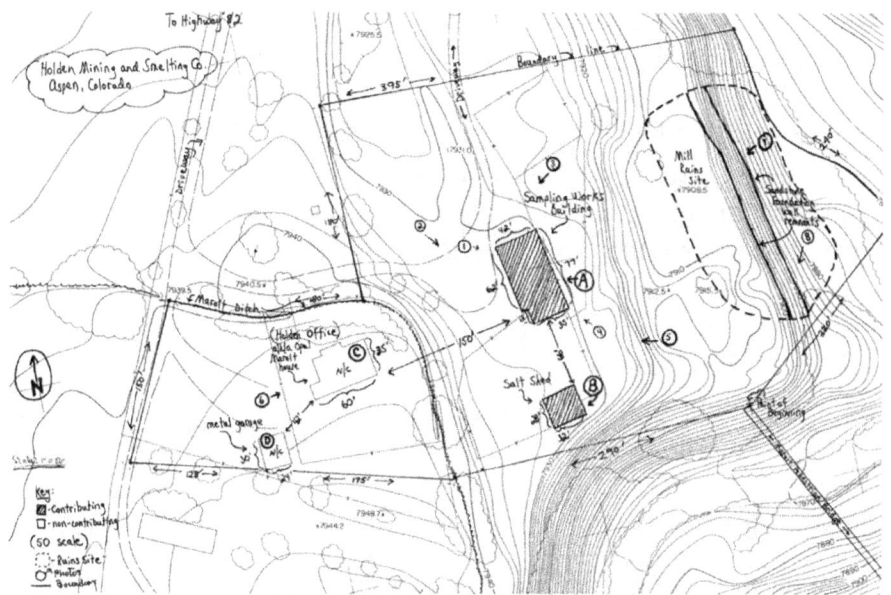

Source: National Register of Historic Places Registration Form OMB No. 1024-0018 dated May 10, 1990 – National Register Number 90000867.

Scrub Triangle and Junk

The three roads – the main road, the granary road, and the lower granary road – created a triangle of open land. This triangular area was mostly covered in sagebrush, jack oaks, and boulders on the sloped areas. The western half, next to the main road, was higher than the eastern half until the two levels converged near the cattle guard.

In the spring, reddish-orange Indian paintbrush and yellow alpine sunflowers with their fuzzy mossy green leaves covered the area. By the time I started school, a section of the upper area, directly east of the house, was the site of the garden, two playhouses, and the pet cemetery. Cottonwoods bordered the north-south lateral ditch used by the garden. The lower half of the triangle was the future site of the bale shed, and it was the future site of a small potato cellar wedged in a ravine created where the two levels converged.

We used the flat area of the scrub triangle nearest the granary for storage or junk. On the west of the flat area was a steep slope leading to the upper level, and on the east was a raised area parallel to the lower granary road that had been part of a spur of the Midland Railway. Next to it were large, corrugated pipes between two and three feet in diameter and many yards long. Dad intended to use them for culverts. Dad and Steve stored hay wagons and the horse trailers in this area. Behind the bale shed were abandoned shells of cars, trucks, farm equipment, and rusting equipment from the lixiviation works cluttered the area. Trees and shrubs grew out of them.

On the northernmost end of the flat areas was a strange-looking rusted metal object about the size of a small car. It looked like a square pyramid with a hole in the top and a door on one side. It, along with the corrugated pipes, was a good hiding spot for playing Hide and Go Seek. I assume it was a piece of equipment from the lixiviation works.

Another odd item, across the granary road south from the junk area, was a big piece of rusting iron. It rested against the hillside leading up to the house. It was about six feet wide and eight or nine feet long and at least a half an inch thick. It was curved as if it was part of a huge cylinder. A seam with welded bolts was a third of the way down. It looked like a rocker for a giant teeter-totter. As a kid, I'd climb on it and run from curve to curve, trying to get it to rock, but it never budged. Over time, dirt slid down the sides and sat in a pocket on the bottom. Eventually, vegetation grew in the dirt.

It never occurred to me to ask what it was. It is only now that I realize it was probably a section of one of the iron tanks from the lixiviation works. This tank probably was about 15 feet in diameter.

When the lixiviation works were in use, there were twenty or more iron tanks, some as big as twenty feet in diameter. I'm guessing the ruins were the source of iron for various ranching projects, mostly related to irrigation and water. There were six or seven iron diversion boxes. There were two headgates on Castle Creek, both with iron gates. There were iron water troughs in the corrals, barns, and pastures. There were several iron culverts.

Water

The lifeblood of a ranch or farm is water. We were fortunate. Water surrounded and crisscrossed the ranch. As anyone who lives in the west knows, water rights are often more valuable than land or buildings.

There were two rivers. Castle Creek was on the east and Maroon Creek on the northwest. Castle Creek ran through our property from the southern border to the Castle Creek Bridge. Besides the two rivers, there were the Marolt Ditch and the Holden Ditch.

Marolt Ditch

The Marolt Ditch was originally the Aspen Ditch and part of the Midland Railway's "Aspen Ranch." The appropriation date for the Aspen Ditch was 1902. It brought water from Castle Creek to the plateau north of the Midland Railway. When the Marolt brothers bought the ranch, they obtained the rights to the Aspen Ditch. In 1934, they adjudicated the water rights and renamed it the Marolt Ditch.

By the time I was born, the Marolt Ditch curved around the northeast corner of our house and went under Highway 82 at the confluence of the highway, the Castle Creek Road, and the Maroon Creek Road. I assumed it had always been that way. We called it the big ditch. We did not refer to it by its former name, the Aspen Ditch, nor its new legal name – the Marolt Ditch. Other than the hours of fun it provided, I never thought much about it or its origins.

The Aspen Ditch had been part of the water system supplying water to the lixiviation works. The lixiviation water supply originated about a mile south of the mill, which is the same location as the headgate for the Aspen Ditch. Photographs of the lixiviation works taken from the east shows what appears to be a ditch along the eastern edge of the plateau above Castle Creek at the same location as the current ditch. The water was for a flume running along the southern edge of the complex. The flume supplied water for power and throughout the facility.

After the lixiviation operations ceased, the water was diverted to the west, away from the buildings. The 1912 Aspen Ranch map shows the Aspen Ditch taking a sharp turn to the where the Midland roadbed bed met the Castle Creek Trestle. That was the location of the earlier flume.

On the map, the Aspen Ditch ran south of the assay office – between it and the main tracks. It followed the main track west until it made a relatively sharp turn to the north along the east leg of a wye switch. In railroad terminology, a wye switch is a spur that looks like an inverted "Y." They are used to change the direction of a train. The ditch followed the tail of the wye and eventually dumped into a reservoir north of the current highway. The large lake on the existing golf course is at the site of the original reservoir. When I was born, the reservoir was dry, and a potato cellar in the basin.

The western leg of the wye switch met the main railway tracks east of the current intersection of Highway 82 and the Castle Creek Road. As can be seen in the following 1934 photograph, Highway 82 used that leg of the wye switch after the highway first connected to the converted Maroon Creek Bridge.

By the time I was born, the highway was moved to its current location north of the spur, thereby flattening the curve. The ditch next to what was the eastern leg of the switch is also visible in the 1934 photograph. Until recently, I was unaware there had been a wye switch in the big field.

Aspen Historical Society

When I was growing up, the section of the ditch next to the eastern leg still existed and was used from time to time. Dad referred to it as the "old ditch," but he did not elaborate. The old ditch was perpendicular to the Marolt Ditch. It was not like the lateral ditches in the fields. It was deeper. It was narrower than the rest of the Marolt Ditch. An isolated willow was on the bank between Marolt Ditch and the highway. The old ditch and the willow are visible in the postcard in the Prologue. I do not remember how often there was water in this ditch, and I never played in it.

The relocation of the Marolt Ditch from south of the assay office to the northeast of it occurred before I was born. After finding the Aspen Map showing the ditch south side of the assay office, I spent hours perusing photographs and newspaper articles trying to figure out when the change occurred. None of the lixiviation photographs showed the ditch in its present location. For a while, I believed my uncles changed the channel after they bought the Holden Tract. That would explain why the formal entrance was on the north side of the house next to the ditch. I surmised they built the formal entry before the change.

I now have a photograph that clearly shows the newly excavated ditch northeast of the assay office. In that photograph, the Midland railroad trestle was still intact. Because the trestle was razed in late 1920, the channel change occurred somewhere between 1912 and 1920. It was unquestionably before my uncles owned the property. I still have no explanation for the front porch of the north side of the house next to the ditch.

Holden Ditch

The Holden Ditch was the other one on the property. It did not come into existence until the late 1940s. It was appropriated in 1950 and adjudicated in 1952. Dad and Steve built it to irrigate the flat land south of the elevated Midland railroad bed. Before that time, the area was only useable as pastureland because there was no irrigation. It was covered mostly with sagebrush. The extra water irrigated the south half of the big field and all the little field.

The Holden Ditch headgate was 750 feet further up Castle Creek from the Marolt Ditch headgate. It was across the river from the Newman Mine ponds and the current Aspen Country Day School campus. The ditch hugged the edge of the slope below the Castle Creek Road and met the Marolt Ditch at the intersection of Highway 82 and the Castle Creek Road. The two ditches went under the highway and became the Marolt Ditch. The place where the two ditches converged had a small sandy "beach" frequented by sandpipers.

Dad and Steve took several years to build the Holden Ditch. I heard stories about its construction. Most of the stories involved dynamite. Dad hired someone for that purpose. The blaster may have been Russell Holmes. Dad raved about the blaster's skill in placing the charge to expend the least amount of energy for the desired result.

Dad precisely engineered the Holden Ditch. He learned to survey while attending the engineering school at the University of Colorado. He had a survey transom and used it for many ranch projects, including the ditch and the wooden fence in the yard.

Dad was surprised the part of the ditch in the field turned out to be the most difficult to dredge because of hidden boulders. One would think the upper section was the challenging portion because of the steep banks on the edge of the ravine. While some of the construction involved blasting, red sedimentary rocks in this area were not as challenging as the granite boulders buried in the field.

Dad was able to build much of the upper part using the Caterpillar bulldozer. This part of the ditch was noticeably wider and shallower than the Marolt Ditch. I complained. Unlike the Marolt Ditch, it was too shallow for tubing. Dad explained using the bulldozer made it that way. The ability to get the bulldozer up the ditch made spring-cleaning possible. In the spring, rocks sloughed from the upper banks. The Cat or the John Deere removed them.

Dad planned on putting the corrugated culvert pipes in the scrub triangle through this section to avoid the need to clear the rocks each spring. He never got around to using them.

Dad dug the lower part of the Holden Ditch at the perimeter of the field, mostly with a ditch digger attachment or by hand with the help of strategically placed dynamite charges. It was deep and narrow. That part of the ditch was not tubing friendly either because most of it was under low overhanging brush on the hillside below the Castle Creek Road.

The final appropriation date was in 1950. At that time, Dad and Steve officially named it the Holden Ditch. With the completed Holden Ditch, the southern part of the big field and the little field were now useable as a hayfield.

Dad added three diversion boxes for lateral ditches crossing the southern fields. The easternmost diversion box was below what would become Bill and Celia's house. The ditch was wide and shallow to allow vehicle access to the hill below Castle Creek. The area had rich, dark mud and was the largest mosquito breeding ground on the ranch. Peggy set up her mud pie operation using the metal diversion box as an oven.

The next box created a lateral ditch parallel to the west side of the dividing fence. It was on this box Peggy took a break from bringing the milk cows to the red barn for milking to stand and direct an imaginary orchestra. A couple of times, when the cows did not arrive when expected, Keith came and got them. Peggy didn't notice.

Judy caught a small fish sitting the last box used for a lateral ditch bisecting the southern half of the big field. The box was next to the deepest part of the ditch and shadowed by overhanging brush. Judy brought the fish home only to lose it in the window well in the car. It is unclear why she had the fish near the window well. The smell remained in the car for quite some time.

The Characters

The Characters

Picnics with the Extended Family

My immediate family was Mom, Dad, my sisters, Judy and Peggy, and my brother Keith. But we also had daily contact with a large extended family of aunts, uncles, and cousins. The event that brought us together was picnics.

From Memorial Day until Labor Day, there was a picnic nearly every Sunday somewhere. Sometimes, picnics were planned as part of a family reunion when relatives arrived from California, Denver, and Salida. We particularly liked it when Dad's relatives, who owned the Coca Cola bottling works in Salida, showed up with cases of Coke.

Sometimes the picnics were a holiday celebration. Otherwise, we decided on the location a day or two before or after Mass. Some picnics were traditionally on a specific day and at a specific place.

At first, there were different locations. Most were up Castle Creek. There were picnics at Pine Creek and Ashcroft. Although we went up Maroon Creek and the trail to East Maroon Pass, we never had a family picnic at Maroon Lake. I remember a few picnics up Independence Pass at the Difficult Campground, Lincoln Gulch, and the Grottos.

The first picnic I remember was at Pine Creek. We were near an area that was currently dry but covered with rounded stones as if it had been under the river that often flooded. The picnic was in the pine trees on an improvised table. I was walking around wearing beer cans on my feet. We stomped on the middle of the can and molded the ends over the instep. This was supposedly something fun to do, but I cannot for the life of me remember why. I was eating black olives off my fingers.

Edmund was in a tall pine tree. Albina had an ax and was either threatening to chop down the tree or was in the process of doing so. I got the impression everyone thought it was funny. Edmund survived his ride to the ground.

I recall a picnic or two in the river bottom Steve owned below the Midland and north of the Maroon Creek Bridge. These picnics also included the Bishops. We took a steep road down to the river and past beaver ponds cut off from the main river. I played with Gary and

Barney. Dad and Albert fished. When Steve sold the Midland, he sold the river bottom property to Sam Caudill, a renowned local architect.

One of our favorite picnic spots was the Montezuma Mine mill and bunkhouse, near the headwaters of Castle Creek, and Steve's 320-acre "pasture," off Owl Creek Road. The pasture was between what became the Buttermilk and Snowmass ski areas.

Montezuma Picnics

Bill organized the Montezuma picnics. Bill was Dad's oldest living brother, who was seven years older than Dad. He was a handsome, quiet man. He, Steve, and Dad looked similar – no doubt they were brothers. They favored their father. Bill had softer features than Steve, who had a chiseled look. Dad looked like both but looked a little more Slovenian and probably like Frank, Jr. At one time, I thought Dad looked like an older Glen Ford. Ted was the youngest living brother and had more delicate features like their mother.

All the brothers were about five feet seven or eight inches tall. All were bald from their foreheads to the back of the top of their heads. Dad said, "I comb my hair with a washcloth." Undoubtedly, their hair loss was part of their motivation to wear hats.

Other than Steve, who sounded a little like John Wayne, I do not remember anything distinctive about the brothers' voices.

Bill was no longer involved in ranching. During the Montezuma picnic era, he, Celia, and their children lived in town in a cute two-story yellow Victorian across Bleeker Street from what used to be the Washington School. Their children were Beverly "Bev," George "Bud," Max, and Bill "Billy." At that time, everyone called him Billy. When I was little, only Max and Billy were living full-time in Aspen. Max was Keith's age, and Billy was Peggy's age. Bud and Bev were older. They came to Aspen frequently; they both had children near my age.

During the time we were having picnics at the Montezuma, Bill worked as the bartender at the Red Onion – a bar on Cooper Street. To supplement his income, Bill went "junking."

Early each morning, he drove his red Jeep to the dump. At that time, the dump was on the west side of the Maroon Creek Road just after the road makes a right-angle bend to the south. It was across the river from what is now Tiehack in the Buttermilk Ski Area. Currently, it is the site of the recreation center. Townspeople were free to go to the dump any time and drop off their trash. Around mid-day, someone bulldozed the new deposits into the perpetual smoldering fire. That burning garbage smell lingered over the west end of town when the winds were right.

When Bill went to the dump, he looked primarily for items containing recyclable, semi-precious metals like copper, brass, and iron. Sometimes he found other treasures, such as furniture, tools, equipment, and appliances. One time, he found a brand-new upholstered headboard in its original shipping carton that he and Celia used in a spare bedroom in their house.

When not working at the Red Onion, Bill removed the metal and sorted it into piles. Once or twice a year, he loaded Dad's pickup with barrels of the sorted metal and drove to Denver to sell the scrap metal to dealers. On his return trip, he brought back supplies for Dad and Steve, including a case or two of whiskey.

Celia also went to the dump. She went to the old part overhanging the river to find and excavate antique bottles. There was no smoldering garbage there. The bottles were layered like sedimentary rock. From time to time, Mom and I went with her. Celia knew just how far down to go to could find the best antique bottles.

She mostly excavated beer bottles that were brown, dark green, or clear, turning shades from light blue green to pink. Then she found the most prized bottles, the pharmacy bottles. The Al S. Lamb "druggist" bottles were some of the more popular ones, especially those with the emblem of a lamb.

Over time, Celia excavated thousands of bottles. She filled the high windows in her house and the spaces above her kitchen cabinets with her collections. Some of the bottles were particularly valuable because they dated back to well before the Civil War.

Later she began collecting specialty bottles. She focused on whiskey bottles and Jim Beam collection sets – some in figurine decanters that were more like sculptures than bottles and some flask-shaped bottles with reproductions of old masterpieces.

In the late fifties, Celia and Bill built a modern split-level house on an elevated piece of property on the hillside at the end of the little field. The house was just off Castle Creek Road north of the big curve above what used to be the Newman Mine and is now the Country Day School. The building site was on the side of the hill between the road and the field. They leveled out a nook in the aspen trees for the house and added an apron of fill dirt to accommodate a driveway. It was a split-level house with old brick and siding and a deck on the front. There was a matching two-car garage south of the house, also nestled in the trees. They had a view of the side of Aspen Mountain, our field, our house, the golf course, and Red Butte.

Before Dad sold the property to Bill and Celia, they started leveling another lot about 1,000 feet to the west but realized it was too close to the city water line. As was typical for Dad's real estate transactions, when the house was complete, Dad had Gerry Pesman, the local surveyor, provide the legal description so Dad could prepare a deed.

Sometime after they moved into their house, Billy, who was an Alpine ski racer, got a trampoline for dryland training. For a short while, it was in the aspens in their back yard. Billy found that to be a difficult place to practice and appeared dangerous for solo practice. Therefore, he made a wood-lined pit in a flat below the steep slope of the driveway apron. The trampoline sat in the hole and was even with the ground. Billy covered it with a tarp anchored by two by fours. It certainly seemed a lot less intimidating than when it was three feet above the ground.

After Celia and Bill built their house, I walked across the field to visit. Once Billy got and moved his trampoline, I was motivated to stop and jump even when I was on my own. I rarely did anything courageous. I only did a few knee flips – never any real flips. For the most part, I just practiced "drops" – stomach, back, knee, and seat. The goal was to see how many hundreds I could do. If it was just me, after a half-hour or so, I got bored.

If I saw Bill's Jeep, I climbed up the steep driveway apron. Bill was usually in an alcove in the trees near the garage. He was working with the junk from the dump. I sat on a stump and watched him unscrewing or dislodging small pieces of metal or stripping the coating off the wires. Then he sorted the bits of metal into coffee cans which he later transferred to the metal drums.

He stored the drums across the Castle Creek Road in a shed that was part of the city water system. The shed may have stored chlorine for the water plant at one time. A stream for run-off from the tanks ran under the shed and disappeared under Castle Creek Road.

I enjoyed talking to Bill. He was always interested in what I was doing and asked about other members of my family. For some reason, he called me, "Slick." His son, Max, also used that nickname. Sometimes, Max teasingly calling me "Icky Sticky Vicki." I did not mind. It beat "Silly Willy Wet Spot" Keith used to tease me when I did not make it to the bathroom on time.

My visits were not just about conversations. After a while, Bill said, "Do you want a spud?"

"Sure."

I followed him into the lower level of the house. Bill disappeared into the utility room, where there was a large chest freezer, and returned with two frozen candy bars – one for each of us. His favorite was, ironically, an Idaho Spud. An Idaho Spud had marshmallow nougat covered in chocolate and frosted with coconut in the form of a potato. The Idaho Spud was ironic because Bill took the lead in the Marolt family potato operations.

Bill liked candy; it may have been an alternative to having a drink or two. Despite being a bartender, Bill did not drink. I heard he stopped after getting into trouble when he was young. Mom said it had something to do with him flipping a car. Maybe I am thinking of Ted, who I know flipped the car when he was a teenager but not from drinking. Bill, being a Marolt, may have just stubbornly stopped drinking when someone said he couldn't do it.

Despite not drinking, Bill always had beer at his house. Sometimes he shared the gifts of beer he received from August "Augie" Busch of Anheuser-Busch. I am not sure if it was Auggie Busch II, who was around Bill's age, or if it was Auggie Busch III, who was around Max and Keith's age. I think it was the younger Busch. He was fond of Bill and got to know him on skiing trips to Aspen, where they chatted across the bar at the Red Onion. He gave Bill many items related to the brewery, including new beers. Therefore, besides the candy, before I went home, Bill handed me one of the gifts or a new beer to take to Dad.

For a while, Bill did not talk to any of the brothers, although they all attended the same events. I never knew the reason. I wonder if any of them remembered why they did not talk to each other. I bet it had a lot to do with the time Frank, Jr., Rudy, and Steve more or less forced Bill to sell his share of the ranch. It seemed like most of his angst was directed at Steve and, because Dad and Ted were always with Steve, it rubbed off on them.

At gatherings at Bill's house, the four brothers sat in the living room. Two on the couch and two in separate chairs. Steve, Ted, and Dad talked to each other, and Bill listened. From time to time, Bill said something to me like, "Slick, ask your dad if he liked the Champale."

Dad responded, looking at me, "I thought it was too sweet. I liked that Michelob a helluva lot better." At the time, Michelob was Budweiser's new premium beer.

If Bill was not around, I enjoyed visiting with Celia when she was home. Unlike Mom, who was home most of the time, Celia cleaned houses for many of the newer people in town, including Elizabeth Paepcke, Betty Oakes, and Edgar and Polly Stern. She always had interesting stories about what went on in her clients' homes – her tales would have made a reality show premise today. She shared more than they would have liked about their habits and lack of cleanliness. "You wouldn't believe the gunk I mucked out of the rubber around their refrigerator door." I thought, perhaps, her observations could be the origins of "Airing Dirty Laundry" about famous domestic employers from the perspective of their workers.

Celia was a tall, handsome woman with medium-brown long hair she wore on top of her head in a bun. I took an iteration of her name, Cecelia, as my confirmation name, and she and Bill were my godparents. Celia had a distinctive, lyrical voice with melodic inflections and a quizzical upbeat. It had a recognizable cadence. One expected that she could soon break into heartfelt laughter, which was often the case. She could imitate people and "got a kick" out of the things they said and did. She was a great storyteller. I can still hear her voice in my head. Several of her children and some of her grandchildren have the same inflections in their voices.

Celia came from a family of daredevils. Her brother George hiked up Mount Hayden to ski and did so in the dead of winter without gloves. George was in the 10th Mountain Division in Italy during World War II. Celia's children carried on the tradition with their ski racing and mountain climbing. Celia's bravery was not unlimited. She claimed, "That Maroon Creek Bridge scares the shit out of me. I close my eyes when I drive across it." This was not hyperbole. It was true.

Bill was a picnic fan and organizer. He organized the picnics at the Montezuma Mill. There was always one and sometimes two picnics a year at the mill's bunkhouse up Castle Creek. The Montezuma Mine was below Castle Peak at around 13,000 feet. The bunkhouse and mill were about 3,000 feet below the mine. Bill had connections that allowed him to get keys to the bunkhouse. Going to the Montezuma was like going to an amusement park. I could hardly wait until a Montezuma Sunday rolled around.

We drove our Jeeps, packed with kids and picnic foods, up the Castle Creek Road, and turned off a couple of miles above Ashcroft. Then we went on a Jeep road for a few more miles bordering Castle Creek to the right. Just before the split in the road leading to the Montezuma Mine and Pearl Pass, we turned off the main road onto a rugged trail. We went several yards through the trees and crossed a large stream below a waterfall coming off a steep hillside. When we forded the stream, the Jeeps swayed from side to side. I gripped hard to the edge of the seat and closed my eyes, fearing we would tip over and float away to where the stream joined Castle Creek below. I opened my eyes when I felt the Jeep climb out of the water.

Before us, in the distance, set against the hillside, were the Montezuma mill and boarding house. The buildings were dark brown timber with rusted iron roofs. I was always surprised to see them. In my mind, they should have been on the opposite side of Castle Creek. As we approached, the mill was on the left side of the road, and a bunkhouse was on the right. Castle Creek ran below the bunkhouse and had not yet joined with the stream from the hillside.

Marolt Family Collection

    Bill took out a key and unlocked the rusty padlock on the bunkhouse door. The main room was two stories high with tables, benches, and a heating stove. In the modern world, it would have made a great ski lodge. I think the sleeping quarters were below this room, but I never went down there. We set up the picnic food, beer, and the yellow and silver, slightly dented Thermos jug filled with Kool-Aid or lemonade on one of the wooden tables.

    The older kids went over to the mill. It was a large mining building. The inside of the mill went up several stories. Despite having been idle for many decades, it was much as it had been at the time it was abandoned. It was filled with large equipment, most of which appeared to be rusting. Some of the equipment looked like giant squared funnels – probably some sort of hopper. There were stairs and metal ladders and conveyor belts. It was dark with a few rays of sunshine coming in through the windows near the top and defusing in the dust we stirred up. I only went in there a couple of times and mostly just to look around. I was too little to play with the teenagers.

They played army and espionage games. The games included dividing into teams throwing metal objects at each other or dropping the items on unsuspecting opponents on the ground below. They hid in the equipment. One year, Cherie almost got stuck in one of those funnels. As I heard the tale of combat and triumph, I could hardly wait until I was old enough to participate. Miraculously, no one ever got seriously injured in these games, but it is likely there were a few near-fatal misses. I can imagine the headline: "Fourteen-Year-old Local Child Critically Injured by Half-pound Bolt Dropped from Window."

Sometimes, I hiked above the mill with my sisters and Cherie, but usually with Albina, Celia, or Polly. That was the shortest distance to the mine at the base of Castle Peak. It was not an easy path. It had been the site of a tram from the mine to the mill.

Albina was shorter than Celia. She had long, coal-black hair, which like Celia, she wore it in a bun on top of her head. In later years, a single gray streak came from her temple, and she enhanced it on special occasions with a little white shoe polish. Though most of the time she wore pants and shirts, when she dressed for special events, she was stunning. Unlike Mom and Polly, neither Celia nor Albina wore housedresses. They wore slacks and shirts.

I liked being around Albina and Celia. They were both notoriously late to everything, but when they finally arrived, they were fun. They made up for the late arrival by staying late.

Albina was married to Edmund Gerbaz. The Gerbaz family came to the valley from Italy and had a large sheep ranch about 10 miles "down the valley" toward Glenwood Springs. The location of their ranch is known today as Gerbazdale. Edmund was tall and lean and often wore a billed military-styled work cap. I had the impression he may have stooped over just a bit to reduce his height.

The hike was steep and covered with timbers and rusted tram cables used to transport the ore from the mine to the mill. Shortly after completion, the tram collapsed under snow. We used the cables to help climb the steep hill. At this high altitude, it was hard to climb up the gravelly surface, especially in sneakers or my Mary Janes. Mine were not prissy Mary Janes, just hand-me-down leather shoes with a leather strap. They were my shoes of choice.

I do not think we ever made it more than a few hundred feet up the steep hill behind the mill. I never made it to the mine using that route. We could reach the mine by Jeep by going up a road that clung precariously to the steep hillside. It was scary, and I only rode up there once when we picnicked at the bunkhouse. There was a sizeable permanent snowfield above the mine at the base of Castle Peak. In later years, Max got permits from the Forest Service and used it as a summer skiing and training center he called the Montezuma Basin.

Instead of participating in the "mill games," I spent most of my time with my cousin, Rodney "Rod" Barnes. He was Celia and Bill's grandson and a year younger than me. Rod was a handsome boy.

Bev was the oldest of Bill and Celia's children and Rod's mother. She was a tall, regal woman with a distinctive, heartfelt laugh and a voice like her mother's. Rod's voice is similar. Bev was a true combination of a Marolt and a Tekoucich. She pulled her long, dark hair on top of her head in a French roll. She maintained a slender figure by drinking a lot of coffee and smoking a lot of cigarettes.

Bev was married to Bob Barnes. Bob was a tall, quiet guy, who I thought, in later years, looked like Clint Eastwood. Bob was from another Aspen family. By the time of the picnics, Bev and Bob were living in California. Bob worked as a smelter supervisor for American Smelting and Refining Company in Tormey Village, a company town near Crockett, California. It was also known before that time as the Selby Smelting and Lead Company and boasted a 606-foot smokestack. Smokestacks seem to be a family theme. Bev, Bob, and Rod came to Aspen for a few weeks every summer. Rod and I spent virtually every day, all day, exploring or playing on the ranch.

At the Montezuma, Rod and I scurried up the ladder leading into a loft overlooking the main floor of the bunkhouse. From there, we could spy on the adults and listen in on their conversations. After a while, they forgot about us, and their conversations got a bit louder and bit bolder. Sometimes we went down from the loft long enough to return with our fingers capped with black olives – obviously my favorite picnic food. For years, the only "vegetables" I ate were olives and tomatoes.

Usually, Rod and I went outside to find Bob. Bob did not participate too much in the conversations. He did target practice over the hill below the bunkhouse with a pistol shooting beer cans or bottles leaning against the creek bank. He was probably a good marksman. I remember shooting a gun only once in my life, and it was under Bob's supervision at the Montezuma.

Dad owned two guns that I remember – a .22 pistol and a .22 bolt-action rifle with a scope. He may have had a shotgun as well. I saw a few shotgun shells in the dresser drawer in Keith's room with the rest of the ammunition and the pistol.

I was disappointed in the pistol. It did not look anything like the six-guns the cowboys used. It looked more like something out of *Dick Tracy*. I never touched it. By that time, my parents told me in no uncertain terms never to touch a gun. Additionally, when I was in grade school, Butch Lowderback, who was a day older than me, was accidentally shot in the leg by his brother. The rest of the time, I knew him, Butch limped.

In our house, the rifle hung in Keith's closest behind the razor strop. The razor strop had a leather side and a canvas side held together with a metal ring on the end. It used to hang in the back porch sink when Dad used a single-blade razor and the sink for shaving. I think the placement of the razor strop in the closet was intentional. "If you touch this gun, you will get this on your backside." I never touched the gun. I never got the razor strop for this or any other infraction. I don't think anyone in our family ever experienced it. The threat was sufficient.

Bob also took a coffee can and his pocketknife into the forest to excised nodules from the pine trees. I believe those nodules were pine resin. When he inserted the knife under the edge, flicked his wrist, the nodules popped into the can. They had a pleasant pine smell. I do not know what he did with them, but in my memory, he did something with closets either as a deodorizer or as a means of inhibiting pests.

After watching target practice, Rod and I sat on the moraine-like hillside below the bunkhouse above the creek and tried to entice camp robbers, gray jay type birds, to swoop in and grab bits of bread or leftover food. The challenge was to have them take the food directly from our hands. These were the only birds we were aware of that could be held.

At that time, I had never heard of cockatiels. At most, I hoped the legend was true that if you put salt on a magpie's tail, you could catch it. Duh, if you got close enough to put salt on the tail, you were close enough to catch it. I also heard that if you split a magpie's tongue, it could talk. I never tried that either because I never got close with a saltshaker. Other than camp robbers, there were many chipmunks, but they were not nearly as friendly.

There was a cabin nestled in the pines downstream from the bunkhouse. My sisters, Cherie, and I looked through the windows to see it was well preserved. There was an iron stove, an icebox, a metal bed frame, tables, benches and pots and pans and dishes on open shelves. I wished it could play inside.

Across the creek, in the distant pines, was another structure – a modern "A" frame building with a shiny metal roof. It belonged to Stuart Mace as part of his Toklat dogsled operation. We never went across the stream to that building. It seemed out of place.

After our mill adventures, the Jeep caravan wound down the road, past Ashcroft, and returned to Aspen. Sometimes, Rod spent the night at our house. I am sure that by the time the adults closed the bunkhouse and filled the Jeeps, they had consumed their fair share of beer. It never occurred to us that it might be unsafe. As far as our family was concerned, it never was.

Rod and I were contradictions to each other. Bev and Bob raised him to be neat. When he came to our house after a picnic, the kids took turns taking baths. We used Vel soap because it was the only thing that lathered in the hard water.

When Rod took a shower or a bath, he brushed his teeth, combed his hair, and looked neat in his pajamas, bathrobe, and slippers. He precisely folded the sash on his robe.

On the other hand, when I got out of the tub, it had to be rinsed to remove the remaining sand and grime. Even after a bath, I had messy hair, my fingernails were not completely clean, and my legs and arms were scratched and dotted with small black and blue bruises and mosquito bites upon which I slathered pink Calamine lotion. My pajamas were mismatched. Usually, I wore a white boy's T-shirt and hand-me-down pajama bottoms from Barney and Gary. I do not remember having a bathrobe until I was in high school. Before that, in the winter, one of my sister's old moth-eaten cardigan sweaters worked just fine.

One year, probably 1961, we got devastating news – the mill and the bunkhouse burned to the ground. To think the Montezuma was gone was distressing. We had stopped going there a few years earlier when the owner of the mill leased the bunkhouse to two miners working the mine. The newspaper reported the probable cause of the fire was lightning. The two miners escaped, but their dogs did not.

After we no longer used the Montezuma bunkhouse, Bill continued to organize small picnics at ski touring huts built or associated with Fred Braun. These huts were also in the Castle Creek area south of Ashcroft.

I remember one Sunday picnic on a lovely fall day. It was probably some time when I was in junior high school. Mom, Dad, Celia, Bill, and I were the only people attending. We went to the Lindley Hut, which was in the mountains south of Ashcroft near Star Peak. At the time, it was an A-frame with a tin roof tucked in the trees. It had a big sunny deck on the south side in front of a wall of windows.

Dad and Bill sat on the bench outside next to the big window. Bill was whittling. Dad was nursing a beer from a glass bottle. I sat crosslegged on the deck as I sketched the scenery. Mom and Celia were inside the open door, talking.

The daylight was brilliant in that fall sort of way, especially when accentuated with the long dark shadows. The sky was cobalt blue. The colors of the Aspen leaves were intense, and they sparkled in the sunlight. The trees were mostly yellow and orange, but on a steep hillside across a small draw was a bright red vertical strip of aspens. Bill said the color had to do with a vein of some type of mineral below the roots.

Celia and I hiked up the hill and retrieved branches for fall bouquets. I took a few leaves to school for show and tell. Having never seen bright red Aspen leaves, some people said they did not believe they were real. I was disappointed.

Years after the Montezuma fire, I hiked up to the site of the old bunkhouse and mill. It was littered with rusted metal. The location of the mill and bunkhouse was as always on the opposite side of the trail from where I imagined they should be. The cabin had collapsed into a random pile of timber. The modern A-frame across the creek was still there.

I sat on the hillside below where the bunkhouse used to be – the one where Rod and I fed camp robbers. I closed my eyes and imagined being back there feeding camp robbers and hearing the laughter of the people inside a now missing building.

The Picnic Grounds

After the Montezuma was no longer available for family picnics, we started having picnics on the ranch. Bill picked the location. South of the potato field below Bill and Celia's house was a small meadow bordered by the Holden Ditch to the east and a small stream running along the base of the hill. The run-off stream was from the water tanks and reservoir on the mountain above. Cottonwoods, near the Holden Ditch, outlined the meadow. There was a grove of aspen trees to the south and along the hillside.

The first picnic in this meadow was in 1957 when Dad's sister, Elsie, and her husband, George Rinker, visited from Encino, California. They came to build a summer cabin on the property below Aspen Mountain, which Dad sold to them for $500. Their adult daughters, Audrey, Dorothy, Dorothy's husband, Chuck Clifton, their children, and another grandson, Johnny Rhode, joined them. Chuck was a retired navy pilot, and Dorothy was a former WAVE. Chuck was a handsome man who reminded me of John Kerr from *South Pacific*. Dorothy was pretty. She looked like a movie star with dark hair, dimples, and deep red lipstick. Audrey was younger than Dorothy and had a career at the Department of Social Services in Los Angeles.

Much older than my siblings and me, Dorothy and Chuck had three boys all about my age – Gary, Tim, and Loren, whom we called George. Johnny Rhode was the son of another sister, Mary Elisabeth, and was Judy's age. Until these cousins showed up one day, I did not know they existed. During that summer and the next summer, we had a great time playing on or around the ranch.

Picnic guests parked their vehicles in an area on the northeastern side of the Holden Ditch. To get to the picnic area, everyone crossed the ditch on a couple of planks. For the first picnic, Dad or Bill built a fire ring from rocks upon which they placed an iron mesh. They made a seating area with a couple of logs. Dad brought up an old wooden table from the granary, and they strung tarps in the trees for extra shade.

The aspen trees on the hillside behind the picnic area were a great source of amusement. My favorite activity was to find a young aspen tree, reach up, and hang on it until it bent enough for my feet to touch the ground. Once it was low, I climbed on, straddled it, and rode it like a horse – pushing off and bouncing several feet above the ground. After being ridden, the trees never wholly recovered. In later years, trees bent at unusual angles interspersed the aspen forest. They looked like victims of some haphazard snow slide.

Another fun aspen tree activity was carving pictures or words on the big trees. The dusty white bark was soft and easy to score with a pocketknife. The bark pulled away from the wood. The wood was moist and had a sweet smell. By the next year, black scars formed over the writings and drawing, making them stand out against the white bark.

Sometimes, Dad made whistles out of willow branches. The kids gathered around and watched him work. He cut off a small section of a branch about six or eight inches long, making sure there were no knots. He cut one end at an angle for the mouthpiece, moved a few inches to cut a small notch, and scored the circumference of the bark. Then he tapped the bark with the butt of his pocketknife and magically removed a skin-like piece of bark. Then he carved a long u-shaped notch below the first notch and planed a small channel from the notch to the angled end. Finally, he replaced the skin, and the whistle was ready for use. The process repeated depending on the number of kids, followed by the cacophony of whistles.

One of the more memorable picnics at the picnic grounds was when the adults decided to polka. Someone brought a portable record player or went home to get it. It was one of those like they had in school that looked like a suitcase. For a power source, they stretched together extension cords over the hill from Celia and Bill's newly constructed house. The extension cords were all lengths and types. That day it ended up drizzling. The tarps in the trees were filling with water, and we went around dumping the puddles using a long pole. Given the strange assortment of cords, it is unbelievable no one was electrocuted. The only damage from that day was the grass was trampled into a muddy mess, and it took years for the grass to recover completely.

After the first picnic, the picnic grounds evolved. Dad built a lean-to that was built like the bale shed and could support either tarps, corrugated metal, or fiberglass as a temporary roof. The panels were removed before the snow and immediately after each picnic, so they did not blow away. The inside of the lean-to had a counter-high wooden bench for food and space underneath for coolers and picnic baskets.

One summer, Dad and his good friend Buck Parsons hosted an Elk's picnic at the picnic grounds. That may have been the year Buck was the Exalted Ruler. Dad built a special barbeque. He used iron railroad rails and welded a metal base and topped it with mesh racks. It was big enough to cook 25 steaks and dozens of foil-wrapped ears of corn and potatoes.

There were at least ten picnics at the picnic grounds each year. To get to the picnic grounds, everyone but Celia and Bill, who could walk the hundred or so feet over the hill through the aspen trees, drove their cars and Jeeps past our house, past the cattle shed, up the dirt road on the east side of the little field, and past Bill's potato patch.

When we loaded the Jeep with the oilcloth-lined bushel baskets and coolers, Nipper went crazy with excitement. He loved picnics in the field. When he saw the baskets and us climbing into the Jeep and backing up, he ran full speed past the cattle shed toward the picnic grounds.

It was sad when Nipper realized there would be no picnic for him that day. He came back to the gate past the cattle shed and realized no one was following. He stood looking longingly as we disappeared in the opposite direction. Nipper could have gone with us to other picnics, but he refused to ride in vehicles. I wish we had trained him to do so when he was young.

Steve and Polly's Pasture

The other designated picnic location was what Steve and Polly called the pasture. We referred to it as Polly's pasture. For years, it was the preferred location for the Fourth of July picnics. Steve bought the 320 acres sometime in 1949 for $6,000 when he and Dad were concerned about ever diminishing grazing rights on Federal land.

Steve's property was on Owl Creek, which is off the Brush Creek Road. It was on a hillside between what became Buttermilk Mountain and the Snowmass ski area. Steve wanted a place to take his cattle during the summer. Over the years, when he wasn't working the Midland, Steve and Polly worked at the pasture. It was a summer getaway. The rest of the year, they lived in town in a white Victorian house on the corner of 6th Street and West Smuggler.

Polly's real name was Olive. She was four years older than Steve. She was a small handsome woman who was feisty and smart. She had curly, light brown hair. Despite some premature wrinkles, she was exceptionally spry and walked fast. Over the years, she did not seem to age. Sometimes she wore jeans and a plaid shirt for these picnics, but for the most part, she wore housedresses, often with an apron, knee socks, and a hairband.

Polly came to Aspen in the summer of 1932 to visit the Wentworth family, who owned a lovely two-story yellow Victorian house across from the Washington School – the one Celia and Bill eventually owned and sold to build their Castle Creek house. Mr. Wentworth came to Aspen in the summer and wrote *Aspen on the Roaring Fork*, which he published in the 1930s. He was a postman in Connecticut and knew the Nieman family. Their daughter was Polly's friend. When she lived in Connecticut, Polly taught at a "normal school" to train teachers.

On one of her summer visits, Polly and her friend wanted to ride horses, and someone suggested Steve Marolt had horses. Steve, who exemplified the Marolt brothers' shyness around women, offered to let someone else take a couple of his horses to the "young ladies from the East." He ended up being the one who delivered the horses.

Polly and Steve hit it off. Polly readily participated in horseback riding and helping with ranching operations. Her only complaint was that, because of her narrow hip configuration, it made her extremely saddle sore. She did better riding Steve's favorite steed, Snake. In later years, Polly underwent two hip replacements well before they were a standard procedure.

After a few more of Polly's summer visits to Aspen, Steve traveled by train to Connecticut to meet her family. They married in a civil service in New York City Hall. Polly said they chose that location to avoid a "fuss" with her family, who frowned on her marrying a Catholic.

Years later, Steve's neighbor, Frances Kalmes, conspired with Polly to arrange for her to marry Steve in the Catholic Church. Frances told Steve to put on dress clothes because there was an event he wanted him to attend downtown. They went to St. Mary's, where the priest was waiting for Steve to hear his confession. He then married Steve and Polly in a private ceremony. That was many years before the picnics.

To get to Steve and Polly's pasture, we turned off the Brush Creek Road near Bernard "Bernie" Stapleton's home. Bernie was one of many Stapletons. Besides being a rancher, he drove a school bus and parked it behind his house in the summer. Many ranchers had similar winter jobs. Edmund worked as a lift operator on Little Nell.

Steve had an easement through Bernie's property. Immediately after turning off the road, there was a wooden gate. If we were following Steve and Polly, the gate was unlocked. I got the job of jumping out of the Jeep, opening the gate, and closing it behind us.

Owl Creek was to the right of the road for several yards, and then the trail crossed it over a small culvert. I think of the water in Owl Creek as being gray. I do not know if that was the color of the water or the small shale-like stones over which it flowed. About halfway to the cabin was another gate separating Steve's property from Bernie's property. The cabin was at the top of a large sloping meadow set in a grove of aspen trees. The road went up a steep incline impossible in winter.

Originally the cabin was one room with a red concrete floor. There was a wood-burning cookstove, a small propane-powered refrigerator, a counter with a washbasin, and upper and lower cabinets with sliding Masonite doors. Two twin-sized beds at right angles in the corner were used as couches during the day and beds at night.

Several Coleman lamps hung from hooks in the ceiling, and others were readily available for a trip to the outhouse. I was fascinated by the white mantles in the lamps, which to me, looked like the cobwebs in chokecherry bushes. I liked watching the color going from amber to bright white as they heated.

Below the window facing Woody Creek and the Roaring Fork Valley, was a large table covered with a checkered oilcloth. Polly always had a bucket or vase of wildflowers on the table. Columbines were the most prevalent flowers in the pasture. The first thing she did when she came into the cabin after they had been away for a week or two was to sweep up dead flies. She used a brush and a dustpan in the windows and on the floor below to pick up fly carcasses.

Steve built a liquor cabinet on the wall behind the door. Like Dad, Steve was a good cabinetmaker. He made the liquor cabinet with light-colored wood with a matching wooden knob. The cabinet opened, creating a serving shelf supported by small brass chains. Steve's liquor of choice was whiskey – Jack Daniels or Jim Beam. Polly liked sherry which she kept it in a cut-glass decanter in the liquor cabinet. They had a similar liquor cabinet at their house in town.

A couple of years later, Steve added another room to the cabin connecting directly with the original room on its northwest corner. On the west end of the new room was a brick fireplace. Steve had a knack for building efficient heating fireplaces with the bricks from the big chimney on the ranch.

On the south and the north wall were two built-in sofas used as beds. There were a couple of chairs and end tables and a coffee table between the beds. The north wall had large windows overlooking the valley.

The new room had its own outside door opening perpendicular to the outside door from the old section. Each room had a stoop, which was connected by a wooden bench good for storage or sitting. Antlers hung over the door to the old section. I am not sure if it was an animal Steve shot or the remains of one Polly found on one of her numerous hikes throughout the property. I suspect it was the latter. My family wasn't much into hunting.

Marolt Family Collection

Steve built a fence out of aspen poles to surround the cabin that kept out the grazing cattle. I loved walking on this fence, and Steve and Polly encouraged it. The rail poles were only about three to four inches in diameter and of irregular shapes. Baling wire secured the poles to the posts. As a result, some of the rails tended to rotate. Another problem was that some of the poles had silvery bark, and when I stepped on it, the bark rotated and broke off, causing my feet to slip and me to fall.

Walking on this fence was challenging. I walked facing forward and arms outstretched like a circus tightrope walker. If I fell off, I had a rule I must start over again. I eventually walked from the woodpile around the "yard" without falling or touching anything with my hands.

Steve built a brick barbeque in the backyard in which he used aspen wood for cooking steaks. Steve and Polly spent much of the year collecting and cutting wood. They used the wood at the cabin and their house in town. They had a room on their house that looked a lot like the new cabin room and was heated exclusively by aspen wood. Steve was proud of the design of that fireplace, its glass doors, and the way it regulated the heat.

Behind the cabin was a faucet connected to a spring. Springs were the only source of fresh water at the pasture. A gate led to a path to a naturally cleaning outhouse Steve built over the Owl Creek ravine. During the summer, there was little water, so the waste accumulated and dried in the creek bed. There was not much waste because it was usually only two people using it. In the spring, Owl Creek ran high, and the waste disappeared – not a pleasant thought for those downstream.

When I think of the outhouse, it reminds me that much of what we did was not eco-friendly. Steve had an outhouse over a small stream that made its way to another stream. The sewer system in our home was sewer pipe running 150 feet from under our house and dumping out on a hillside overhanging Castle Creek. It was unintentionally hidden from sight by a stand of stinging nettles. I sometimes thought that nasty plant thrived on sewage. The end of the pipe, which was near the barn, seemed always to be dripping.

We burned our paper trash in an incinerator, which was an oil drum with a couple of holes near the bottom and a screen on top. We dumped the wet garbage in the ditch, and the coal furnace belched black smoke. At the granary, Dad, Steve, and other relatives repaired their vehicles and drained oil directly on the ground making rainbow-colored puddles. Old tires and other junk filled in the empty pits under or behind the granary. As the years progressed, our environmental stewardship improved.

Above Steve's cabin was a road in the aspen trees leading to a dam Steve built across the open eastern end of a mountain cove. The dam created a several acre-sized reservoir. Its primary water source was the spring run-off, but it remained topped off with other springs on the hillside. The water from the reservoir was piped down below the cabin and used for irrigation. Steve used sprinklers like the ones found in urban parks.

We called the reservoir Polly's Lake. Today on maps, it can be located as the Marolt Reservoir. Polly recounted how, when they first owned the property, she and Steve came up to work on the pasture or the cabin and took breaks by skinny-dipping in the lake. For me, that was too much information.

On the south and west side of the lake were aspen trees and deadfall littering the edge of the water. The north side had a grassy, south-facing hill with a small grove of large aspen trees on a knoll above the lake. That's where we drove the Jeeps and Albert's truck and sat under the trees on a big log and looked out over the lake. From that view, the lake looked navy blue.

Most of Steve's acreage was aspen forest above the cabin and the lake. A bit above the lake and to the south was an abandoned cabin Steve used to store tractors and equipment. Polly called it Harry Holmes' cabin. Harry Holmes homesteaded the property sometime before they bought it. Beyond this cabin was another body of water. It was a large swampy area Polly aptly named the cattail pond because among the deadfall in the water were stands of cattails. Skunk cabbage surrounded the boggy outer perimeter. Skunk cabbage is a tall broad-leafed plant on a stock. Despite the name, it is inedible. It stinks and looks a little creepy and sort of alien.

Further to the south was White's Lake, which was on someone else's property, but Polly and Steve had access. We hiked to Burnt Mountain, taking this route. Burnt Mountain was on the east side of what became the Snowmass Ski Area. In retaliation for the encroachment of settlers, the Utes intentionally burned it. Evidence of the fire was visible. Skeletons of burned trees dotted the hillside.

Although we went up to Steve and Polly's from time to time for small get-togethers, the big event was on the Fourth of July. Everyone gathered at the cabin. The guests included all the Marolts – Steve, Ted, and Bill and their families, along with Edmund, Albina, Jimmy, and Cherie. The Bishops were also part of the tradition. Barney and Gary were cute kids a year and two older than me. As children, we spent time with each other several times a week, either at their house in town or on our ranch.

Pearl was three years younger than Mom, had light brown short hair, was about Mom's height but thinner, and wore wire-rimmed glasses. She had an adorable smile and a sweet personality. You could tell she and Mom were sisters.

Albert was a nice-looking man with dark hair and a cleft chin. During World Warr II, he was a merchant marine. Albert's contribution to the picnic was the watermelon from his store. Albert owned Beck & Bishop Food Market along with Henry Beck. Alton Beck sold both his share of the store and his house to Albert.

On the Fourth of July, Albert loaded Gary and Barney and the picnic food in the back of Beck & Bishop's red delivery truck and drove it to the picnic. A canvas top covered the truck bed. Usually, Al Prechtel parked it at his house across the street from the Bishops' house. Al was the Beck & Bishop deliveryman.

I was excited to see the hood of the red truck come over the hill to the cabin. Once Albert parked the truck, I clambered up and over the back to see what Gary and Barney were holding. The watermelons were enormous – at least two feet long and a foot in diameter. In addition to watermelon, Albert brought bottles of Coke and Hires Root Beer. Of course, Pearl prepared picnic food.

Everyone made or brought food, and they were good cooks. In later years, the main course was meat for barbequing. Early on, fried chicken and Albina's famous spaghetti and meatballs were the main courses, along with sides of lettuce salad, potato salad, and baked beans. There were desserts – cakes, apricot bar cookies, brownies, and pie. Sometimes we made ice cream. We had plenty of cream.

Ted always brought a case of beer. Sometimes, he got an eight-pack of seven-ounce cans of Coors for the kids. At the time, I was not crazy about beer and sucked on candy to mask the bitter taste. The cool part of the beer, as far as I was concerned, was that they had those new Pull Tabs. We collected them and made belts.

For an hour or so, the adults drank beer, talked, and told stories. This was a good time for fence walking. Sometimes, the kids went over the hill to see how far they could throw dried "cow flops," much as we throw Frisbees today. If the timing was right, we picked coneflowers and threw them at each other. When some of the boys threw them, and they hit, they could create a rather nasty bruise.

After dinner, the women did the dishes in the large dishpan with hot water from the stove. When the dishes were done, we headed up to the lake with the watermelon. It was time for swimming.

From a distance, the lake was pretty with a navy-blue sheen, but up close, it was murky. That's because it was mostly stagnant water. There was one large raft made out of logs held together with boards. It floated about a foot above the water. There was a smaller raft that was not nearly as buoyant. We usually brought large inner tubes as well.

I rarely went out on the raft, and that was okay with me. I found it unpleasant and scary. To get to the raft, we had to wade into the lake. The mud was dark and slimy. As you stepped into the mud, your feet got sucked in almost as if it was quicksand.

Someone steered the raft out into the middle of the lake with long poles. I did not like swimming in the lake. For about a foot below the surface, the water was warm, but then it met with a layer of ice-cold water. It had some slimy catfish and a bunch of leeches. After swimming, we checked for leeches. Around the rim of the lake in the tall grass were blue dragonflies. I did not like them either.

At Polly's insistence, the little kids – that is, Gary, Barney, and I swam or sat in inner tubes in a small area near an aspen stand naturally fenced from the main lake by a ring of cattails. After an obligatory time in the water wading and having our feet sucked into the soft mud Polly called "muck," we were free to have other adventures.

Sometimes we skipped flat rocks from the dam. I was never good at this. I could get it to skip two or three times tops. Gary and Barney were better. Rod Barnes was the best. I suspect Rod was the best because he played baseball. He became a competitive baseball pitcher in high school in California.

Because I did not like going all the way in the water, I spent most of the time around the edges of the lake catching small frogs and putting them into coffee cans to bring home as pets. The frogs were less than an inch long. Once I got home, I made a habitat for them in a galvanized metal tub. The habitat had bridges and tunnels, plants, rocks for sunning, a swimming hole, and a little beach. I covered it with wire mesh so the frogs could not jump out. I caught grasshoppers and flies to feed them. Despite my best efforts, the frogs never survived for more than a few days or disappeared overnight.

The older kids played on the raft in the middle of the lake. They played pirates. The pirates swam to the raft, which they tried to capture. Those on the raft tried to prevent the capture by throwing the pirates into the water. No one ever got hurt, and no one drowned, which is kind of surprising because none of us were great swimmers. One time, Albina jumped in the lake and joined the kids in the pirate escapades. Upon capturing the raft, she tied her red sweatshirt on a pole and stuck it in the raft. With that flag, she claimed ownership of the vessel.

After the lake fun, Albert cut the watermelon with a huge butcher's knife into round slices, which he then cut in quarters. We sat on a large log overlooking the lake and spit seeds on the ground. Every year I came back hoping to find a watermelon patch. It never happened.

After consuming watermelon, besides the mud from the lake, my forearm and clothes were now covered with sticky juice. Before we returned to the cabin, I went behind the aspen trees and changed into something dry.

We stayed at the cabin until it was dark and ate leftovers. That meant we missed the fireworks in town. For the most part, that was okay with me. I did not like the crowds in Wagner Park or waiting for what seemed like hours for the show to start. I also wasn't crazy about the people setting off fireworks on the lawn of the park. The final waterfall display near the south end of the park was spectacular for its time. When I was a teenager, there were more reasons to leave early and go to the park.

As we left, Steve and Polly stood in the door, waving good-bye. They would spend the night in the cabin. It was dark as we wound our way down from the cabin. The Jeep lights reflected off the loamy banks near the gate. The light exposed bright white, almost fluorescent, snail shells the size of dimes. Dad stopped so I could pick a handful for a collection I kept in a metal tin in my room. At the time, I assumed the snails crawled on the banks of the hill and died. Now, I realize they were fossils of sea snails from thousands of years ago. In 2010, a few miles from Steve's cabin near the Snowmass Village, a massive burial ground for ice age mastodons was discovered. I wish kept the snail shell fossils.

At home, we lit a few sparklers. They were the kind of sparklers that got hot and could burn a finger. They also burned a long time. At one time, the kids had Roman candles. One year, Judy was holding one that backfired and burned her stomach.

After a few minutes of our mini fireworks, I got a wood tick check and took a much-needed bath, scrubbing away the dirt-encrusted watermelon streaks on the back of my forearms.

Riley and Stella's House

The only Aspen family members who rarely attended picnics were Riley and Stella.

There was a time when Riley would have loved the picnics, and everyone would have enjoyed his company. Riley had been a party person. He was a tall, large man with slicked-back light brown hair and wore wire-rimmed glasses. Riley looked happy, and his nickname fit perfectly.

By the time I was old enough to know him, he had come to terms with his major demon – alcoholism. No one ever described him or what happened to him when he drank, but I am inclined to believe he became extremely drunk. I never heard of him being violent or a danger to anyone other than himself. When he was drinking and living with Grandma, Mom and Pearl searched out and hid his whiskey bottles.

When I was old enough to know him, he no longer drank and avoided any situation in which drinking was part of the activity. Although the family picnics were never drunken orgies, they always involved generous amounts of beer. When we had a family get together, including Riley, alcohol was served well before he arrived, if at all. I do not know if this was something Riley requested or if it was something Mom and Pearl thought was in his best interest. We had no alcohol by the time Riley and Stella arrived for Thanksgiving and Christmas dinners.

I am not sure if Riley stopped drinking and found religion or if he found religion and stopped drinking, and I am not sure if he met Stella before or after he started going to church. For whichever reason, he and Stella were devout Baptists.

Stella was a sweet, quiet woman with a slight southern accent. She had short, curly dark hair and wore glasses. She was from Kentucky and worked for Hod Nicholson at the Aspen Laundry & Cleaners on Hopkins and Monarch.

Riley and Stella married after Grandma died. They moved into Grandma's house, which they decorated in a decidedly religious theme. There were many pictures of Jesus and Bibles on end tables. Despite the devotion to their religion, neither Riley nor Stella preached outwardly to us or criticized Catholicism.

Mom stopped to see Riley and Stella when they were home, but because they both worked, it was not a daily visit like the ones she had with Grandma. At the time, Riley worked as a butcher at Elder's Market and, which became Tom's Market. I understand he was a great butcher and extremely adept at cutting up frying chickens. It seems like an obvious question now, but I never asked why he did not work for Albert at Beck & Bishop.

I did not spend much time with Riley and Stella. They did not have kids, and that was where all the action was for me. Gary and Barney, on the other hand, went with Riley to what he called the claim. Riley had a mining claim, which he and his brother, Elmer, inherited from Grandpa Peterson. The claim was above the Midnight Mine. Maintaining their claim rights required that he or Elmer spend a certain amount of money and time working the claim. Although, as far as I know, he never made any money there, he enjoyed going up and tinkering around. Gary and Barney liked getting in his Jeep and going to the claim with him.

My involvement with Riley and Stella was mostly stopping at their house when Mom visited. Their favorite activity was sitting on the front porch, which they later screened in, and watching the traffic on Main Street and the restaurant across the way. Originally the restaurant was Guido's, then for a short time, the Toklat restaurant, and in later years, the Hickory House.

As we sat on the porch, nobody did much talking. Stella offered cookies. Sometimes they came out to visit at our house on Sunday afternoons from fall to spring. Summer Sundays were for picnics.

Riley and Stella had a few picnics in their back yard, but those were mostly when Elmer and his family came to town from Denver. They were like the picnics Grandma used to have.

Although there was no beer, there was plenty of good food. Riley and Elmer were competitive in their cooking both as to quantity and quality. Meals at their houses usually featured Kåldolmar, a type of Swedish cabbage roll stuffed with beef, pork, and rice.

When Elmer entertained at his house in Denver, he had a fully stocked bar in his laundry area in his garage. Elmer had been one of the Exalted Rulers at the Elks Club when he lived in Aspen after the war.

Another activity we shared with Stella and Riley was car rides down the valley. We did this with the Bishops as well. On Sunday afternoons, usually in the fall and spring, when there wasn't much else to do – like picnics or skiing – we got in one of the cars and drove down the Highway 82 to Glenwood. The rides were usually after our Sunday dinner.

The kids crammed into the back seat. For me, riding in the back seat on twisting mountain roads induced carsickness in and of itself. With added cigarette smoke, the situation was intolerable. Mom, Dad, and Albert smoked. I believe Riley did for a while, but I don't remember him smoking when they were with us for the ride. Because our rides were usually in cold weather, we closed the windows, and the car filled with smoke. I think Pearl sat in back, thinking she would be somewhat protected.

The cars did not have seat belts. The back had a bench seat, and there was a rope stretched across the back of the front seat. I used to think you held on to the rope if the car was going fast around a corner. I have since learned that the design was known as a robe rail for a robe coat. It held a blanket or robe to use because there was no heat in the back.

The best part of the Glenwood trip was the end destination – the soda fountain at the Glenwood Creamery. We got malts and shakes. I liked the machine they used to make them. Because I was usually car sick, I rarely drank the whole thing. Although tempted, I never got a banana split. I never got a float. I never liked floats – root beer or otherwise.

Although I am sure we went to their house for some other meals, I only remember one meal inside Riley and Stella's house. It was dark outside, so I assume it was in the winter. After dinner, Gary, Barney, and I sat on the floor near the dining room table playing a board game.

I was sick. I had one of the worst colds I can remember. I brought a spray bottle of decongestant that was new on the market. I sprayed it in one of my nostrils about every five minutes or as soon as my nose clogged. I started feeling woozy from the liquid draining down into my throat. At some point, I looked at the bottle, read the instructions, and realized I was overdosing. For the rest of the evening, I wondered if I would die. I never again used spray decongestant.

Being sick was unusual for me. As a child, I was rarely ill. Mom would have attributed my good health to my daily dose of Homocebrin vitamin syrup. When I got sick, Mom made eggnogs out of a beaten egg, milk, sugar, and vanilla. I only remember a couple of times where my illness warranted that treat. The persistent problem for me was cold sores, which appeared as a side effect from chapped lips from skiing. The only known treatment was Campho-Phenique. I dabbed it on with a cotton ball. It only slightly numbed my lip and smelled medicinal. When I was in high school, the doctor gave me a smallpox vaccination to help reduce the number of instances. It seemed to work, although I still had a small one from time to time after skiing.

I avoided many of the childhood diseases. When I was beginning school, they were giving polio vaccinations. We lined up in the gym, and a doctor and or a nurse gave us a shot. Later we got our boosters with sugar cubes drenched in a liquid.

I had a mild form of measles and chickenpox. I do not believe there were vaccines for them at the time. The worst of my childhood illnesses was mumps. I was extremely ill. I had massively swollen glands and a sore throat. I was too sick to swallow, let alone care about eggnog. I had a high fever. I was so ill I felt like I was hallucinating.

Mom had me lay on the sofa, so I was closer to the kitchen if I needed anything. Despite being hot, Mom insisted on covering me with many blankets and gave me lots of baby aspirin and ginger ale. While lying on my back looking at the ceiling, sweat suddenly broke out on my forehead. Mom was pleased that my fever broke. I was out of school for a week – the longest I was ever out of school for an illness.

Part II

Life Before School

On the Ranch

I have a smattering of early memories. My first identifiable memory was when I was in my crib in Mom and Dad's room. The crib was in front of the east-facing window from which I could see Aspen Mountain. The long side of the crib was down, and I was able to climb in and out. I guess I was three or four.

Keith came into that room while I was in the crib and to say goodbye. My memory suggested he was leaving for college or the army. I doubt that was the reason given the timing. When he went to college the first time, I was five and was in my own room. He went to the army even later. I'm guessing he was leaving for Boy Scout camp or a visit with Denver relatives. Whatever the reason, I was sad. I adored Keith. Keith was nice looking. He was tall with wavy blond hair, bright blue eyes, and a smile like Mom's smile.

I called him Kee Kee. He read *Doctor Goat* to me - "... he went to the house of a mouse with mumps. He cured a frog who had the jumps...." Besides reading to me, Keith played the *Happy Farmer* on the piano. He told me he wrote that song; Robert Schumann would probably disagree. When I learned to play the piano, I was frustrated I could not write something as simple and as good as the *Happy Farmer*.

In an early memory, I was sitting in the dirt at the bottom of the path from the house to the granary below. I was on the perimeter of the parking area where Mom left me while she fed the chickens.

The day was warm. The earth was dark and dry. There was a faint smell of motor oil. I was alone. I took off my shoes and white anklets and was scooping dirt into one of the anklets and sifting it through the fabric to make it even finer. My socks were turning a darker and darker shade of gray.

Because I was engaged in the sifting process, I did not notice that little pigs had come to surround me. The little pigs were snorting and sniffing at me. A particularly menacing looking sow trotted toward me. I was startled, and I cried. Mom swooped in and saved me. She shooed the pigs back toward their pen under the granary porch.

Many of my earliest ranch memories involved animals. We had many Hereford cattle. In the winter, there were cattle in the big field. From late November until April, snow covered the ground, and the cattle sheltered in the cattle shed. To feed the cattle, Dad hitched a hay sled to the workhorses. The sled was like the hay wagon, but it had runners instead of wheels. Dad drove the sled up from the granary and stopped in front of the house to pick up whatever children were around – including his children and their cousins and friends – most often Gerbazes or Bishops or Marolts. We snuggled under a few blankets with our backs against the front of the sled; Dad stood driving the team. Our breath hung in soft clouds in the air. Someone opened the gates to the fields, and, as we crossed the wide section of one of the lateral ditches, the wagon rocked from side to side.

There was a big stack on the south side of the elevated railroad bed opposite the cattle shed. Dad drove the sled next to the fence surrounding the stack and used the pitchfork to load hay on the wagon. In the process, he "accidentally" covered the kids with hay. We laughed and giggled. By the time the sled was full, the cattle were starting to wander over the railroad bed for breakfast. Dad steered the wagon in a large, previously trampled circle. This is where our job began. The kids got up and unloaded the hay by armful or kicked it off the edge to the growing group of cattle. They stood along the path of hay for the next several hours, enjoying their meal.

Spring was calving season and was always a tense time. Dad fretted about the condition of the calves and the possibility of losing calves or cows because of changing weather conditions. Every morning, he went out early to check on the herd.

On one occasion, Dad returned, carrying a tiny calf in his arms. He fixed a spot in the basement with straw and an old blanket on the backside of the furnace. He fed the calf milk from a beer bottle with a nipple. The calf survived, but unfortunately, his mother and twin did not.

I saw the mother when Dad went to bury her. She was in some brush on the southwest side of the field above the ditch. Her body was next to a twin calf, mostly covered in the filmy white covering from the placenta.

Eventually, all the calves were separated from their mothers. The sound of the mothers and babies crying was horrible. At night, I closed my window and covered my head to avoid hearing the sound. If this was not bad enough, before the calves could rejoin their mothers, Dad and his brothers dehorned and castrated the males and branded all the calves.

I avoided watching the branding. Our brand was XIII and ingeniously engineered on purpose, so Dad could make the brand by using only one iron. Although our brand looks like a Roman numeral 13, its registration was as "X One Eleven." Steve also used the same iron in his brand, which was Ul/ and its registration was as 'U one slash." He had a separate U iron. Dad and Steve burned their brands on the inside of the southern granary door.

I remember the smell of burning hair and the blue liquid they painted on the spot on the calves' heads after removing their horns. The blue liquid was iodine or potassium permanganate to keep out infections from the wound.

I did not like to see anything happen to the cattle, and fortunately, I was never present when they were killed. To this day, I do not know how they were killed or by whom. I'm pretty sure Steve or Bill did the killing. Dad may have done it too. I like to think he did not do it, but he was a rancher, and it went with the territory. Regardless, it was something Dad had a hard time doing. That's why he rarely hunted. I remember him shooting one elk, and I think it may have been out of season. Somehow, I did not connect the steaks, roasts, or chops with the animals in our field or corrals.

I did have an unfortunate experience seeing what happened to one of the pigs. One day when I was out in the back yard, I wandered onto the granary bridge and looked down at the corral surrounding the barn. In an area near the watering trough west of the barn, I saw the front loader of the tractor rise with the carcass of a pig suspended over a large vat of boiling water. Steam was coming off the body.

Without knowing its purpose, I had played in the vat when it was empty. It was made from an eight-foot length of three-foot diameter iron pipe, sealed at the ends, and a side section removed to create an opening. The vessel was placed over a fire, filled with water, and heated to boiling. After it was killed, they dipped the pig in scalding water to scrape off its hair. What is remains is the skin or rind.

Until I saw the pig hanging from the tractor, I had no idea of the purpose of the metal tub. I wished I did not have that image of the dangling pig in my mind. I worried it was one of those little pigs or the mother pig that surrounded me.

I didn't feel better despite knowing we used almost all of a pig. Bill made blood sausage and head cheese. Besides the roasts, hams, and chops, Dad made the klobasa. Mom made lard. She cooked the trimmed fat in water until the brown cracklings rose to the top. We stored it in lard buckets in the refrigerator.

As with any ranch, the most important animals were the horses. Before my grandfather moved the family to the old ranch, everyone had horses and wagons. When they lived in town, the family kept their horses in Bill Tagert's livery stable across Spring Street from the saloon. Horses played an even bigger part in ranch operations. We had several cattle horses. Dad and Steve broke and trained them.

A few of our horses stood out. Probably the most famous was Steve's horse, Snake. Snake was pure white and with flaring nostrils. He was big and strong. I have an impressive photo of Snake with Steve wearing his hat and chaps. He and Snake are high in a mountain col covered with moraine. The background is of high peaks devoid of vegetation. Snake is alert and standing strong, his tail and mane are fluttering in the breeze, and his nostrils are flaring. They are on top of East Maroon or Pearl Pass. Steve looked like a movie star. He boasted Snake was the best horse ever for riding or cutting cattle; he was probably right.

Marolt Family Collection

While Steve had Snake, Dad had Pet. She was a large bay with a black mane and tail and distinctively pointy ears. She was smart, and, like Snake, a good cow horse. Bill had a handsome black horse he rode up Maroon Creek and waded into pools so he could fish from his back.

At the same time, we had another mare named Penny. She was famous mainly because she was the mother of Patty, a family favorite. Somehow a rogue stallion managed to get with Penny. There was a claim that, because Patty was a small horse, the sire must have been a "pony." For a long time, I thought they meant a Shetland pony. They were referring to an Indian pony or a pinto. Regardless, Patty was a surprise.

One day, Dad went down to the corral between the granary and the milking barn and noticed something odd about the horses as they gathered in the corner of the shed next to the granary. He went in closer, and there standing with splayed legs next to Penny was a tiny black, white, and brown pinto foal. No one knew Penny was pregnant. Dad came running back to the house. He brought the entire family to see the surprise. I missed out because I was not yet born.

Patty was forever a part of the family and the ranch. Dad broke her when she was old enough to ride. At that time, Dad and Steve broke, trained, and shod all the horses. She was easy to break. Besides being a good kid's horse because she was short, Dad said she was, "One helluva little cow pony." She, along with Pet and other horses, was used in the cattle operation.

During this time, Dad took our cattle up Maroon Creek to graze in the summer. Dad and a couple of other ranchers shared federal range rights up East Maroon. I vaguely remember Dad, Keith, and others gathering the cattle together at the west edge of the big western field. They drove them across the ditch and out the gate onto the Castle Creek Road and went north for a few hundred feet until it joined the Maroon Creek Road. Then they continued up the Maroon Creek Road.

The first phase of the drive was to go to what they called the first gate next to a cattle guard above the T-Lazy-7 ranch. That phase took most of the day. Judy was lucky and got to help take the cattle to the first gate with Keith when she was in her early teens.

They had to drive the cattle past the T-Lazy-7 barns and buildings. Many of the buildings were only a few feet from the Maroon Creek Road. As the cattle passed the barns and buildings, Lamplighter, our bull, saw his reflection in one of the windows and thought it was a competitor. For a tense minute, it looked as if there might be a stampede, but somehow, they were able to urge the bull past his nemesis.

Our grazing area was beautiful. The first pasture was in a meadow with a view of Pyramid Peak above an Aspen outcropping. The higher summer pasture was on the other side of Maroon Creek and up East Maroon on the backside of Pyramid Peak.

Throughout the summer, Dad, Keith, Steve, and Ted brought up horses in the horse trailer and checked on the cattle. Larkspur grew in the area, and they wanted to make sure the cattle stayed away from this deadly plant. After grazing an area, Dad moved the cattle from one area of the range to another when the forest ranger found it was time to move. Sometimes, we rode with Dad in the Jeep to check on the cattle. We took the opportunity to have a picnic lunch near where they were grazing.

Once the cattle were on the range, the focus of the ranch was raising crops. Most of the crops were grown on the Midland part of the ranch, which was a patchwork of crops separated by lateral ditches. In the spring, there were red patches from the recently tilled red earth planted with potatoes. There were patches of varying shades of yellow and light green sown with oats, wheat, and barley. Of course, there were many patches of emerald, green hay.

Hay was the main crop. I have a few memories of hay before Dad got a baler. Much of that time was anecdotal. In the early days of the ranch, horses powered the hay operation. The hay was mowed, raked, and stacked using them. Sometimes Mom and Polly drove the bucker or stacker and accidentally dropped the hay on their husbands as they stood atop the stack. I remember me and my cousins encouraging Mom to drop hay on Dad when he was on top of the pile. We thought it funny. I doubt he did.

The most significant early haying story involved Max. In the late forties, the haying operation involved mowing the hay and letting it dry. Then someone raked the hay with a dump rake drawn by workhorses. The dump rake had curved metal teeth between two large wheels. The operator sat in a metal seat and drove the team. When the rake was full, the operator lifted a lever and dumped the hay in a pile. These piles were placed end to end by driving back and forth perpendicular to a row of hay. The hay was then picked up by the bucker and taken to the haystack.

One year, Max, who was probably twelve years old, was operating the dump rake and driving the horses back and forth. Something spooked the team, and they took off running. Max was thrown from the seat and ended up under the rake. The team drug Max tumbling in the area under the bend of the teeth. Everyone stood by helplessly watching. They knew this was probably not going to end well. There was nothing they could do.

The team continued in a dead run into the field. Then, miraculously, it crossed one of the lateral ditches, into which Max dropped from under the rake. The horses and rake continued without him. Although he was badly scraped and bruised, he had no broken bones.

For that matter, it was remarkable that none of my family, friends, or ranch workers were killed or severely injured in ranching operations or in playing dangerous games in dangerous locations. While we had a fair share of broken bones, for the most part, those were the worst injuries anyone suffered except for Steve.

One day, Steve was working near the granary with some metal and wood. He was not welding because he did not have on a shield or glasses. He hit something with a hammer or a crowbar, and a piece of wood flew off and pierced his eye. The doctors were unable to remove all of the fragments. The doctor said it would have been better if he hit his eye was a piece of metal that could be extracted with a magnet. Steve was blind in that eye.

As a result, Steve had a glass eye. I had a hard time telling it from his other eye. Both eyes moved together. It was when I looked at Steve's eyes trying to figure out which one was the glass eye that I realized, unlike the other Marolts who had brown eyes, Steve's eyes were gray blue. Rudy also had blue eyes. He was the only one to wear glasses when he was a young man.

As for the cattle operation, in the fall, we brought the cattle home. During the summer, the cattle stayed together because of Lamplighter's influence. He was a prized bull. In the fall of 1954, Dad and Keith went up East Maroon to bring the cattle home before hunting season. Lamplighter was missing. Dad, Steve, Ted, Keith, and others searched and searched for hours and then for days looking for him. Dad's primary focus was on the area near what they called the high bridge. He feared larkspur poisoned Lamplighter.

Unable to find Lamplighter on horseback, Dad enlisted the help of Art Pfister, a local rancher and pilot, to fly over the area in the hope of spotting him. Art flew up the Maroon Creek and East Maroon Creek valleys several times over several days. Neither Lamplighter nor his carcass was ever found.

At some point, Dad saw tire tracks that did not match our vehicles. His conclusion was someone poached or stole Lamplighter. It was disheartening. A bull is essential to a cattle operation, and to replace him would be expensive. He was not insured. Dad concluded someone from another cattle operation, outside of the area, stole him. Dad eliminated the idea that someone poached him for beef because it was easier to take a steer or a cow. Someone stole Lamplighter because he was a bull and a prized one at that.

A year or so later, while Keith was at the University of Colorado in Boulder, in the Colorado Bookstore, he found a postcard of Pyramid Peak taken up East Maroon the previous fall showing our cattle and Lamplighter. I recognized the location as one of the spots where we had our impromptu picnics. Forrest Neville Yockey, a famous Colorado photographer known for his postcards, took this photograph. He probably took it a few days before Lamplighter disappeared.

Forrest Neville Yockey

Lamplighter's disappearance coincided with increased grazing restrictions imposed by the United States Forest Service. The Forest Service was limiting the number of cattle that could graze an area. Land use and grazing rights were now conflicting with a burgeoning tourist industry. As it was, the government reduced the number of cattle that could be on our range. With a reduced heard size, ranching was no longer economically feasible as a primary income source. It would now become a gentleman's hobby.

The combination of events led Dad and Steve to conclude they could no longer operate a cattle ranch. When their primary business was cattle, they needed many acres to grow hay and grain to support a large cattle herd in the winter. Once they concluded they could no longer support a year-round cattle operation, Dad sold off the breeding stock.

With the end of the cattle operation, Dad and Steve began selling pieces of the ranch. Today, the land they owned is worth close to a billion dollars. It is ironic that in the 1950s, owning this much land was a liability. As Polly said in an interview, when asked how much property Steve and Dad owned, she answered, "Hell, I don't know how many acres they owned. All I know is that they had to work them." In 1955, Dad and Steve sold the land on the north side of Highway 82 – the part we called the Midland. It became the golf course and the Snowbunny subdivision.

My strongest memory of that part of the ranch was while we were still in the year-round cattle business. I was four or five. It was late summer. I was sitting on a flatbed wagon, dangling my legs over the side. It was hot, and there were no trees in sight. We were near the potato cellar parallel to Highway 82. It was a massive structure. I'm guessing it was at least 70 feet long and sat in a stony depression that had once been a reservoir.

Dirt and growing grass covered the outside. Inside, it was dark and musty and cool, and the sides were stacked high with sacks of potatoes. The ceiling was low, probably less than seven feet high. Single low-wattage light bulbs dangled along the center aisle. It smelled good.

There were several potato patches – one near the potato cellar, one near Red Butte, and another northwest of the cemetery. During the harvest, there were rows of dirt mounds with potatoes sitting on the top left after the potato digger went through the rows of plants. Potato pickers were usually high school students who picked the potatoes and put them in baskets and filled strategically place burlap gunnysacks.

As I sat on the wagon, I smelled the burlap from the newly filled gunnysacks. It was a hot day for Aspen. The ground was tinged red from the cellar to Red Butte in the distance. From the Red Butte area, Pyramid Peak was visible. I do not remember seeing it on that day, but Peggy recalls one of her most vivid memories was being awestruck at the sight of it while she sat on the sled while Dad fed the cattle one winter morning.

After selling off the northern part of the Midland Ranch, Dad continued to raise cattle in the summer on the remaining portion of the ranch south of Highway 82. Each spring, he went to Glenwood Springs or Rifle to buy steers at livestock auctions. We fattened the steers in our pastures and the pastures at the old ranch supplemented with hay and grain. In the fall, Dad took the fattened cattle back to the auction and sold them. Dad made sure the cattle were always calm. He did not want them to be running anywhere, as they would lose weight.

For a while, Steve bought cattle each spring and let them graze at his 320-acre pasture on Owl Creek. He bought the pasture in 1949 for $6,000. The cattle often grazed below the cabin or on the hill above the lake. Polly warned us to watch out for "cow flops." Although Steve's downsized cattle operation did not last more than a couple of years, he kept the pasture for decades.

Bill continued a small potato operation on the remaining part of Dad's ranch. Bill grew potatoes at the south end of the little field. The potato patch was below the house he built off the Castle Creek Road. In the late fifties, he made a small potato cellar in the ravine between the bale shed and the main road near where the two roads split by the cattle guard.

This cellar was probably fifteen feet long and maybe six feet high. It, too, was covered with dirt and brush and blended into the hillside. It had a single wooden door. It was a great place to hide while playing outlaws. Years later, someone wanted to designate this potato cellar as a historic structure. They had it confused with stories about the big potato cellar on the Midland.

I think we were one of the last real ranching operations in Aspen. Some of the ranchers on Woody Creek may have lasted a little longer. While someone took over the Maroon grazing rights, they raised cattle as a hobby. These changes overtook this short-lived part of Aspen's history. Like the Utes and the miners, the farmers and ranchers would or could no longer thrive in this valley.

Going to Town

Our ranch was across Castle Creek from the City of Aspen. We went to town daily and sometimes several times a day.

Before I was in school, I spent my time with Mom. Our morning routine was to go to town, drop off my sisters at school, and on our return, stop and visit her mother or her sister, Pearl, or some of Mom's other friends.

Mom drove a cream-colored 1949 Chevy. I sat on the edge of the front seat but could not see over the dash. Immediately at the end of the main road, we turned right and crossed the Castle Creek Bridge. The paved, wooden bridge had narrow walkways on the side. The walkways were impassable for foot traffic in the winter because of piled up snow.

The road into town made a sharp right-hand turn at 7th Street - known as Waterman's corner. LeRoy Waterman owned a small store, with a couple of gas pumps and some motel cabins on the southeast corner of the intersection. The area within the inside of the turn on the southwest was a vacant lot.

My grandmother, Alma Peterson, and my grandfather, Andrew Peterson, lived in a small house on the south side of Main Street. It was the third lot east of Seventh Street. The left-hand turn from Seventh Street to Main Street was known as Stitzer's Corner. My grandparents' house faced Main Street. The house to the west had been my great grandmother's house, which Gene Robison, one of Aspen's mayors, later owned. There was a vacant lot next to him on the corner where Hans Gramiger built a real estate office a decade later.

My grandparents lived in a typical Victorian house. It was set back behind a couple of the cottonwoods lining the length of Main Street. The sidewalk crossed one of the small irrigation ditches feeding the trees. A large lilac was on the right of the sidewalk. The house had a small front porch that shared a side with one of the front interior rooms. The interior of the original house had four rooms and no halls. The rooms lead directly into each other. This configuration of connecting rooms and no halls was typical. Many of these houses were built from kits sold by Sears, Roebuck & Company.

In Grandma's house, one room was a kitchen and was in the southeast corner. The other rooms were interchangeably a sitting room, a dining room, and a bedroom. Since there were no closets, they used wooden wardrobes in the designated bedroom. Most houses had an outhouse in back and a washing room on a back porch. At some point, my grandparents added a bathroom and another couple of bedrooms in the back. The addition's construction was primitive. The walls were varnished plywood with little insulation.

Steve and Polly had a two-story Victorian. They converted one of the four downstairs rooms into a bathroom. The bathroom, on the southwest corner, was so large it not only held the toilet, sink and claw foot tub, and it was big enough for a washer and dryer. One of the main outside doors came through this room, but it was no longer functional. The "front door" of the house was on the north side facing Smuggler Street.

The big bath made up for the fact that the upper story, in which there were two small bedrooms, had no bathroom. There was plumbing available, but Steve and Polly used that space between the two bedrooms as a walk-in closet. Stairs for the second floor were enclosed and accessible from the living room.

They added a room along the width of the south side of the house. It had a door to the kitchen and a fireplace as the only source of heat. As was typical of the construction at the time, the addition had high windows with a peek-a-boo view of Aspen Mountain and an outside door. Although there was a "formal" door on the north side of the house, we entered their house through the addition. They furnished it like they furnished their cabin.

Pearl and Albert's house was once a Victorian, but when they bought it from Alton Beck, it was "updated." Before the update, Alton claimed each room had an outside door. I think that was kind of typical because Victorian houses did not have central halls and needed a means of escape in case of fire. The Becks took down the wall between the dining and the living room and made it into a single room. They moved the original entrance from Hopkins to Center. What used to be the front porch was replaced with a large picture window looking over City Park, which is now known as Paepcke Park. Albert planted a blue spruce that eventually obliterated the view.

Like our house, the entrance to Pearl and Albert's house was through a "porch," which contained the washer and dryer, a pantry, and stairs to the basement. The porch, like our porch, led into the kitchen. Over time rooms were added. The original doors, windows, and gingerbread were gone. It was ironic that in later years Gary had to fight a "historical" classification to sell it. A few years earlier, when Riley sold Grandma's original Victorian, the buyer razed it without a single objection. They built a "Victorian looking" duplex in its place.

My memories of Grandpa Peterson are vague because I was two when he died. I remember seeing him one time in his house. He was suffering from what Mom called "miner's consumption." He was in the darkened bedroom, which at that time was at the front of the house. I tip-toed behind Mom close to his bed. He was lying on the bed, slightly propped up with pillows with wild gray hair and a large gray mustache and said something to me I did not understand.

Grandma was the quintessential grandmother. She was a little stooped and had white hair she wore in a bun behind her head. Like Mom, she always wore housedresses. I remember her in the kitchen. The door to the wood-burning stove rested on a log standing on end to keep it from falling to the ground. She usually had something freshly baked like the sponge cake she called "scrub cake." She named it scrub cake because she made it on the day allotted to "scrub" the floor. We ate sitting at the small kitchen table with an oilcloth cover.

There was a trap door in the northwest corner of the kitchen floor that had an embedded handle. When lifted, the door exposed steep steps into a small cellar. The cellar was dark and had a dirt floor and smelled musty. There was a bare light bulb on the ceiling and shelves with jars of home-canned food and other stored items.

The cellar was a hazard. Once when Mom's cousin, Harold Horstmann, was visiting, the door was open. He took a step backward and fell into the cellar. He was severely injured and taken to a hospital in Denver. After that, Mom was careful to keep me away from the opening on the few occasions the door was ajar.

While Mom and Grandma kept up their Swedish coffee drinking tradition, I played in the dining room, which, at that time, was to the west of the kitchen. Grandma kept toys in this room. There were the small trunk and iron bed Mom's uncle, Charlie, made for her dolls, a doll buggy, and a few baby dolls. In a wooden china cabinet with rounded glass doors, there were items I could touch on the bottom shelf. There was a six-sided, elongated red coffin about two inches long. Inside was a mummy. If I hovered the lid of the coffin over the mummy, he suddenly stood up. It was truly amazing. I had no idea magnets were involved.

Sometimes when I came by, if Grandma had not baked a treat, she gave me slices of American cheese. American cheese was a new grocery store item. I did not like it, but I did not want to hurt Grandma's feelings, so I pretended to eat it, nibbled at the edges, and then hid the uneaten cheese under a cardboard insert in the doll buggy.

In the spring of 1955, Grandma fell and broke her hip. At that time, doctors could do little for her, and she did not recover. I did not understand the significance, but I knew Mom was upset. She cried a lot. A part of my life seemed empty.

After Grandma died, Riley moved into her house. Once when Mom was visiting with Riley, I was playing with Grandma's toys and lifted the mattress from the baby carriage to find several shrunken bright orange squares of American cheese. I felt sad and guilty.

When we were away from the ranch, besides visiting Grandma, we sometimes visited with Pearl and Polly. Most often, we went to Pearl's house when Gary and Barney were home. When they were in school, it wasn't as much fun, and the visits were short. Once I went to school, I walked to Pearl's house almost daily.

Mom and I went to Polly's house a few times before I started school. While Mom and Polly visited, I played in their living room. Polly let me play with a brass ashtray shaped like a lily pad with a removable frog sitting on the edge. It reminded her of the frogs at their lake.

One day before I started school, when I was coming home from town with Mom, we stopped at another house on Main Street. I often wondered about this house. It was a three-story bright red and deep green Victorian with a front porch sweeping around its front and side.

I noticed the house because of the unusual stairstep lawn. The house and yard were on the Main Street Hill. Instead of following the natural slope, the lot had three flat steps – top, middle, and bottom separated by nearly vertical grass-covered risers. The house was on the top level, and a matching carriage house, next to the alley, was even with the middle step. On the street side of the lawn, a stone retaining wall mirrored the steps in the lawn. I thought it would be fun to walk on that wall.

Mom and I walked up the sidewalk and onto the large covered front porch. Mom knocked. A few minutes later, a woman with blondish coronet braids on top of her head opened the door. She was about Mom's age, and, like Mom, she was wearing a housedress. Peering out from behind the woman was a girl about my age. She had blond braids in two loops at the side of her head tied at the top of the loop with ribbons.

Mom said, "Vicki, this is Mrs. Elisha."

Svea Elisha turned to her little girl, "Ingrid, this is Mrs. Marolt and Vicki. You two are about the same age."

We both shyly peaked at each other and then looked down at the floor. Mom and Svea talked for a while, and then we said goodbye and left.

Svea, like Mom, was Swedish, and Laurence, her husband and Ingrid's father, was Assyrian. At the time, he was the owner and manager of the Hotel Jerome. He was a nice looking, impeccably dressed man. Laurence was related somehow to Albert through their mothers, and Svea's brother, Reinard Elder, worked for Albert at his store.

Like me, Ingrid was the baby in her family and like me, not by a couple of years, but by many. I suspect we were mistakes. Ingrid had three older brothers. M.J., who was a year older than Judy, lived at home. Lowell, who had been the Pitkin County Superintendent of Schools, lived in the Denver area. Don lived out of state.

I did not become friends with Ingrid until third grade. We somehow managed not to run into each other at Church before we went to school although both families were involved in the Catholic Church. Dad and Laurence were Catholics. Svea converted to Catholicism and became the parish bookkeeper. Mom was not Catholic but honored its traditions. Our family always went to 7:00 a.m. Mass and Ingrid's family went at 9:00 a.m.

Besides visiting with people, we went into downtown Aspen. I never knew the names of most of the streets in town except Main and Hallam, which went by the school. I first learned Galena Street when a teenage dance club was named Galena Street East. Until that time, we knew where things were, and we gave directions relative to landmarks. "The bank – well, it's kitty-corner to the Aspen Drug across from the post office." The Elisha house was "on the Main Street Hill – the one with the stairstep lawn." Beck & Bishop was "two blocks up from the Jerome toward the ski hill." I use street names now because many of the landmarks we relied upon for directions are gone – like Hansel and Gretel's breadcrumbs.

Z-12799, Western History Department, Denver
Public Library, Bachman Collection

During that time, there were sporadic landmarks. Most of the town was vacant. Block after block was empty or with only dilapidated houses or buildings. That did not seem unusual at all. There was a big yellow house near Grandma's with boarded windows and an overgrown lawn. There was a similar abandoned house across from Steve's. It was dark and scary. I fantasized about how nice it would be if someone fixed up these houses and mowed the lawns. I later learned the yellow house belonged to Dorothy Shaw, Judge Shaw's wife.

Many vacant lots dotted downtown as well. Part of the block with the Wheeler Opera House, the lumberyard, and the laundry was empty. The lots where the Washington and Lincoln Schools used to be were vacant. We used vacant lots for school activities. The homecoming bonfire was on one such lot near Little Nell. Another lot near the high school was the ice-skating rink.

When the carnival came to town for two summers in the mid-fifties, it used the half-block behind Guido's restaurant. The carnival had a row of games and booths with carnival food; there was a small Ferris wheel, a small roller coaster for little kids, and an octopus ride. The octopus ride was one of those rides with arms and spinning seats that undulated up and down while the entire contraption revolved. I rode the octopus once, and it made me sick. I vomited. I never went on it or anything like it again, but I did get more than my fill of cotton candy.

Before I had some independence, my trips to town were with Mom or Dad. In the morning, after his early chores, Dad went to the Aspen Drug to pick up the Denver Post. He never got the Rocky Mountain News because Dad was loyal and had always read the Denver Post. It was necessary to get the newspaper in town. There was no home paper delivery. We paid the Aspen Drug to put a copy of the paper in a designated pigeonhole inside the store. The other newspapers and magazines were on the west wall perpendicular to the front window.

We got the Sunday paper on Saturday afternoon, but we held it unread until Sunday. When I was old enough to read, I looked forward to reading the "funnies." I could hardly wait to get home from Mass and spread out the newspaper pages on the living room floor, lay on my stomach, and read every word – from *Peanuts, Dagwood and Blondie, Beetle Bailey, Prince Valiant, Brenda Starr, Dennis the Menace,* and *Dick Tracy.*

During his winter weekday trips to the Aspen Drug, Dad "chewed the fat" with Buck Parsons and Frank Loushin. He did not do much fat chewing in the summer because there was too much work.

Buck and Frank were pharmacists. Buck's father, Jimmy Parsons, owned the Aspen Drug and the ISIS Theater. The Aspen Drug was on the corner of Galena and Hyman across from the Elks Building. At some point, the Aspen Drug was painted blue. At that time, the Elks Building also housed the post office.

Although Buck was quite a bit younger than Dad, they were good friends and spent time together having a drink or two across the street at the Elks where Buck had once been the Exalted Ruler. Elmer and Albert each held that position after the War. Buck and his family lived in the apartment above the ISIS Theater.

The ISIS was the only theater in town. It was on the corner of Mill and Hopkins across from Aspen Lumber & Supply, which we called Sardy's for Tom Sardy, the owner. In the tradition of the previous owners of the building, Tom was also the town's mortician. Initially, part of the building was used as a mortuary and may have been the reason Tom Sardy bought it. By the time I was born, the mortuary was in the Sardy house on Main Street. It was like the situation in *Six Feet Under.*

Judy and Peggy worked at the ISIS in high school, making popcorn, which was the only food option. Plain popcorn cost a dime, and buttered popcorn was a quarter.

When my sisters set up for the evening, they put in oil and popcorn and started the popper and put several cubes in the heated container for buttered popcorn. I liked the finely ground popcorn salt. I liked salt – a lot. Judy usually stayed and watched the first run of each of the movies.

The movies started at 8:15 p.m. and included a newsreel, a cartoon, and a preview of the coming attractions. Two heavy curtains separated the theatre from the lobby. A similar curtain, above a stage, covered the screen. There was an upright piano to the right of the stage.

Buck or John Crosby, who administered the ether during my caesarian birth, operated the projector. The projection room was behind an apartment above the theatre in which Buck, his wife, Carletta, and their three children, Buck, Dave, and Nancy lived. Buck's kids were known for being kind of wild.

The popcorn operation stopped about the time I went into junior high. That was the first time I saw bats in the theater flying near the ceiling. When the lights went out, and the bright light from the projector hit the screen, bats flew through the shaft of light and were visible against the backdrop of the screen. Some of the teenagers tried to encourage the bats by making loud sounds. I did not like it when they came out. I was afraid they would come down during the movie and get stuck in my hair. Someone told us that is what happens with flying bats. Besides being in the ISIS, bats hung on the fence behind the Jerome Pool.

Frank Loushin, another person Dad visited with at the drug store, was also an Elks Exalted Ruler. Frank was a pharmacist at Aspen Drug and was one of the ushers at Church. Once a month, Dad returned from the drugstore with stacks of comic books missing their covers. At the end of the month, the store removed the covers from the unsold comic books and magazines and sent them back to the publisher for credit. They were supposed to destroy the rest of the booklets. Missing the first page of some of the stories was a price I paid to have a copy of every comic book I ever wanted. I liked the Disney comics with *Mickey Mouse, Donald Duck,* and *Scrooge McDuck,* and in later years, I liked *Archie, Superman,* and *Batman.* Eventually, I got *Mad* magazine, which sort of creeped me out. I spent hours reading these comic books on my bedroom floor, and I stacked my collection behind my bedroom door in orange crates.

I was reading one of these comics one day when I was sure I saw a ghost. I sat cross-legged on the linoleum floor in my bedroom on the hall-side of my bed. The linoleum looked like an area rug. I was six or seven because it was before Mom redecorated my room

As I sat on the floor, I sensed something. I looked up toward the ceiling above the west wall. Floating there ever so briefly was a diaphanous shape. It moved down from the ceiling, stopped for a second or two, and disappeared through the outside wall. I was awake. It was daytime. I did not imagine it. It was not smoke. I only saw it once, but I knew it was a ghost, or more accurately, a spirit.

Like Dad, Mom went into town at least once a day. Once a week or so, she might go in quickly in the morning after seeing Grandma, to either the Mesa Store or Waterman's for a few groceries. Waterman's had a few canned foods and a small selection of penny candy and soda. I mostly remember it had motor oil.

For a short time when I was in grade school, a small-shed like building with a drive-through was on the corner of the mostly empty lot across Seventh Street from Watermans. For a summer or two, it had soft-serve ice cream and soft-serve ice cream cones dipped in chocolate. This was like Tasty Freezes in Glenwood and Denver. As a special treat, we stopped there after supper and then drove up Independence Pass while we finished our cones. It felt like Aspen had finally hit the big time. They tore the place down when the actress, Hedy Lamarr, built a motel complex named the Villa Lamarr on the spot.

The Mesa Store was further down Main Street from Grandma's on the other side of the street. It was a two-story red building that had a covered front porch. It looked like an old-west building with the false façade in front of a gabled roof. There was a covered staircase on the west side leading to the apartment for Elizabeth "Liz" Callahan, who owned it at the time.

I liked stopping at the Mesa Store. Liz was a tall, stout woman who had been a nurse at the hospital and was now a widow. She was a little older than Mom and one of Mom's good friends. Mom had lots of friends. Another good friend was Connie Lewis, who was Dr. Lewis's wife. The Lewis family lived in a Victorian house across from the school gym later owned by the Berko family. Albina was probably Mom's best friend because, unlike Celia, who worked outside the home, she was home during the day.

One of Celia's jobs was at the Mesa Store. She and Bill lived in a yellow Victorian house across the alley and across from a large empty lot with a dilapidated fence. The lot had been the site of the three-story Washington School, which was the high school from which my parents graduated. It was a majestic building; it was a shame they tore it down. Supposedly, it was too expensive to retrofit it to meet fire code requirements. The bricks were reused in the new single-story modern redbrick school at the northeast corner of Center and Hallam. The D.R.C. Brown house, which was also used as a high school, was once on that site. Steve went to school there and remarked it too was a beautiful building, and he especially liked the chemistry lab at the top of the round tower.

The Mesa Store had some canned goods, bakery items, dry ingredients like flour, soda, salt, and sugar, and a limited amount of meat cuts. From time to time, there were a few pieces of fresh fruit and some root vegetables. There was a cooler for ice cream and one for soda. Inside the door was a set of shelves and counters. They separated the store from the cash register operator and the goods on high shelves typical of a western general store. To the east were some shelves parallel to the counter set aside for the penny candy, vegetables, fruit, bread, and other self-service items.

I loved the penny candy shelves the best. My favorites were the coconut "watermelon" and "bacon" slices, the wax lips and teeth. There were also small rolls of Smarties, wax bottles filled with liquid, and licorice whips, pipes, and babies. There were candy cigarettes and bubble gum cigars, suckers with soft braided handles, Hershey kisses, and jawbreakers, Beemans, Blackjack or Clove gum, Bazooka Joe, candy buttons, Nonpareils, Pixy Stix, rock candy swizzles, jawbreakers, and Necco wafers – so hard to choose. I could only get a couple of pieces at a time. I bought most of my penny candy at the Mesa Store. When I was older and running around town, my penny candy came from Tiedeman's on Hyman Street next to the White Kitchen.

The Mesa Store had a round wood stove in the northeast corner where Mom, Liz, and Celia stood and talked. I laid on my stomach next to the stove and drew on the Red Chief tablet Liz kept for me behind the counter.

Every afternoon after dinner, Mom got cleaned up and went back into town. By cleaned up, that meant she took a bath, put on a clean house dress, put on some red lipstick, and splashed on some Chamberlain Lotion. Chamberlain Lotion was a clear liquid – probably mostly alcohol – in a clear bottle with a red pump spout. Later she changed to Jergens Lotion. I loved the almond smell.

While she primped, I sat on the edge of the bathtub and admired her and her beauty routine. I do not recall Mom doing much with her hair except brushing it. Even when I was young, she treated herself to a weekly trip to the Klip & Kurl to get her hair "set."

Every trip to town included a stop at the post office. The post office was in the Elks building across from the Aspen Drug and the Pitkin County Bank. It had wooden floors and two walls of post office boxes. The boxes were on the north and east, and radiators and counters were on the west and south. The room smelled of oiled floors and the metal doors of the mailboxes.

Our box was "423," and it had a combination lock on a sunburst pattern. There was a service counter on the east side of the room for stamps or picking up packages. There were bars on the window. I am not sure how we got our packages. I think they opened the door and brought them out. I was always concerned about the arrival of packages around Christmas. Although I believed in Santa Claus, I knew there was a direct relationship between packages at the post office and presents under the tree. Mom picked up and deposited Keith's laundry box here when he first went to college.

Across from the post office was the Pitkin County Bank in the Cowenhoven Building. We did not bank here. We banked at the First

National Bank in Glenwood Springs. Part of the reason, I was told, was because there had been a problem with one of the local banks – someone embezzled money from it and went to jail. Dad worried about losing his money. Another reason for not using the local bank was Dad had a credit arrangement with the First National Bank of Glenwood to cover expenses until the crops or cattle sold. He was loyal to the bank and refused to open even a savings account in a local bank. Therefore, my savings accounts were in Glenwood.

Because we did not have an account at that bank, we were not permitted to write counter checks. At the time, there were blank checks in which a customer could put their account number, and the bank honored the check the same way it honors printed checks today.

After picking up the mail, Mom went grocery shopping at Beck & Bishop, which was on the north end of the Wheeler Opera House building. The main floor had a high ceiling big enough for a loft on the west end. The basement was for storage and the compressors for the freezers and refrigerator units.

On the left of the store was a small produce section in front of the windows and in an "L" along the south wall. The produce section was usually sparse – mostly root vegetables and seasonal fruits and vegetables in late summer and fall. The dairy cases were also on the south wall.

Beyond the dairy case was a metal door leading to the rental meat lockers. The meat locker part of the store was probably partially behind the library. We had a meat locker. The room was icy and so cold my nostrils stuck together, and the fog of my breath hung motionless in the air. Mom did not linger long in there. I remember one time when she had what I thought was an unreasonably long conversation with Trude Baar in the locker while I froze by her side.

Next to the meat locker in the western third of the store was the butcher shop with another meat locker and a meat display counter. It was not unusual to see a beef carcass hanging above the sawdust floor behind the counter. Albert was a butcher, and he and Reinhard Elder butchered the pork and beef we kept for our family's consumption.

The part of the meat counter which faced the front of the store had glass to view the meat cuts. I liked the "lunch meat," which consisted of salami, bologna, and what Mom called "boiled ham," which was a brick-shaped block of ham that could be thinly sliced. There were several varieties of cheese, including Swiss. Because I did not like cheese, I paid little attention to it. When I was older, I went into the store and bought ten cents worth of dry salami – sliced thin – for a snack. It was the kind of hard salami with a casing around it and peppercorns inside. Next to the butcher area was a back room with a coffee pot, stairs leading to an office overlooking the store, and access to the basement storage.

The rest of the store had two or three shelving units for canned goods running perpendicular from the meat counter to the front of the store. There was a frozen-food bin in the north wall for frozen vegetables, ice cream, ice cream treats, or sherbet. There were a few more shelves along the wall and a tall Coke machine. There was a small candy section near the front by the two cash registers next to the northernmost window.

At that time, we charged our groceries. Instead of paying with cash or writing a check – no credit cards yet – the clerk went through an alphabetical box and pulled out our ledger card. They ran it through the cash register machine. Once a month, Mom got a bill from Bea Zick, the bookkeeper. Bea had an office above the meat counter with an opening looking out over the store. From time to time, you could see her or Henry Beck working in the room.

Bea and her husband Bob lived across from Steve and Polly, as did Wayne Habermann, who also worked at the store. Wayne's wife, Ruth, and Bea were sisters. Wayne was from Wisconsin, and whenever he went home to visit his family, he brought back several pounds of German wieners for Dad. They reminded Dad of wieners he had when he was a boy. They came in long strings and looked like the sausages a cartoon dog would steal from a butcher shop and run away while the receding butcher shook his fist.

The store had most of the staples – canned food, baking supplies, and spices. From time to time, they got in novelty items. I remember going into the store and wasting some of my prayers to urge God to make sure they stocked that new drink – Tang. I was disappointed. It was sold out. I had to settle for black cherry Kool-Aid.

On the front sidewalk, metal doors concealed an opening below the sidewalk. Such metal doors or grates were on the sidewalks throughout town. The ones at the store had disks of prism glass. When the doors were open, cases of groceries could be unloaded and slid on ramps to the storage area in the basement. Gary, Barney, and I slid down the ramps a couple of times. Unfortunately, there was no elevator or lift out of the basement, so the heavy cartons were carried up steep stairs into the store.

In the summer, there was a pop machine in front of the store with Orange Crush, 7-Up, Hires Root Beer, and Squirt. I now call it soda because I live in California, but it was pop when I was a kid. The machine in front of the store was a chest type unit. One lifted the lid, chose the pop, drug it through a maze to the trap area, and pulled it up and out. Barney and Gary could get a key to get extra pops stored in the bottom of the machine. The Coke machine inside the store was one of those tall machines. It was cold, and ice crystals formed in the neck of the Coke bottle instantly when opened. It was so good.

Besides going to Beck & Bishop for daily shopping, Mom often stopped at the library. Although she was a voracious reader, she did not read to me and left that chore to my siblings. Reading was her single greatest pleasure, and she loved mysteries, romances, and poetry. A book was usually open on the kitchen counter while she was cooking.

The library was on the first floor of the Wheeler Opera House south of Beck & Bishop, slightly higher than the Beck & Bishop side. The door was on the southeast corner. The steps had curved concrete sides that were fun to walk up and down instead of using the stairs. Climbing the sides of the library stairs was not as fun as climbing the side of the courthouse stairs; they were twice as long.

The inside of the library was dark and gave the false impression it was dusty. The stacks were to the left, perpendicular to the western wall. The librarian's table was straight ahead. Renate Braun, a short, German woman, was the librarian. Big arched windows and radiators were opposite the stacks. Near one of the northernmost windows was a small section of lower shelves forming an alcove filled with children's books. While Mom looked through the stacks, I sat on the floor and read or looked at picture books. My favorites were *Dr. Seuss* and *Babar the Elephant*. When we checked out the books, Mrs. Braun let me stamp the due date on the flap inside the book and on the book card. Sometimes when Mom shopped, I stayed and read.

When I was older, I got *Nancy Drew* books from the young reader section. That section also included the *Hardy Boys* and the *Tom Swift* series. It may have included Jack London stories as well. I never got into *Tom Swift*, but I loved the *Hardy Boys*. Barney and Gary had a complete set, and I borrowed their books. When I read the *Twisted Claw* one night, I had a hard time falling to sleep. As far as Jack London, Keith had several of his books that I read in his room – *White Fang* and the *Call of the Wild*.

From time to time, Mom and Dad bought liquor either from Louie's Liquor or Magnifico Liquor. Mostly they only bought beer because Mom and Dad got bourbon from Harry Hoffman's in Denver. They never bought wine unless it was a bottle of sherry or port because we had a supply of Zinfandel in our basement.

We got our hardware at the Aspen Lumber & Supply across from Beck & Bishop. It was a typical hardware store – lots of displays with gadgets and tools hanging in display cases – everything from paint to pots and pans. We did not go daily, but we went there often.

It was another one of those places where I prayed that they had the item I wanted. Because when you needed something – you needed it. This happened most often at Christmas when we discovered the fuse was out on a strand of Christmas lights, and none of the lights worked without it. One year when they did not have a fuse, I worried it would be a dark Christmas. Thankfully Dad was able to jury-rig a work-around, and we had lights after all. After that, I made sure there were extra light bulbs and fuses. To this day, when I open the Christmas tree box, I have a heart-stopping moment when I plug it in and worry my pre-lighted Christmas tree will not work.

The Aspen Lumber & Supply lumberyard was across the street from the hardware store and across the alley from the Beck & Bishop. I went in there a few times with Dad. I went with him when he bought a couple of pieces of Masonite pegboard to use for a school project.

On that same block, but west on Hopkins on the corner was the Aspen Laundry and Cleaners. That is where we got our wool clothing cleaned. Riley's wife, Stella, worked there for Hod Nicholson for years. I was fascinated by how they pulled the clothes into the plastic bags on a large roll above the counter. In winter, large plumes of steam came out of the side of the building.

Sometimes, Dad and I went to Tomkins Hardware. Tomkins Hardware was on the southeast corner of Galena and Cooper. It seemed more industrial than a typical hardware store – more geared toward farm and mining equipment and supplies. I bought two boxes of yellow Calcimine, a type of powdered paint, for fifty cents a box, mixed it with water, and used it to paint the interior of Judy's playhouse. I only painted part of the walls because I ran out of yellow, and on the return trip, they only had green. Therefore, the playhouse had two-toned walls.

During the winter of 1965, the building collapsed after a massive snowstorm. A modern building that housed the new Mountain Shop replaced it. In sixth grade, I got my English racer, three-speed narrow-wheeled girl's bike from the older Mountain Shop when it was next to Tomkins Hardware.

Another store we visited was what we called The Kalmes Store. It was a "dry goods" store. It was the place to buy Levi 501's. Knowing the statute of limitations has now expired, I confess I stole a package of needles from the store. I was standing in front of a blond wood display case in the northwest corner with lots of slots for needles, pins, spools of thread, rick rack trim, and zippers. Suddenly, I had an overwhelming urge to take something. I looked around. No one was watching. I reached in and grabbed a package of needles. I looked around again. I stuck them in my pocket. When I got home, I worried about getting caught, so I threw them away. I never confessed this sin, but I worried about both the sin and my soul. I knew if I confessed to Father Bosch, he would make me tell my parents, and they would make me go into the store and admit my crime. I remember Peggy's parent-imposed humiliation when she took a piece of candy from Beck & Bishop.

There were a few other stores we went to from time to time. There was a gift store known as the Pack Rat. That is where Mom bought Peggy her doll furniture in a going-out-of-business sale. The Aspen Jewelers, owned by Lottie and Kurt Bresnitz, was behind Sardy's Hardware across from the ISIS Theater. This store is where Dad bought special gifts for Mom – earrings and a watch.

Keith was the source of Mom's silver jewelry. He worked for Jim Hayes, who, besides owning an earthmoving business, was a silversmith. He was famous for his belt buckles and aspen-leaf jewelry. Keith designed a snowflake, and Jim made a unique set of earrings for Mom, using the design. Keith gave me one of Jim's aspen-leaf necklaces.

We went into Matthew Drug occasionally, but mostly for ice cream. Matthew Drug was on the opposite end of the Hotel Jerome block on the other side of the *Aspen Times* building. It had a small soda fountain. Sometimes I checked out their supply of comics. As for drugs and sundries, our allegiance was with the Aspen Drug. We did not make purchases from Matthew Drug if it was available at Aspen Drug. We had brand allegiances as well. We did not read the Rocky Mountain News. We read the Denver Post. We did not use Miracle Whip. We used Best Foods Mayonnaise.

We frequented two restaurants – the Red Onion and Guido's. The Red Onion had a small dining room east of the bar where Bill worked. It had red-checked tablecloths and served steaks, chops, burgers, and deep-fried shrimp. We loved the homemade Roquefort dressing so much Dad got the recipe from Werner Kuster, one of the owners. I still make it.

For fancier food, we went to Guido's Swiss Inn. It had a Tyrolean decor. Like the Red Onion, it had red-checked tablecloths except here there were matching cloth napkins folded like fans. I deconstructed how these napkins were folded and recreated them for fancy holiday dinners at home.

Originally Guido's restaurant was in a log building across from Grandma's house on Main Street. When I first went to it, it was on the corner of Galena and Cooper across from Tomkins Hardware. We dressed nicer when we went there. Dad put on his sport jacket and tie, and Mom wore a dress with heels.

Guido's had a variety of Swiss and German food such as sauerbraten, wiener schnitzel, and stroganoff. Dad liked the food. He liked the owner, Guido Meyer, although he thought Guido could be a bit cranky. His wife, Trudi, was the hostess and seemed glad to see us. She always gave me a piece of Swiss chocolate when we left. Guido's was the place I first tasted a Toblerone candy. A piece or two of Toblerone wrapped in foil became a must-have item to stick in my pocket for a skiing snack.

I do not remember much about the food except for dessert. I got a Swiss chocolate parfait. It came in a tall clear stemmed glass with vanilla ice cream alternating with a sauce made from Swiss chocolate bars, topped with whipped cream, and of course, a maraschino cherry. For his dessert, Dad liked the apple strudel.

On a shelf behind the front counter was an Austrian wine decanter known as a *wein heber*. The decanter was made of etched glass shaped like an upside-down teardrop and set on a wrought iron stand. It had matching glasses with etched grape leaves. Mom liked it so much that when she found one in an antique store, she immediately snatched it up. We kept it on the buffet in the dining room. Peggy still has it.

Although we got most of what we needed in town, we supplemented with trips out of town and mail-order catalogs. Once a month, we went to Glenwood Springs, which was 40 miles from town, to do business with the bigger stores and do our banking.

Unlike today, banking required being there in person, so Mom and Dad went to the bank to deposit checks and clip bond coupons. Some of our important papers, such as stock certificates, were kept in the safety deposit box. They stored the other valuable documents in an old red-and-cream metal breadbox on a shelf in their bedroom. They told us to grab it in the case of a fire.

Sometimes, Dad went alone or with one of the kids. Sometimes Mom might go with one of her friends and us. Dad frequented the Farmer's Supply Store, across the Colorado River. It was the source for farm equipment and supplies and where Dad bought his farm clothing, such as bib overalls and hats. One time when I was with him, I saw a small pedal-powered John Deere tractor. Although we had no sidewalk upon which to ride this thing, I still wanted it. Not only did I not get it, I also did not get my second choice of a toy John Deere tractor with a trailer.

We went to Bullocks for "dress" clothing. Bullocks was the premier department store in Glenwood and was where Dad bought his dress western shirts– the ones with the mother of pearl snaps. I always got my first day of school outfit here.

J. C. Penney was another "department" store where we got underwear, sewing patterns, fabric, and notions vital to our 4-H projects. We stopped by Hested's 5 and 10. I was usually disappointed in their merchandise. Even as a kid, I knew it was mostly junk. The best "toys" we got were coloring and sticker books. There wasn't much there that I wanted – except when they got hula-hoops.

In later years, we went to one of the two new "supermarkets" – Safeway and City Market. Mom bought supplies such as toilet paper, detergent, and canned foods that were not available at Beck & Bishop. When she learned we were going to Glenwood and she could not go with us, Polly asked Mom to bring back Morton frozen pies – fruit, cream, and pot pies for her and Steve.

Mom and Dad stopped to fill the cars with gasoline. By doing so, they preserved the gas at the ranch and got S&H Green Stamps. S&H Green stamps were available at about all the Glenwood stores we frequented. With those stamps, Mom bought a rocking chair, a spinning wheel planter, and several lamps. I still have one of the milk-glass lamps she purchased with S&H Green Stamps.

Across the River

Our property not only included the area we ranched. Dad also owned many acres on the east side of Castle Creek at the base of Aspen Mountain.

When I was little, there was one house in this area. It belonged to Albina and Edmund. Albina's grandparents, Joseph and Julia Skriner, lived there before them. Although Dad technically owned the property, there was no doubt the Skriner family lived there long enough to claim it through adverse possession. At some point, Dad deeded the property to Albina and Edmund.

Their house was across Castle Creek at the same elevation as the granary and barns. When the river was low, the kids from our families could either walk across the river by placing wooden planks between boulders or taking off our shoes and wading. The crossing was downstream from the path Dad took for to reach his fishing holes. The trail on the Gerbaz side was not as steep.

This low-water crossing should not be confused with the spot further up Castle Creek where, Billy, and his high school buddies, Tom Moore and Don Neil Stapleton, put boards across giant boulders through which the water boiled. These boards were five or six feet above the water. The water was so swift that droplets hung in the air making the boards slick. I never crossed up there. They did. They survived.

Like our side of the river, the other side had terraces. The houses on the eastern side were on the same elevation as the granary and barn terrace. The one below the houses matched the elevation to the lixiviation cooling floor. This doglegged terrace ran mostly north-south along the riverbank with a northeast curve, which once supported the Midland Railway trestle.

Inside of the dogleg curve was a large group of chokecherry bushes and was a prime source of chokecherries. We picked them, collected them in lard buckets, and sold them to Mom, Celia, or Albina to use for jelly. It took a long time to fill a lard bucket. The going rate was twenty-five cents per bucket. I was vocally annoyed when Bud's daughter, Jamie, got the same amount for less than a cup just because she was little.

The Gerbaz house and barn were a few yards away from the base of Aspen Mountain and little south of a raised portion of the Midland railroad bed. There were abandoned sawmill buildings to the north.

The sawmill buildings were like huge sheds, now with gaping holes and large openings in the swayback roofs and sides. The roofs were rusted metal. There were some big, rusted saws. Going through and around the sawmill buildings were ore-cart sized rails. There were a few small flatbed carts that could be pushed around on small sections of tracks. In a little glen near the sawmill, there was a rhubarb patch and a spot where Albina harvested spring dandelion greens for salad.

The carts may have been like the ones used by Albina's aunts and uncles to gather hay for their milk cows. Before Albina and Edmund lived in the house, Albina's grandparents, Joe and Julia Skriner, lived there. When the Skriner children were young, the family had milk cows and sold milk in town. The Midland tracks and trestle were still in place. The children crossed the trestle pushing a small railroad cart. Once they got to what was then known as the Aspen Ranch, they went along the ditches and roads and chopped down the hay that could not be reached by the mower. They piled it on the cart and pushed it back across the trestle to the waiting milk cows.

Albina and her siblings ended up living with her grandparents after their mother became ill. Before that, they lived in a small house up Castle Creek near the coke ovens. Albina stayed on in the house after she married Edmund.

The Gerbaz house was next to the original Castle Creek Road, which was a southern extension of Seventh Street. West of the house was a walkway to a barn. The barn was two stories tall. I never went upstairs. The shed held everything, including beehives. The downstairs was filled with storage, tack, and livestock supplies for Cherie's horse, Dutch, the sheep, chickens, and the lambs they kept in the summer in a small pasture behind the shed. An outhouse was attached to the front of the barn to the left of the door. Inside the were stacks of magazines and catalogs for reading and wiping.

My first memories of the Gerbaz house were before they had an indoor bathroom. At the time, they took baths in the large kitchen sink. I took a bath there once and thought it was fun – sitting up high looking out the window.

At that time, it was a three-room house. One room included the kitchen and a dining and living area – not to be confused with a modern, great room. The entire area was probably twenty by ten feet at best and also included an upright piano and a heating stove. On occasion, Albina dried homemade noodles above the stove.

Besides the main room, there were two bedrooms. Edmund and Albina's bedroom opened into the main room. Jimmy and Cherie walked through their parent's bedroom to get to their room. Albina stored extra pots and pans and home-canned goods in a cellar accessible from the outside.

In the fifties, they extended and nearly doubled the main room and added an indoor bathroom and a bedroom for Jimmy. The new area was slightly below the old part of the house and separated by an angled step.

The addition came about after Edmund kept promising Albina to build one but never got around to it. One day or maybe one night, Albina had enough. She took a meat cleaver to the outside northern wall and pretty much destroyed it. Edmund had no choice but to build an addition. John Morris, Bud Marolt's friend, helped with the construction.

This event was not unusual for Albina. She was known for her spontaneity with household chores. It wasn't unusual for her to decide to paint a room in the middle of the night or to drag all the furniture out on the lawn to facilitate spring housecleaning.

Albina loved her home. Despite the size, she had a knack for decorating. Mom accurately described the inside as a dollhouse with white cupboards and blue walls and crisply ironed white curtains at the windows. There were open shelves with blue willow dishes. Albina was a good seamstress and made beautiful clothes for Cherie. She probably made some of Jimmy's shirts as well.

Outside the western kitchen door and several yards to the south was a large mound or small hill in what was otherwise or should have been flat land. The mound consisted of large boulders that rolled off Aspen Mountain years before. By large, I mean, these boulders must have been the size of pickup trucks. Someone filled the top spaces between the boulders with dirt and planted grass. It was a chore to mow with the push mower. Several pine trees and two or three transparent apple trees topped the hill. Transparent apples are bright green, about an inch and half in diameter, and tart and tasty. They made excellent pies, cobblers, and applesauce. I ate them until my stomach ached.

The trees on top of the mound provided hiding places during games of kick-the-can or gray wolf.

On the level below the mound was a page wire fence beyond which was a vast garden at least three times larger than ours. Not only did Albina plant the same vegetables Mom planted, she also grew tomatoes, corn, cucumbers, and zucchini. The vegetable garden was on the south side of the barn. The fact that the garden was on the south side of the building may have provided some shelter and heat for the tomatoes and corn to get an early start and survive till harvest.

Then there were her flowers. While Mom described Albina's house as a dollhouse, she described her yard as heaven. Against the page wire fence next to the road and in front of the house, she planted sweet peas covering the fence with every pastel color imaginable. In front of the sweet peas in the same beds were petunias, small marigolds, and white and blue alyssum. On the south, east, and north sides of the house were gladiolas, tall marigolds, asters, zinnias, and her favorites – baby's breath and dahlias. The dahlias were her pride and joy and grand prize winners at the local P.E.O. Sisterhood flower show.

In the exposed rocks east and south of the hill, she planted every imaginable color of nasturtium. Bordering the wooden sidewalk leading from the house to the shed, clothesline porch, and outhouse were calendulas in rust, apricot, peach, and yellow. Sunflowers bloomed next to the outhouse and a corner of the shed. Judy remembers the clothesline porch was surrounded by pansies.

Because she liked a white contrast, Albina stuck white candytuft here and there throughout the flower beds. She knew what to plant and when to plant it to keep a colorful array as long as possible. For instance, Icelandic poppies bloomed in the spring, dahlias and gladiolas lasted all summer. Other than her dahlias and gladiolas, she did not plant bulbs like tulips or daffodils because they took up too much space and did not last long. Nor did she use greenhouse plants like geraniums.

Seemingly the only white flowers she did not have in her yard were daisies. There was no need. Oxalis daisies covered the banks of the Hoaglund Ditch on the east side of the road. The Hoaglund Ditch was about a fourth the size of the Marolt Ditch and was used for a pasture near the music tent and supplied water to the small ditches irrigating the cottonwoods flanking Main Street.

Besides the flowers and vegetables, there were a few animals. Cherie had horses, and they raised a few lambs and their dogs – Nipper's brothers. A car killed Tip when he was young. Although another car hit Sandy, he survived with a broken tail. Because he could not wag it effectively, he seemed sad. At one point, the family had some geese. God knows why. The geese were horrible. Without any coercion, they chased me around the lawn, flapping their wings and nipping at my butt or ankles. They chased me up and down the hill.

I spent a lot of time at Albina's when Mom went to visit or when she watched me while Mom ran errands. When I visited, Albina brought out some of Jimmy's toys. I either played with Jimmy's miniature lead army men he molded and painted or with his toy farm. His farm had a barn with a hayloft with a hoist, plastic hay bales, a couple of cows, some horses, pigs, and chickens. One of the pigs had a leg that we slightly too short, so it needed to lean against the barn.

There were fence sections that snapped together to make corrals or pens. To make it even more authentic, Albina went into the cupboard and brought out a bag of chocolate chips and sprinkled a few around the barnyard. "What's a farm without some road apples?" she said. Part of the cleanup included consuming the chocolate chips.

I liked lunch at her house. She had bologna from which she sliced a piece, put it on homemade white bread, and slathered it with yellow French's mustard. Every time I see bologna, I think of those sandwiches.

Not every moment was perfect. One time while playing at the house, I ran through a dust pile in the kitchen, disbursing the dust over an area Albina just swept. She yelled at me. I guess this was an unusual event. I remember being so ashamed that she got mad at me that I thought I saw the floor drop from under my feet.

When the family went to the Gerbaz house for an event, it was fun. We played outside on the hill or at the sawmill. We played hide-and-seek, gray wolf, or kick the can. Supper was good because everyone knew how to cook and bake. Albina picked up a knack for cooking Italian food from Edmund's family.

When it got dark, the kids got tired. While the adults continued talking and laughing, the kids went in and laid down on Edmund and Albina's bed. In the winter, Albina put a large silky red comforter on top of us. It was cozy. When it was time to go home, Dad picked me up, and I rested my head against his shoulder. When we began to leave, they opened the door and continued talking while I froze.

Ted's House

After I was born, Ted built a house near the Gerbaz house. He was the youngest of the twelve Marolts and looked like his brothers but had a slight build and wore glasses. Like his brothers, he was bald on the top of his head and, like them, he wore hats. He was smart and read a lot. Whether it was because of a hearing problem or just being a Marolt male, Ted was shy.

His hearing problems developed after he learned to speak because he did not have any associated speech problems. Someone said severe untreated ear infections caused his hearing loss as a child. Perhaps he had one of those conditions that today could be remedied by some minimal surgery or one of the newer hearing aids. Instead, he wore a bulky headband contraption that sat behind his ears and had a chord leading to a metal transistor radio looking device he kept in the pocket of his work shirt. The device was slightly larger than a pack of cigarettes. He continually reached into his pocket and turned a dial on the device because it buzzed and was annoying. I think that is why he often preferred to be alone in his peaceful world without the hearing aid. In later years, his hearing aids improved and became smaller and higher quality, but he still did not like them.

Because Ted did not have his own family, he volunteered to help with community projects using his team of workhorses. He helped level and build the City Park, which eventually became Paepcke Park, and helped clear Ruthie's Run on the ski hill. He attended daily Mass and served as an usher on Sundays.

When Ted sold his ranch, Dad sold or gave him a piece of property across the river. Ted's lot was about fifty yards south of Albina's house on the same side of the road. It included the house site and a bit of the terrace below. Dad considered the property on the other side of the river to be more or less worthless, and he practically gave it away. It was "worthless" because it was not suitable for farming or ranching and was in the shadow of the mountain for much of each winter day. He eventually sold a lot between Ted and the Gerbaz house to Bud, who built a small vacation house. Dad sold a lot across the road to his sister Elsie for her vacation house.

Ted's house was west of what had been the original Castle Creek Road. It was before the spot where the road had a steep incline along the edge of Aspen Mountain. The road crossed Castle Creek at the Newman mine. A new road was built on a spur of the Midland, going from the main tracks to the mine. It was on the western, flat side of our ranch. For a while, both the original road and the new road were open.

Before Ted built his house, Alf Chesley, one of the original ski patrolmen, was killed south of what would be Ted's lot where there was a steep cut in the side of the mountain above the river rushing in the gorge below. Two local boys were climbing on a rocky ridge above the road and throwing rocks at a boulder. Alf was returning from a fishing trip. A few minutes, whether on purpose or by accident, the boulder broke free, hitting Alf's truck. He was thrown from the truck before it plunged into Castle Creek. Alf was killed.

Within a short time, the county closed the road and abandoned the right-of-way. The rocky hillside was too dangerous with or without human interference. Some of the land reverted to Dad. He sold a parcel on the road incline to Bud's friend, John Morris, who built a chalet-style house. Peter Vought eventually bought it. Robbie Albouy built another chalet higher on the hill that was later owned by Keith Hefner – Hugh's brother. I do not believe we owned that property.

Ted's house nestled between the first incline of the road on the south and a huge boulder and chokecherry bush to the north. Once there was a small house in the same location, but after the big boulder came down off Aspen Mountain, the people who lived there moved to the east end of town far from falling boulders. Their house was long gone before Ted decided to build.

The presence of large boulders, such as the ones in Ted's and Albina's yards and the one that killed Alf Chesley, was not at all surprising. The land was at the base of Aspen Mountain, and the spine along the top of the mountain was staggered layers of rock outcroppings. With freezing and thawing, boulders broke off and plummeted to the flat below.

Ted's boulder was the size of a delivery van. Over the years, chokecherry bushes grew around the boulder and partly obscured it. Ted used the boulder and chokecherry bush as his primary landscaping feature and was a source of chokecherries. Because they benefitted from pruning and fertilizing the nearby lawn, the chokecherries were big and plump.

In choosing his lot, Ted played the odds that no other big rock was going to find its way into his yard or his house. He reasoned, to hit his house, another boulder would have to get around the existing boulder.

Ted started building his house after he moved from our house. He had help excavating his basement, pouring the foundation, framing the house, and adding a roof. After it was framed and insulated and had electricity and roughed-in plumbing, he moved in and did all of the finish work. It took years to complete.

The garage and furnace room were below the house on the lower terrace, and the living area was on the upper level. The driveway leading to the garage curved around north of the boulder. From the road, it looked like a single story-house.

Ted rarely used his garage because his gray Corvair and Jeep were in the two parking spaces near his front door. Both he and Max had Corvairs. One summer, when it was new, Max drove his yellow Corvair to Alaska on the Alcan Highway. That may have been the trip where he climbed and skied one of Alaska's highest mountains. After that, the locals referred to it as Max's Mountain.

Ted loved his Corvair because General Motors made it, and he owned General Motors stock. Ted was loyal and was furious when Ralph Nader claimed Corvairs were *Unsafe at Any Speed*. It was unusual for Ted to get angry. He was usually calm and quiet. Ted took Nader's criticism personally. When he talked about it, he raised his otherwise soft voice, and his face flushed.

The upper part of the house was like many of the homes built during this time. It had a flat roof, vertical cedar siding, and the high bedroom windows provided ventilation, but no view. Bill and Celia's house had the same high windows. I remember similar windows in the Wally Mills' house built on the Midland. Ted's main door was in a covered alcove near the boulder and tree.

The small house had two bedrooms, a bath, and a galley kitchen with a view of the boulder and the chokecherry bush. There was no dining room, only a space at the end of the kitchen for a small table.

The table was often covered with the newspapers Ted was reading. Although I got a drink of water from time to time there, I never ate anything there and do not think he did much cooking. When I looked in the refrigerator, there was usually a six-pack or two of Hamm's Beer, a carton of milk, and eggs. He probably had the beer on hand for when his friend, Tony Kastelic, visited. Tony was the son of the Anton Kastelic, who walked to Aspen with our grandfather, and, like Ted, had hearing problems. Both were devout Catholics.

The living room had a brick fireplace with a raised hearth covering most of the eastern wall. I suspect Steve helped build the fireplace – at least he helped with its design. Between his cabin and his house, Steve built efficient heating fireplaces. The bricks were from the big chimney.

The living room was surrounded on the south and west by windows, starting a foot above the baseboard radiators and extending to the ceiling. Ted had a view of cottonwoods across the river and the hills to the south and west of our ranch. There was a deck outside the western windows and the sound of Castle Creek in the background

Ted designed and built a metal spiral staircase descending from the deck to a concrete pad in front of the garage. Although there was in the internal enclosed stairway to the garage level, the spiral staircase allowed access directly to the upstairs from the parking area below. Ted, like Dad and Steve, had a knack for building things.

Ted's living room furniture consisted of a chair and an end table. Guests could drag in one of the kitchen chairs or sit on the raised fireplace hearth. When television arrived in town, he had a tv with rabbit ears on a portable stand equipped with headphones.

With Dad's advice and equipment, Ted tiled his kitchen and bathroom. Celia talked him into tiling the kitchen in pastel pink, which was fashionable at that time. Nothing could have been worse for a bachelor. The bathroom, however, was tiled in dark hunter green with chrome details. Of all the bathrooms Dad and his brothers tiled, it was the most handsome. There were only two sparsely furnished bedrooms. Many years later, one of Ted's sisters took him to Glenwood and made him buy furniture.

Elsie's cabin, which was across from Ted's house, abutted the edge of Aspen Mountain in an area that appeared to be a turnout for the road. Elsie's husband George was a contractor from Encino, California, and may have designed the cabin. His son in law, Chuck Clifton, did most of the construction over a couple of summers.

Dad was not impressed with southern California construction techniques. There was no basement, and the walls and attic had little or no insulation. The cabin was simple with shellacked high-grade plywood. It was a rectangle with the broad facing side toward the driveway and a small mudroom and laundry room entrance attached on the east end. The main "great" room was the length of the front with a row of large windows and a view toward Ted's house. The main room had a fireplace on one end and a kitchen on the other with a window overlooking the side Aspen Mountain only yards away. A table and chairs, a sofa and easy chairs filled the spaces in between. The northern half of the house included two bedrooms and a bath. The structure was adequate for a summer vacation home but lacking in winter.

Part III

Grade School

After the Midland

New People – New Friends

I was five when I started first grade. The rule was a student could start first grade in the fall if they turned six by the end of December of that year. School always started the day after Labor Day and ended the Friday before Memorial or Flag Day. I turned six in September.

By that time, Aspen was seeing an influx of new people Many of the new people seemed to have a lot of money. At least it seemed they had more than we had. The new families came from cities that had kindergartens. Therefore, one of them started a private kindergarten in the basement of the Community Church. It cost money or a donation to attend. I have no idea how much, but it was more than we could afford. So, I did not go to kindergarten.

My teacher for first grade was Patricia Lumsden. Miss Lumsden put the kids who had gone to the kindergarten automatically into the top reading group. I was relegated to the slow group even though I had been reading Barney and Gary's first-grade readers for a year. I learned to read by following the books I made my sisters and brother read to me over and over.

My group sat in a circle on our small chairs and took turns reading a page or two. It was painful. I waited and rocked back and forth until some of the slower kids read their page with six words in the *Dick and Jane* reader. They stumbled over words like ball, play, and run.

For a while, our class was in the big room on the west side of the red schoolhouse closest to Center Street. That room, which later became the library, had a small stage. In the afternoon, Miss Lumsden rolled out a cart with small bottles of milk and stacks of graham crackers. After our snack, we pulled out mats and took a nap on the stage.

School for everyone, whether you were in first grade or a senior in high school, was from 8:30 a.m. to 3:30 p.m. The hours coincided with the bus schedule. Most of the down-valley farm and ranch kids took the bus. Our ranch was too close to town for the bus, so Mom drove me to school.

I liked some of the newer kids. I liked Nora Berko and Nora Gallagher. I played with some of my Catholic friends, such as Martha Coble and Christine Sparovik. I even went a couple of times to Ray Weidenhaft's house. Because his father was the District Forest Ranger,

Ray lived in the living quarters attached to the ranger station, which was kitty-corner to Waterman's store. We played with his electric train that puffed out real smoke. One time when I came to play, he gave me a small glass of Mogen David wine. I doubt if it was authorized.

I went to several birthday parties. The most memorable was for Pat Herwick's birthday. His father was the sheriff. The family lived in the basement of the courthouse. To get to the living quarters, we passed the jail cells. On the day of the party, there was a blond woman in a cell sitting on her bed. I wondered if she was a bank robber or a murderer? Someone said she wrote bad checks. I had no idea what that meant.

The living room area of their quarters was dark because the only windows were high up on the wall. We played spin the bottle. Fortunately, as the bottle spun around, it never landed on me. I used up a few prayers avoiding having to kiss someone. I had the idea that there were a finite number of prayers, so I had to use them wisely. We ended the party with cake and ice cream and had fun climbing the sloping sides of the courthouse steps as we waited for our parents.

In first grade, Suzy Tekoucich was my best friend. She was Celia and Albina's niece. Her father, George, was tall, gangly, and funny. When I think of him, I think of Kramer on *Seinfeld*. Pepper, his wife, was small with curly blond hair. She was sweet and talked with a bit of a lisp. When I remember her, I think of Bernadette Peters.

Suzy was smart. Her older sister, Linde, was a talented artist. Linde drew paper dolls on cardboard so we could design and color our paper clothes for them. Suzy's family lived in Lenado, a small mining and logging community over the hill from Woody Creek. Suzy, Linde, and their little sister, Jo Jo, took the bus to school along with John and Tom Marsing, who also lived in Lenado. I believe Tom, Christine Sparovik, and I were the only people who started first grade together and graduated together.

Once I rode the bus to Lenado with Suzy and spent a few nights in the Tekoucich's cabin. Their cabin was sparse, and they had an outhouse. I remember we ate Grape Nuts for breakfast. That was unusual because we did not eat boxed cereal and only occasionally had oatmeal and Cream of Wheat. Usually, I did not miss having cereal because, for the most part, I did not like milk – the drink. Despite my dislike of the beverage, the word "milk" was, at the time, my favorite word. I like how it felt in my mouth when I said the word out loud. I liked how it sounded, going from soft to smooth to hard.

One weekend early in the year, I took some inspiration from Linde and sat down with a large blank piece of butcher paper and drew a picture of our house. Albert supplied matte butcher paper from his store. I used it for drawings and making murals. I also used it for cardboard televisions – paper taped to two broom handles and rolled to reveal new scenes in a "screen" cut out of a large cardboard box.

The drawing I made that day was the view of the south side of our house. I had every detail – each window, each pane of glass, the siding, and the shingles. The perspective was off – I was only six. It was almost an aerial, two-dimensional view with the house appearing to lie on its side. The *pièce de résistance* was Nipper lying on the ground between the clothesline and the house.

My drawing was sophisticated for a six-year-old, and I got rave reviews at home. I was so pleased with my picture that I took it to school. I showed it to my friends. They were impressed. During class, I rolled it up and put it in my desk. It was one of those metal desks with an open shelf under the wooden seat, a wooden top, a hole for an ink bottle, and a groove for pencils.

At some point, the drawing unrolled and fell on the floor. Just as I noticed it and reached to pick it up, one of the new girls came down the aisle and stepped on it. I asked her to move. She refused. Instead, she began twisting her foot tearing and smudging the picture. I asked her to stop. She refused. Instead of stopping, she tore the picture in half with her feet. I started crying. It felt like she was destroying my house, my family, my dog, and me.

Miss Lumsden intervened. Instead of reprimanding the girl for ruining my picture or asking her to apologize, she chastised me for bringing the picture to school in the first place. The new girl went scot-free, and I had a ruined picture. With this incident, Miss Lumsden earned the distinction of being my least favorite teacher – ever. I truly believed, and still do, that she favored the new people and looked down on me and the other farm and ranch kids.

I am in the minority concerning my feelings about Miss Lumsden because I see the rave reviews from others who had her as their teacher. Seeing her name mentioned on social media for the first time in decades created a visceral response deep in the pit of my stomach. Maybe I am unfair. On the other hand, actions have consequences, and because of Miss Lumsden's actions that day, my lasting memory of her was negative. Nothing redeemed her in my mind.

After his wife died, Earl Kelly, the principal, dated Ms. Lumsden. Eventually, they married. He was okay. He saved me from falling from the Little Nell chairlift the first time I rode it. That is another story.

The next year, I had a much better teacher experience – Mrs. Johnson. She was a kind older woman who put me in the highest reading group. The worst part of that year was that Suzy Tekoucich left – her family moved to Glenwood Springs. I was sad and lonely.

By third grade, I was reasonably popular. Mrs. Johnson salvaged me from my disheartening first-grade experiences. My third-grade teacher, Mrs. King, was fair.

In the fall of third grade, our class made a mural on butcher paper with crayons. We worked on it all the time, and it spanned one of the walls in the classroom. I suspect it had something to do with Indians and maize and feasts. The mural was going to be the prize for the person with the best Halloween costume.

In past years, Mom made me elaborate costumes. The most memorable was a Little Dutch Girl dress with the curled-up hat made from starched organdy and braids made from yarn attached to the hat. It had a dress and apron and striped stockings. We could not find wooden shoes, and at the time, no one sold clogs. This year, however, I was wearing a bright yellow nylon Indian Princess costume Mom and Dad bought for me at a Woolworth's in Denver. It was not nearly as cute as previous costumes, but I believed store-bought things must be better.

Mom and Svea Elisha were the volunteer mothers for the Halloween party. Parents in the PTA put on parties for each of the holidays. We had apple dunking, glazed donuts, apple cider, and I won the coveted mural for my costume.

I invited Svea's daughter, Ingrid, to spend the night. This was the first chance we had to get together since the day Mom and I walked up to their front door and Ingrid peered out from behind her mother's dress. The first thing we did was to hang the mural in my bedroom, and then we jumped on my double four-poster bed. I do not remember what else we did, but, from that day forward, Ingrid and I were best friends. That was but the first of hundreds of sleepovers at each other's houses.

Over the years, we did many activities together, such as catechism, skiing, and 4-H. We played on the ranch like all kids played on the ranch – riding Patty, playing in the playhouse, exploring the barns and the river bottom, camping in the yard, walking the flume, and swimming and tubing in the ditch. Dad and Steve called her Ingie.

Sometimes she was at our house when we had steak dinners. Steak dinners were an everyday meal. A few times, Mom let us take our plates outside to eat. We sat in the bed of Dad's red International Harvester pickup parked under the Chinese elm by the gate and ate our dinner. Remember, dinner was the noontime meal. I suspect we would have rather spread a blanket on the lawn to eat under the willow tree, but we ate in the pickup as a defensive mechanism to avoid Nipper begging for or eating our food. After dinner, we stayed in the pickup and played *Authors*.

Authors was "go fish" with thirteen authors and four of their works for a total of 52 cards. We played Authors about every time Ingrid came over. Because of playing Authors, I can answer questions on Jeopardy about Nathaniel Hawthorne, Louisa May Alcott, and Robert Lewis Stevenson. For a long time, I knew all the authors and at least four of their books. I read some of their poems and all the Charles Dickens and Mark Twain books listed on the cards.

Going to Ingrid's house was a treat. First, the house was more spectacular than I thought it would be. To the right of the front door was a stained-glass window. Through the front door was a large foyer with a staircase on the right that turned 90 degrees halfway to the next floor then turned 90 degrees again to a third floor. It was like looking through the center of a squared-off spiral staircase. There was a closet under the stairs for hide-and-go-seek. It was also where Svea stashed Santa presents.

On the left of the foyer was a large room facing Main Street. Other than a sizeable oriental-looking carpet, I remember a few pieces of furniture and a piano in that room. It did not appear they used it much. Straight back from the foyer was a sitting room. The sitting room had a bay window on the east wall. To its left, on the west side of the house, was the dining room. It connected to the big room at the front of the house and could be closed off from it by large pocket doors. The dining room had a large table and matching china cupboards and sideboards.

The neatest thing as far as I was concerned was that the sitting room and the dining room shared the same fireplace flue. The fireplaces were angled, so each side faced a different room. One fireplace had a blue tile face, and both had ornate mantels.

It was in this area that Svea sometimes set up and used the mangle iron. The mangle was a desk-sized device with heated rollers and was used to iron flat pieces and came from the Hotel Jerome laundry. Svea used it to iron sheets, pillowcases, doilies, and tablecloths. In our house, we ironed pillowcases and tablecloths by hand. The machine looked like a torture device, and Svea warned us to stay away while it was heating.

Beyond the sitting room to the north was a large kitchen with two walls of picture windows. The sink was under the eastern window and had a view of the town and Ajax Mountain while another window looked toward Red Mountain. There was a basement entrance under this window, and it was not unusual to see Ingrid's Chihuahua, Chico, looking in the window after she climbed up on the slanted roof. Yes, Chico was a girl. After all, Butch was our girl.

There was a set of enclosed stairs to the second floor behind the west wall of the kitchen. The servants for the previous owners used these stairs.

The area between the kitchen and dining room contained a half-bath with black and white tile and a pedestal sink, a pantry, and access to the cellar. The kitchen floor was painted gray and with dollops of red paint applied with a sponge – the same colors as my bedroom, and the cupboards were rose beige. The best part of the kitchen was a metal-lined drawer with a sliding top that held store-bought cookies and baked goods – such as Twinkies, Hostess pies, or powder-sugared donuts.

Ingrid's room was on the second floor, at the front of the house. The open attic stairs rose outside the door to her room. It was a small room that was probably designed as a sitting room because it had no closet. Therefore, Ingrid used a large antique wardrobe for her clothes. There was only enough room for a single bed. She had a little covered porch area outside her room. We got on the porch by climbing through the windows. It was a good place to sleep outside in the summer.

There were two bedrooms on the west side of the landing. Each room had a lavatory set in the wall next to the closet. Ingrid's brother, M.J., was in high school, and his room faced Main Street. Model airplanes hung from his ceiling. These were not plastic airplanes from kits. He made them from balsawood, cloth, and wires, and some had tiny working motors. The room smelled of paint and airplane glue.

The adjacent bedroom mirrored M.J.'s room but with twin beds. When we had overnights, we slept in the twin beds in this room, and the only window faced a neighboring house. The master bedroom was on the opposite side of the hall facing east. It was directly over the sitting area and had a matching bay window with a view of the ski hill.

At the end of the hall was a large linen storage room, and to its right was the only full bathroom. It was "modern" with a bathtub shower with a sliding door, tiled in blue and white plastic tiles, and a laundry chute to a utility room. The back stairway came up by the linen room.

The third floor was the attic, which was not like attics in most houses. It was open with ornately carved railings from which you could look down all three flights of stairs. Most of the attic was high enough for an adult to stand with headroom to spare. The walls and the ceilings were finished, and the floor was hardwood. The dormers created alcoves – some of which were enclosed for storage others were open. We played house and dolls in one, and M.J. made model airplanes in another.

A carriage house, with paint matching the house, was on the level of the second step of the lawn and had a flagstone patio. It was the size of a three-car garage with heavy sliding double doors off the alley and horse stall dividers topped with ornate iron grills. Stairs to the second story were inside a door leading to the patio.

Once we got television reception in Aspen in the late 50s, Ingrid and I spent many mornings in the sitting room by the kitchen watching children's programs such as *Sky King*, *Sea Hunt*, and *Roy Rogers*. Besides the Twinkies and store-bought baked goods, I learned about interesting foods at her house. At Christmas, Svea ordered a supply of Mr. Elisha's traditional ethic food such as apricot leathers, pistachio nuts, and Jordan almonds and peas.

The first time I ate an artichoke was at Ingrid's house. I am ashamed to say it frightened me and looked awful, so I pretended to eat the leaves and put them upside down on the plate so no one would know I hadn't tried them – kind of like the hidden American cheese my grandmother gave me.

Another memorable steak dinner was one at the Elisha house on the patio. What made it memorable was that Svea made French fries. We rarely made French fries at our house, at least until years later when we got a K-TEL Veg-o-Matic food cutter.

Mr. Elisha was wearing a white dress shirt with his sleeves rolled up and offered me a second helping of fries. It was rare for me to see him when I was at the house because he owned and managed the Hotel Jerome and spent long hours there.

Ingrid and I did not spend much time at the Jerome. I wish we had. I was familiar with its public rooms and restaurants, and I rode the elevator because it was the only one in town. I never got out on an upper floor and never went into a single guest room. In later years I went to the pool with Ingrid. We went on a school field trip to the laundry facility in the basement. There were bins of sheets and towels, large washing machines, a lot of steam, and an open elevator platform to the main story.

My favorite field trip was to the *Aspen Times*. It was next to the hotel. I was impressed with the typesetting machines and the rolls of newsprint that dwarfed the rolls of butcher paper at Beck & Bishop. For our field trip, they set up the type and printed a small newspaper we wrote for the event.

Pent-up Demand – Remodeling, Jeeps, and Furniture

Compounding the transition from being at home and going to school were changes in the ranch and the way my parents earned a living. In April of 1955, before I started first grade, Wally Mills bought the Midland part of the ranch from Dad and Steve. The sale of this part of the ranch was important for our family. Dad and Steve could no longer afford to keep this part of the ranch because of range right restrictions. Without a large herd of cattle, there was no longer a need to grow the amount of hay this property produced. Dad made enough to invest in the stock market and put away money to send us kids to college.

Wally Mills built a nine-hole golf course. It later became the 18-hole course that exists today. He also created the Snowbunny subdivision west of the cemetery and on the far northern end of the property. That meant a large part of the Midland remained open. The reservoir depression used for the potato cellar once again became a lake fed by the irrigation ditches.

A couple of years after Dad sold part of the ranch to Wally Mills, Leonard "Lenny" Thomas approached Dad to purchase part of the remaining ranch on the south side of the highway. Lenny Thomas was a wealthy man from New York who moved to Aspen in the early 50s. When the Hotel Jerome denied him membership in its pool, he built the municipal swimming pool.

Dad called him Lenny, and they talked when Dad stopped at the Eagles or the Elks for a beer. Lenny told Dad he admired our property especially the field next to Highway 82. It reminded him of Kentucky horse farms. He especially liked it in the spring after Dad brushed the meadows and irrigated the fields.

At some point, he approached Dad and said he wanted to buy the property and hoped to keep it open and away from developers. If he purchased the property, he wanted Dad to continue to farm it as if he still owned it. He wanted Dad to continue irrigating and growing hay. Eventually, Dad agreed to the sale.

In 1957, Lenny purchased the big field and the property on the west side of the Castle Creek Road next to the old ranch. Dad retained over 40 acres, including all the buildings and the lixiviation ruins, the little field, the picnic grounds, the Castle Creek riverbed, and the remaining property on the east side of the river.

Besides liking the property, Lenny respected Dad. For years when he was in New York, he called ostensibly to check on the property but ended up carrying on a long conversation about books, music, art, and politics. Dad said he thought Lenny was lonely.

For the next ten years, after he bought the property and until he died, Lenny did only two things with the property other than paying the taxes. He donated the land under the water reservoir and the water tanks to the City of Aspen, and he built a white wooden fence along Highway 82 in keeping with the Kentucky horse farm theme. I was so excited there was going to be a fence from the cattleguard to Castle Creek Road. I could only imagine the hours of fence walking. When the fence was complete, I was disappointed because, unlike the one in our yard, there was no board on top, and the fence boards were too narrow for walking. Regardless of that disappointment, Lenny was true to his word. He left Dad alone to treat the property as if it were his own. It was as if it never sold.

The only time we were nervous about the sale was when, a few years later, the school board tried to convince Lenny and Wally Mills to sell their property as a site for a new high school. Fortunately, that did not happen. Instead, Jimmy Moore donated the property that at one time belonged to my grandfather for the school. After Lenny died, the big field remained open because either he or his estate donated it to the City of Aspen as dedicated open space.

Sometime after Dad sold his share of the big ranch to Wally Mills, Mom and Dad began plans to remodel the kitchen. There had been few upgrades to the house except the hot-water heating system, and an electric stove replaced the woodstove.

I'm not sure how they planned it. I was pretty much oblivious to the planning and preparation. In anticipation of the project, Dad made stacks and stacks of knotty pine tongue and groove boards with a router he purchased with the plan in mind. At the time, knotty pine was the style for modern kitchens.

The first noticeable part of the project was to lower the ceiling. The ceilings in the house were twelve feet tall, and they wanted the kitchen ceiling three feet lower. To create the false ceiling, Dad got several of the large hardwood timbers left over from the lixiviation works and planed them until they were smooth. He bolted rails of planed wood to the east and west walls. He then inserted beams at the north and south walls and added six more parallel beams across the expanse.

Once the beams and rails were in place, Dad wired for the ceiling fixtures and put in ductwork for an exhaust fan to the chimney that had been used by the wood stoves. After his preliminary work was complete, he laid knotty pine tongue and groove planks north and south on top of the beams to create the "false" ceiling.

Another structural change involved the southern windows. There were two double-hung casement windows a couple of feet above the sink. Mom wanted a large picture window so she could have an unobstructed view of Aspen Mountain when she washed dishes. She said, "If I have to do dishes, I might as well have something nice to look at."

Dad removed and lowered the windows and replaced them with a single, Thermopane picture window about a foot above the cabinets. Over the decades, we washed thousands and thousands of dishes, appreciating the view.

In the meantime, Dad was busy in the granary, fabricating the pine cabinets. He made everything, from the frames to the doors and drawers. Three of the drawers had galvanized steel liners with sliding lids – one for flour, one for sugar, and one for bread and baked goods. He welded a Lazy Susan out of left-over iron from the lixiviation works and used the rollers from an old hearse as the rotating mechanism.

The kitchen design was a joint effort. The space was rectangular. There was a recess on the west wall over the basement stairwell that was a perfect spot for a refrigerator. On the opposite wall, across from the refrigerator alcove, was the chimney coming from the basement. It was about three feet wide and two feet deep.

They built cabinets along the south wall from the back porch door to the corner and down the east wall until they abutted the chimney. To get the most space and incorporate the chimney, they put the stove perpendicular to it, which created an open divider between the cooking and eating parts of the kitchen. Dad built a cabinet around the electric stove, which had two ovens and a deep well for soup or deep-frying. When cooking, we faced the eating side of the kitchen, which was a clever design ahead of its time.

The first and easiest installations were the lower cabinets without doors or drawers. At the time, the only plumbing necessary was for the sink. We didn't have a dishwasher because they were not common at that time. I remember the lower cabinets being open for a long time.

During remodeling, Mom and Dad took a trip to Denver to buy tile and fixtures. Bud worked in Denver for Floyd Biegert, who owned F.E. Biegert, a tile and patio store in Cherry Creek. Mr. Biegert had a vacation home in town near Steve's house. Bud sold the equipment, supplies, and tile at wholesale, and he gave Dad discontinued tiles for free. We eventually tiled our basement with free tile.

Tiling the kitchen was Dad's first experience with ceramic tile. I'm not sure how the tile was delivered, but I guess it was a typical arrangement. When Bill borrowed the pickup and took his copper and brass scrap metal to Denver, he returned with the pickup filled with supplies the other brothers needed from the big city.

One time when Mom and Dad came to Denver to buy supplies and equipment, they left me in Denver. I spent a week with Mom's brother Elmer and his wife, Noreen, and their new baby, Trent. I then spent another week with Dad's niece, Julia, and her family. She had a daughter Cindy who was a little younger than me. For a while, I had fun. Elmer and Noreen had a TV, and I liked to watch cartoons and Romper Room.

Between the two houses, we did a lot. We went out to eat. We went to the Denver Natural History Museum and to Lakeside Amusement Park. I rode the roller coaster, the Wild Mouse, and played in the funhouse. I loved the bonbons that were golf-balled sized ice cream balls covered in chocolate.

I learned how to ride a two-wheeled bicycle. Unlike the streets in Aspen that were gravel or dirt, the paved Denver streets and sidewalks provided a good surface for learning how to balance. They also had a child-sized girl's bike I used for practice.

While I was gone, Mom wrote me several letters and filled me in on the progress of the remodeling project. I was homesick. I did not like the city. It was gray, hot, and smelly. I missed Mom and Dad. I missed my sisters. I missed Nipper. I missed Patty. I missed my room. I missed Aspen.

I don't remember which of the relatives brought me home, but when I got there, the upper cabinets, without doors, were in place, and

Dad was filling in the soffit above them. After completing the soffit, but before he could begin staining and finishing the wood, Dad wanted to make a finishing touch over the window above the sink.

Below the soffit and between the cabinets, he planned on having a wooden scallop. Dad worked on the scallop for what seemed like weeks. He wanted the scallop to fit perfectly between the cabinets so that each side had precisely half of a scallop – no more, no less.

Dad took out his slide rule to make the calculations. When he went to the University of Colorado, he planned on being a civil or mechanical engineer. As part of his studies, he used the beautiful, ivory slide-rule his father gave him when Dad went to college.

Dad stood at the counter in the kitchen, leaning on one elbow on the countertop. He slid the rule back and forth and jotted down numbers with his carpenter pencil on a scrap of wood. Then he took out and unfolded his carpenter ruler and confirmed the measurements. I liked to unfold and fold the ruler into different shapes.

The figures Dad jotted on the wood scrap did not guarantee success. There were many attempts to make the scallop, and none of them were, according to Dad, right. Mom tried to convince him that it was close enough, but he was bent on perfection. The left-over unused attempts found their way into the lumber pile in the granary. Finally, he got it just right and then meticulously rounding the edges of the scallops. Finally, it was in place.

Then began the staining. The doors and soffit and the cabinet faces were stained and lacquered a rich honey color to match the ceiling. The smell of stain permeated the house. Fortunately, we could open the windows. When everything was dry and finished to the perfect patina, Dad began hanging the doors with hammered copper hardware. They carried over the copper theme to an oven hood with a scalloped edge, two light fixtures, and a built-in clock over the sink. Dad built a cabinet next to the hood for cookbooks and knickknacks. The exhaust from the fan connected to the basement chimney.

Dad built a hutch cabinet on the eating side of the kitchen, especially for Mom. It was built in and filled the space between the chimney and the double-swinging dining-room door. It had a modest single scalloped design in the middle on the top. Dad was not going to get into the same situation, trying to make the scallops match. Mom could display some of the dishes she got from Grandma and collected over time in the grooved, open shelves.

In particular, she displayed what she called her bird plates. These were an old series of plates painted and signed by Daudin, a naturalist illustrator, with various types of game birds – pheasants, geese, ducks, grouse, quail, and so on. There were six small plates and one large platter, all with a subtle pink hue.

The lower half had a drawer and two doors. It was a beautiful piece of furniture. Mom regretted that it was built in like a cabinet and was not a removable piece of furniture. When Dad later made a bookcase that looked like a small hutch intended for the space behind the door to my room, he made sure it was a piece of moveable furniture.

As part of the remodel, Dad built a cabinet under a sink in the back porch for handwashing and hung a wooden medicine cabinet above it. The sink was on the kitchen side of the washer and dryer. He also made a broom closet across from the sink on the sidewall of the refrigerator alcove. For much of the year, the door between the kitchen and the backroom was open, so the broom closet was partially hidden. Dad never got around to making doors for the broom closet.

A half-wall divided the stairwell from the laundry area. It was a good spot for a bench for changing shoes and boots, and we hung the wet coats on the back and to drip on the concrete basement stairs. Windows surrounded the room - two windows over the washer and dryer, one at the top of the stairs, and three over the stairs. Washing the windows over the stairs was a challenge requiring a plank from top of the stairs to a ladder leaning against the backside of the alcove.

With the cabinets in place, Dad began tiling. Most of the tile was yellow. He tiled the countertops and backsplashes. He then tiled all the other walls in the kitchen and about four feet above the floor, including the refrigerator alcove. He tiled the back of the stove divider. He tiled all the walls in the back room, including behind the washer and dryer and the half-wall.

On the walls, there was brown tile as the upper border and, one yellow tile down was a narrow decorative brown strip with a white design. I'm not sure why Dad thought he needed to tile all the walls. It may have been the style at the time. It may have been that he was having so much fun he could not stop. He must have received a good deal on yellow tile.

Steve used the same yellow tile in his kitchen. He trimmed his tile in a soft green instead of brown, which, quite frankly, I thought was prettier. He made knotty pine cabinets using Dad's equipment and stained his a lighter blonde shade. He, too, made a scallop over the sink window in his house.

The tile on the wall was a benefit for the space between the kitchen door and the refrigerator alcove. That space was about three feet wide and was Steve's favorite place to hunker when he, Dad, Ted, and, sometimes, Mom, had their morning confab. He hunkered and leaned against that wall nearly every weekday morning, day after day, year after year. Most of the time, he was wearing his ranching overalls, and I'm sure they had their share of dust and grime. Because of the tile, it was easy to clean.

Almost immediately, Dad made some changes to the bathroom. At the time, we had only one bathroom. It was a narrow room east of the dining room. On the east was a large tub with a high showerhead, and the toilet was at the end of the tub facing the western wall. On that wall, in front of the toilet, was a single porcelain sink with four chrome legs. There was a metal medicine cabinet with a mirrored door above the sink. The remainder of the wall was bare except for a clothes hamper. The wall had plaster made to simulate tan tiles done by Mr. Parsons during the original remodel.

The bathroom remodel was simple. Dad replaced the sink with a counter that extended toward the door and was big enough for two small sinks and storage. It also included a built-in clothes hamper. Dad made the cabinet out of pressboard and laminated it with Formica. I wonder why he did not make it out of wood. I guess he thought Formica would hold up better in a steamy bathroom.

Once again, he went crazy with tile. He tiled all the walls at least four feet above the floor and tiled in the entire shower area at least a foot above the showerhead. The wall tiles were a peach color and included some white accent tiles with peach and green flowers. The countertop was in a coordinating mint green color, the same green as Steve's kitchen. Above the entire length of the sink cabinet was a mirror set flush with a backsplash topped by a fluorescent light fixture. Dad put the wrong kind of tile for a floor; it was slick, and we needed floor mats to prevent slipping.

At or about the same time as the kitchen remodel, we made significant changes in the basement, including removing the coal furnace and stoker and replacing them with an oil-burning boiler and an "on-demand" water heater. Although it was ahead of its time, Mom didn't like it because it took a long time until the first hot water began to flow. Eventually, she got a water heater that delivered water faster, but there was no longer an unlimited hot water supply when it started flowing. Dad removed the coal room and part of the fruit room, put in steel beams to carry their load, and acid-washed the foundation.

Almost immediately, Dad partitioned the entire south end of the basement as the furnace room. He built pocket doors for the furnace room and at the base of the stairs. He put the old metal kitchen cabinets in the west end of the furnace room for storage and a work area.

On the east side of the open area, Dad created three rooms – one on the north was the reconfigured the fruit room; one in the middle was for storage, and one on the south was a roughed-in bathroom.

Because this had been a cellar, the walls were only about seven feet to the base of the upper floor joists. For us, that didn't matter much because Keith was the tallest one in the family at six feet. Dad was five feet eight inches tall, and the rests of us were even shorter. The tallest people we knew were Edmund, Riley, and Elmer, and they did not spend any time in the basement.

The first room Dad finished was the bathroom. He moved the old sink and medicine chest from the upstairs bathroom to an alcove next to a built-in shower with a glass door and a marble seat. There were nooks for the toilet and the sink. It was tiled in blue and white tile and wallpapered in red, white, and blue early American town scenes.

This bathroom was Dad's refuge, including a built-in stainless-steel magazine rack and ashtray. Dad spent a lot of time down there reading and smoking and continued smoking there long after he claimed to have quit. The exhaust fan was strong but not that strong. I could smell the stale smoke. Mom did not notice the smell because she was a heavy smoker. From time to time, when I went into the bathroom, I saw one of Dad's cigarettes floating in the toilet.

Dad put what he called sheetrock on the inside of the new rooms. The outside of the walls facing the big room were open studs and the exposed backside of the sheetrock. Dad covered the floor with free tile from Bud. The tiles were small in several shades of green, attached to a white mesh. It was pretty ugly but better than the stained concrete floor, and it was not slick like the upstairs bathroom tile. For a long time, the basement had finished floors, two walls of exposed red rock, and exposed stud walls. Dad built window wells and replaced the old windows with bigger metal windows with screens. The basement became the repository of all the old furniture when it was no longer needed upstairs.

Although the basement was not finished and would not be for many more years, I could set up my toys, like the American Plastic Bricks, with no need to put them away. It was where I listened to the old 45-rpm records. We had several collections. They were boxed sets with five or six records – essentially an album in 45-rpm format. We had boxed sets of Sons of the Pioneers, Frankie Lane, Mario Lanza, and several Disney stories such as *Snow White*, *Cinderella*, *Sleeping Beauty*, and *Bambi*. They were Golden Records – the records were yellow to simulate gold. The Mario Lanza album belonged to Dad, and I did not listen to it much.

New Jeep

The ranch sale allowed a little discretionary spending. The remodeling was a big project, but between Dad's labor and discounted supplies, it was not expensive. Mom and Dad each splurged on something special.

Dad's guilty pleasure was to get a new Jeep. After World War II, it appeared everyone in town ended up with a Jeep; my family was no exception. Dad, Steve, and Ted each had gray army surplus Jeeps from World War II with canvas tops. Bill, Riley, and Albert each had red Jeeps. They all had canvas tops that Albert removed from his Jeep in the summer. Steve bought a new green Jeep after the Wally Mills sale.

For the decades, Bill worked as the daytime bartender at the Red Onion, his Jeep was in front, and it appears in many photographs and paintings of the bar. Ted was the one who spent the most time Jeeping around the mountains. It took little to convince Ted to take people on Jeep trips up the Midnight Mine Road to the Sundeck or over Pearl Pass to Crested Butte.

In the summer of 1957, Dad got a new Jeep. He picked it up in Glenwood Springs and drove it home. We waited in anticipation as if he was bringing home a new sibling. When Dad and the Jeep showed up, it was a beautiful vibrant blue color. We named it the Blue Goose. For the first couple of days, we had so much fun riding in it because there was no top. Being topless did not last long. Dad strung canvas from the windshield over a support pipe and fastened to the back as a temporary way to keep off the sun.

Within a few days of owning it, Dad drove on a routine trip into the field, and the attached step hit the ditch bank and bent. He took off the steps and the mirrors, saying they were, "Pretty, but worthless."

Not long after he got the Jeep, Dad made a solid top. I'm not sure if it was factory authorized. It was a kit with "much assembly" required. It was like the top Steve put on his new green Jeep the year before. It was metal primed for painting and include two side doors and a lift-up back door.

Once he assembled the top, Dad set up a painting operation in the granary and painted it with matching factory-supplied paint. When the top was complete, he attached it to the Jeep frame. The top made the Jeep more comfortable in winter. Ted put on a similar top on his old gray Jeep.

After "cracking his head" a few times on the open back door, Dad decided to alter it. He engineered a mechanism in which he installed a curved track down the center of the roof. He attached a roller on the top of the door. The door rolled back into the cargo area. Now the door was more like a folding garage door.

The following spring, we realized the top was a mixed blessing. It kept the Jeep warmer in the winter, but it made it top-heavy. For most of its uses around the ranch, that was not a problem, but if we decided to go on Jeep trails, such as Taylor Pass or Pearl Pass, it was dangerous. It even seemed to rock a little more than we liked on a couple of spots on the two-track road leading to Steve's cabin.

On the Jeep trails, when we got to the spot where the Jeep was going to lean to the downhill side, the passengers either got out, or we all moved to the upper side to counter the weight. It was like the crew of a yacht leaning on the high side to keep it from capsizing.

Another problem with the top was that it made driving on icy roads even more hazardous than usual for a Jeep. Jeeps had a short wheelbase, and it was easy to lose control on slick roads. Fortunately, we rarely drove far on icy roads. The Jeep worked great on snowy roads, and the extra weight of the top gave it more traction. Knowing of its problems, we were careful when we learned to drive.

Dad let me start driving the Jeep when I was about twelve – as soon as I could sit on the edge of the seat and work the pedals. I practiced in the driveway learning to shift. Dad taught me how to stop on the upward climb on the granary road. I learned how to keep the Jeep from rolling backward by working the clutch and the gas. I learned to parallel park between oil drums set up near the granary.

Once I learned shifting, I was allowed to drive alone around the ranch. I doubt if my early driving experience included third gear. I never had to use four-wheel drive until much later and in deep snow.

My usual drive was to make the circle on the main road, the granary road, and the lower granary road, alternating directions. I could drive to the picnic grounds and from time to time in the open field. I was not allowed to go to the river bottom because that road was too steep and tippy.

The reason for teaching the kids to drive was not just for our fun; it was for doing chores. Now, Dad could tell me to feed the horses or take a salt block somewhere or bring back something from the granary or the house when he was working in the field.

In the mid-60s, Steve got yet another new Jeep – his third. This one was tan with a lightweight fiberglass top and an FM radio. I went on several trips with Polly not only to the cabin but to Marble and Red Stone. I was surprised she kept a package of Salem cigarettes in the glove box and smoked one or two a week. Few people knew Polly smoked.

If anyone commented on Steve's new Jeep and the lighter top, Dad claimed, "My Jeep is just fine. I think Steve misses his old Jeep." I know deep down Dad wanted a lighter top but wasn't about to succumb to pressure from the kids or Steve; that would be some sort of admission the metal top was a mistake. He was not about to give up all the work he put into it.

New Furniture

Mom's guilty pleasure was buying new furniture. Sometime after the kitchen and bathroom remodels and after the sale to Lenny Thomas, Mom wanted new living room furniture to go with the modern kitchen and bath. Before getting furniture, they decided to refinish the living room and dining room floors. The floors were maple but had been stained dark, and we covered them with large rugs to hide the scratches. I never realized there was wood in either room.

Before finishing the floors, Mom and Dad had a polka party. They moved all the furniture out of the living room and rolled up the rugs so everyone could dance to Frank Yankovic playing on the HiFi. Joe Strauss was in town and had his accordion. Joe married Julia Ambrose, who was raised by Dad's family after her mother, Pauline, died in the flu pandemic.

Knowing they were going to refinish the floors, Mom and Dad were not worried about causing damage. It was a fun night. There was a lot of laughing, and the party got louder and louder as the beer flowed. I took a few polka turns around the living room. Then at some point, while there was still a lot of noise coming from the living room, I went into my room and sprawled on my double bed and fell asleep. The next morning there were the remnants of what had been a fun party.

That was the only Polka party in the house I remember. Mom, however, had canasta or "500" card parties. She belonged to a group of women who rotated the party between houses. When Mom had her party, she set up three or four card tables in the living room and dining room. She went to a store in Glenwood and got scorecards and matching napkins, and several sets of cards in plastic trays. The best part for me was that each table had mixed nuts and Brach's Bridge Mix. We each got to have a small bowl of Bridge Mix.

After the Polka party, Dad sanded the floors with a borrowed belt sander. It was big and seemed to move on its own. I wanted to ride on it. He finished the floor with lacquer and repeated the process a couple of times. In the end, the floors were a honey color. The process must have gone well because I did not hear any complaints about how it could have been better.

Before Mom got new furniture, the living room furniture was sparse considering its size. The furniture had been scrounged together from relatives and friends and included a sofa, a couple of easy chairs with wooden arms – one of which rocked on a stationary base. The chairs always flanked the fireplace. There were several end tables and some floor lamps. The two maple end tables had fold-down leaves and converted to round tables perfect for doll tea parties. There was an old-fashioned cabinet radio about four feet high between the fireplace and the window on the north wall. It rarely worked.

We replaced it with a Motorola Hi-Fi, which opened on the top and included a radio and record storage. I spent hours and hours listening to music on the Hi-Fi. We had all the Oscar and Hammerstein Broadway shows, Burl Ives, The Kingston Trio, Frank Yankovic, and Christmas albums. When Keith came home from college, he brought his Tom Lehrer comedy albums. I listened to my first Beatle albums on this machine.

Mom had a maple writing desk. I'm not sure when or how she got it, but it was one of her prized possessions. Behind the slatted door that opened for writing, there were pigeonholes for sorting envelopes, a couple of little drawers for pens and notions, a small door with a keyhole in the center, and the best were two wooden columns that were secret compartments. That is where Mom hid her bankbook.

Our upright piano sat mostly alone on the eastern wall. There were a couple of low bookshelves next to the piano. Mom was a voracious reader. Although she borrowed most of her books from the library, she had several poetry collections, paperback mysteries from the drug store, and a subscription to the Reader's Digest condensed books.

The telephone table was in the southwestern corner with a seat, top, and space for a phone book. I thought of it as a side-saddle student desk. For a while, we had an upright, candlestick telephone with a stand for the mouthpiece and a hook for a separate earpiece; we replaced it with a black dial phone. At the time, we still had a party line. Before making calls, we listened to make sure no one else was on the line. It was bad form to listen to other conversations. However, when we wanted to make a call, we made sure there was a click, so the other party knew they needed to hurry and end their call.

At some point, a door-to-door traveling salesman talked Mom into a set of the *Encyclopedia Americana* – a knock-off of *Encyclopedia Britannica*. She paid for them with milk money. The entire collection included the encyclopedia, two huge dictionaries, and a set of children's books – Black Beauty, Heidi, Dickens Stories, Kidnapped and Treasure Island, Alice in Wonderland, Tales from Shakespeare, Robinson Crusoe, The Arabian Nights, and Robin Hood. We also had an atlas and a huge bible.

As it turns out, the need for more bookcases may have been the driving force behind the new furniture. On one of the trips to Denver, as Mom and Dad drove on Colfax Avenue on their way into town, Mom convinced Dad to stop at a furniture store, Homestead House. She had seen it advertised in the *Denver Post*. Homestead House sold Ethan Allen furniture. She fell in love with bookcase units that could be mixed and matched into all sorts of configurations for the eastern wall. There were separate lower sections, some with doors and some with open shelving and others with drawers. The smaller units were in varying widths. They then could fit with matching upper units. Not only would these units hold lots of books, but they also held special dishes and knickknacks. They bought four bookcase units, two each of the doored units, and two with open lower shelves and added a matching credenza in the middle. The units covered the entire 13-foot-long wall and cost $545.

In addition to the bookshelves, a year later, Mom bought two sections of a sectional-type sofa. Two loveseat-sized couches with only one arm each. She wanted them to face each other with a table between them in front of the fireplace. There were two matching floor lamps with double milk-glass shades and chimneys. Finally, she got two matching wing-back chairs covered in an early American print. Dad teased her that he didn't think much of the wing-back chairs because he said, "They make me feel like I am a horse with blinders." The chairs sat on the southern wall between a table with a fancy "Aladdin's Lamp" with a pleated shade. Mom loved to sit in these chairs, by this lamp, and read.

They bought several braided rugs – two for the two living room seating areas, one under the dining room table, and a runner from the hall to the kitchen. Although it was a tight fit, the piano was now in the dining room.

A couple of years earlier, Mom and Dad brought home some furniture from a relative in Denver. The furniture included a television. It had a blond-wood cabinet. At the time, there was no TV service in town. We put it in the dining-room at first and put on the set of rabbit ears enhanced with tin foil. From time to time, we got a fuzzy image in the snow and could hear sounds. Eventually, a group of local men got together and put up a television booster on Smuggler Mountain, and the town was able to get KREX television from Grand Junction. It was a big deal.

The image was improved, and Dad installed an attic antenna and ran the wire running behind the fireplace. We moved the TV to the space previously occupied by the radio. The only problem with the TV service was that, if there were a bad storm, the booster would either fall or get disturbed, and we lost reception until the local men could make their way up the mountain to fix it. That could be days or weeks.

We had television service in time to watch *Gunsmoke, Wagon Train, Rawhide, Huckleberry Hound, Father Knows Best, Ed Sullivan,* and *The Red Skelton Show*. We missed out on some of the other shows because KREX was primarily a CBS affiliate but was able to get a few other programs as well.

When television became more a part of our life, the furniture arrangement changed. The sofas were moved together in a long line on the southern wall to allow more seating for TV. Dad liked to sit on the east end of the couch. I often sat next to him and snuggled against his shoulder and arm. We also got a set of TV trays that we used for Sunday night supper with all the good programs. I used them for doing homework in front of the TV. We moved the wing-back chairs on either side of the fireplace. Mom was content to read by the fire.

Dad got a recliner he sat in from time to time, although it was too far away to be suitable for watching television but good for reading. It was near the bookcase and the hall. When Dad sat in his chair, he had one of those smoking stands with a large clear, amber-colored ashtray. We moved the phone to the end of the bookcase next to the hall, and Dad used the chair when Lenny Thomas called from New York.

The next furniture was for the bedrooms. Before getting new furniture, we painted them colors. Gone were the dark ceilings. We thought about finishing the bedroom floors, but the wood was pine and not suitable for finishing, so we left it alone and used area rugs. I got a piece of yellow wall-to-wall carpet for my room because the "oriental rug" linoleum was glued to the floor. They left the cream-colored rubber or asbestos tile in the hall. There was a time when I borrowed a unicycle from Billy, and, using the walls as support, I learned to ride it.

All the new furniture was Ethan Allen from Homestead House. Mom and Dad got a double bed with a headboard, a large dresser with a mirror with a railing, and a highboy they called a chest of drawers. They moved their blond bedroom set into Keith's room. My sisters got a corner desk unit, one side with doors and another side with drawers and the corner desk with a rail. They got two twin beds attached to a bookshelf headboard. When changing the linens on the beds, the beds swung apart. I got a small Ethan Allen dresser and twin beds on Hollywood frames for each side of my window. I had dust ruffles, and the bedspreads looked like patchwork quilts. I soon covered them with my stuffed animal collection.

We moved some of the old furniture, including all the antique double beds and vanities, to the granary. Judy and Peggy's bed was so rickety it went to the dump. Years later, Mom refinished one of the antique four-poster beds and returned it to Keith's room.

I loved my new bedroom arrangement. I chose the bed on the west side of my window. The bottom of the window was at the height of my bed. When I was in bed, I could scoot down a little, lie on my side, and see the trees at the end of the yard, and then Aspen Mountain rising above them. On full moon nights, the mountain, the trees, and the yard were washed in moonlight. There was no light pollution. In the summer, with my window open, I fell asleep to the soothing sound of Castle Creek in the distance.

Although they refurnished the rooms, Dad did not seem to care about putting doors on the closets. The closets were small and had single-door access. Eventually, Mom got some folding accordion-style vinyl doors she had Dad install over the openings. Later she replaced it with louvered, wooden doors.

Not seeing the need for closet doors was one of those odd things about Dad. He was a perfectionist in so many ways, yet it did not seem to bother him that the closets were open. He may have felt a door was an excuse to hide a mess. Further, the closet in his and Mom's room was usually not visible, because when their bedroom door was open, it obscured their closet opening.

Because my room was small, Mom asked Dad to build a bookcase to put behind my door for storage and to replace the orange crates I used for comics. She was expecting something basic. After several weeks' work, Dad brought the unit up from his granary workshop. It was a miniature version of the living room bookcases with three drawers, a removable shelving unit with adjustable shelves. It was too nice to put behind the door, so I put it at the end of my bed and filled it with knickknacks and books.

In the bookcase drawers, I kept a "treasure" box where I held my snail and tooth collections. After a period of leaving teeth under my pillow and receiving a dime, I decided it was not worth it, so I kept my baby teeth in a Scotch Tape metal canister. The tooth fairy still brought the money.

After remodeling the kitchen and bathroom and with the new furniture, our house was comfortable and cozy and became the place for family gatherings. It was and always will be home.

The Seasons

Fall

When I envision a year, I see something like a game board with a rounded track with twelve spaces along the perimeter. Each month has its own space arranged in counterclockwise order. September is in the lower-left, December is in the upper-left, March in the upper-right, and June in the lower-right. For me, a year starts in the lower left-hand corner – September. Perhaps it's because that is the month of my birthday, but it is more likely the beginning of the school year. When I think of my elementary school years, I remember them not by years but by seasons. The first season was fall.

When I started school in September 1955, there was one school building in town. It was a single-story red brick building on the corner of Hallam and Center. Neither street was paved. On the east end, a recent addition included three classrooms, a gymnasium with a stage, and a cafeteria and locker rooms under the stage.

For hot lunch, we went down the stairs on the east side of the gym under the stage. Local women cooked the lunches – mostly casseroles and soups, and occasionally a boiled hotdog with sauerkraut and always an orange slice. They posted the weekly menu on the wall at the top of the stairs.

After filling our trays, we walked past the locker rooms and up the western stairs and a short flight to the stage, where we ate our lunch at folding tables.

Sometimes, I brought lunch from home. I had a lunch box with Trigger on the front. For a while, I had a matching Trigger Thermos, which I dropped and broke a day or two after I got it. I could hear the broken glass rattle in the lining. My packed lunch of choice was a salami sandwich wrapped in waxed paper. I added some fruit, carrot sticks, and perhaps a homemade cookie. We rarely had anything like chips.

My Trigger lunch box worked only for a couple of years because the subject matter did not age well. Ingrid, on the other hand, had a red Scotch-plaid lunch box and matching Thermos. She was able to use hers into junior high. I have no doubts her lunch contained Twinkies.

I looked forward to lunch for the food and recess. I also looked forward to returning to the classroom. The teacher read a book for half an hour. At first, it was a storybook. Later it was a novel read in half-hour installments. I could hardly wait to get to school the next day to hear what happened. Perhaps that is why I enjoy audiobooks.

The old part of the school had wooden floors and interior doors with windows. Lockers lined the dark-seeming halls, and the floors smelled of oil polish. The main entrance was in the middle of the south-facing wall with a short hall with restrooms on each side. A trophy case sat in the central corridor perpendicular to the short hall. The office was to the right. Inside the office were a couple of chairs in a waiting area by the door. The principal's office was to the left. His door was often closed. Maude Twining, the school secretary, had her desk beyond a high counter. She was an older woman who wore her steel gray hair on her head in tight finger waves like someone from the 20s. Some of the kids thought she was cranky. I liked her okay. There was a telephone on the counter where, with her permission, we could make emergency calls home.

I was in the old part of the school, at least until third grade. First grade was in a room with a small stage that later became the library. Both second and third grades were on the other side, looking toward Aspen Mountain. The high windows above the radiators had small panes and opened for fresh air. The southern rooms looked toward Aspen Mountain and the northern toward Red Mountain.

For a short period, one of my early grades was in one of the new rooms on the school's east end. I remember the supply closets with blond sliding doors. That's where the teacher kept a big jar of school paste. She used a tongue depressor to scoop dollops on a scrap of paper for art projects. I liked the smell and taste of the paste.

Mom drove me to school. At first, I was sad I was not going with her on the errands that had been such a big part of my life. Grandma was dead by the time I started school. Even so, there was no stopping at Pearl's or the Mesa Store. Usually, Mom picked me up at the end of the day, but sometimes I walked to Pearl's house with Barney and Gary, and Mom picked me up there.

Pearl's house was south on Center Street (now Garmisch), across Hopkins from City Park. The park eventually was renamed Paepcke Park. There were no stoplights in town, and there were no crossing guards. We looked both ways and ran across Main Street when it was clear. Pearl's house was three blocks from school and one block south of Main.

Going to Pearl's after school was a treat. She had snacks we ate at the kitchen table. She made tea – Lipton or a new orange and spice tea, Constant Comment. She made her tea in a clear, bluish, Pyrex teapot. She brought out homemade cookies or cake and yes, sometimes fruit cake. One of my favorite snacks was Hi-Ho crackers and Kraft chive cheese. Hi-Ho's were like Ritz crackers. The chive cheese came in either small foil packages or in glass jars designed to become juice glasses when empty. After Mom and Pearl visited for a few minutes, we headed to town for our daily downtown errands – always groceries and the post office. Mom was an at least once-a-day shopper at Beck & Bishop.

The school playground was outside the old part of the school near the elementary classrooms on the west end. This part of the playground had two sets of swings, a merry-go-round, a slide that got hot and had dents in the metal, and two or three teeter-totters. I never liked the merry-go-round because it made me sick unless I stood in the middle.

One of the swing sets was tall. Some of the boys stood up in the swings and swung so high they were parallel to the top bar. A few times, they got above it, and it was scary when the chains went slack. Sometimes they purposefully bailed out of the swings. I stood up on those swings a few times but never got that high.

Another part of the playground that could be deadly was the teeter-totters. One was high with the fulcrum about three feet off the ground. The others were about a foot and a half high. There were no seats, so kids straddled the boards and held on to the sides. If your teeter-totter partner was inept or untrustworthy and got off when you were on the high side, you crashed to the ground. A jungle gym made from galvanized pipes and an extension with a trapeze was behind the home-economics room.

One time when playing on the trapeze, I lost my Pope Pius XII medal. When Max was in Europe with the United States National Ski Team, the team had an audience with Pope Pius XII. Max brought back medals for family members he said were blessed by the Pope. The medals were slightly larger than a dime with the Pope's image. At the time, I thought the audience was just Max and the Pope. I imagined Max said, "Your Excellency, would you bless a medal for my cousin Vick?" The Pope proceeded to bless it just for me. I was so thrilled with the medal I wore it every day around my neck on a chain and swore I would never take it off.

After recess, I came into school and realized the chain was broken and was down my shirt. The medal was no longer on the chain. I could hardly wait to get outside to find it. It must have happened when I was hanging by my knees. After school, I ran out to the jungle gym area, but I could not find the medal. I went to the office to look for it and told my friends. Every day at every recess for a week, at least, I looked for it. I was heartbroken. Years later, I still walked back behind the school, hoping to find it. I even thought if I ever had access to a metal detector, I would look for it.

Besides the equipment, the best part of the playground was a brick wall against which we played 7-Up. It is a ball game involving bouncing a ball against the wall and the ground in many different configurations and to see if you could get to 7-Up without missing.

We also played in a blocked-off section of Center Street to the west of the school. It was the place for jumping rope or playing hopscotch. I played marbles there a couple of times. I don't know much about marbles, and I wasn't very good. I had a bag with cat's eyes and a couple of slightly chipped aggies. Like a lot of my toys and clothes, they were hand-me-downs from Gary and Barney.

After one of these days playing marbles, Mom came to pick me up near the barricade. I came running over to the car. By this time of the day, my socks were at different heights, my hair was messy, and my dress was twisted to the side and probably had some smudged dirt. Mom looked and me and said,

"Oh, Vicki. Look at you! Look at all the other little girls who look so nice and neat. Why can't you look like them?

"Let me tell you something, Mommy. Those little girls aren't having any fun."

She couldn't argue with that.

The first part of the school year was fun. I got new clothes and school supplies – a new box of Crayola crayons and a Red Chief tablet. I just loved the new crayon smell. I did not get one of the 64-count boxes with the pencil sharpener until I was in fourth grade. The old and broken crayons went into a Crayon jar at home. I was disappointed with how dirty the white crayon got, although I never used it. It was also disappointing because you could not use it to lighten a darker color. When no one was watching, sometimes I melted crayons on the back of the radiator in my room. It was fun to watch the slow-moving colored liquid flow down one of the back columns between the radiator sections. I worried Dad might notice the crayon marking when he came to bleed the radiators before winter.

Another good part of the fall was my birthday on September 15. There was a celebration at school for our birthdays where our mothers brought cupcakes, ice cream, and Kool-Aid for the class. Mom usually coordinated the party with Kim Howell's and Butch Lowderback's mothers because our birthdays were within a day of each other.

My real parties were at the ranch. I invited eight to ten boys and girls to arrive after lunch. In the early years, we played games like Ring Around the Rosie and London Bridge is Falling Down. Later we had cake and opened presents. Judy, Peggy, Cherie, Jimmy, and Billy chaperoned and organized these parties.

In later years, the parties involved a couple of rounds of "Try to Get in the Granary" after the present opening. That was one of the games we survived. One team went into the granary and guarded against an invasion by the opposing team. It could involve merely shouting a warning if an area was about to be breached, thus causing the invading kid to back away. Other times, it might involve pushing an invader out a window. If someone got in without being noticed, they opened the doors, and their team won that round. The game involved strategy and stealth. I remember sneaking on my belly through stinging nettles so as not to be seen from above. Stinging nettle rashes and a few scrapes were the worst injuries anyone sustained. I cheated once. I unlocked the back doors and hoped the inside team did not notice. My team won, but I felt terrible.

The parents came to pick their kids much too soon for me. One year, I convinced Mom to get some bologna and bread at Watermans so we could make sandwiches and extend playtime into the evening.

About this time, the colors began to change. Most of the changes occurred in the mountains. The back of Aspen Mountain visible from the kitchen was unchanged because it was mostly covered with evergreens. The area that eventually became Highlands and Tiehack had aspen trees that turned yellow and gold.

The trees in our yard were disappointing. The willow changed to a pale yellow, and the leaves fell before they were dry. The cottonwoods were slightly darker yellow and dryer. Some years there were enough leaves from the cottonwoods across the ditch to rake into a leaf house. In retrospect, I was lucky not to have too many leaves to rake.

School Carnival

The fall was also the time for the PTA's school carnival. Mom was heavily involved in the event. Everyone in the school participated. For one Saturday night, the school rooms had different attractions. The kids purchased red tickets from a big roll at the entrance to the school.

In one room, there was a fishing pond. The kids took "fishing poles" and dropped a line with a bucket attached behind a divide made to look like a pond. A few seconds later, there was a tug, and when we pulled up the line, the bucket contained a prize. There were games with balls and pins, beanbags and cans, milk bottles, and clothespins. There was bingo. Bingo was big, and it was in the gym. Another attraction was a dark room with drapes and a fortuneteller whose face was mysteriously lit from below. Albina was the fortuneteller. She was perfect with her long black hair. She had lots of costume material with scarves and shawls and long skirts and costume jewelry

In another room was the cakewalk. Each of the PTA mothers contributed a cake. The person in charge selected the cake for the round, and we played musical chairs until the last kid in a chair won the cake. The single cake I won was a yellow cake with green icing.

I had so much fun running around with my friends; I was disappointed when it was over. On Monday, following the carnival, I was sad about going back to the same old boring school.

Teacher's Convention - Going to Denver

Every October, the school was dismissed for a Thursday and Friday for the teachers to attend the teachers' convention in Denver. That was our opportunity to go to Denver to run errands and visit relatives.

Some years we were lucky, and we could go over Independence Pass before the first snow. At the time, the pass was unpaved. It was finally paved in 1967. Much of the road was rough like a washboard. On the downward grade, it felt as if the car was going slightly sidewise. If we were unfortunate enough to get behind another car, light brown dust billowed from behind. The dust found its way into the car, into our hair, and into our teeth. Despite these drawbacks, the trip over the pass saved about an hour and was scenic.

However, if the snow came early and closed the pass or if it looked like the weather might get bad, we drove through Glenwood Canyon. That route gave me problems. I was prone to carsickness, and, about halfway through the canyon, I would start feeling ill. We pulled off by the side of the road, and they gave me some time to get out and walk around a while. My tight jaw started slacking, and the warm metallic feeling in my mouth would subside. One of the traditional stopping points was a pullout with a stone monument and a model of a California Zephyr Vista Dome car. The Zephyr itself traveled on tracks across the river. I thought the model was cool.

We stopped for lunch at the Moon Valley Lodge on the Blue River near the town of Dillon. Dillon was between Vail and Loveland Pass. During these early trips, the town of Vail and the Vail ski area did not exist. The ski area did not open until 1962. There was, at the time, skiing at Arapahoe Basin and Loveland Basin. At the Moon Valley Lodge, I got a salami sandwich on white bread, a handful of chips, and a Coke. With this stop, we knew we were halfway to Denver.

In the late fifties, the Denver Water Board built a reservoir over the town of Dillon. They razed the town and the Moon Valley Lodge. In later years, it was eerie flying over the lake and seeing the old highway go into the reservoir and be visible below the water for several yards and disappear. The road reappeared near the site of the Moon Valley Lodge.

From the Moon Valley Lodge toward Arapahoe Basin, we passed the turnoff to the Ski Tip Lodge owned by the parents of one of Peggy's school friends, Sonny Dercum. Then we went over Loveland Pass. Because of the twists and turns, I needed a stop in Georgetown to recover. I wonder why Mom and Dad never thought about having me sit in the front seat or, more important, for them not to smoke in the car.

We usually stayed with Elmer and Noreen – Mom's brother and wife and later their children. They lived in a new tract home on the west end of Denver. In the early 50s, Elmer moved there to work for the Denver Post as a Linotype machine operator. Noreen had Aspen connections. She was related to Carletta Parsons, Buck's wife. Noreen and Elmer were generous people who loved to cook and loved to eat.

We rarely stayed with Dad's relatives on these short trips, although we may have stopped briefly to see Dad's niece, Julia, and her family. Julia and her husband, Joe, had four children – Bonnie, Ronnie, Cindy, and Marty. Bonnie and Ronnie were Judy and Peggy's ages. Cindy was a little younger than me. Marty was the youngest. Dad's sister, Rose, a nurse at St. Joseph's Hospital, was like Julia's surrogate mother and had been from the time Julia was an infant. She spent a lot of time with Julia and her family.

The focus of many trips was to visit Bud at the tile store in Cherry Creek and pick up supplies. The store was on Detroit Street. The treat after waiting around for Dad, Bud, and Mr. Biegert to wheel and deal was going to the Cherry Creek Shopping Center. The shopping center had something for everyone – The Denver Dry Goods for clothes, Fontius Shoes for dress shoes, and Woolworth's for Halloween costumes and decorations.

We stopped for lunch at a cafeteria near the Denver Dry Goods, which anchored the shopping center. Going to a cafeteria was impressive. You could go down the line and have anything you wanted. I could have fried chicken, and someone else could have spaghetti, and there were all types of desserts. The food itself was marginal.

Finally, and most important, was a stop at Anderson's Toy Land. It had all the newest toys. These toys were not available in catalogs. It had towering shelves of dolls from Madame Alexander to the latest thing from New York. That's where I first saw a Vogue fashion doll and a year or two later, where I saw for the first time the strange insect-looking Barbie. I drooled over hula-hoops and coveted Etch-a-Sketches. The store had complete Lincoln Log villages. There were mounds of stuffed animals, including Gund bears and a Steiff eight-foot-tall giraffe and Noah's ark filled with stuffed animals.

They had a play area on the roof with small amusement park rides. I found it kind of tame compared to Lakeside or Elitch Gardens. These parks, however, were not open in the fall. Sometimes we took a trip to the Denver Natural History Museum to see the dinosaurs and the dioramas. The museum smelled like the science room in the school.

The final destination was to pick up a couple of whiskey cases at Harry Hoffman's Liquor Store on Colfax – one case for Dad and one for Steve. If Steve thought Dad paid too much, he left Dad holding the bag and the case of whiskey. However, Steve was not shy about drinking that same overpriced whiskey at our house one glass at a time.

The last day of the trip involved going to Mass. We needed to find a church near Elmer's house. Neither he nor Noreen was Catholic. I had the impression they did not think much of religion and thought Catholicism was kind of a cult. At the end of one of our trips, they had an argument with Dad about the Catholic Church and God. Dad didn't talk to them for a while, but fortunately, not too long.

After Mass, we went to breakfast at the International House of Pancakes. That got me filled up with all the stuff that was going to make my ride home particularly miserable. It always did. If I went for the pancakes, they were too sweet. If I went for the breakfast meats, they were too fatty. Who was going to go to the International House of Pancakes and have toast and cereal?

Halloween

Halloween was the next event, but not one of my favorite holidays. I liked the costume part.

For years Mom made me cute costumes, or I borrowed the ones she made for my sisters. There were poodle skirts and the Dutch girl outfit. In later years, I wore a store-bought costume for a while like the one I was wearing the year I won the costume contest, and Ingrid and I became best friends. By late grade school, we made our costumes. One year I went as a Yankee baseball player, and Ingrid went as a football player. I don't remember her team.

Most years, the costumes were only good for the school Halloween party. It was cold and often snowy by trick-or-treat time, and we stuffed our costumes into snowsuits or put on heavy coats and boots. One of our parents drove us around because if we had to walk from inhabited house to inhabited house, it would take most of the night. There were few sidewalks in town, and the houses were far apart with vacant lots in between.

We knew who had the best treats. Svea gave out Hershey Bars. Not miniature Hershey bars – the real full-sized nickel ones. They were substantially bigger than a modern grocery store Hershey Bar. Peggy Rowland made popcorn balls. That was a special treat because I had tried to make them at home. Even when we buttered our hands, it still burnt. Better to have someone else go through that torture. We drug around our CARE milk cartons decorated in orange and saying, "Ghosts and Goblins go out to scare, but we go out for CARE." Svea gave out rolls of pennies. No one ever came to our house to trick and treat, so we never bought candy.

After trick and treating, we did not linger long at any house. We came home early. The next day was All Saints Day, and we had to go to 7:00 a.m. Mass. Driving home from Mass, we saw the results of the "tricks" played by the older kids soaping windows on the downtown buildings. The streets were empty and sad.

One year. Gary, Barney, Ingrid, and I had a Halloween party at Celia and Bill's house. After they built their house, Celia offered to let us make a haunted house before they finished the lower level. To get to what we called a spook house, the guests slid down a slide on the steps leading to the basement. We separated the rooms with blankets and sheets attached to the upper floor joists, added eerie lighting, and made gory things to touch. Building the haunted house was far more fun than the event itself.

The same was true for the other party Gary, Barney, Ingrid, and I had when we were in high school. One spring, we decided to have a barn dance in the barn. We cleaned it from top to bottom and put tarps on the leaky roof. The east side was for dancing with hay bales for seating and flowers in the water trough for decoration. The refreshments were next to the milking stanchions. We used the bowl from the milk separator as the punch bowl and set it next to the fixings for submarine sandwiches. One of my friends, Diane Pierce, made a cake featured in *Seventeen Magazine* that looked like half of a watermelon. The party was a success.

Thanksgiving

The biggest fall event was Thanksgiving. By that time, we may have had some snow, but it was rare to have the ski areas open. If they opened, skiing was not good. Sprigs of yellow grass poked through the dusting of snow. Rocks were also visible.

About a week or two before Thanksgiving, the Elks Club held their annual Turkey Roll at the Armory Building. It was a bingo game, and the winner of each round won a raffle ticket, and eventually, there was a drawing for turkeys. I loved playing bingo. Because each card cost money, I was usually limited to one card. I could have played all night. At first, people had cardboard bingo cards and used wooden disks. Later they got the fancy wooden cards with the sliding metal doors. The balls were turned in a spherical wire cage until a ball popped out into a chute. I liked it so much; I got a home version as a Christmas present when I was in junior high.

After bingo ended, the Elks women served cold turkey sandwiches and a dollop of cranberry sauce on paper plates. Turkey sandwiches were the best Thanksgiving food as far as I was concerned. They also made hot coffee that smelled good.

The Elks Club was part of my parent's social life. They often went to dances there. On dance night, Bill and Celia and Edmund and Albina brought their kids to our house for Keith and Max to babysit – that meant they had to watch Peggy, Judy, Billy, Jimmy, Cherie, and me. Our parents stayed out until the wee hours of the morning, roust the sleeping kids, and go home. Mass came early.

The Elks supported children's activities and scholarships. The Elks owned a significant section of the Red Butte Cemetery – surrounding a statue of an Elk. Mom and Dad reserved their plots in the Elks section. The Marolt family plot is just to the southeast of the Elks section.

Dad was also a member of the Eagles. It was where he might go for an hour to get a beer and "chew the fat." The Eagles were not as formal as Elks. Sometimes Dad stayed too long, and Mom worried. She worried because Dad was not away from home that often. There was a time or two when Mom had me call to see if Dad was there. I heard the bartender shout out, "Hey Mike. Your kid wants to talk to you."

On Thanksgiving Day, our family tradition was to go to Grandma's house. After she died, Pearl took over hosting the dinner. The occasion included our two families, plus Riley, Stella, and Ted. The entrance to their house came into a porch like the one in our house. It had a washer and dryer, a pantry, and access to the cellar. A bar stocked with bourbon and mixers such as ginger ale and Coke sat on the washer and dryer. During periods when Riley was having problems with his drinking, the bar disappeared before Riley arrived. Ted always brought a box of Russell Stover chocolates.

Because she and Mom were sisters and learned from the same mother, Pearl's Thanksgiving meal was similar to Mom's Christmas meal. Pearl started her dinner with her version of antipasto – carrot and celery sticks, pitted black olives, green pimento olives, and pickled cherry peppers. She served them in oblong and diamond-shaped cut-glass serving dishes. The dishes originally came from Grandma or Albert's mother, Georgie Bishop, who we called Gi Gi, his grandmother Lenora Healy, or his great aunt Lu Lu Buffehr Wilson.

The dinner included turkey, stuffing, mashed potatoes, gravy, candied sweet potatoes, steamed green beans, a molded Jell-O salad, and canned jellied cranberry sauce cut in slices. Besides the jellied sauce, Mom also made cranberry sauce from fresh cranberries. Dessert was pineapple sherbet and Swedish cookies.

Pearl's dressing was slightly different than Mom's – Pearl did not use pork sausage. If you closed your eyes, it was hard to tell the difference. Because Albert was a butcher, he carved the turkey at the table. Dad carved ours in the kitchen using a wooden board, which one of us gave him as a present. It was one of those presents at which he rolled his eyes. It had spikes between wooden grooves on the bottom and a spiked arm on top to hold the turkey. I wonder if someone thought the turkey would get up and walk away.

Dinner was finished by 2:00 p.m. The women and older girls did the dishes. Their house was hot because the heating system primarily heated the combined living and dining room. I felt sleepy even without the l-tryptophan from the turkey. Before my conscription into dish duty, Barney, Gary, and I played board games, pick-up sticks, or Tiddlywinks on the living room rug. The men also sat in the living room, but I mostly remember them napping and smoking. After TV came to town, they watched the only football game on TV. The Detroit Lions always played on Thanksgiving regardless of whether they were any good.

After doing the dishes, we gathered around the dining room table and played poker. We played for penny's represented by buttons from Pearl's button jar. Pearl loved poker, especially seven-card stud. Usually, she was the big winner. The game would go on until dark. After dark, before the earlier meal settled, Albert carved up the rest of the turkey, Pearl put out the fixings for sandwiches and made a pot of coffee in her electric percolator. There were more cookies. I remember sitting on the carpet near their big picture window feeling so stuffed I thought I would explode.

The nice thing was that there was no school the next day, but rarely any skiing. It was time to start planning for Christmas.

Christmas

I'm not alone in this – Christmas was one of the best times of the year.

By mid-October and through the first weeks of December, the landscape in Aspen was bleak. The earth was brown or tan and dotted here and there with snow. Dead grass stuck through the snow. The headgates were closed, and the ditches were empty. The trees around the ranch and town were bare. The most common trees on the ranch were aspens, cottonwoods, and jack oak. Most of the evergreens were on the mountains. Although the sky was often blue, it was just as often a blustery gray. There was not much to do outside except a short hike or horseback ride before the fields were inaccessible.

In most years, it was too early for downhill skiing. While they tried to open the lifts on Thanksgiving Day, the conditions were marginal - lots of rocks and grass. It was challenging to find a path to the bottom.

We didn't have the equipment or knowledge for snow hiking or cross-country skiing. One improvement since I was a kid is snowshoes. I would have loved the modern small variety.

Instead, we filled the time with a month-long preparation for Christmas. Christmas preparation did not start with the shopping season; it started with, of all things, Church.

It started on the first Sunday of Advent. Each year we got an evergreen Advent wreath from the church. It had four candles – three white and one pink or purple. On the first night of Advent, we lit the first white candle before supper and said Grace. We did this each night for a week. The next Sunday, we added another white candle on and on until the final Sunday before Christmas when we included the pink candle. That was an exciting time – Christmas was just around the corner.

Besides the wreath, sometimes we had an Advent calendar and opened a door each morning to see a small picture. Four weeks seemed like a long time to wait for the big day. I'm sorry to say, the big day for me was much more about the tree and presents than Church.

In the meantime, we were getting into the Christmas spirit at school. The Monday after Thanksgiving, we took down the brown and orange fall decorations and started putting up Christmas decorations. We hung green and red construction paper chains around the room and put up a small tree with paper ornaments and no lights. We cut out white snowflakes and taped them to the windows. We began practicing for the Christmas pageant. That meant each class wore costumes and sang Christmas songs for a presentation before vacation.

The town also started getting into the spirit. I do not remember a lot of decorating in town – mostly strings of colored lights strung from lampposts across the streets. There were evergreen garlands on the balcony of the Hotel Jerome. Several of the stores painted opaque pictures on their windows of Santa, reindeer, trees, or giant white flocked snowflakes.

Although there was no "black Friday" for shopping in town, we rejoiced at the arrival of Christmas catalogs after Thanksgiving – from the Sears Roebuck Wish Book to the ones from Montgomery Ward and Spiegel. There were also gift catalogs Mom liked from Miles Kimball and Lillian Vernon. If I went to the post office with Mom when the catalogs arrived, I'd tear off the brown paper wrapper and immediately turned to the end of the book to scan the toys.

I lay on my stomach on the living room rug and went through each catalog - page by page - several times a day. The catalogs were pretty much the same. I'd say Sears was bigger, Montgomery Ward's was practical, and Spiegel could have a surprise or two. Spiegel had bigger pictures. Within a few days after they arrived, between my sisters and me, the catalogs were dog-eared and wrinkled.

When I looked through the catalogs, I'd glance at holiday pajamas, robes, and slippers. I always received at least one of these clothing items every year, but the crucial part of the catalog was the toy section.

The toys were generic – dolls, trains, and scale modeled filling stations and farms. The individual items lagged what was available at the stores in the big cities. In some cases, the brands were knock-offs. Barbie was not available in these catalogs for years after she was first available at Anderson Toyland in Denver. Instead, Sears sold Mitzi – high-fashion-doll – equivalent from the Ideal Toy Company. She was approximately the same size as Barbie and, therefore, could almost wear Barbie's clothes. Because Mitzi was slightly larger, Barbie's clothes did not fit her quite right. Mitzi had her own wardrobe. Instead of the teeny tiny zippers in the Barbie clothes, Mitzi's clothes fastened with snaps. In proportion to the doll, the snap on a human was the size of a saucer. Improper proportions bothered me.

The arrival of Barbie was a big deal. It was not until then that I cared about dolls. I never wanted a baby doll. There had been a time where I wanted a high-heeled doll with a yellow dress we saw in a gift shop next to a restaurant in Idaho Springs on one of our trips to Denver. I begged for it and was told we could not afford it. I also seem to remember it cost $17.

A few miles down the road, the Highway Patrol pulled Dad over for speeding. The ticket, which happened to be $17.00, had to be paid on the spot. Mom and Dad were able to pay the fine after telling me they could not afford the doll. I was miffed.

From the Christmas catalog, I wanted a gas station with a lift, an elevator, and a ramp. I wanted a toy piano even though we had a perfectly good real piano. I wanted a toy typewriter even though we had a perfectly good Remington. Regardless, I could make up a long list for Santa. The list needed to be prepared in time to get it to him in time for Christmas morning delivery.

Early in December, Mom made her fruitcakes. She made them, wrapped them in cheesecloth soaked in brandy. Fruitcake was a tradition. I'm sure Mom's cakes were good – they had an applesauce cake base. She did not use any candied citron or pineapple because she said they made it bitter. Her cakes had a lot of nuts and dates and cherries. After Mom made the loaves, she wrapped them in cheesecloth and put on the first dose of brandy. She wrapped them in foil and put them in the "doghouse" where it was cold and added brandy every day or two.

The doghouse was a room behind the living room fireplace. As far as I know, no dog ever stayed there. It was a space created when the Marolt brothers added a gabled enclosure to the house's north side. It had a foyer for the front door and enclosed the area behind the fireplace. There was no heat source. Since it was on the northern side of the house, in the winter, it was frigid – perfect for the baked goods. It would hold a frozen turkey all winter.

There was a ladder attached to the wall inside the door to the doghouse leading to the attic. The attic was accessible but unusable. There was no floor, just the ceiling joists filled with sawdust. I never went beyond the opening and the few sheets of plywood resting on the over the joists. There were no lights except light coming through a few woodpecker holes under the eastern eves. I fantasized about opening the attic as a second story.

After making fruitcake, Mom, with Judy and Peggy's help, made batches and batches of Christmas cookies. Early on, I helped by licking the bowl. Mom was one of the best cookie bakers ever. When they remodeled the kitchen, Dad designed it, especially for her baking. There were two large drawers lined with galvanized metal and sliding covers for flour and sugar. There was a space for the mixer next to the stove.

Mom made her cookies with real butter. First and foremost, she made Swedish cookies. Mom was Swedish, and the recipe for these cookies was passed on for generations. Other people call them spritz. Mom mixed the ingredients until she had a perfect consistency only she could gauge. Then she used a star shape for the Mirro cookie press and formed the dough in wreath circles a little over an inch in diameter. She baked them until they had but a hint of gold on the tips – never brown.

Pearl made Swedish cookies on par with Mom except for the year she used Wondra flour instead of regular flour. Wondra was the new flour that, according to the ads, did not need to be sifted. That year Pearl's cookies had the texture of sand. Being frugal, rather than start over, she lived with gritty cookies.

In addition to Swedish cookies, we made other butter varieties – Chinese cookies were butter dough circles, flattened by a glass, dotted with a blanched almond. Cream cheese cookies, also made in the cookie press, look like strips of corduroy. After baking, we dipped the ends in melted chocolate and sprinkles.

Mom made Austrian nut bars, especially for Dad. They had a buttery, shortbread cookie base covered with a walnut and egg mixture like what we spread on potica. They were then baked and sliced into bars.

I especially liked the thumbprint cookies. They were butter cookies formed in a ball, rolled in egg whites, and finely chopped nuts. The ball was depressed with a thumb before baking. At serving time, we filled the impression with red currant jelly – salty and tart. There were some other varieties of cookies, including date pinwheels, pecan fingers, and apricot bars. Mom tried a couple of new recipes every year. Some became part of the tradition. Others did not make it.

Despite the focus on cookies at Christmas, we never made "Christmas cookies." We never rolled cookie dough and cut it with a cookie-cutter and covered with icing and sprinkles - no red and green sugar in our house.

By Christmas, there were at least a dozen varieties of cookies stored in jars, tins, and bean pots nestled in the rungs of a ladder to the attic in the doghouse. Whenever one of our friends or relatives showed up in the afternoon, Mom prepared either Lipton or Constant Comment tea and brought out a plate of cookies.

Shortly after Thanksgiving, we started playing Christmas music on the Hi-Fi – Bing Crosby, Perry Como, Johnny Mathis, Andy Williams, and the Boston Pops. Later we added a compilation of orchestra renditions of religious carols. Those later albums were often giveaways as part of a promotion at one of Glenwood Springs' gas stations. We called gas stations "filling stations."

Gasoline giveaways were prevalent at the time. The oil companies wanted to motivate people to consume more. With one of these giveaways, Dad got me a stuffed tiger. I assume it was the forerunner of the "tiger in your tank" from whatever company became Exxon. One day Dad appeared with this reclining stuffed tiger that seemed to be nearly half my size. His back made a nice pillow. I called him Tigsie.

Tigsie and the stuffed calf, Bambi, who Keith brought home from his first year at college, were special. Bambi had a goofy rubber face with buck teeth, rubber hooves, white and brown fleece covering the rest of him. He had a cowbell around his neck tied with a red ribbon. I slept with them every night. Every time I rolled over; Bambi's bell rang. Tigsie and Bambi were front and center in my fire evacuation plan.

Although Tigsie was from a gas station, we rarely used gas stations in town because we had a gas pump. Near the culvert inside the driveway were a buried gasoline tank and gasoline pump for our ranch use. The pump was tall and orange. There was a ten-gallon clear glass cylinder on top.

We used the pump to fill the car, the pickup, the Jeeps, the tractors, and a glass jug for the lawnmower. We pulled the vertical handle and pushed it back and forth until the glass cylinder on top of the pump was filled with up to ten gallons of orange liquid. A hose extended from the base of the cylinder with a nozzle. It was not precise, but no one cared about calculating gas mileage. At that time, gasoline was less than $.25 per gallon. Although we rarely did so, we could padlock the pump so no one could steal the gas.

At any rate, one of our Christmas-carol albums came from a gas station, and it, along with the other albums, was played continuously until Christmas. Once we finally got some television, I watched a black and white version of *A Christmas Carol* and some Christmas cartoons. I particularly liked the Norelco shaver ads. They were black-and-white animation of Santa swooping down a wintery slope on a Norelco rotating electric razor head. For the Christmas ad, they renamed the company "Noëlco."

Besides cooking and drooling over the catalogs, I worked on art projects such as making cards or unique gift wrap. One year, Ingrid and I painted a Madonna and Child on the window in the front room of Ingrid's house. We used opaque poster paint. The Madonna was tall and long and thin in a dark blue robe holding a baby. There was a halo of light behind her head. I copied a "modern" Christmas card, which I thought had something to do with Jacqueline Kennedy or someone famous. It looked nice from the street.

I duplicated the scene in our dining room window. The painting looked very good from the outside and, at night, on the inside. No one could see it from the outside at our house unless they were hanging clothes on the line. During the day, the sun made the picture look mottled. That bothered me. I would have liked it better if it was transparent like stained glass.

After the catalogs arrived, I worried about presents. I knew that much of Christmas depended on Mom getting packages from the post office. I worried, if I did not see her coming out with big brown boxes, Santa was not coming. It never occurred to me that she might go to the post office without me when I was in school and get those big brown boxes.

In later years, Ingrid and I did the unthinkable – we searched for hidden presents. We always searched a little but never hit the mother lode except for one year. That year, I found a pink GE kitchen stuffed in the back of my sisters' closet. It had four parts – a refrigerator, a stove with an oven, a sink unit with running water, and a unit with drawers and doors below and a cabinet above. Finding the kitchen was thrilling at first but dampened the excitement on Christmas morning. It was indeed a surprise gift, and I never got over the guilt of finding it beforehand. What made it worse is that Ingrid and I played with it and lost one of the refrigerator's main parts. A chemical we threw away was supposed to be poured into the freezer's lining, filled with water, and frozen. It would have provided cold in the toy refrigerator for an hour or two.

About two weeks before Christmas, it was time for Christmas tree hunting. Dad gathered the kids in the pickup and went up either Maroon or Castle Creek or near Shale Bluffs to look for a tree. There was usually no good place near the road for acceptable Christmas trees. Therefore, the trees we got were big treetops.

Dad preferred Shale Bluffs. The trees there were the right kind – evergreens with not-too-hostile needles. He stood on the highway, looked down, and surveyed the treetops below the road. That made it easier to pick the perfect one rather than looking up from the ground. Once Dad found a tree and thoroughly inspected it, he climbed it until he was about twelve feet from the top. Then he sawed off the top. If the very top – the part used for the star – broke off, Dad was disappointed. Depending on how long we had been looking, Dad might look for another tree. Other times, he knew he could do some reconstructive surgery in his shop. Each year, it got harder and harder to find trees in the usual spots because of Aspen residents' earlier harvests. The forests around town were dotted with decapitated trees.

On one of these hunts, Dad climbed a tree on the slope below Shale Bluffs. For the first time, I was aware Dad had health issues. He had trouble breathing and trudging through deep snow exacerbated it.

Once Dad had the tree, we drug it through the snow and loaded it into the pickup. Dad did not bring it directly to the house. Instead, he took it to his shop in the granary, and it stayed there until a week before Christmas.

In his real Santa shop, Dad worked his magic. He cut the tree, so it was 8 or 9 feet tall and put on a custom-made stand. The house's ceilings were 12 feet high, and there needed to be room for the star. Then he began reshaping the tree by pruning a branch here and there and taking extra branches and configuring them to fit into the bare spots. He drilled a hole in the trunk and then shaved a branch to fit snuggly in the hole. The result was a perfect looking Christmas tree. Dad put on the stand on the appointed day, loaded it in the pickup, secured it, and brought it up to the house. I was always so excited when the red pickup arrived with the tree standing in the back.

The tree was usually in the northwest corner between the windows. Dad oversaw the lights and the star. For most of my childhood, the lights were the traditional bulbs about a little less than an inch long. We used multi-color strands. Dad made sure the lights worked, and then he carefully placed them on the boughs, so the bulbs did not touch the needles of the tree. The bulbs we used burned scalding hot. Although the tree was fresh, the heat from these bulbs could dry the needles quickly, and by the time we took it out of the house, the spots near the lights were brown.

The lights were the type that, if one light went bad, the whole string went dark. I worried about the lights. I still do. What would happen if one of them went out? Could we ever find which one it was? What if we could not find replacement bulbs? To this day, I have the same nervous feeling that the tree will not light.

Before we put them on the tree, Mom plugged each strand into an outlet and stretched out the string on the floor to make sure each bulb was working. After the lights were in place, Dad announced he had done everything he would do for Christmas – except enjoy it. Dad, like the rest of us, loved Christmas.

Now the fun part began. Mom drug out the Christmas boxes stored in the back of the doghouse. There were all kinds of ball ornaments. She made a point of buying a few new boxes of glass balls each year. No matter how we tried to avoid it, we lost several each season when they fell and shattered into confetti-sized shards of glass.

I thought the balls were beautiful and expensive, and I pretended I was the owner of a store selling rare ornaments. Mom ordered most of the ornaments from Sears. After the ornaments, we put on "icicles." By that, I mean the silver tinsel strands. At that time, they were thin aluminum foil. Now I think they are silver Mylar.

After each Christmas, we tried to salvage some of the icicles for the next year, but they were lumpy and stuck together. We never used them and instead bought new packages. Each strand was placed one at a time. There were demerit points for throwing on a chunk or if there were too many strands together. Then we put a white bed sheet around the base of the tree.

That was not the only part of the decorating. There were pine boughs on the fireplace, pine boughs on the piano, and pine boughs on a bookcase where we set up the crèche. We hung Christmas cards around one of the arches in the living room. We hung up stockings on the fireplace. Our stockings weren't anything special – usually just large woolen stockings.

There were candles everywhere. For a couple of years, we made some of our own candles. Mom took four bars of paraffin used for canning, melted them enough, so they stuck together in a single block with a wick vertically down the middle. Then the block was placed on end. Several more paraffin bars were melted, and, using an old electric mixer, we whipped it until the clear liquid turned to a white froth. We added a little silver or gold glitter and spread the mixture like seven-minute icing on the outside of the block. When lit, the candles were iridescent.

Besides the homemade candles, we had several glass candle holders that looked like stained glass, and with a votive candle, they cast sparkling light around the room. Every candlestick in the house had either a red or green candle. One year, Mom got a candle at Wax & Wicks – a new store in town. That candle was about a foot tall, white, and it looked like a pine tree covered in frothy snow. It was too pretty to light.

Except at Pearl's house, I do not remember going too much to other houses and seeing their decorations. Albert attached Barney and Gary's train track to plywood and put it under the tree. It was fun to play with the train, although I don't remember it being out except at Christmas. They also had those interesting bubble lights. They looked like clear glass "candles," and as the light heated, they made bubbles.

In the remaining days leading to Christmas, there were presents to wrap, and it was at this time we made the candy. We made Mom's cooked fudge. It was a little temperamental and required cooking until the sugar and Karo syrup formed a perfect soft ball in cold water. We did not use a candy thermometer. We stirred the fudge as it cooked, avoiding the sides lest a single seed of sugar crystal find its way into the mixture and cause the entire batch to become granular. Once it was at the right stage, we removed the pan and added a cube of butter. The butter melted without stirring.

Then the beating began. Dad beat the fudge by hand. He sat in his chair with a towel on his lap, wedged the pan between his knees, and used a spoon to vigorously beat the fudge until it lost its sheen. Before it was done, we added chopped walnuts or pecans for one more stir. We poured it in a pan and set it on the washer in the backroom to cool. The resulting fudge was terrific.

If for some reason, the fudge did not get cooked enough to set up, it made fudge sauce for ice cream. In addition to regular fudge, we made divinity fudge. It was a concoction made from sugar, corn syrup, egg whites, and nuts dropped on a cookie sheet. I was not crazy about divinity – too sweet. Sometimes we made caramels, toffee, and popcorn balls. In later years, we made crackerjack in the oven.

Finally, it was Christmas Eve Day. What could be prepared ahead for the next day's dinner was made and stored in a cool spot. The bread was dried for stuffing, and the turkey was out of the doghouse in the slightly warmer back porch. A few presents appeared under the tree over the week – presents between Mom and Dad and between the siblings or from aunts and uncles and friends. The ones for me were shaken and examined in hopes of guessing their contents. I was disappointed if a package was limp. That meant it was probably something to wear. One year it was a set of hand-embroidered pillowcases from Albina. I wasn't too impressed at the time, but later I treasured them.

Although in later years, we established a Christmas Eve tradition of cheese fondue, when I was little, I don't remember our Christmas Eve dinner being anything other than a typical supper. Once Mom threatened to make us eat the traditional Swedish dinner – Lutfisk. Her description sounded bad – cured in lye, tasteless, and gelatinous. One of the fish I liked, besides trout, was Finnan haddie. It was a smoked fish mom poached in milk and drizzled with butter. We reserved it for meatless Fridays.

For Christmas Eve, we had something simple such as soup or leftovers. After supper, we cleaned the kitchen, turned on the tree lights, lit the fireplace, lit the candles in the kitchen, dining room, and living room. We turned out the electric lights and played Christmas carols.

About 7:00 p.m., the Bishops – Pearl, Albert, Gary, and Barney – came over, and we exchanged gifts for the morning. We put their presents under the tree. We had Christmas cookies and candy, and sometimes we each got a small cordial glass of port wine from the ruby cut glass decanter on the bookcase. It was a beautiful, magical time and even nicer when it was snowing outside.

The Bishops left around 9:00 p.m. Someone read *The Night Before Christmas*, and then it was waiting time. Before we left for Mass, I put out a couple of cookies and a glass of milk if Santa showed up before we got home.

At 11:15, we put on our coats and hats and drove to town for midnight Mass. Mom was not Catholic and did not go to Mass at that time. As soon as we drove down out of the driveway and the main road, I imagine the lights went on in the house, the candles went out, and Mom cleaned up the dishes. She had more work to do.

We got to Church early because Judy and Peggy were in the choir. The parishioners began singing Christmas carols with the choir at 11:30. The main part of St. Mary's, the nave, was upstairs. There were matching sets of stairs from the entrance on Main Street – one set going up on the right and one going up on the left. Halfway up, there was a landing below a stained-glass window, and the stairs switched back, leading to the nave. Inside either door was a holy-water font. I dipped my fingertips and made the sign of the cross. I had a holy-water bottle at home and sprinkled it on my bed at night. I was assured it kept me from dying, or at least, if I died, I would go to heaven.

There were four sets of pews – two on each side with a wooden divider down the middle of each. The padded kneelers could be moved up and away from the floor. There were huge radiators under the stained-glass windows on the side. Between the windows were framed pictures representing the Stations of the Cross. The life-sized statue of Jesus on the cross was at different locations in the church over time. I remember it being on both the west and east side of the altar, and, at one point, it may have been in the back on the west wall near the confessional.

The choir loft was in the middle of the church's back, about four feet above the main level and accessible through side stairs on the northwest landing before the nave. It had a wooden rail facing the altars. On the other side of the stair doors were the confessionals. The confessionals did not have doors – only curtains. The baptismal was on the northeast corner rear a confessional.

The altars covered the front of the church. There were three altars – two on the sides and the high altar in the middle. The high altar had three statues – the Sacred Heart on top, St. Patrick was lower on the right in a green robe with a snake peering out from under his foot, and St. Aloysius lower on the left. Genuflecting angels flanked this altar. The tabernacle was in the middle behind a gold starburst.

The Madonna and Child were above the left altar, and St. Joseph was above the right. When I was small, the altars were behind a communion rail that spanned from side to side. The rail was about two and a half feet high with another unpadded kneeling platform beneath. The hardwood rail had two hidden gates to access the altar. There was a white cloth, like a curtain, hanging the length of the backside. The altar boys brought the cloth over the rail for communion to prevent host crumbs from falling to the ground.

At Christmas, pine trees provided by men from the parish filled the area behind the communion rail next to the altar. There were twenty or thirty trees at different heights, making it look like the altar was in a forest. They were decorated with blue lights. The rest of the church was dark. When we arrived for midnight Mass, it was spectacularly beautiful. Our family sat on the left section of the pews closest to the windows. Our chosen spot was always about a third of the way toward the altar.

The crèche was on the right-hand side in front of the St. Joseph Altar. It had ceramic figurines each about a foot tall – Mary, Joseph, the three wise men, some shepherds, angels, and livestock. Baby Jesus was in his manger, and there were sheep, cows, and donkeys. The figures were under a structure that looked like our bale shed with a thatched roof. It was open on all sides and had a slanting roof covered in straw. Lights outline the front of the structure. There was a kneeler in front.

After singing, the house lights went on, and the high Mass began. For a long time, it was in Latin. The choir sang a lot, including all the verses of the carols. Father Bosch gave the sermon. At Christmas, he was pleasant and uplifting. On that night, he did not yell at tourists or someone he did not think was dressed appropriately.

Dad said Father Bosch was nice because he wanted the big check we delivered for the offering. I believe it was $25.00 on Christmas and Easter. Otherwise, he put $2.00 per week in the offering envelopes.

Finally, Mass was over around 1:00 a.m. We went downstairs and outside. White crystalline ice crystals were suspended and sparkling in the sky under the streetlight. Much to my chagrin, Dad stood outside and talked to people for what seemed like hours. It was cold. I was tired. I wanted to see if Santa arrived while we were gone.

When we got home, the house was dark except for one lone light over the kitchen table. There was the faint smell of butter, onions, celery, and sage. While we were gone, Mom made the stuffing, so it was ready to put in the bird in the morning. It was cooling on the back porch on the washer.

The Christmas tree lights were off, and the fire was out. It was cold because we did not dare close the damper until there was no doubt the fire was out. As I came out of the kitchen, I peeked around the corner toward the tree. The room was dark, and the tree was a slightly discernable shadow before the reflected snow-light through the window. We were not allowed in the living room, but in the light created by the glow of the snow, there was no doubt the pile of presents had grown while we were gone.

I could hardly wait until morning. I threw off my clothes, put on my pajamas, gave my nightly nod to Aspen Mountain outside my window, said a rosary, and grabbed Tigsie and Bambi. I just knew I would never get to sleep. Miraculously, however, I fell asleep within minutes.

Usually, I woke somewhere between 6:00 and 6:30 and jumped out of bed. It was still mostly dark, but a bit of light might be breaking. Yes, indeed, the pile under the tree had grown. The stockings were misshaped with lumps and were no longer hanging but instead arranged neatly on the hearth. Only half of a Swedish cookie remained on the plate by the fireplace, and the glass of milk was half gone. After surveying the situation, I ran from room to room, waking everyone.

Within 15 to 20 minutes, the family was getting up. Someone turned on the tree lights. The extent of Santa's largess was now known. There were boxes of all sizes wrapped in a variety of green or red papers. Some years the pile was three feet high and tumbled into the room. I sat by the pile anxiously waiting for everyone to get up and for Mom to make a pot of coffee.

During the wait, I got to open my stocking. It had nuts to be shelled and perhaps an orange or two. The nuts and orange were holdover traditions from when Mom was a child. Sometimes there were a few pieces of chocolate candy and some candy canes. There may have been a toy or two, such as a tiny working flashlight. One year, I got some nesting characters from Little Red Riding Hood, including the wolf, the grandmother, and a strange-looking child. I also got a set of nesting cats that got smaller and smaller until there was a tiny mouse. One of the best stocking gifts I ever got was a wooden apple the size of a real apple. When opened, there was a wooden apple cross-section that made a little table. Then there was a tiny wooden teapot with a lid and four even tinier wooden cups and saucers.

As soon as the coffee was poured, the unwrapping began. One of the older siblings passed out presents. Our tradition was for one person to open one present at a time. I got the first gift, a Santa gift of my choice. Over the years, I was pleased with what I received. Santa got several items on my list. I was disappointed when I got Lincoln logs and an erector set because the sets' size was so small that I could only make a cabin and a small crane.

One year, I got the toy gas station I wanted so badly. I never did get a toy piano or typewriter. It was probably just as well. The gas station was one of the most worthless toys ever. The car wash did not wash the cars, and the cars did not move on their own. The elevator moved up and down by manually rotating a crank. I think I got most of the amusement out of unwrapping the parts and putting it together.

I had much more fun in the summer playing with toy cars and trucks in the dirt. It could not begin to compare with the fun I had the year Dad had several yards of sand delivered to the edge of the driveway for some project. I played on the tall mound for several days, making roads around the "mountain" and could even make tunnels in the moist sand in the middle of the pile.

As far as the gas station, I pretended to play with it long enough to avoid a lecture about asking for things I never used. The gas station soon made its way to the back of my closet, and eventually, I gave it away.

One year I got a Betty Crocker baking set. It was a large package with small cookie sheets, loaf pans, pie tins, and cake pans, including three pans for a wedding cake. It also had several different packages of cake, cookie, and muffin mixes. The baking set was for the toy oven my sisters received years earlier. Their toy oven was real; it did not run on a battery or warmed with a light bulb. It plugged into a wall and was ready to catch fire at any minute. It was among the many dangerous toys prevalent during that era – like chemistry sets, lead toy-soldier molding sets, or wood-burning sets.

One year, the best present was the Vogue Jill doll. It was one of the first fashion dolls. I saw her on one of the Denver trips when we went to Andersen's Toy Land. The one I got was blond and had feet pre-bent for high heels. She was proportioned to be a "healthy" young woman. She came dressed in a bathing suit. I got two or three sets of clothing, each in a separate box. There was a red shirtwaist dress with a full skirt, a white felt hat with a red ribbon, and red heels. There was also a tropical Capri set – a Hawaiian shirt and some khaki capris.

The best part of the gift, however, was the clothes Judy made. She was a gifted seamstress who won all the purple ribbons in 4-H. Using a Vogue pattern, she made the complete set – lace adorned underwear, a pink sheer nightgown and negligee, a faux fur coat, a blue and white miniature checked shirtwaist dress, and a bridal gown with a veil. I played a lot with this doll. Unfortunately, a year later, Jill was replaced in the toy market by a new strange-looking creature – Barbie.

Another year, after I was finally interested in Barbies, I got the four-piece pink, GE kitchen set for her – the one Ingrid and I found early. I have no idea where Mom and Dad found it. I did not ask for it, but it was one of the best presents ever. It worked with Barbie, although the proportions were a little off. The set included a refrigerator that was supposed to work if the freezer drawer frozen in the real freezer. It never worked for me because, as I said, we lost the chemical capsule weeks before Christmas. When batteries were fresh, the range burners turned red, the dishwasher spewed water, and the sink had a reservoir that pumped running water. The set also included dishes, pots and pans, utensils, and plastic food, including vegetables, fruit, pork chops, and fried eggs. Everything was accurate except the turkey – it was green.

Where I got an hour's worth of fun out of the gas station, I got days and weeks of enjoyment out of the kitchen and the Barbie dolls.

The presents with the longest shelf life were the puzzles, board games, stadium checkers, and art supplies, including paint-by-number sets, John Gnagy Learn-to-Draw books, storybooks, and of course, American Plastic Bricks. The brick sets provided plans for a small village. Gary and Barney each received sets of these bricks for years on end, and as a result, they had quite the collection. They could build the school and at least three or four buildings.

I had so much fun playing with their bricks at their house that Santa started giving me a small set every year. The brick sets came in a round canister. Each set had instructions for many of the buildings, but a small set could only build a small house. Every year I got new sets, and the possibilities expanded. I played with these continually. When Gary and Barney grew out of their toys, they gave me their huge box of bricks. I was in heaven. I finally had enough bricks to build the entire village. Even when I was in junior and senior high, I went down to the basement and played with the bricks.

We never played with our presents on Christmas morning because we needed to clean up and get ready for dinner. We picked up the boxes and wrapping paper and burned them in the fireplace. Then we made up piles of our gifts to give a tour when the relatives arrived.

Christmas mornings, Steve and Polly, the Gerbazes, and Ted stopped briefly and gave us presents. Albina gave homemade items, and Ted and Steve gave us envelopes, usually containing $5 to $10. I am not sure what Bill, Celia, and their family did for the day. Steve and Polly spent the day with their friends Jens and Gladyce Christiansen. Jens was a rancher who had a ranch on Owl Creek. Albina, Edmund, Cherie, and Jimmy spent the day with the rest of the Gerbaz family down the valley.

In the meantime, we set the tables – the main table and the small table for the kids. The big table had a linen tablecloth, and we used Mom's wheat-patterned dishes and crystal goblets Dad gave her one Christmas and her silver-plated flatware. We dressed for dinner, which was for Mom's family, and Ted. The adults had a cocktail before Riley arrived.

Dinner was the same as Thanksgiving – turkey, dressing, mashed potatoes, giblet gravy, sweet potatoes, a vegetable, a salad of molded gelatin of some sort, two kinds of cranberries – freshly cooked and jellied – and an antipasto plate of olives, celery, carrots, and sweet peppers. Until later, when Mom came up with some fancy mousses and whipped cream and coconut concoctions, dessert was pineapple sherbet and a tray of cookies and fruitcake. Mom brought out her electric percolator for coffee.

After dinner, the men loosened their belts and went into the living room and smoked and napped. There was no TV, so there was no football to watch. They may have listened to a game on the radio. The women cleaned up. I began helping when I was ten or eleven. Gary and Barney, being boys, were never expected to help.

There was a time when the ISIS Theater accommodated tired and stressed parents. On Christmas Day, they had a free matinee for the kids. That's where I saw most of the Disney movies like *Bambi* and *Old Yeller*. Talk about sad movies. My favorite Christmas Day movie was *The Living Desert*. I particularly liked the tarantulas. They were creepy, and I was glad there were none in Aspen.

By about three in the afternoon, the kitchen was clean, the kids were back from the movie, and it was time for games. We played bingo for a couple of years after I got a set with round balls in a cage. Most of the time, however, we played poker. We played at the dining room table. It was penny ante using buttons from our button jar as chips.

Poker could last for hours. Then as if our bodies could stand any more food, turkey sandwich fixings were put out on the table. Everyone retired to the living room for a little longer. The room was fully lit. While the tree lights were still on, it just was not the same. Every Christmas night, I felt sad and let down and thought, "I have 364 days to wait until next year."

The next day was okay. I usually stayed home and played with my new toys. I could take out the art projects or spread out a jigsaw puzzle on the dining room table. We had warmed-over leftovers for our noon dinner and turkey noodle soup for supper. The week after Christmas, I went to Ingrid's house, or she came to mine. Although it was not the best time for skiing because of crowds and the cold, we might ski at least once or twice during the remainder of the vacation.

New Year's Eve was a bit nostalgic. I never did anything that night as a child. It was a bitter reminder of how excited I had been a week earlier. Mom and Dad, on the other hand, partied. They went to the Elks Club and stayed out late. In the morning, they looked tired and smelled of bourbon and cigarettes. They brought home an assortment of noisemakers and paper hats from their party. Although it was a holy day, Dad did not make it to Mass.

New Year's Day was a good skiing day. The tourists were in about as good of shape as Mom and Dad, and therefore the slopes were empty. The kids, who got plenty of sleep, had a full day of skiing.

Other than parental hangover recovery, we had no tradition for New Year's Day or evening. Food-wise it was like any other day. Our tradition was to take down the decorations and the tree on January 2. We worried about fire and, quite frankly, I wanted to get back to normal – at least, until next year.

Winter

After Christmas and New Year's, it was winter. Winter was quiet. Everything was white – the ground, the roofs, the paths, and the roads. The nights were light. The snow reflected the starlight. With a full moon, the night glowed.

One thing I liked about winter was being home. When I was away from home, and it was snowing and dark, I longed to be there. I felt the same, whether I was two miles away or twenty. On such evenings when I was in town, I was happy when the car crossed the Castle Creek Bridge and turned for home. I knew home was cozy and secure. I could not imagine ever feeling like that anywhere else.

When I went to bed, Aspen Mountain looked like it was rising out of the trees at the edge of the yard. It was always visible from my bedroom window except when it was snowing. When it snowed, a curtain of snow and cloud descended over the rock face and obliterated the mountain from view. It made me feel like the snow enfolded me into a snuggly, white blanket.

Not everything about snow was positive. With the snow came plowing. Dad started plowing as soon as snow started collecting on the roads. He used either the D2 Caterpillar or the John Deere tractor with a loader. He kept both in the shed attached to the granary. Dad always was nervous before confirming whether they would start. Frequently the process involved swearing, but then they started.

The Cat did the best and was the quickest to get the job done. Dad plowed the driveway in front of the house, the main road from the highway, the granary road, and the lower granary road from the granary to the bale shed.

Dad waited until there was enough snow to raise the Cat's blade enough above the dirt to avoid stirring the gravel on the roads or plowing so deep that it would produce ruts. As the winter progressed, the snowbanks got higher and higher around the driveway near the house. There were times when Dad plowed near the house, and he was pushing the snow so high that the Cat, belching black smoke, looked like it was climbing to the sky. When he needed more height on the snowbanks, and the Cat couldn't climb higher, he brought out the John Deere and used the front loader to raise the snowbanks' height. In some years, the snowbanks in the driveway were eight feet tall. Regardless of their height, snowbanks were always fun for climbing, jumping, burrowing, or skiing.

Playing on the Ranch

In a typical season, the ground was not completely white until late December. What made Aspen a perfect ski resort, light, fluffy snow, made it difficult for other traditional snow activities. When the heavy snows started, I was disappointed the snow was not suitable for making snowballs or snowmen. When it worked for a snowman, we had plenty of coal for his eyes and mouth. Snow angels were always possible.

One year, the early winter snow was moist. It made perfect snowballs. That year, Gary, Barney, and I spent an entire weekend rolling snowballs in the yard. They were the size of the middle section of a typical snowman. The dried yellow grass from the dormant lawn on the balls looked like cat hair on a jacket.

We put the big balls together in a ring near the willow tree. Then we added another ring offset slightly inside, followed by another ring and another until we had a mighty fine-looking igloo, although the top was more pointed than round. We built an arched tunnel as an entry. For a moment, we thought about camping inside. We hoped Nipper would use it. I doubt if he spent any more time inside than was needed to extract the treat used to lure him inside. The igloo lasted into spring. The ring was visible after most of the lawn was bare.

To build our igloo, we needed our winter clothing. Our snowsuits were bulky. They were made of crushed or condensed wool that looked like modern microfiber, and they were lined with flannel. They were heavy, to begin with, but, as the wool collected globules of snow, they became heavier and heavier the longer we played.

The snowsuit pants were like overalls. They were high waisted and had crisscrossed straps or suspenders. Some of my snowsuits had a strap under the foot so they could be tucked into the overshoes. They had to be big enough to pull over regular clothes and shoes. The snowsuit jacket was a matching parka with a hood. Our outfits could have been the inspiration for the giant Stay Puff Marshmallow Man in *Ghostbusters*.

We wore black rubber overshoes buckled over street shoes and over the snowsuit pants. My feet froze even if they managed to stay dry. The nylon mitten covers did not prevent the woolen mittens from getting wet. So, we came into the house often to readjust or replace our gear with dry items. When playtime was over, we draped the mittens, shoes, and snowsuits on the radiators. The dining room was overwhelmed with the smell of wet wool. The overshoes stayed upside down, draining on newspapers on the porch.

We did many outdoor activities on the ranch in the first snows. There was plenty of snow, but it was not so deep it was impassable. We took out the wooden sled and tried to go down the main road, but it was not steep enough for the sled to gather momentum. So, we went down the granary road between the house and the garden. It was a short ride.

The "flying saucer" sled worked better than a traditional sled. It was a circular aluminum dish about three feet in diameter with two canvas handles. Our saucer was not entirely smooth on the bottom. It was heavily pitted and dented from hitting rocks and debris. That made it reluctant to move in anything but bone-dry snow. The best flying saucer hill was behind the granary. However, it had hidden debris that caused many of the dents.

That area had what I called a "cliff." One time when Gary, Barney, and I were playing, we took the flying saucer to the flat below the granary. One of them asked, "Hey Vicki, do you want to be an honorary Marine?"

I would do just about anything to be one of the boys. They already believed they were honorary marines because their dad was a merchant marine in World War II.

"Sure. How?"

One of them said, "You need to jump off the cliff into the snow."

The cliff was the remains of a sandstone foundation of the lixiviation works. The snow covered the building debris. Most of the wall was about fifteen feet high.

"Are you sure it's okay?"

"Yeah, we did it," one of them responded.

After surveying the situation, I found a spot in the wall closest to the riverbank that was lower than the rest of the wall. Dad destroyed several rows of the sandstone blocks when he dynamited the little chimney. This damaged section was probably ten feet above the next level. Without a bit of verification that Gary and Barney passed this test, I crossed myself and jumped into the snow. I imagine they were snickering.

Fortunately, I did not hit anything, and the snow cushioned my fall – another near-fatal event averted. It took a while to get out of the snow and make my way up to the top of the wall.

"Now, Vicki," said Gary. "You need to walk back up the house barefoot."

I complied. By the time we got home, my feet were bright red. I warmed them for a while. Then to complete the induction ceremony, I played a one-handed version of the Marine Hymn on the piano. They sang along. I thought the "Halls of Montezuma" in the lyrics referred to the Montezuma Mine, where we had our family picnics.

There were other winter ranch activities. One year we had a "skating rink." The ditch either did not get completely turned off, or a board in the headgate broke. The ditch flooded a large portion of the big field near the highway. Dad was annoyed and went up to the headgate to close it. The trip was difficult.

For us, the mistake provided a couple of days of fun skating on the undulating surface. The ice-covered area was about half a football field from the edge near the highway and east of the old ditch. After a light snow, Gary, Barney, Ingrid, and I swept paths on the ice and played Duck-Duck-Goose. I got up early for several mornings in a row to skate by myself and play fantasy games of castles and kings and princesses.

Winter at School

In my mind, winter officially began after Christmas vacation. School started the first Monday after New Year's Day. For most of my school years, girls had to wear dresses to school, even in high school and even when it was twenty degrees outside. Therefore, in elementary school, we wore our snowsuits over our dresses to play outside at recess.

Recess involved swings, slides, and monkey bars. One winter, a girl got her tongue stuck on the monkey bars. One of the kids said she was going to have it cut out like in the *Mummy* movie. That did not happen, but it took a while to get her separated from the metal bars. I suspect she pulled off some of the surface of her tongue.

The school also had giant snowbanks. There was one on the edge of the playground looking over toward Hallam Lake. The snowbank was about ten feet high and was where kids played King of the Mountain. That game involved pushing and shoving to get to and stay on the top. I tried hard, but I did not win big or lose badly. It was a game that would be frowned upon today.

School Activities

The best part of school in winter was Wednesday afternoon activities. They started right after Christmas. Every Wednesday afternoon, students participated in one of three activities – skiing, skating, or indoor activities, including art, gym games, and tumbling. For a couple of years, when the Aspen Pool was open in winter, some people swam. The kids who broke their legs skiing spent their Wednesdays indoors.

There were usually at least 15 kids with broken legs in plaster casts every winter. One year, both Gary and Jimmy had broken legs at the same time. I was jealous Gary had crutches. They looked like fun. He got pretty good at doing tricks with them.

All my siblings skied. Keith was on the ski team as was Judy for a while. Keith excelled on the team and placed on the Junior Nationals Ski Team. People remarked they knew it was Keith coming down the hill. He was taller than most of the team, and his baggy black ski pants flapped in the wind.

Judy's experience was not as good. She was the only person on the team who did not get a ski pass even though she was as good or better than the other women. They explained they had a limited number of passes. No one explained why Judy did not get a pass. Because she had no pass, she was not able to compete. It seemed passes were awarded based on popularity or political expediency rather than merit.

Peggy skied for fun. My cousins Bud, Billy, and Max raced. Max and Billy skied in college and were respectively on the 1960 and 1964 Olympic Ski Teams.

Despite being from a family of skiers, my first-grade Wednesday activity was skating. That decision was based on equipment. I skied earlier when I borrowed skis and boots from Gary or Barney, and I even took a trip up the T-Bar on Little Nell. When I did not have access to their equipment, my skis were essentially toys. They had no edges and were attached to overshoes with rubber straps. There wasn't even a bear-trap binding. The poles were made of wood dowels with pointed ends and "baskets" made from wood circles. I did, however, have a pair of Barney or Gary's used black ice skates.

On Wednesdays, everyone came to school dressed for their activity. We leaned our skis next to the school or in a snowbank. We had regular classes until noon and hot lunch of chili con carne, oyster crackers, and milk. On chili day, Mom said, "Do not drink any milk with your chili. It can make you sick." I believed that for years. I passed the same warning on to my children. Mom never said why the chili-milk combination was lethal. I never tested the theory.

After lunch, we met our instructors near the school and followed them like ducklings to one of the lifts. The older kids went to the base of Lift No. 1, and we went to Little Nell. Parents picked up their kids at the base of the lifts.

Skating

The skaters walked across the street to the rink, which was kitty-corner to the red brick school. The rink was on the corner of Bleeker and Center – the former site of the Lincoln School. The Lincoln School had been a large two-story wooden structure. Neither of my parents mentioned going there. Instead, they both went to and graduated from the Washington School.

The skating rink was on a large empty half lot someone plowed and surrounded with snowbanks. When the temperature was right, the fire department flooded it. I am not sure how they did it, but they made remarkably smooth ice. Someone took care of it by shoveling or plowing the snow. I think they used a Jeep – no Zamboni. When there was a skiff of powder, kids helped sweep with brooms.

There was a small building on the east end of the rink. It had a potbelly stove and benches for taking off and putting on skates. My first-grade skating experience was not memorable. The most memorable moment on the ice was a few years later at Ingrid's birthday party.

Ingrid's birthday was on December 29. I was jealous because she got an extra round of presents after Christmas. That is how I looked at it. She argued that they just spread the Christmas gifts over two occasions, so in the long run, she was cheated.

One year, she had her birthday party at the skating rink. About ten kids met at the rink at night. The plan was to skate for an hour or two and walk to her house for cocoa and cake. Her house was a little over two blocks from the rink. I was invited to spend the night.

I am not sure of the source of light on the rink at night. There may have been a light pole with a floodlight, and there were lights from the skating shack and a nearby building. Although it was not brightly lit, there was enough light, so as we skated around, we could see where we were going. Someone played music from the skating shack. At that time of year, the air was cold, and my nostrils stuck together.

On the night of Ingrid's party, I put on my black hand-me-down figure skates in the warming shack and put my shoes and overshoes under the bench. I wanted white skates like the ones Ingrid got for her birthday the year before. I put white skates on every Christmas list. I wanted to look like Carol Heiss, the famous American skater who I read about in the *Weekly Reader*. She wore white skates with a skating skirt. At least the black skates I was wearing that night were not the hockey skates I borrowed once. It was almost impossible to turn hockey skates. Forget trying to make figure eights.

We did free skating for a while. I was thrilled because I was learning how to skate backward, and, going forward, I could balance on one leg in a crude arabesque. After a while, some of the kids decided it would be fun to play Crack the Whip. The group of kids joined hands, and someone took the lead and started skating, and they would start making sweeping turns as they accelerated. Everyone followed. The farther back in the whip, the harder it was to hold on. The tail of the whip had a lot of movement. The point of the game was to hold on, but everyone knew the kids at the back of the line would eventually fall from the whip – the question was how long you could hold on – kind of like how long a cowboy can ride a bucking bronco.

We had been playing for a while. Then it was my turn to be at the end of the whip. One of the boys was leading. It may have been Gary or Barney. The line was going faster and faster. I lost my hold and was propelled airborne and landed on my face and skittered down the rink like a hockey puck. When I came to rest, I was dazed. I got up on my hands and knees. Then I sat on my heels with the blades pressing slightly into my buttocks. I put my hand up to my mouth – it felt odd. In the low light, I looked at my red canvas mitten. It was dark – very dark. Dark, expanding drops appeared on the ice. I could taste and smell blood. The kids came over to me. Someone said, "Gross!" or "Yuck!" Someone else helped me up, and I cupped my hand over my mouth as we made our way into the light outside the shack. Someone said they should take me across the street to Frank Garrish's house and call a doctor.

Frank was the school janitor. Frank, his wife, Maxine, and their son, Nick, lived on the corner across Center from the ice rink and across Hallam from the school. Everyone liked Frank, who kidded with the kids at school. Maxine got a towel and wiped off my face. There was lots of blood. Ingrid said she thought I must have been kicked in the mouth with a skate. Maxine called Mom and Dr. Baxter.

Mom showed up a few minutes later and looked at me and gasped, "Oh my! Oh, my God."

Maxine reassured Mom, "We called Dr. Baxter. He said, 'she'll be okay. He can't do anything tonight. Stitches won't hold. You should call him in the morning.'"

Mom looked at me, "We need to get your stuff and go home. Maxine, I'll wash the towel and bring it back tomorrow."

Ingrid, who was with me, said, "Please, Mrs. Marolt, can't she come to my house. We are going to have cocoa and open presents, and she's supposed to stay the night. Please."

"I don't think that's a good idea."

I was teary, "Please, Mommy, Please, can I go for the cocoa and presents." I'm not sure if I was crying because I was disappointed, in pain, or embarrassed.

"Please, Mrs. Marolt. Please. Just for the cocoa," Ingrid begged. Mom looked at Ingrid and at me.

"Okay. We'll get your stuff at the shack, and I'll take you to Ingrid's for a little while, but not the night."

When we got to Ingrid's house, Svea commented, "Oh, Vicki. What happened to you? Your mouth looks like it really hurts." Today she would have been calling her attorney and insurance company. Instead, she rinsed out the towel, gave it back to me. As I sat in the sitting room holding the towel on my lip, I wished I was walking home from the rink with my friends. Mom and Svea went to the kitchen and smoked.

Ingrid and the rest of the kids arrived a few minutes later. Once everyone was at the house, Svea brought out a tray of steaming cups of cocoa, each topped with marshmallows.

By this time, the shock of the injury was wearing off, and I was in pain. My lip was swollen, and I could feel the inside of my mouth was cut. There was a hole through my lip. I tried to drink the cocoa, but my lip was swollen. It was like trying to drink after a Novocain injection, and everything drizzles out. This time, my lip was not imaginarily swollen; it was swollen. I could not drink any cocoa even with a straw. I stayed for a while and watched Ingrid open a few presents. Soon, I wanted to go home.

When we got home, Mom cleaned me up and put some ice in one of those cloth, ice bags with a metal screw-on lid for me to hold over my lip. It was like one of those bags cartoon characters put on their heads to treat hangover headaches. She covered the fabric bag with a clean dishtowel so I would not ruin it with blood. The next morning, my mouth all the way below my chin was black and blue and swollen. My pillowcase was covered with blood. The ice had melted.

Mom took me to Dr. Baxter's first thing. He confirmed there was nothing he could do. He said my teeth had gone through my lower lip. The wound would just have to heal the way it was going to heal. He trimmed off a little of the tissue hanging out both inside and outside of the wound. He put some stinging antiseptic on the outside of my mouth and a bandage. He told me to swish my mouth with warm salt water several times a day for a few days. That was fine with me; I loved salt.

For the next several days, the outside of my mouth looked awful with different colored tissue, ranging from purple to red to yellow surrounding the ragged wound. The inside looked like raw hamburger. Fortunately, it was several days before school, so no one would make fun of me.

Several people commented that I was lucky. They told me stories about how another little girl lost the tips of several fingers when someone accidentally skated over them while playing the same game. She apparently lost her mitten when she fell from the line. All things considered, I agreed – I was lucky.

The next year I did not ask for skates but got a pair anyway. They were white with fake fur around the tops and red laces. Mom and Dad got them from a discount catalog. They were the closest to white skates available. They were not what I had in mind and, in so many ways, were worse than the black skates. I hid them under pants. I wished Mom and Dad would forget getting presents if they were poor substitutes for the "original." Mitzi was not Barbie, and white skates with fur were not the white skates Carol Heiss wore with her skating skirt.

Although I continued to skate from time to time, I never played Crack the Whip again. When the ice rink moved to a vacant lot across from Little Nell, my favorite thing to do after a few turns on the rink was to hike half-way up Little Nell in the moonlight and skate ski down the hill. It was fun being alone on the mountain at night. Besides, when I fell, it was soft.

My lip eventually healed but left a permanent horizontal scar below my lip. At first glance, it looked like it was cut with pinking shears. On closer inspection, it is the exact shape of three of my lower teeth – two incisors and one canine.

Skiing Activities

I started skiing as a school activity in second grade. By second grade, I had real boots, real bindings, and real poles previously used by Barney and, before him, Gary. I had a pair of baggy, black ski pants with a stirrup under the foot. I wore long underwear. I had a goldenrod nylon parka Mom got at the Thrift Shop – the used clothing store.

At the time, the Thrift Shop was at the east end of the Independence building. Svea volunteered there and did its books. We went in there mostly to donate items, but we looked around for used ski equipment and clothing. In later years when wealthy people came to town, we went to the Thrift Shop to check out their discarded expensive items, especially those that were barely worn or the ones with original price tags.

Beneath the goldenrod parka, I wore a sweater or two. I had a wool hat that tied under my chin and red canvas mittens with leather palms I wore over wool mittens. Before school on Wednesdays, I put on a pair or two of wool socks to fill up the still-too-large black ski boots. I grabbed the laces and hobbled out to the kitchen.

After breakfast, Dad sat at the table next to the window. I pulled up a kitchen chair and put my boots up on his knees. He pulled the inside laces tight and tied them. Then he methodically laced the outside laces until the boots were tight, and my ankles were secure and not able to wobble. That's the way the boots stayed until skiing was over for the day.

On my first day of activities, I sidestep up the hill with a group categorized as beginners to see how well we could ski. I was able to make several snowplow turns, so I was approved to learn how to ride the chair lift.

The Little Nell chairlift was new and replaced the old T-Bar. It was a red Riblet-double chair with a pole in the middle between the two riders. There was no safety bar. In order to teach people how to ride the new contraption, there was a wooden structure with two ramps. A chair was suspended over a landing area. The chair went back and forth like a swing.

The instructor operated the chair. Each person learning to use the chairlift sidestepped up the back side of the structure, stood on the landing, looked back over their inside shoulder, and watched the operator slowly move the chair forward. The skier grabbed the middle pole, sat down, and wriggled to the back of the chair. After the instructor swung it a few times, it was time to exit. We then wriggled forward and pushed off the edge of the seat and skied down the front ramp. Because I was short, I had to drop a little to get off the chair. After a few successful tries, I was off for the real thing a few yards away.

My first trip up the lift was with Earl Kelly, the school principal. Mr. Kelly was a large man. I was nervous as we approached the loading area. He was on the inside closest to the lift attendant. I was on the outside. I looked back over my left shoulder as the chair came around the bull wheel. As Mr. Kelly sat down, my side of the chair rose, and I was not able to get completely on the seat. As the chair swung forward, I began sliding out of the chair. Somehow Mr. Kelly grabbed me under my arms and hoisted me up. Not only was this terrifying, but I was also humiliated because when he pulled me up, my bare belly was exposed to everyone waiting in line.

After that experience, I insisted on being on the inside closest to the lift operators who could help lift me into the chair. Eventually, the operators encouraged the shorter riders to take the spot near them. I believe that became the procedure generally but have no idea whether my experience prompted the change.

Unfortunately, my first year of Wednesday activities on Little Nell was marred by yet another bad lift experience. A few Wednesdays later, I was riding the lift. This time, I was with another equal-sized kid. We were supposed to get off at Midway. The lift did not stop at Midway, so you had to be ready – tips up and on the edge of the chair to push off on the flat area and ski down the incline while the chair passed overhead.

This time, I moved from the back of the chair to the front. I dangled my legs over the edge, unwrapped one arm from the center pole, and wiggled forward, dangling my legs over the edge. For some reason, I could not get off in time, and both me and the chair passed over the landing. I was left barely sitting on the edge of the chair. I was not able to wriggle back. I was stuck. I was alone – no Mr. Kelly to hoist me into the chair. No one bothered to stop the lift.

The chair was headed to the top of Little Nell. The view of what I faced was daunting. The lift began climbing up a steep incline getting higher and higher above the ground. The terminal towered above the ground and looked to be far off in the distance. The back of the top terminal ramp sloped downhill with a wooden dam at the end. If a skier was unfortunate enough to slide down the back incline, the theory was the dam would catch them before they tumbled twenty or more feet to the ground below. Good luck with that.

I sat on the chair half-way on and half-way off. I managed to wrap one arm around the center pole while still holding my poles and the side rail. I squeezed the rail and did not breathe. I thought a hint of breath could cause me to plummet from the edge of the seat. I was at least 30 feet above the ground, and the snow below was hard. I closed my eyes and prayed. I snuck a peek every so often, hoping I was at the top. I was so alone. I was so high. I was so scared.

While I was still dangling on the edge – or so it seemed, I approached the ominous looking upper terminal. Someone must have called the lift operator in the top terminal. As I approached the landing, the lift slowed, and it came to a stop on top of the landing. I was able to scoot forward that extra inch or two and get off. Even at that, I had to drop nearly a foot to reach the surface. I had never been to the top before. The forward ramp was steep. I moved to the edge and tried to snowplow, but instead, I slid down on my back.

Now I was stuck at the top of Little Nell. This was not a great place for skiing because it was situated on the mine tailings from a mine in the Silver Queen area – perhaps the Compromise Mine. There was a spot near the base of the terminal that always had blue ice – probably from a spring of some sort. The upper part was rocky even in the best winters because it was steep and made up of mine tailings.

I was able to snowplow down a service road for several yards. But when it looked like it was going to head far away from Little Nell toward "the big mountain," I knew I had to turn onto another service road and go down part of the upper slope. Once I got back to the hill, I sidestepped down the hillside about twenty feet until I felt comfortable making a few snowplow turns and rejoin my group at Midway.

I am not sure how long I was stuck in the beginner classes on Little Nell. As the year progressed, we were moved from class to class as our skiing skills improved. There were lists of who was in who's class posted on Wednesdays. I was doing a pretty good stem christie by the end of the first year in activities. By third grade, I graduated into the intermediate group, where we did a combination of stem christies and parallel skiing.

After we mastered the basic techniques, the activities involved following the instructor down the mountain. Albina taught for a while, but I did not have her as a teacher. Mrs. Thorpe and Bill Dunaway were my teachers. The ski instructors were teachers at school, parents, and businesspeople from town. Bill Dunaway was the editor of the *Aspen Times*. His stepson, David Jones, was in one of my groups. He had a crush on me, and Mom was impressed when he asked to carry my skis when she dropped me off at school in the morning. Bill Mason was one of the owners of Mason and Morse Real Estate. He was the teacher everyone aspired to have as his or her instructor. He was a good powder skier and took his group – the top group – all over Bell Mountain after it opened in 1959.

My skiing experience improved when I graduated to Lift No. 1, which was a single chair. What a pleasure. I had grown some, so it was not as hard getting into the chair. The chair had a safety bar that the lift operator closed after boarding. The chair was covered with a light orange canvas for warmth if it was snowing or cold. The cover was very heavy and stiff. It had a small clear window that was positioned over the head, but it pretty much obscured the view. Pulling it over my head was more trouble than it was worth.

The lift was quiet. It was mostly flat when it passed over Fifth Avenue. It rose through the original Roche Run, and it ran alongside Ruthie's Run. I liked to look back and watch the town disappear. Lift No. 1 took 20 minutes from bottom to Midway. I never had a bad experience on this lift.

The terminal at Midway was gentle. Next, we took Lift No. 2 to The Sundeck. At first, it too was a single lift like Lift No. 1, but a few years later was replaced with a double Riblet like the one on Little Nell.

The single lift was not for the faint of heart. Immediately after loading onto the lift, it crossed a high spot over Tourtelotte Park. It was probably nearly 100 feet above the ground. The area was exposed and prone to wind. It was a long distance to the next tower. It had originally been a mining tram that was jury-rigged to hold chairs for a chair lift.

Once past this spot, however, it was not too high above the ground and was deep within a pine forest. I liked this part. It was silent except for the sound of a clump of snow dropping from the pine boughs and the muted squeaking of the gears as the chair approached the towers. In the spring, greasy water dripped from the melting snow on the towers. This lift had a gentle terminal at the Sundeck.

The octagon-shaped Sundeck was a warming hut and restaurant. There were a few stairs leading to the main floor – one large room with a fireplace surrounded by tables. Eventually, it added a new concentric octagonal section on the perimeter for more seating and cooking. The restrooms were downstairs. A deck attached to the back overlooked the Castle Creek and Conundrum Creek valleys.

In elementary school, we spent most of our time on the short beginner or intermediate slopes toward the top of the mountain. Most of the bad weather skiing I ever did was on activity days. I doubt Wednesdays were snowier than other days, but we skied regardless of weather conditions. There was someone to follow, so flat light was not a really big factor. Further, misery loves company. On the other hand, when I was paying for a ticket, I thought twice before going out on a really cold day or when it was snowing. I knew once I committed to buying a ticket, I had to stay all day. On Wednesdays, I liked the snowy days with the school group.

Recreational Skiing

During weekends and vacations, I usually skied with Gary and Barney. Sometimes I skied with Ingrid and other girlfriends. The usual plan was to get to Lift No.1 and be one of the first on the lift when it opened. When Mom dropped me at the lift, she gave me $1.25 or $1.50. The ticket cost $.75. Luds Loushin sold tickets at this lift – he was one of Dad's friends. The tickets were made of cardboard about an inch and a half by an inch with a reinforced hole punched through the top. Luds stamped the date on the ticket. I took a metal ball chain from a box and hooked it to a zipper on my parka. The goal was to get a new chain every time we skied so we could snap them together to see who had the longest chain at the end of the year.

The routine with Gary and Barney was to head straight to the Sundeck and ski the top of the mountain until lunch. We went down One and Two Leaf, Dipsy Doodle, and my favorite, Silver Bell, and rode up Lift No. 3. Lift No. 3 was a completely different kind of lift. It was double, but there was no pole in the middle, no safety bar, and it was green. It also led to The Sundeck, but it had a kind of scary high span over Dipsy Doodle.

Our last run of the morning was down Buckhorn or on the Buckhorn Cut-Off, which was on the westernmost ridge of the mountain. From this run, there was a road to the top of Ruthie's run. If we went fast enough, we could make it without having to herringbone up the slight incline at the end.

Sometimes when we were on Ruthie's, we schussed from the second tower, depending on the tracks and the crowd. We then went down Ruthie's to what we called Howard Awrey's at the bottom. Its real name was the Skier's Chalet or Skier's Café. Lunch there was about half the price of lunch at The Sundeck. Howard did not have to pay the cost of bringing in supplies by chair lift. With my remaining money, I bought a hamburger for a quarter and a Squirt for a nickel. That left enough for cocoa at The Sundeck in the afternoon. After lunch, we went back to The Sundeck for more skiing. The goal this time was to see if we could make it down to the bottom for the last ride on the No. 1 lift. The lift closed at 3:30 p.m.

Most of the time, the last run was down Ruthie's, but sometimes we came down Sparr Gulch and took the Magnifico Cut Off to Magnifico or Fifth Avenue and down to the base of the Lift No. 1. If I skied with Gary and Barney, we skied as far as we could down the streets to their house. It was only about four or five blocks from the ski hill, and usually, there was plenty of snow on the streets because although they were plowed, they were not plowed down to the dirt street.

When we got to their house, Pearl made Ovaltine, cocoa, or tea. I could finally loosen the tight boots. It felt so good. I rubbed my toes, which were always numb, either from the cold or from lack of circulation.

If I was not skiing with Gary and Barney, Luds let me use his phone to call Mom, and she met me at the parking lot below the lift. I opened a window in the back seat of the car so the skis could stick out.

When I skied with Ingrid or other girlfriends, it was more casual. We laughed a lot and did our fair share of "timber bashing," especially near One and Two Leaf. It was not real timber bashing – skiing fast in a heavily wooded area through powder. It was more or less walking through the deep snow between trees to the next run. It often involved falling over and giggling and expending our energy, trying to stand up in the soft snow. Sometimes, I pretended to timber bash as an excuse to get out on my own and relieve myself behind a tree if I had been laughing too hard.

When the Bell Mountain lift opened, we talked the lift attendant into letting us ride three in a chair because the seat on that lift was extra wide, and there was a safety bar to hold in the middle person. That was a good thing because the span over Copper Bowl was pretty scary. I think that distance to the ground was not as high as the Tourtelotte Park span but high enough. I closed my eyes or looked straight ahead going over it and prayed it would not stop or bounce. The sound of the far away wheels on the tower was reassuring.

Skiing was a normal part of my week. It was an unusual weekend when I did not ski at least once. This continued until the lifts closed in March or sometimes April. Ironically, that is when we could get heavy snows, and we would finally get that great wet snow for making snowmen.

Winterskol and the Torch Light Parade

Christmas was a busy time in town. It was the prime season for tourists. The town was bustling. Then a day or two after New Year's Day, the town was dead.

Although it was the coldest time of the year, it was the best time for skiing. After Christmas, the tourists had gone home. Often, we could ski up to the chair without waiting in line – talk about getting in a record number of runs. The business owners were not happy because it meant with no tourists; they were not making money. Therefore, someone came up with the idea of having a winter event that would bring people to town during this off-season. They started Winterskol. It was four or five days of events in which the residents and businesses participated.

As with many manufactured "events," there was a parade. Restaurants and businesses sponsored floats on hay sleds emulating their businesses festooned with partying employees. There were snow bunnies and snow piled high on wagons and trucks. There were high school bands and bagpipe players. One year, soldiers from the Army's 10th Mountain Division marched, followed by marching ski patrolmen and instructors. Individuals wore costumes and walked their dogs. There were the dog sleds from Toklat and horses and riders and horses pulling decorated sleds. Frequently, we loaned our hay sled for one of the floats.

During the festivities, there were dances, movies, talent shows, and there may have been a queen. There were ski races both for bona fide racers and for novice skiers including costume and three-legged races. I don't remember ever attending any of these events. I went to the parades but never participated in them.

The best and most exciting part of the Winterskol for me was the fireworks at the opening – or was it the closing – ceremony.

The fireworks display was situated in the same place it was for the Fourth of July – shot off from the road near the Straw Pile on Aspen Mountain. The color and reflection against the white snow on the broad mountain slopes was spectacular. The side of the mountain ranged from pink to blue to yellow and green matching the showering lights in the sky.

Before the fireworks display was the torchlight parade. This was the only event in which I participated. I was one of the hundreds of people who took part. About any Aspen person who could ski showed up. We boarded the Little Nell lift in the dark without poles. I liked not having poles because I could hold on more tightly. As we started up the hill, we could see our shadows in front of us moving up the mountain. The lights from the town and at the bottom of the hill were enough to make these shadows that slowly disappeared the higher we rode. The lift ride was quieter than during the day. Maybe it was because no one seemed to talk. As I rode, I fantasized how nice it would be to ski on a moonlit night. It would be so cool to have the bumps and moguls highlighted with moon shadows.

We rode the lift to the top of Little Nell. The ride was not too long, and that was good because the January nights were exceptionally cold. When we got off the lift, we went down the Magnifico cut-off, took the first switchback toward Little Nell, and waited in line. When we got to the front of the line, people were igniting the ends of long torches and handing two to each of the skiers. We held them up and out in front at the same level our poles would have been. Each skier followed the skier in front and zigzagged down the hill.

The skiing was easy – just snow plow and follow the person in front. I doubt if many fell. I didn't. In later years, I think they added some more choreography to the event by having the skiers start at different sides and crisscrossed each other's lines. When I was taking part, it was simple – just one line. The line grew until there was a continuous line of light on the side of the hill. From Red Mountain, it looked like lights on a child's drawing of a Christmas tree. At the bottom, we turned in our torches and received our reward – hot cocoa.

St. Patrick's Day Dinner

The final event of the winter season was Saint Patrick's Day. The Church held a Saint Patrick's Day dinner in the classrooms and sold tickets to tourists and townspeople. The meal, prepared in the kitchen, was beef and pork roasts, coleslaw, mashed potatoes, rolls, cake and ice cream, and a few beverages. Parish women baked the cakes.

The diners sat at long tables running north and south in the two rooms. Svea Elisha and Frances Kalmes were usually in charge of the meal preparation. The Catholic women and men sat in the church kitchen and peeled potatoes, sliced cabbage, and cooked the meat.

The junior high and high school kids served the meals and bussed the tables. We wore white shirts and black skirts or pants and something green. The tables were covered with butcher paper and decorated with paper shamrocks. I served meals a couple of times. I remember it being fun but a lot of work. For the most part, no one fussed too much when the food did not come out right. However, given that limited experience, I was pretty sure I did not want to wait tables on a regular basis.

The Catholic Church was a big part of our lives. Everyone was concerned when the roof nearly collapsed from heavy snow in 1956. They added iron rods near the ceiling to keep the walls from spreading apart because of the weight of snow. They also added a metal roof to prevent snow buildup.

Then, sometime after Vatican II, the upstairs of the church underwent a major remodel. Parish men, including Dad, did most of the work. They removed the pews, the communion rail, and installed a new heating system. While the work was in progress, we attended Mass in a chapel on the first floor's west side. To accommodate the small space, there were several extra masses on Sunday.

Once construction was complete, they installed red carpeting over the creaky wood floors. Although the high altar and the two smaller altars were left as they had been, because of Vatican II, a table-like structure was added in front of the high altar so the priest would say Mass facing the parishioners. Because of changes both in the method of delivering communion and because laymen and women were allowed in the sanctuary as lay readers, there was no need for the communion rail, and it was not replaced. I was disappointed; I liked it. It fenced off the sanctuary and made it mysterious. Besides, it was pretty.

As a girl, I would never be allowed back there; the only female who ever had that right was Mary Babic, who was in charge of the linens on the railing and the altar. I do not believe even the nuns were allowed to enter that area. At the time, I did not think too much about the fact that girls were treated differently than men and boys. In fact, I was not jealous of the altar boys because they had to go to daily Mass when it was their week to serve.

The St. Patrick's dinner was the start. In the spring, the Church dominated our lives.

Spring

After the first major snow, we no longer had access to the fields. Because we stopped raising cattle year-round, they were no longer in the fields in winter, and the horses wintered in the corral between the barn and the granary. There were no other animal trails across the fields. No one in my family ever used snowshoes or cross-country skis to access the field. Why would they need to?

The only time I heard of any family using large wooden snowshoes or skis to trek across the snow was when Mom, Polly, and Albina went to Polly's cabin for a night. They packed food, raided the liquor cabinet, built a fire with the wood stored by the fireplace, and lit the Coleman lamps. I wished I could have gone with them.

During the winter, our house, the small field, and the south side of the big field were in the shadow of Aspen Mountain until late morning. At first, spring looked a lot like winter. Everything was covered with snow, and we could still get some of the heaviest snows of the year. What set spring apart was the noticeably increasing hours of daylight.

About a month after the shortest day, Mom began following the location of the sun as it moved north along the ridge of Aspen Mountain. She stood at the kitchen window, mentally marking the spot on the ridge where the sun appeared. Once the sun rose on a certain spot, she knew there would be many more minutes of direct sun on the house and the fields within a day or two and would increase each day thereafter. By the time Mom was monitoring the sun, I had a pent-up desire for uninhibited movement around the ranch.

With the increased sunlight, there was a lot of freezing and thawing. The surface of the snow formed a crust layer about an inch thick. It was strong enough to hold my weight. Norwegians refer to this phenomenon as Skaresnø. It is created either from thawing and freezing or from sustained winds.

With Skaresnø I had instant access to parts of the ranch unreachable during winter. There were one or two optimal days and then only a very short window during the day for crust walking. I could only walk early in the morning when it was light but before the sun hit the surface of the snow. Once that happened, the crust weakened and would no longer support my weight. I might be trapped in the middle of nowhere.

The morning after a warm and sunny day, I got up at first light and put on my jeans, shoes, a jacket, hat, and overshoes, which I really didn't need unless the crust broke. I climbed to the top of a snowbank on the south side of the driveway and descended to the undisturbed snow on its backside. I tested the surface, and if the snow was solid and hard, I could stand and walk as if on concrete. As I stepped, there was a hollow sound. It was like the sound when I rolled down one of the Great Sand dunes near Alamosa. A couple of days earlier, I would have sunk up to my armpits.

I headed directly to the small cattle shed as the crow flies. In summer, I would go a hundred feet to the end of the driveway and through a gate to get there. A direct path would have involved climbing through the barbed wire fence and climbing in and out of the rocky cocklebur-covered ravine next to the Midland railroad bed. Because of the magic of crust walking, I could step over the one exposed wire of the fence, which was only a few inches above the snow. The ravine was now only a slight depression in the blanket of white.

I was fascinated by the first look inside the cattle shed. The snow angled down past the entrance for a couple of feet to where it drifted into the shed's opening. Beyond the apron of drifted snow, the ground inside was dry. That's where the baling equipment and the pickup were stored. There were still horseshoe and boot prints undisturbed since the day Dad decided to move the horses. As I looked at the footprints, I imagined I was an explorer stumbling upon this scene frozen in time because of some apocalyptic event. It reminded me of the photograph in my archeology book of a dog from Pompeii turned to stone as he scratched his ear. Both scenes gave me a shiver.

After a few minutes in the shed lending my own footprints to the mix, I climbed the gentle incline out of it and walked to a mound of boulders about a third of the way into the little field. There was no explanation for the mound's existence. The boulders were big, but unlike the ones on the other side of the river, there was no obvious reason for them to be in the middle of flat land. Like the boulders on the other side of the river, they were surrounded by chokecherry bushes and were the best chokecherries on our side of the river.

In the summer, I used the rocks as a place to mount Patty when bareback riding. This was Peggy's favorite part of the ranch. She spent countless hours sitting on the rocks shielded by the bushes and daydreaming. I now suspect these were some of the boulders Dad encountered when he built the Holden Ditch, and he decided to pile them in one place. In the winter, the boulders were barely visible. On the back side, there was a small cave. I fanaticized it was a home for a family of foxes.

From there, I crossed the rest of the little field to the picnic grounds. As far as I knew, no one had ever seen the picnic grounds in winter. The Holden Ditch was barely visible, covered in white. The lean-to was nestled in the bare aspen trees. I could not get closer than the end of the parking area near Bill's potato patch because the crust stopped. The picnic area did not yet receive any direct sun, so there was no rapid melting and freezing. For most of the winter, it was in a permanent shadow.

I turned around and stood at the potato digger. Its rusty seat was just above the surface of the snow. I looked out on a vast ocean of white. I could see the house across the little field and Red Butte beyond the big field. I walked quickly directly into the big field, stepping over a barbed wire separating the two fields. I moved to the center of the south half of the big field and wondered if anyone but me ever stood in this very spot on top of three feet of snow. It never occurred to me that my sisters, who had also been crust walkers, also stood there.

Now it was critical to keep an eye out for the sun because this is the first place the sun hit when it rose over the ridge of Aspen Mountain. Once it came up, there were only a few precious minutes to get home before the crust began to soften. If that happened, I might get caught in chest-high snow.

One time I waited too long. I was within 20 feet of the snowbanks. As I stepped, the crust broke, and one leg suddenly dropped below the surface. On the way down, my pant leg went up, and the crust scratched and scraped the bare skin of my shin. I threw myself forward on my stomach and pulled my leg out from under the crust. I moved in a combination of crawling and swimming until I made it to the snowbank – a beach of solid ground.

There were maybe one or two more days of unobstructed crust walking. The second day was not nearly as fun as the first. Sometimes,

I could see a faint impression of my footprints from the day before and was fascinated that they were larger than my feet. I might check to see if there were signs of foxes in the snow cave and then spend most of the time in the big field. As I stepped over the barbed wire, I noticed it was several inches higher than it was the day before. Today's challenge was to see how much territory I could cover in the big field before having to return home.

Within a few days, the white ocean faded as once buried brush popped out of the surface. Areas on the south side of the boulder pile were getting bare. A second wire appeared on the fence. As the days went by, the bare areas grew so that there was more brown than white in the fields. That signaled the time to begin my next favorite spring activity – playing river.

When the patches of dirt started appearing behind the snowbanks and in the driveway, I knew there soon would be puddles of melting snow forming in the dark earth. A few days later, the tracks from the cars began to melt down to the dirt. Mom would say, "The bottom fell out of the road."

Now the goal was to take the water from the big puddles in the driveway and create a series of "rivers" to drain the water further and further down the main road – all the way to the cattle guard.

I could spend hours with a garden hoe and my rubber overshoes creating a series of locks from the driveway, down the main road, and ending in the open space under the cattle guard. The main road was perfect for this activity. It declined slightly its entire length. It was only recently that I realized why playing river only worked on this road and not on the other roads around the ranch. The granary road was mostly flat from the main road and then dropped precipitously to the granary. It was flat from there to the cattle guard.

There was something meditative about playing river. Once the series of locks were complete, I started at the driveway and broke the gates of each lock on the main road allowing the water to drain to the next lock – break that gate and on and on until a large stream of water cascaded into the concrete-lined area beneath the cattle guard. It continued flowing for an hour or more.

Unfortunately, often, someone drove on the main road before the process was complete. If Mom or Dad saw me playing river, they did their best to avoid disturbing my work. However, if someone else came up the main road, they destroyed large sections I had to repair.

The next morning, I returned to the project, but until the sun came out, much of it was frozen with panes of ice over empty puddles. Once it started melting again, I went back to work. I repeated this process day after day until no more puddles formed and the snowbanks subsided into the drying land. I doubt if my hard work hastened the melting process, but it was satisfying, nonetheless.

This was about the time of the year Dad kept his eye on the rivers to see how high they were getting. I don't think he had a concern for our property because the river was so far below the main part of the ranch; flooding was not an issue. There may have been some worrying about the headgates breaking.

One time after supper, Dad said, "Let's go see what's going on up the Roaring Fork. I hear it's flooding up the Pass." We loaded into the car and drove through town toward Independence Pass. Starting above Christine Sparovic's house, the dark water was fanning out from the normally meandering river over what had been meadows. The Sparovic house was on the bank of the Roaring Fork in an area known as Stillwater. Below their house, toward town, the river made a steep descent and broke into rapids. The drop saved their house from flooding.

The Sparovic house was a new single-story ranch house. On the long south side, big windows overlooked Stillwater and the mountains in the background. It was a gorgeous view. Besides the view, their kitchen was a big open room with enough space for a couch and some chairs by a fireplace. It was a "great room" design before its time.

Below the Sparovic house was another noteworthy piece of property. About a half of a mile closer to town, the rapids stopped, and the river made a sharp turn toward the west. There was more deep, still water and an island at a bend in the river. The still water went in front of a long sloping meadow. A house sat at the top of the slope overlooking the water. Dad commented that he thought this piece of property was nearly as pretty as our ranch. At one time, it belonged to Roger Dixon, a Texan who spent only part of the year in Aspen. Celia cleaned the house. One time I went with her, and while she worked, a friend and I swam and sunbathed on the island.

We passed the Sparovic house and continued further up the Pass to the bridge to James Smith's property, which is now the North Star Preserve. Mr. Smith owned a lot of acreage in the Stillwater area. He built his own private bridge from the highway across the river to a higher spot on which he built a modern house. The Smiths were new to town and were trying their hand at ranching. I remember them as having red hair.

At the Smith's bridge, the water began lapping at the edge of the road. It was nearly to the bottom of their bridge. Dad commented, "In all my years here, I've never seen anything like this." He added, "I hope their bridge doesn't wash out. I bet they spent a bunch of money on it."

From here for several miles, all the way up the river to the end of the Stillwater, most of the valley floor was covered with water. The meandering river was gone. Fortunately, there were no major structures to flood. I never saw it like that again.

For some reason, a lot seemed to happen in the spring near Stillwater. When looking for signs of spring, we looked for flowers on a hillside above Christine's house. Her father owned a trailer park across the highway, and much of it was on the hillside. When we hiked up the hillside in early spring, we found spring beauties and what we called "May flowers." The May flowers were about 6 inches tall, blue blooms, and soft fuzz on the stems and under the bloom. The delicate blooms rarely survived being picked, let alone being transported to our houses.

They may have been Pascal flowers, which was appropriate this time of year. Easter was a big holiday for our family. During Lent, besides giving up something such as candy or dessert, we went to the Stations of the Cross every Friday evening. The stations went around the outside aisles of the nave where the statues and crucifixes were covered with purple cloths.

Then there was Holy Week. Quite frankly, I did not look forward to this week. Some of the services were in the evening. I would rather be doing just about anything other than going to Church. Holy Thursday was one of the events. It was a reenactment of the Last Supper. The most interesting part was when the priest washed the feet of twelve men from the community. Dad participated in this part of the service a few times, but the ritual embarrassed him.

Good Friday services began early in the afternoon. The service seemed to last for hours – it probably did. It did not include a Mass. I remember walking home after one of the services. Apparently, I must have gone alone. I only went in the first place because part of the deal, for Catholic kids to get out of school, was we had to go to Church.

That Good Friday in late spring, I walked home up Main Street. The street was paved down the middle but had gravel shoulders. Most of the snow had melted, and the ground was bare. The grass in the adjacent lawns was yellow and matted. Flies buzzed near my feet, where I stepped. The sun was surprisingly hot.

Good Friday and the next day were big days for cooking for Easter breakfast. In today's terms, we would call it brunch, but at the time, we did not use such fancy words. Dad's Slovenian background was the source of our Easter breakfast tradition. Mom made potica and krofé, two traditional Easter foods. Both involved raised dough.

Mom made potica using her basic roll dough. She spread a sheet on the kitchen table, sprinkled it with flour, and rolled it to the edge of the table. She painted on beaten eggs, followed by butter, and sprinkled it with a dusting of cinnamon. On top of that was a cooked mixture of chopped walnuts, cream, sugar, and cinnamon with a few graham cracker crumbs. Then she sprinkled on white raisins. The potica was rolled into a long roll. She circled it around in an angel-food cake pan and let it rise. It was baked golden brown until it sounded hollow when tapped.

Krofé was made with richer bread dough – it had more butter, sugar, and eggs. It was rolled until it was about three-eighths of an inch thick and cut into rounds with a water glass. The krofé was cooked in lard in a deep fat fryer. It expanded to make a slightly flattened ball. I liked watching them cook and then flipping them over. They were drained on brown paper. We ate krofé like a donut by rolling it in sugar or cinnamon sugar. Otherwise, they were cut open and piled high with ham and horseradish and eaten like a sandwich. Bill made good horseradish from plants he found in a secret place in the woods.

We boiled eggs and dyed them. We did nothing fancy; we used one of the Paas dye packages. The dyes were from a tablet that was dissolved in water with a little vinegar.

Unlike Christmas, where we went to midnight Mass, I only remember going to the Easter vigil Mass once. It was another one of those long Easter-week ceremonies. It started with a long procession with lots of prayers to bless the Paschal candle and the holy water. At our Church, part of the procession lead down the stairs, and the blessing occurred on the lower landing. Those in attendance watched from the stairs. Then everyone returned to the main church for Easter Midnight Mass.

As far as I was concerned, there was no benefit to going to this service. There was no reason to be able to stay home in the morning. While there may have been Easter eggs to hunt, it was not even close to the excitement of Christmas morning. Besides, I liked wearing my new Easter outfit. I got a new dress, a new coat, a hat, and new white socks to go with my black patent leather Mary Janes.

On Easter Sunday, there was no early Mass. The first Mass was at 9:00 a.m., and there may have been another Mass at eleven. Therefore, in the morning, we had time before getting ready for Church to hunt for "eggs." We never looked for the real eggs because the egg hunt was always indoors. Instead, our Easter Bunny brought jellybeans. One of his favorite hiding places was in crevices in the basalt rock fireplace. The Easter Bunny also brought each of us a chocolate bunny or a chocolate egg in an Easter basket with green cellophane straw. Because we could not eat anything before communion, we had to wait until after Mass for a taste of candy.

Then we got dressed for Mass. My sisters were in the choir. Although Mom was not a Catholic, she went to Church on Easter. Everyone wanted to wear their new Easter clothes. When we returned from Mass, we set out the food that had been simmering while we were gone. The food was replenished for much of the morning and into the afternoon as people stopped by. There was no formal sit-down time to eat, and people ate what they wanted when they wanted as if it were a buffet.

Our breakfast was heart attack central. There was potica, krofé, and eggs. Also, we had a bone-in ham – one of those hams with a rind and marbled with lots of fat. We also had klobasa.

There was absolutely nothing green on the holiday menu unless it was a green dyed Easter egg. The food was good and seemed especially good after the restrictions from Lent, but after one piece of everything, I had a bit of indigestion. Fortunately, we did not have to go for a ride down the valley after that meal.

Besides Easter, spring involved more participation in special events at the Catholic Church. In May, we had the living rosary and the crowning of the May Queen. The Madonna statue from the little altar was placed on a high platform in the yard between the church and the rectory. The platform was draped with a white cloth. There was a set of white stairs leading to the platform.

The crowning of the May Queen came after the living rosary. The rosary was made up of children and young adults from the Church. The ten bead sections were ten girls, each wearing different pastel-colored dresses -- pink, blue, green, yellow, and lavender. The dresses were sleeveless cotton covered in a layer of nylon tulle and then dyed. The girls wore matching veils made with nylon tulle on headbands. The dresses were used year after year and stored in a closet on the main floor of the church. From time to time, they needed to be replaced. One could always tell the new dresses because the colors never quite matched.

The "Our Father" and "Glory Be to the Father" beads were made up of altar boys. The priest represented the crucifix and carried the processional crucifix. Three high-school girls were selected to be the "May Queen" and her attendants. They represented the initial three Hail Mary beads. There were also two little-girl attendants.

Peggy was the May Queen one year. I was a little-girl attendant when I was five. The May Queen was dressed essentially as a bride with a white dress and a veil. The older attendants were like bridesmaids, and smaller attendants carried the flower crown. The event culminated when the May Queen ascended the stairs and placed a crown of flowers on Madonna's head. The flowers were almost always carnations dyed to match the rosary beads.

When I was an attendant, I remember it was bright with the sunshine reflected off the draped white platform and the attendants' white dresses. My eyes could not stay open, and they watered. I never got a chance to be May Queen because the tradition stopped before I was in high school.

Not everything in the spring revolved around Church. Spring was a busy time on the ranch. One of the first tasks after the snow was gone was to turn on the irrigation ditches. The Red Butte Cemetery Association was instrumental in getting the ditch turned on in the spring to make sure water was flowing on Decoration Day, now known as Memorial Day. Kenneth Maurin, who took care of the cemetery, wanted to make sure there was a water source for flowers placed on the graves by relatives and friends. The Marolts gave some water rights to the cemetery in exchange for the Marolt plot and perpetual care.

Dad and the other men walked the Marolt Ditch bed up-stream from the house and removed any debris, which consisted of fallen trees, branches, and dead grasses. They removed patches of silt from the previous year's flow. This ditch had a few sections that included wooden flume-like structures overhanging the bank. These needed to be thoroughly checked for any decay or damage and repaired.

The Holden Ditch by the picnic grounds was much more exposed and therefore did not have nearly as many problems with vegetation. However, the upper section was below the Castle Creek Road and a steep hillside. Rocks sloughed from the hills into the ditch bed. Some of the rocks could be removed by hand. Others required the tractor or the bulldozer.

Dad had a plan to place large pipes in the ditch in this area to prevent rocks from filling the channel. That's why he collected large corrugated-metal pipes he stored in the scrub triangle. While stored, they provided hours of fun. I walked on them and hid in them. Some were the perfect height for getting on Patty to ride bareback.

The ditch clearing took days, and I was always impatient. Once the ditches were clear, Dad went to the headgates and opened the gates' sections. In the spring, because of high water, the gates only needed to be opened a little. As the high water receded, they were opened wider, so we got our allotted amount of water. Mom worried about this process. She worried Dad might slip and be swept away by raging waters.

Often, upon picking me up at school, Mom announced, "Daddy turned on the ditch today." I was delighted when we crossed the culvert and saw the water flowing.

Sometimes I was there when Dad came back and said the ditches were on. I expected the water to start flowing immediately, but it took hours before the water made its way to the yard. I ran up the ditch to find the leading edge. Even after Dad cleared the larger items, there were still leaves and other detritus making it look like flowing lava. It was so exciting lying on the granary bridge to see the brown water approaching. It would be many weeks before the water finally cleared. In the meantime, the settling silt made the little nooks perfect for minnows.

Another spring activity was to walk along the ditch to find pussy willows while they still had the fuzzy catkins. Pussy willows were our primary spring flowering plant. From time to time, if the conditions were right, we had some spring beauties such as the ones above the Sparovic trailer park in the melted areas in the upper scrub triangle. They were visible for only a short time. When we found them, we were assured that spring had arrived on the ranch.

We used pussy willow branches for the early spring bouquets around the house. Often the bouquets stayed as they were when they were picked weeks or months without any water. One of my favorite spring projects was to make pictures using the soft furry catkins. The easiest way was to draw a fence and glue a vertical catkin on the fence and draw a tail dangling over the top rung. Next, I added on a round head made of half a catkin and drew some pointy ears and whiskers. The cats always faced away from the viewer, looking toward a distant horizon.

Once the ditches were full, the next spring chore was for Dad to "brush the meadows." Once the snow left, the hay stubble was flat and yellow, and the area was covered with dirt piles made by gophers over the fall and winter. To bring the fields back to life, he knocked down the goffer holes, broke up the dead vegetation, and stirred up the soil. Originally, he literally dragged brush lashed behind the tractor – hence the name. Later, he built a device that included heavy chains dragged behind the tractor. After brushing the meadows, Dad brought out the manure spreader and covered the ground with a thin layer of dry manure he had prepared near the red barn. Then it was time for the first round of irrigation.

Within a few days, after Dad completed brushing the meadows, adding the fertilizer, and having the first round of irrigation, the ground turned an emerald green with the new alfalfa sprouts. It was the beauty of Dad's newly brushed meadows that cause Lenny Thomas to convince Dad to sell the big field to him.

The next important activity was horseshoeing. Because the horseshoes were removed before the winter, we could not ride the horses for more than a short ride in the field until they were shod. I was anxious to ride, so I got a bridle or hackamore and put it on Patty. I did my best to brush her back. This time of the year, it was still covered with her winter coat and was dusty. It was fun to use the currycomb to get the big clumps of hair off her. I then climb on her back for a short ride. Regardless of how much I brushed her before those first spring rides, I got off her, and the inside of my jeans was covered with hair and dirt.

It was a treat to come home from school and have Mom report, "Daddy shod the horses today." I'm not sure she liked making this announcement. For as free as we were to run around the ranch and the bodies of water without any restriction, Mom had a fear of horses, and her warnings and fear made me a little timid at times.

At first, Dad did the shoeing. He and Steve had lots of horses to shoe over the years, including the workhorses. They had an anvil and all the farrier tools. I liked watching Dad when he put the horse's hoof between his legs and trimmed it. The horses didn't seem to mind. I could not watch when he nailed on the shoe even though I knew it did not hurt.

In later years, Dad had Bob Zick or Jack Ray do most of the shoeing. Bob Zick was Bea Zick's husband. She was the bookkeeper for Beck & Bishop, and the Zicks were Steve's neighbors. Jack Ray was a local cowboy who owned a stable in town. He also owned a café across from Little Nell. Dad exchanged horseshoeing for a small pasture by the river bottom Jack used for his horses. Both Bob and Jack were efficient farriers. Dad approved of their work.

Then it was time for Dad to go to Glenwood or Rifle to the livestock auction and buy 25 steers to fatten throughout the summer. He had them shipped to the ranch and off-loaded on the cattle chute by the red barn. I never saw them delivered. Suddenly, the red barn corral had a new group of Herefords. Later, we moved them from pasture to pasture around the ranch. In the spring, they spent most of the time in or near the corral eating hay. Once the new grass was established, we moved them across the field to the property on the other side of the Castle Creek Road next to the old ranch.

I remember a few years when we also took the cattle to a field on the west side of the old ranch now owned by Jimmy Moore. In later years it became the location of the Aspen schools. These fields provided most of the pasture the cattle needed until the hay was harvested.

In conjunction with the arrival of the cattle, one of my favorite chores was to get on Patty and follow the fences in the pastures and along the hillsides to make sure they did not need repair before the cattle arrived. If I spotted a problem, I marked it and reported to Dad. Breaks were rare.

Besides ranch chores, there were house chores. Each spring, Dad removed the storm windows on the house. They were wooden-framed panes that covered the entire window and hung from the top on bracketed hinges from which they could be lifted and removed. Dad stored them in the granary, and Mom washed the outside of the regular windows. She washed the sheer curtains and took them to Mrs. Babic to put on the stretchers she used for the church linens. We also washed the blankets and bedspreads and aired the pillows on the clothesline. It was sheer heaven to sleep on a fresh pillow after a day hanging on the line.

Eventually, Mom and Dad decided it was too much work to remove the storm windows. Instead, we left them on and propped them open for fresh air. They had a hinge at the top, and we held them open with a board wedged in the windowsill. If there was no board available, a book worked. We ended up with quite a few warped books that fell out of the windows onto the damp ground. I loved having my window open at night. Not only was the air cool and fresh, but there was also the soothing sound of Castle Creek in the distance.

Like the field, the yard needed to awaken from its winter sleep. We raked and fertilized it by hand. Then Mom planted the garden. Dad brought up the walk-behind tractor to prepare it for planting and stirred up the dirt with the disk harrow attachment. This was the only time I remember him using the walk-behind tractor he normally stored under the granary porch. I suspect others borrowed it.

After Dad turned over the soil, he added some of the dry fluffy manure from behind the red barn. He made sure there were trellises for the beans and peas. He dug the trenches for irrigation water to come from the small diversion box from the main ditch. After marking the rows, I helped plant the seeds and some of the starts. Mom planted according to the weather and made sure nothing came up before the last frost.

We also planted flowers such as nasturtiums by the sidewalk and sweet peas along the back of the house. In early summer, not only was there a hedge of lilacs in the yard, we filled the house with bouquets of them everywhere. The smell of lilacs filled the air. In July, we filled the house with bouquets of the pink, lavender, white, and yellow sweet peas. Mom was famous for their size and colors.

Mom also put geraniums in planters on the porches. Dad's cousin, Pauline "Sis" Davis, and her husband, Gene, owned a greenhouse in Salida. When they came to Aspen for "Decoration Day," they brought small geraniums along with wreaths and flowers used for the family graves in the Red Butte Cemetery. The geraniums stayed in the backroom until Mom was sure there was no more frost. She brought some of them in the fall, and we had flowers on the low wall in the back porch for most of the winter.

In the spring, I do not remember any significant events at school – except getting out. There were no special spring sports or games. There may have been a softball game or two and a picnic in Wagner Park, but that was about it. School always ended the Friday before Decoration Day. For most people, that was the beginning of summer vacation – not for me. Remember, for me, spring was about Church.

Unlike the rest of the school, the Catholic kids' summer vacation had to wait two more weeks. The week after regular school was out, we attended what we called "sister school." We did not get enough religious training from our weekly catechism classes to make up for not going to parochial school.

I liked going to catechism class mainly because Ingrid's mother picked us up at school to take us to the church. She brought treats – candy bars, Twinkies, powdered-sugar donuts, or fruit leathers. Women from the Church taught the classes – some of them, such as Elva Fitzpatrick, also taught at school.

Sister school wasn't nearly as fun. Several nuns from the archdiocese parochial schools in Denver came to Aspen to provide enhanced religious training. We went six days a week from 8:00 a.m. to 12:00 p.m. I don't remember too much about what we learned. There were coloring books with bible pictures. We memorized a lot of the prayers that I can recite to this day. When it was time for our first communion or confirmation, the sessions became a lot more intense. In preparation for confirmation, we needed to memorize prayers and be prepared to answer any number of questions.

We had recess and jumped rope and played seven-up. The nuns, who wore full habits, watched with their hands in their pockets, under the scapular, or fingering the wooden rosaries attached to their belts. Some of the nuns ominously swung their rosary beads when they looked angry. They made loud clicking sounds with their hard shoes when they walked down the first-floor hall. Some of the nuns were nice, but most were stern, and some were downright mean.

One of my first experiences was not good. I believe it was in my first or second year of school. One nun was lecturing us about why it was important for us to be good all the time. She then went on and on about how our parents should be good too. The reason was that it was possible we might wake up one morning, and our parents would be dead, and they would go to Hell because they died with sins on their souls.

I was troubled. At that time, Dad was a sporadic Catholic. He went to Church on the holidays but did not attend weekly Mass. Instead, I went to Church with my sisters. So, he had a problem "keeping holy the Lord's Day." Mom was not a Catholic, so that was an even bigger problem. Besides, until that day, it had never occurred to me that my parents could die.

That day after sister school, I went to play with Martha Coble. She lived with her mother, her brother, and her grandmother, Mrs. Elder, in a little house on Francis across the alley from Steve's house. We apparently had a good time because we decided to have a sleepover at her house. This was going to be my first sleepover. Mom stopped by with my pajamas.

That night after we went to bed, I started thinking about what the nun said. I started worrying that Dad or Mom would die that night. I started sobbing and told Mrs. Coble I had to go home. I wanted to save my parents or, at the very least, to see them before they died.

Nothing she said could stop me from being afraid. Eventually, she called Mom, and Mom came and brought me home. Mom must have said the right thing to me once I got home because I was later able to spend the night with Martha and other friends without fretting over whether I would see my parents alive in the morning.

Summer

Finally, with sister school over, this is what it was all about. There are obvious reasons to love summer. No school. No snowsuits. No gray skies. Opportunities galore. Freedom. So much to pack into a short time.

One of my favorite parts of summer was the change of environment in my bedroom. The storm-door windows came off so we could have fresh air. We replaced them with screens. A light breeze circulated between the bedrooms, down the hall, through the living room, and out the kitchen. We hung the Hudson Bay blankets and the feather pillows on the clothesline and pounded them to get rid of any dust. After a day outside, they smelled so good.

At night, my window opening was a few inches from my head, and I heard Castle Creek rushing through the canyon in the distance. I listened to the birds before daybreak and the change of their songs with the growing light. I felt the cool air and snuggled into my blankets. I smelled the lilacs. I never worried someone would come to get me. Despite having no screens, I do not remember any insect problems.

In the summer, the nights were dark unless there was a full moon. I could see no lights out of my window. The only lights we could see from our ranch were an occasional headlight in the distance on Highway 82 to the north and a slight glow in the east from the town. Because there was little light pollution, the stars were intense. The major constellations disappeared in the mass of lesser stars.

Some mornings I got up and went outdoors before starting my day. I ran into Nipper as he strolled up from the bale shed for his breakfast. Nipper and I often shared part of the same breakfast. I ate some of his Sunshine coconut-chocolate chip cookies Mom bought for him as a special treat. I dipped mine in coffee. At that time, no one knew chocolate could be deadly for dogs. No one mentioned it to Nipper because he never got sick. The only time he ever got sick was when he got in the trash and consumed the remains of a ham bone.

Nipper's usual breakfast was dried bread soaked in milk. Pearl saved all the heels from her store-bought bread and gave them to Mom. Mom loved how, if she mixed up white bread with brown bread, Nipper patiently took out the brown pieces and put them on the floor. When telling the story, Mom pantomimed delicately picking up the bread between her index finger and her thumb and setting aside.

Besides one of Nipper's cookies, my breakfast was the same as it was throughout the year. Yes, we had eggs and bacon sometimes, but most of the time, it was routine. I ate homemade white bread dipped in coffee with cream. Later I made cinnamon toast with the bread.

Even when I was a child, I drank coffee with more milk than coffee. I did not care much for cold milk. I liked ice cream, but not glasses of milk. When I stayed with Pearl when Mom and Dad were out of town, the only part of staying with her that I hated was she made me drink a glass of milk in the morning. I stared at the white liquid. Eventually, I gagged it down. How I wished I could cut it with some coffee.

Mom worried about my lack of interest in milk – especially because she took over much of the milk operation. If I didn't drink milk, I would become a sickly invalid. So, she decided I needed vitamins. Because I fought drinking milk, I got a teaspoon or two of Homocebrin, a liquid vitamin supplement, every morning. It was a thick, orange-flavored liquid. It came in a brown-glass bottle Mom kept on the door of the refrigerator. I thought it tasted good. I used to lick the drips off the side of the bottle.

Sometimes I stayed in the house after breakfast, but often I tagged along with Dad on his morning chores. My favorite was irrigating. I had this thing for moving the water around, but it was also good to have alone time with Dad.

Dad loaded the Jeep with several canvases, his irrigating boots, and a shovel or two. He made his canvases from the orange canvas he was able to obtain from the Aspen Music tent after repairs in the spring. The tent was a source of used rope as well.

He went out in the field and drove to one of the sites where he regularly placed the canvas dams. They were placed in small lateral ditches that branched out of the big ditches. The same sites were used year after year and day after day. He knew where to place the canvases for maximum and complete coverage. He spanned the lateral ditches with canvases sandwiched between two-by-fours that hung like a curtain. He weighed it down with rocks ready for that purpose. Sometimes he cut out a chunk of sod from the stream bank and tamped it near the dam to guide the water into the field.

We started at one side of the fields and followed a regular pattern. He irrigated twice a day – placing the dams in the morning and removing them in the evening. He irrigated every day after he brushed the meadows – stopped during haying season in July – and irrigated again through the second cutting and into the fall.

When he was busy doing the digging and hauling, he usually did not say much, but what he said was philosophical or nostalgic. I remember one day. Dad drove the Jeep on the road toward the picnic grounds and stopped at the first diversion box below Bill and Celia's house. He turned the water into the first lateral ditch running north and south from the box along the Jeep road on the east side of the little field. We turned around and stopped about halfway down the road by a group of serviceberry bushes. Dad put in a canvas and angled it just so, placed the rocks to hold the canvas, and dug out the chunk of sod. As the dam filled and the water began to flow, he made a small adjustment. The water spread in a silvery sheen over the southern-most part of the little field. There was something meditative about watching the water flow and listening to it gurgle.

Before moving on from this location, Dad leaned on the shovel. His foot rested on its edge. He put both hands on the top of the handle, leaned forward, resting his chin on his hands, and looked around. He moved his head slowly from side to side and focused on the side of Aspen Mountain above the hedge of cottonwood trees and sighed.

"God. Isn't this something? I don't think I could enjoy doing anything more than what I am doing right now in this place."

He stepped on the shovel, loosened a piece of sod, picked it up with the shovel, and tamped into a space near the canvas dam. He looked across the road toward the mountain and motioned to an opening before the trees, and wistfully said, "That would make a good spot for a house."

Then he stood up, grabbed the shovel, and loaded it into the Jeep. We moved on to the next lateral ditch west of the little field parallel to the dividing fence. This is the lateral ditch we crossed near the cattle shed to get to the big field.

I didn't know whose house he was talking about, but, in later years, I chose to believe he intended as the site of my future home.

Haying

Irrigating was about hay – alfalfa, brome, and Timothy. Brushing the meadows was about hay. Spreading manure in the fields was about hay. Hay fed our cattle and became a cash crop. July was haying season.

Unlike the days when Max was operating the dump rake, haying was now less about physical danger and more about timing. In the first few weeks after Dad brushed the meadows and put on the fertilizer, the fields started to get green. First, there were a few shoots, and in a while, the alfalfa was like lettuce growing about ankle deep. Then it began turning into stocks of grass. Then the fields started growing high. As we drove down the highway, it was like looking over a big lake or an ocean. The bright green grass waived from dark green in one direction to silver-green in the other.

There were times I went into the field and got lost in the hay. I was small. The hay was taller than me, and the only thing that bought me home was the sun or a glimpse of Aspen Mountain. Dad feigned anger when I romped in the hay. I weighed in at about 50 pounds, so any damage was minimal. It was a problem only if or when I tromped with legions of friends.

By early July, the hay hit its optimum height. Dad had to pick when to mow. After cutting the hay, the harvesting window was three to five days. The year's crop could be lost if, in those days, it rained. I do not know how Dad decided when to cut. I know he worried about it. I'm sure it had to do with the Farmer's Almanac. Or it had something to do with the barometer on the kitchen wall or the color of the clouds over the mountains.

We watched as he made the decision. He sat in his chair in the corner and ruminated and, in his words, stewed. Steve and Ted put in their two cents. I said one or two extra rosaries at night. As the old adage goes, you need to "make hay while the sun shines."

Each day he looked out the window. Sometimes, he tapped the barometer on the kitchen wall. I thought it seemed pretty worthless. If you tapped it enough, it seemed to go whatever direction you wanted it to go – kind of like a bathroom scale sitting on a carpet when you lean from side to side.

As he weighed his options, Dad smoked one or two or ten cigarettes, and then one day, he finally said, "It's time." That day he went out and hooked up the mower to the tractor. He went out the gate to the big field and headed south along the dividing fence, then west next to the Holden Ditch, turned east at the Midland railroad bed, and followed it back to the beginning. He continued in concentric triangles until the entire section was mowed. Then he went to the corner of the big field near the intersection of Maroon and Castle Creek Roads, east along Highway 82 to the original Marolt Ditch channel that bisected this section of the field. The section on the other side of the channel was the last of the big field to mow. The little field south of the house waited another week.

The hay lay flat for a day or two. It turned from bright green to silvery green and emitted a lovely sweet grassy smell. "Please, no rain." Then came the rake pulled behind the tractor and angled, so it deposited the hay in long windrows. This was the time when the hay is the most susceptible to damage. The rows can absorb water and, if the hay remains damp, it will mildew or mold. Mildew and mold cause dust, which is bad for livestock. It was deadly for Patty.

Once the hay was in rows, he started baling. Dad no longer stacked the hay in haystacks. That ended when he and Steve decided the ranch and range rights could no longer support a year-round cattle operation.

Dad kept the baler in the horse and cattle shed in the little field. The first baler used wire and Dad hated it and cursed, "It drives me nuts." Every ten or fifteen bales, it would break or seize-up. Even if it worked, the bales were difficult to handle. The wires tore the hay haulers' hands and were difficult to remove without wire cutters. As we fed the livestock, we cut or untied the wires and hung them on the fence posts. The wires were used for repairing fences, especially the aspen-pole fences Steve built around his pasture. For a while, there were folded, rusting lengths of wire hanging off every post in the corral near the hay cribs. We endured two years with the wire baler. Then, Dad got a newish New Holland twine baler. It was much more forgiving, and the bales were easier to handle.

Our hay operation required manual hauling and stacking the bales. Dad tried to make them weigh about 70 pounds. The hay haulers varied. For the most part, Keith, Max, and Billy were haulers, along with help from school or skiing friends. Hay hauling was pretty good conditioning. Sometimes, there was help from town or down the valley. In later years, Dad enlisted the help of his sons-in-law and Gary and Barney. Hay hauling was particularly challenging for both sons-in-law because both had hay fever. Judy's husband, Chuck, could barely open his eyes, and Tom, Peggy's husband, wore a bandana around his mouth and nose. It was a miserable job, even without hay fever.

Dad fantasized about having an automated system. He almost drooled looking at farming journals and at the modern, streamlined systems of a baler that automatically deposit the hay on the wagon and then designs where the hay was transferred to the bale shed on a series of conveyors. None of these systems completely did away with the need for hay haulers. If Dad were alive today, he would be amazed at the one-person system designed to do everything from collecting the bales in one spot, stacking the group of bales on a wagon, then moving the blocks of hay into the shed with the same device.

In our day, the operation required a hay wagon pulled by the tractor or Jeep moving slowing through the rows of bales. The men hoisted them onto the wagon as it passed. One or two men made rode on the wagon and placed the bales in neat rows. Once the wagon was about four bales high, they returned to the shed. If the hay was too high, it could tip when the wagon crossed a lateral ditch near the new cattle shed. I remember a couple of times when many bales dumped into the ditch and were pulled out and dried in the sun.

Once the wagon was at the shed, the haulers unloaded it a bale at a time and placed them in crisscross patterns under the roof of the bale shed. Then they returned to the field to start the process over again. It took about ten days from cutting to being stacked in the bale shed. If there was no rain, it was perfect hay.

When it rained, or the bales sat outside on a humid night, we went out in the field after the sun was up, and the ground was dry and turned the bales one turn. My sisters and I could do this by rolling them one turn to expose its underside. Regardless, from time to time, we opened a typical looking bale to find black mold inside. We tossed it.

The hay filled the shed and overflowed out one end and even to the red barn in a good year. Dad covered any exposed hay with black plastic sheets. He made sure there was a small room on the south end for Nipper and the barnyard cats. That is where they slept most of the year – especially in winter. Dad commented that in the early morning when he went to the shed to get hay for the livestock, he saw Nipper curled up with the same cats he chased away from the milking barn the day before.

Chores

Despite no longer attending school or sister school, other commitments kept me from free rein with my time. Ongoing household chores took some of the time.

One of the primary year-round household chores was making over the beds each Saturday. Before the new furniture, each of the bedrooms had a double bed. At the end of the hall, the linen cupboard had a shelf with flat, white, double-bed sheets. On bed-making day, we took off the bottom sheet and moved the top sheet to the bottom, and secured it with crisp, tight hospital corners. We put a new sheet on top and replaced the pillowcases. The pillowcases were not only clean; they were ironed. They were in matching pairs and, while they were white, they had different embroidery patterns and colors on the edges.

Ironing the pillowcases and the rest of the laundry was another chore. When the laundry was dry, it was sorted and folded. Other than towels, underwear, pajamas, sheets, and jeans, we ironed just about everything. We put the ironing in an oilcloth-lined bushel basket for sprinkling. That involved laying a shirt or piece of laundry on the table and using a Coke bottle with a sprinkler head to sprinkle water on the item. Sometimes Mom used a pan of water and dipped in her fingers and flicked the water onto the garments. Each piece was folded and rolled it tight and put in a plastic bag in the "doghouse." If we didn't iron the clothes within a day or two, we had to dry the dampened clothes to avoid mildew.

My first ironing job was pillowcases. They were an easy and satisfying task. From there, I moved on to Dad's work shirts. They didn't have to be ironed quite as nicely as his dress shirts. Each of us learned the specific steps in ironing a shirt. Dress shirts and some of the girls' dresses were starched. There were lots of dresses and blouses to iron because we wore only dresses to school since the school forbid girls from wearing pants of any kind.

The kitchen involved daily chores - dishes at each meal, sweeping after each meal, and mopping once a day. We cleaned the bathroom daily. The living room and bedrooms involved weekly sweeping or using a carpet sweeper. Later, when we had carpeting, we used a vacuum. These rooms also involved dusting. We set up the chores in tandem. One person swept and the other dusted and polished.

Then we cooked. Mom did much of the cooking, but we made vinaigrette dressing and the hollandaise sauce. Before meals, we took out a large pot, went to the garden, and filled it with the vegetables – lettuce and green onions for salad, a root vegetable or two, and a green vegetable. We knelt on the garden bridge, scrubbed the root vegetables, shucked the peas, and broke off the ends of green beans. If we were not using the vegetable tops, we threw them into the water.

If Nipper was around, he went crazy. He loved to jump in the ditch and retrieve floating vegetable parts. If we did not have vegetables, I threw in a few dandelion blossoms, so he had something to chase. His favorites vegetables were peas. If we sat on the bridge and shucked peas, we threw the pods in the water, and he not only caught them, but he ate them.

We also baked. Baking was not a chore. It was fun. Dad and Mom designed the kitchen for this activity, especially with the built-in sugar and flour bins and the spot near the stove for the mixer. We all baked. Judy made most of the bread. Mom made the pies. As she said, her pie crusts were not pretty, but they were flaky and tender. She specialized in raspberry, rhubarb, and peach pie in the summer. Fall was the time for apple pie.

We all made cakes. They were a little tricky at high altitude. We adjusted the recipes from *Betty Crocker* or the *Better Homes and Garden* cookbooks to keep the cakes from falling – raise the temperature twenty-five degrees and reduce the sugar. Mom made a yellow cake with seven-minute icing. We also made a chocolate cake with a cooked fudge icing topped with ground walnuts. I liked to use the nut grinder. One of the easiest cakes we made was a chocolate depression cake made with vinegar, oil, cocoa, flour, and sugar. It was similar to the yellow "scrub cake" our grandmother made without butter, eggs, or milk. After we went to California in 1960, the Nut Tree chocolate cake took over as the family favorite. The Nut Tree cake was from a restaurant halfway between Sacramento and San Francisco. It was a light chocolate cake with a rich buttercream icing.

Then there were cookies. Cookies were popular all year round, although we kept the Christmas cookies pretty much for that time of year. The rest of the year, there were other varieties. We had a brownie recipe that I could still make in my sleep today. The brownies were the kind that rose and settled down with a cracked surface. They were chewy and rich and did not need to be iced. Another favorite, especially in the summer, was apricot bars with an oatmeal crust and a tart apricot filling. We made many cookie varieties from the cookbooks. Dad's favorites were *Betty Crocker*'s jubilee jumbles, which were cake-like, caramel-colored drop cookies with a browned butter icing. Everyone liked the traditional cookies, snickerdoodles, oatmeal, peanut butter, and chocolate chip.

Not all the chores were inside. The family women no longer did too much with the hay except turn the bales or haul a small number of bales to the barn or the horse shed. We were, however, responsible for the yard. The yard was big – about a quarter of an acre. In the spring, we raked it. Then we fertilized it with Weed-N-Feed. Throughout the summer, we set and moved the hoses with the sprinklers.

We tried all kinds of sprinklers. The best ones for coverage were the propeller, turnstile type sprinklers, and they were also the most fun to run through. Propeller sprinklers, dome-topped sprinklers with small holes, and oscillating sprinklers only worked for a while and then got clogged. For a long time, Aspen water contained solid particles. That is why we made sure we had screens on each of the faucets that we routinely cleaned. Although I dreamed about having one of the newer sprinklers that drug the hose behind it as it moved around the yard, we knew it would be a waste of money. In the end, we bought and used owls-eye sprinklers with the two holes. They were small, cheap, and efficient. There was another benefit to the owls-eye sprinkler. We could flip the sprinkler over and drag it to a new location and flip it back without getting wet or having to walk back and forth to the hose bib. There were only two hose bibs for our entire yard.

Until I was in junior high, Peggy and Judy mowed the lawn with a Montgomery Ward gas-powered mower with the rope starter. Peggy remembered the mower for how temperamental it was to start. We had an old wooden hand reel mower we used in some tight corners. We did not pick up the clippings. They seemed to disappear rather quickly.

Years later, we got a self-propelled Toro with a key ignition – first class. We never got a riding mower. Dad thought that was a ridiculous idea. As far as he was concerned, we could use the exercise.

When I mowed, I cut it in different patterns to keep it interesting. If needed, we used hand trimmers for the long grass under the fence if the horses on the outside of the fence did not kept it in check. They stuck their muzzles under the lower boards and nibble on the grass inside. The only other chore was some minimal pruning and weeding the flowerbeds and garden.

The main outdoor chore was fence painting. The fence needed painting every two to four years, depending on its exposure to the sun. That meant each summer we scraped and painted 10 to 15 sections. I did not mind this chore because I spent a lot of time walking on the fence. Besides, like most kids, I liked to paint.

That was all the outdoor painting going on by the time I was old enough to be involved. Dad replaced the wooden siding on the house with aluminum siding with insulation. He ordered enough for a future garage, and for many years there were cartons of Kaiser Aluminum siding stored in the granary. Dad used it for the garage he built in 1963. The aluminum siding looked good and beat chipped and graying paint. We continued to paint the window trim every few years.

Piano Lessons

In addition to the summer chores, I took piano lessons and participated in 4-H. I took piano lessons all year long. My lessons were on Saturday morning at 8:00 a.m. I chose that time to not interfere with playing or skiing, but it did have a dampening effect on sleepovers with friends. Given my involvement in school, piano lessons, and Mass, I rarely had a sleep-in day.

My teacher, Mona Frost, also taught sixth grade and was the principal for a while. She had salt and pepper hair and was thin and boney. I had my piano lessons in her house next to the high school gym. The parlor, where I had my lessons, smelled slightly musty because of the stacks of books and sheet music.

Mrs. Frost was concerned about correct posture and obsessed that her students kept their fingers high above the keys. "Play as if you are holding an orange under your palm!" If I forgot and let the palms drop, she took her long finger-nailed hand and poked into my palms until I raised them. If I learned a piece of music in my book and played it well, she gave me a star. The color of the stars meant different things. The purpose was to give my parents something to judge how well I was doing.

At the end of the lesson, she took my spiral notebook and wrote my weekly assignments. She had beautiful cursive handwriting - a perfect specimen of the Palmer method. I liked to watch her write. I can still hear her lead pencil on the paper. Sometimes she tore off a sheet with numbers and asked me to take it to my parents. That was the bill. The next week I returned with an envelope.

It was hit and miss on my practicing. I did just enough to get through the next lesson without a lecture. Now, I regret not practicing more. I was never in the league of my sister, Judy. She practiced all the time and was good enough to get a summer scholarship for private lessons with a renowned pianist associated with the Aspen Music Festival. Her name was Edith Oppens. She was a tall, stout woman with wild red curly hair. She was arrogant and told my sister, "You're a pig." Judy did not play like Mrs. Oppens' daughter, Ursula, a famous concert pianist in her own right as a concert pianist but calling Judy a pig was beyond rude. That experience went a long way in undermining Judy's confidence.

Her confidence was tested again at church. During choir practice, Judy was playing the organ and made a few mistakes. Celia piped in and said one of the older girls should play. It hurt Judy's feelings, and she was embarrassed. I don't think Judy ever tried to play for the choir again. Cherie and Sigrid Braun eventually took over playing the organ.

4-H Club

In addition to chores and piano lessons, another summer commitment was 4-H. My sisters were both in livestock and sewing.

Before I joined, I went with them to the joint 4-H meetings at the Woody Creek School. Dad took us. He enjoyed spending time with down-valley ranchers. George and Alice Vagneur and George's brother, Allen, and his wife Ruth, Alice's twin sister, were 4-H leaders. Both families had ranches in Woody Creek.

4-H met in a one-room schoolhouse, which was no longer used for regular school. The meetings started with the 4-H pledge, "I pledge my head to clearer thinking, my heart to greater loyalty, my hands to larger service and my health to better living." After that, there was old business – people reporting on things they said they would do at the last meeting. There was new business. Sometimes that included a demonstration of some type or a report. There was a discussion of upcoming events. Where was the summer picnic? When was the livestock show? What were some money-making activities to pay for trips and ribbons and trophies? When were the district meetings? Who was going to be delegates at the convention in Fort Collins? Who was going to the State Fair in Pueblo? Who was bringing refreshments to the next meeting?

All the 4-H members attended the joint meeting. It was also our chance to play with the down-valley ranch kids. Between those two Vagneur families, there were seven kids in 4-H. I was always confused with who were sisters and brothers and who were cousins. Although they were reputed to be raucous and rowdy, they were fun to play with at the meeting. After the meeting, we had refreshments of Kool-Aid and cookies or cupcakes.

The adults chatted while the kids played games of kick the can or gray wolf near the old school. It was dark, and the only light was what little came from inside the school or a weak fixture at the building entrance. We had three of these big meetings each summer and a weekly meeting for each of the individual clubs. Most of the clubs met in town.

When we were not meeting in the schoolhouse, it was used for square dances. I went to see a square dance once. I was impressed by the women's dresses with the bright colors and tiers of ruffles and petticoats. Unlike polka, square dances were not a part of our family tradition.

Thankfully, I never participated in raising livestock. I could not possibly have gone through the agony of raising an animal, treating it like a pet, and knowing it was going to be slaughtered. My sisters raised steers, pigs, and sheep. They fed them, groomed them, and practiced showing them.

The summer livestock project ended with a show at the rodeo grounds. The rodeo grounds had a white fence suitable for sitting, a few bleachers, animal chutes, and gates. It was next to Highway 82 west of the Maroon Creek Bridge and east of what became the Buttermilk Ski Area parking lot. Later it was the site of the Pomegranate Inn.

The judges, who were 4-H leaders from Carbondale or Glenwood Springs, awarded ribbons to the participants and their animals. Purple was the best in the entire category. Then for each group, there were blue, red, and white ribbons. How sad it would be to get a white for an animal – was it defective or deformed? Did the owner just not try?

When I went to these 4-H livestock events, it was not nearly as fun as the rodeos. We went to a few rodeos. I did not know any of the cowboys. For the most part, they were from down the valley. We drove in our pick-up. Dad backed it the fence. Instead of sitting in the bleachers, he put the wooden slat sides on the bed and placed planks between the slats to make our own small bleachers. The best part was getting food from some vendors and playing with friends under the big bleachers. The barrel-racing riders impressed me. I tried it once down by the granary, where I set up a couple of oil barrels. I do not think I even trotted around them – so much for that skill.

After the awards, the local restaurants and grocery stores bid on the animals. I'm not sure who got the money – the 4-H office or the member. One year, Judy's purple ribbon was for her special lamb, which was now the size of a full-grown sheep. She named him Mr. Christopher, and he looked particularly good when he was washed and fluffed. Peggy named her blue-ribbon lamb Bill. Beck & Bishop bought them both.

No one mentioned what we all knew – Mr. Christopher or Bill would end up as lamb chops. That evening Judy and Peggy returned the lambs to the ranch. We still had the rest of the lambs we raised that summer to send back to the Gerbaz ranch. At our ranch, the lambs and sheep were in a small pasture bisected by the Marolt Ditch west of the culvert. It had an A-frame shelter under the cottonwoods by the ditch. We called it the sheep pasture.

The next morning, I awoke to a commotion. I heard Dad shouting. The sound got louder and louder as he came running into the house.

"I need the gun. Dogs are killing the sheep!" He added, "Grab Nipper. Keep him inside."

Dad headed to Keith's bedroom and grabbed the .22-rifle from the hook in the closet. He reached into the top drawer of the dresser, stuffed a box of shells in his pocket, and ran down the hall and out the front door.

When he reached the pasture, he aimed the gun at the pack of dogs but slightly above them. There were five or six mid-sized to large dogs. Dogs had never been a problem before, but more and more dogs ran free as new people moved to town. Dad shot the gun. He reloaded, shot again, reloaded, and shot again. The dogs stopped, backed away, and sprinted over the field toward Highway 82.

My sisters and I ran to the edge of the pasture. The sheep huddled near the "A" frame on the other side of the ditch. Lying on his side in front of it on the ditch bank was Mr. Christopher. He was breathing heavily. Blood smeared his beautifully groomed white fleece. His underbelly was open, and intestines tumbled on the ground. He looked at us with big black eyes.

Dad stood paralyzed. He yelled to Judy, "Get Bill. Get Bill." He was talking about his brother Bill who lived in town. Judy turned and ran to the house. Dad knew what needed to be done, but he could not shoot Mr. Christopher. A few minutes after Bill arrived in his Jeep. He went into the pasture. I heard a single gunshot.

I remembered that horrible day and the dilemma when I watched *Old Yeller* a few years later. Dad could not shoot Mr. Christopher. He knew it had to be done, but he could not do it. Thankfully, Bill was able to do it. Poor Travis. He knew what needed to be done, but he had no choice. I sobbed all night after Mr. Christopher died. I sobbed all night after I saw *Old Yeller*.

Because I didn't raise animals for 4-H, I started with the sewing club and later joined the cooking club. For the one year it was available, I was in a new club having something to do with home management – cleaning, decorating, table settings, menu planning – probably training to be a good homemaker. I cannot remember the name of that club. It was not that much fun.

Our sewing and cooking club meetings were held weekly in the basement of the Community Church. We had the usual refreshments – Kool-Aid and cookies. Every meeting, two members brought the refreshments.

Alice and Ruth Vagneur were in charge of sewing. The first year's project was to make a sewing box and an apron with two pockets. We made our sewing box out of a Roi Tan cigar box covered with fabric stuffed with batting and glued on top to function as a pincushion. We lined the inside with fabric, glued in small dowels for thread spools, and there was enough room for a pair of scissors and a tape measure. That year we made an apron and a scarf with a fringed edge. The next year we made a skirt with a simple seven-inch zipper. The last project I made was another dress using sheer fabric, which required French seams. If I stayed in the club, I would have eventually made a tailored jacket.

By the time I was in the sewing club, we had an electric sewing machine. Although it only sewed forward and backward, it was an excellent machine. It was a new Singer and had a buttonhole attachment. It replaced the treadle sewing machine Mom used. Mom got rid of the treadle machine but kept the cabinet.

As far as sewing was concerned, Judy won most of the purple ribbons and Cherie the rest. Although I was never as good as Judy, I was a decent seamstress and won my share of purple ribbons. This was remarkable because I did not like sewing. Besides, I never liked wearing anything I made. The clothes never looked on me like they looked on the models on the front of the pattern envelope. I was not nearly as skinny as the drawings in the patterns.

Ingrid was also in sewing. She had a difficult time with the sewing-technique aspects and lacked the patience to make perfect stitches. Even with Cherie's tutoring, Ingrid got mostly red ribbons on her projects. However, when it came time to model her dress, she looked great. Ingrid was my height but thinner than me. She had a small waist, blue eyes, and blond hair. Her "sheer" blue eyelet dress looked cute despite her ragged French seams. She got the purple ribbon for wearing the dress the best. I felt dumpy in my light blue organza striped dress with the perfect French seams and pin-tucked bodice.

Cooking was the new club for my age group. Christine Sparovic, the mother of my friend and classmate, also named Christine, oversaw this club. Neither Judy nor Peggy was in this club because it was not available when they were in 4-H. The cooking club was fun. We made biscuits one year and chocolate cake the next. One year, we made jelly clarified with shredded Kleenex. We did cooking demonstrations as in modern cooking shows.

At the end of each season, we went to Glenwood Springs for a district meeting to have our projects judged and give a cooking demonstration. After one of those events, we stopped at the Glenwood Creamery, the Main Street soda fountain. We went to get banana splits. When I visited this soda fountain on family Sunday drives, I usually got a sundae or a milkshake. I was not all that fond of bananas and did not like the pineapple sauce. However, this time I decided to get the banana split.

On our way back to Aspen, I was in the back seat of Mr. Sparovic's car, along with four or five other girls. I started getting sick. She pulled over, and I got some air and felt better. She offered me an egg and green olive sandwich left from "little" Christine's demonstration. The salt from the green olives hit the spot, and I was able to make it home. I swear that was the best thing I ever ate. I still make her egg-and-olive sandwiches.

In addition to the individual clubs, the district had a retreat center at Camp Tigiwon in Eagle County near Mintern on the backside of what became the Vail ski area. At the time, Vail did not exist. The camp was available for Garfield, Eagle, and Pitkin County 4-H groups. Camp Tigiwon was like a Girl Scout or Boy Scout camp. Going to camp was exciting. It was a Friday through Sunday event. Both boys and girls attended.

We loaded into the back of one of the Vagneurs' trucks. It had high wooden sides, like the ones Dad put on our pick-up for the rodeo. The truck was probably used for hauling hay and small farm animals.

Then the kids – probably 10 to 12 of us – climbed on piles of camping gear for the 100-mile ride to camp. The trip involved going to Glenwood and through Glenwood Canyon. Thankfully whoever was driving the truck was sober, the tires had tread, the breaks worked, and no one swerved a little too far or too quickly, so the truck flipped. We would have been dead. No one ever questioned the practice of hauling people in trucks.

While we were in the Glenwood Canyon, I stood up from my spot near the front of the truck, and the wind hit my head, and my plastic headband blew away. I wore a heavy-duty headband, so the breeze from being outside of the truck would not beat my hair into my eyes the entire trip. So much for that plan.

Camp Tigiwon had several permanent tents and a camp building. We went to our tents and chose our cots. Then we learned about camp meetings, activities, such as softball, kick the can, hiking, and arts and crafts. My most memorable part of the Camp Tigiwon experience was that I took the wrong pair of pajamas; my old ones were now too short, and they rode up in my crotch, and I was uncomfortable all night long.

In arts and crafts, I made a coin purse out of leather with stitching along the edge and an image I burned on the side. I also made several lanyards. One was particularly ugly – yellow and brown. As usual, I excelled at kick the can.

As was often my fate, the Catholic kids missed out on part of the fun. On Sunday morning, while the others were still sleeping and anticipating breakfast, we put on wrinkled dresses and "chapel veils" and got into Mrs. Sparovic's car to go to Mass in Minturn.

At the end of the year, we had a 4-H picnic and swim day at the Glenwood Hot Springs Pool, attended by all members. The pool was huge and heated by natural hot springs. It smelled of sulfur. It was over a football field length and a quarter again as wide. On one side of the pool, opposite the dressing rooms, was a sloping lawn. That is where we set up our picnic baskets with sandwiches, potato chips, potato salad, cookies, and a jug of Kool-Aid. After lunch, we waited an hour before swimming so we would not get cramps and drown.

By that time, I taught myself to "swim" in the Aspen pool by adding arms and legs to a dead-man float. I never got the proper technique for effective breathing. I raised my head out of the water when I needed to breathe. I later tried to breathe to the side but got water in my mouth and nose.

At the time of our picnics, the pool had a couple of diving boards – a high dive and a regular height board. There were also a few water slides. The metal slides seemed high, maybe thirty feet, with two bumps on each, and cascading water. I jumped off the lower board once and was told I was too young for the slides. That saved me because I was afraid of them anyway.

Another device meant for older kids was a large yellow floating disk with a horizontal wheel in the middle. Kids climbed on the contraption, held onto the wheel, and ran in a circle to get the disk spinning. As it spun, kids lost their balance and flew off into the water. I only remember these disks being in the pool one year. I can't imagine why the pool did not want flying teenagers smashing into smaller dog-paddling kids.

One year, the City threw a monkey-wrench into these organized activities. Aspen decided to go on daylight savings time. It was the only town in the state to do so. Dad was furious. As a rancher, he felt that instead of adding an hour for recreation, it added an hour of work. Besides, it simply did not work with animal schedules. He refused to allow us to change the clocks in our house. We stayed on standard time. Others in town were similarly perturbed.

Because of daylight savings time, before any event, we asked, "Is that daylight time or regular time?" Dad refused to ask the question, so anyone who wanted him to attend an event had to give him the time in regular time. At our house, the noon siren blew at 11:00 a.m. during that summer. This meant that whoever was going to come to the granary bridge and yell, "Dinner," came an hour later. We went to 6:00 a.m. Mass during the summer. I don't remember how long Aspen continued the experiment. It did not play well with ever-increasing tourism.

Playing with Friends – Away from the Ranch

Summer in the City

I went to town less in the summer than in the winter. I no longer accompanied Mom on her errands. When we went downtown, music from the Aspen Music Festival and School filled the air. Walter Paepcke started the music school and festival, which featured famous classical artists. It also trained talented musicians from around the world. The students had classes and practiced their music in the upstairs of several buildings– the Wheeler Opera House, the Aspen Block, the Independence Building, and the Brand Building. We heard singers practicing their scales and the sounds of stringed instruments coming through open windows. On Sundays, there was a concert at the music tent at the west end of town.

The music tent provided a location for one of my annual in-town activities when I played with my friends in town. Much of our town play involved riding bicycles. We mainly went from Barney and Gary's house to downtown and stopped along the way to get treats from their grandmother, Gi Gi, or their great aunt, who they called Aunt Lou. Both women lived in small houses near downtown. Aunt Lou lived in the house that became La Cocina – a favorite Mexican restaurant now gone.

We always made at least one bicycle trip to the music tent in the spring. In the early days, the Music Festival put up the concert tent at the beginning of the season and took it down at the end of the season. It looked like an orange and white circus tent. Ingrid's brother M.J. worked on the crew that put it up, maintained it during the summer, and took it down in the fall. As part of the winterizing, they removed and stored the wooden benches. Before they erected the tent in the spring, we could ride bicycles around on the saucer-like concave concrete floor.

In my opinion, riding my bike was the most enjoyable aspect of the music tent. I was not interested in attending concerts. In all the years I lived in Aspen, I went to two or three concerts. The last thing I wanted to do on a Sunday, after having gone to Mass, was to sit quietly for several more hours listening to music I did not like or understand. I may have gone to a concert with Ingrid. I specifically remember going to a few concerts as Nora Berko's guest. She was the daughter of the famous Aspen photographer, Franz Berko. It was a nice gesture, but I was miserable. I dreaded she might ask me to go again.

My most memorable bike ride was when Gary, Barney, and I rode bikes from my house, across Highway 82, down Cemetery Lane, past the Red Butte Cemetery, past Red Butte, and down the hill to the Slaughterhouse Bridge. We planned on riding toward Woody Creek for a while, turn around, and hike up Red Butte. Red Butte was always a good hike if you wanted to get hot, thirsty, and collect lots and lots of wood ticks from the sagebrush.

At the time, I rode Keith's old orange Schwinn. It was a boy's bike that was too big for me. I was too short to sit on the seat and ride, and the seat could not be adjusted any lower. I had to stand all the time or straddle the bar if coasting. If I hit a bump, it hurt – a lot.

For the most part, the bike worked okay for downhill, but I had a hard time getting enough leverage on the pedals to make it up a steep hill. I had to move from side to side to get leverage on each pedal.

Riding was all the harder because the streets, including Cemetery Lane, were not paved. The roads and streets were dried, somewhat rutted dirt, with pieces of gravel here or there. Sometimes in the spring, the county "oiled" them. That was the process where, after they graded the road to take out the ruts; they sprayed dark thick, tar-like oil on the road. It smelled terrible. After it was freshly sprayed, if you drove over the oil, it splashed on the car; we had to use kerosene or lighter fluid to remove it. We avoided the oiled streets as much as we could until they completely dried. All the streets in town got this treatment from time to time. The only paved street was Main Street and then only down the middle. There were no curbs on Main Street. In 1962 the city paved the downtown streets and added curbs and gutters.

On the day we rode down the hill to the Slaughterhouse Bridge, we stopped at the bridge and decided not to go further. I did not want to have to ride that bike up the hill on the other side of the bridge. Even at that, it was a long trip home. Gary and Barney zipped past me on their bikes, heading back up the hill while I pushed the heavy orange bike. When I got to the top of the hill, I was so thirsty I thought I would perish.

We still had to ride on Cemetery Lane back to our house. It was dry and hot. There were no trees at that time except for those in the cemetery. Finally, after what seemed like forever, we crossed the highway and the cattle guard at the end of our road. I dropped the bike and opened a small wooden gate to the horse pasture near the cattle guard. I fell on my knees and scooped up handfuls of water from a small ditch inside the fence. I do not remember being thirstier or feeling such relief. Every town biking or hiking excursion to or through town included a stop at Beck & Bishop for a pop.

Swimming Pool

Besides going to 4-H meetings in the Community Church, another destination in town was the swimming pool located on the south side of the Prince Albert building. The pool was above the ground behind a concrete wall. The pool was surrounded on the east, south, and west with three-foot walls with glass above. There was an unobstructed view of the ski hill.

Stairs led to the ticket office. The changing rooms were on the north side with a shower curtain here or there for privacy. The rooms were damp with an intense chlorine smell. The floor was wet and seemed slimy. The warning not to run made sense.

For some reason, it seemed as though we always went swimming after lunch, or as we called it, dinner. That meant that after putting on our swimming suits, we had to wait for an hour before swimming. Otherwise, according to Mom, we would get the cramps and drown.

My first experience in the pool was sitting on the concrete steps in the shallow end. I held on to the edge and moved slowly back and forth along the end of the pool. I was too short to touch the bottom even in the shallow end. I remember being stuck across from the steps and not getting back in time to make it to the bathroom. I peed in the pool. I found it interesting the urine was warmer than the pool water. Eventually, Judy showed me how to "swim" in this pool – dead man float, add kicking and arms, and breathe when necessary.

Playing on the Ranch

For me, summer play was mostly on the ranch. Living on the ranch was like living in the Adventure Land at an amusement park. There was the house, the yard, the barns, the granary, playhouses, fields, pastures, and ditches. There were the lixiviation works ruins to explore, Castle Creek, and the flumes. There were horses, a dog, cats, and other animals.

Despite having cousins and friends with whom I played, I was content to spend time alone entertaining myself. I played in the playhouses. I sat on the bridges, on the porches, and in lofts reading and drawing pictures. I walked on the fence around the house. At first, it was to see how fast I could do it. Later, it became a form of meditation. There wasn't much to do but listen to the sound of bugs, the rustling of the grass, the gurgling of the water, and feel the sun's intensity through the thin mountain air. Sometimes I daydreamed. Most of the time, I wasn't conscious of thinking, and there was no internal conversation scraping the inside of my skull. My thoughts were shrouded by pleasant sounds, sights, and smells.

Besides walking on fences, I played in the granary. I sat for hours hammering roofing nails in patterns on the floor. I built chipmunk traps on the porch. They consisted of a box with a hinged top and side held up by a stick. The stick was tied to a string, and when the unsuspecting chipmunk went into the box to get some of the oats, I would theoretically pull the string and trap the chipmunk. Surprisingly, I never caught one. In fact, I do not think a single chipmunk ever went into the box, and why would they? They had a whole oat bin in the granary.

I killed time riding Patty. I rode her about every day. For daily rides, I rarely rode her with a saddle. And, often, I rode in shorts. Riding in shorts avoided getting cockleburs, or as mom called them, "beggar lice," on my clothes. The downside was I was vulnerable to horsefly bites. I have an image of riding toward the little field from the hillside near Celia's house and crossing the ditch. I looked down at my tanned legs covered with horseflies. Their bites were multiple times worse than mosquito bites. Some welts were the size of quarters.

Before I went to school, we had several horses. There was Pet, Penny, and her baby, Patty, an Appaloosa named Annie, and a few others, including one or two that belonged to Steve. At that time, we still had Shorty and Bess – the workhorses.

Although I refer to Patty as my horse, she was one of our horses and available for all of us to ride. Judy was over eight years older than me, so she had done a fair share of riding Patty and Pet with Cherie and other friends, including Fleeta Rowland. She attempted some overnight trail rides, and I am not sure which of the horses she rode.

Peggy, like me, was fond of Patty. Before Patty developed asthma, Peggy and her friend, Ellen Feinsinger, rode up Castle Creek to Ellen's family's mountain house. When she left for these rides, I looked forward to making similar long rides when I was older.

I was never closer to any other horse than Patty. She was like a pet. Almost every day when she was in the granary corral, I sat on the granary porch, dangled my legs into the corral, and whistled to her. She trotted across the corral. I spread a handful of oats on the edge of the granary porch. As if her head was the return carriage of a manual typewriter, she began licking on one side to the end, then start all over again.

Usually, I dropped into the corral, put my arms around her neck, and leaned into her as she leaned into me. She nuzzled my hand and sniffed my face. Sometimes these encounters included her stepping casually on my foot. I patiently tapped her leg and said, "Foot." And repeated, "Foot." Sometimes she removed the offending foot, but often, it seemed she purposefully lifted every foot but the one I wanted her to lift.

One time, Ingrid and I rode double to the picnic grounds for a picnic lunch. As we sat on the ground, talking, Patty walked around grazing. She came near to me, but I didn't pay much attention. Then, without warning, she stepped on my thigh, briefly put her weight on it, and moved on past me to another patch of grass without missing a beat. I was astonished. Was this intentional? For the rest of the summer, I had a purple horseshoe-shaped mark on my leg.

Before I was old enough for school, Dad caught her for me and put on the kid's saddle. I rode around in the corral and the driveway in front of our house. At that time, Patty was about ten years old. In later years when I was riding her on my own, I grabbed a small can of oats and walked out to wherever she was pasturing. I put on a hackamore or a bridle and found a stump or a rock to get high enough to jump on her back. In later years, because she was short, I could get on her back by jumping up, resting my stomach on her back, and swinging my leg over her.

I rode Patty to perform my spring chore of checking the fences. When I checked fences or if I was going to be on Patty for a while, I put on a saddle. We kept the saddles in the barn. There was a tack room in the northwest corner. It was not exactly a room, but a fenced-off area to keep the animals out. There were hooks for bridles, hackamores, halters, and leads. There were two rows of saddle racks and enough room for seven or eight saddles. There was a barrel of oats.

Steve kept some of his saddles and saddle blankets there. He had a Mexican saddle. It reminded me of an English saddle because of its small size, but it had a small metal horn. The pommel and cantle were almost vertical. Steve also stored one of his best saddles there. It was large, in reddish colored ornately tooled leather. It looked like the ceremonial saddles used in the Rose Parade. I had a feeling that saddle had been a gift to him. I don't think that was the one used when he rode his horse, Snake, around the mountains.

In addition to these unique saddles, there were four or five working saddles. My favorite was a small, basic saddle – perhaps it was made for a woman. It had a small horn with rawhide thongs wrapped around it. It was light brown, lightweight, and comfortable.

When I was going on a longer ride, I cinched the saddle on Patty, rode around the corral for a few minutes, and then got off and cinched it again. By that time, she lost the air she purposefully pumped into her belly. In addition to Patty intentionally inflating her stomach, by this time, she was getting a little plump. Her weight gain was because she had developed asthma, and we could not ride her as much as necessary to keep her trim.

For my daily rides, I rode around the perimeter of the hay fields and on the hillside below the Castle Creek Road. I rode to the picnic grounds. I rode up and down the elevated Midland railroad bed. A few times, I rode down to the river bottom below the lixiviation ruins. There was something about this area that disturbed Patty. She seemed alert and anxious. It was clear she wanted to get out of this area and go home. It may have been that same creepy feeling I sometimes got down there. Maybe for both of us, it was claustrophobia. Maybe it was the deafening noise from the river. I wondered if there was something buried there – such as a body.

One of my favorite rides was to go through the gate on the west end of the big field, cross the Castle Creek Road, and go through a gate on the other side of the road. The gate led to a section of property east of the old ranch. There was a small runoff pond near the entrance. It was full in the early summer, but it was mostly empty with dark muddy water by the end. The dry mud cracked in a jigsaw puzzle pattern. There were salt licks near the pond, and by the end of the summer, there were remnants of salt blocks.

The fence dividing our property from the old ranch ran almost true north to south from the intersection of the Maroon and Castle Creek Roads. The old ranch was on the west of the fence. The old ranch house was about twenty yards away. The northernmost part of this pasture, which overlooked the roads and highway, became the site for Prince of Peace Church.

On this ride, I followed the fence to a pasture extending east and south below the Maroon Creek flume. It was a beautiful spot – emerald, green grass from runoff from the flume and the reservoir. The stream softly gurgled and meandered through the grass and the exposed sides of granite boulders. Jack oak and chokecherry bushes surrounded the meadow. Sitting on a rock, I could see the west side of Aspen Mountain in the distance above the bushes, but I knew no one could see me. The meadow was concealed from the rest of the world, making it a sanctuary. It was one of the prettiest spots on the ranch and perfect for daydreaming.

My sisters chose this spot for an outdoor slumber party. They and several of their friends, including Cherie and Fleeta Rowland, decided to spend the night here. They set up a canvas tent on the dry edge of the meadows. Mom, Albina, Celia loaded the Jeep with equipment, food and delivered dinner. I went with them and was jealous I would not be staying for the s'mores and ghost stories.

Unfortunately, it started raining. Celia dug trenches around the sides of the tent to divert the water. We returned home but left the pots and pans so they could make breakfast in the morning. When we joined them the next morning, from the looks of them, I was glad I spent the night in my bed. Celia's trenches didn't work that well, so it took weeks to dry out the sleeping bags.

In later years, after Lenny Thomas' estate sold this section of the property, the meadow became the parking lot for the new hospital replacing the Aspen Valley Hospital that had been on Red Mountain. Seeing it, my heart ached. Whenever I heard Joni Mitchell's *Big Yellow Taxi* – "They paved paradise and put up a parking lot" – I thought of this spot.

While we were still ranching this area, I went here often. Dad kept cattle in this pasture during haying season. When I rode Patty to check on them, she transitioned into her cattle horse mode and immediately tried to round them up. Patty was a good little cow pony – quick and good at cutting. Therefore, I always used a saddle if I went there when cattle were around to stay with her quick moves.

Sometimes on the way home, I cantered in the field but not for long. Dad did not think it a good idea to run a horse in the field. He worried that, despite his best efforts at grooming the fields, there might be a hidden gopher hole, and a horse could step in it and break its leg. Also, because of her asthma, Patty coughed and wheezed when she ran too much.

Like skiing, sometimes the best part of horse riding was quitting. I rode Patty back to the barn and pulled off her saddle. I could imagine how good that felt. Like taking off the ski boots, Dad laced for me in the morning for skiing. I took the saddle back into the tack room, hoisted it and the blanket on the rack, and grabbed a brush to brush down her back that was now wet with sweat.

Brushing her back in the middle of summer was not nearly as satisfying as doing so in the spring. In the spring, I went out with the currycomb and removed vast quantities of her winter coat. It seemed like enough for a full-sized sweater.

After I took off the bridle, I gave her a handful of oats making sure to keep my hand flat so she could not grab the skin with her teeth. She either sauntered away or if she had been in the saddle a long time, she rolled around on her back – so much for having brushed her.

Playhouses

Besides having a horse to ride, I was lucky because I had the use of two playhouses. In the mid-fifties, Dad helped Judy build a playhouse using one of the several small animal sheds scattered around the ranch. The A-framed structures were about six feet tall at their peaks. They had wooden floors and were used for sheep, pigs, and poultry.

Keith moved one of the sheds to the upper scrub area northwest of the garden. Dad and Keith took off the western half of the roof and added and squared-off addition west of the A-frame peak. The addition tripled the size of the shed.

Judy and Cherie, who were now teenagers, did much of the carpentry work under Dad's supervision. They added walls, a flat tin roof, a door, and two windows. One window was next to the front door, and another was on the west side. They hung the door with leather straps because they could not find suitable hinges when they wanted to hang the door. Inside, they built a bunk bed under the slanted part of the structure. Therefore, the top bunk was narrower than the lower bunk.

Dad built a plywood cabinet in the corner. The lower part had a door and shelves and open shelves above. It was perfect for holding a washbasin. Someone found a potbelly stove to use for pretend cooking. There was a small table under the window.

Next, they built a fence around the house. The fence had a few new posts, but it mainly relied on the garden fence and a tree here and there for support. The fencing material was bark-covered boards from the sawmill at Lenado. The gates were wooden wagon wheels rolled in front of the openings.

Once their house was complete, Judy and Cherie decorated it. That meant some curtains, some mattresses and bedspreads, and bouquets for wildflowers from the "yard." They also did some entertaining.

One night they made a macaroni and cheese casserole and a salad for entertaining the Strauss kids in the playhouse. Whoever carried the casserole through the wagon wheel gate tripped, and the casserole went sprawling over the dirt. They scraped up as much as they could and pretended it was edible. Cherie and Judy may have slept there once or twice. I never stayed in the house overnight; the bunks looked like they could crawl with spiders.

Not surprisingly, Peggy wanted her own playhouse. Her situation turned out to be somewhat easier. Peggy was more interested in decorating than building. There was a tool shed behind the red barn. It was taller than Judy and Cherie's playhouse with about the same square footage. It already had a door and a window. It may have been one of the original buildings from the lixiviation works and was of sturdy construction. Keith moved it north and west of Judy and Cherie's house next to the main road at the top of the rise from the cattle guard. It was nestled in some cottonwoods to the west of Bill's potato cellar. The small irrigation ditch used to water the garden ran behind it.

Dad added a set of bunk beds. In this house, because the walls and roof were square, the bunks were the same size. There was space above the top bunk, and it did not look nearly as spider friendly. Because both houses needed to be equal, he built Peggy a cupboard and supplied another, nonfunctioning potbelly stove. This was Peggy and Jimmy's playhouse. Neither of them nor anyone else spent a night there. It was, however, a nice place to decorate and to pretend it was a real house.

When I was in junior high, I went there to write and draw. I pretended it was my studio. I planned on turning it into a place to paint and sketch. Therefore, I was shocked when one day when I came home from town and, as I walked my bike across the cattle guard, I saw the playhouse sitting in the bucket of the large front loader – a large piece of earth-moving equipment Keith was operating.

At the time, Keith worked for Jim Hayes in his earth-moving business. Besides his earthmoving business, Jim was a silversmith. His wife, Mary, was a photographer and wrote a weekly column for the *Aspen Times*. The Hayes family lived in a little house on Bleeker Street behind the Community Church.

I couldn't believe what I was seeing. I dropped my bike and ran up the hill.

"What are you doing?" I yelled.

"I'm taking this to the Hayes kids."

"You can't do that. It's mine."

"You're too old for playhouses. Besides, you still have Judy's house."

"I like this one." I cried. "Why didn't you ask me?"

He didn't have much to say. He continued down the road, and I saw the playhouse sitting high on that earth-moving equipment as it crossed the Castle Creek Bridge.

Keith delivered it to Jim and Mary Hayes for their children. He set it up in their back yard. The children got years of enjoyment from the playhouse, and perhaps it still exists. But as a kid, I was angry no one consulted me or, for that matter, Peggy. Whoever decided to give the house away assumed we did not care or, more accurately, they probably never even thought of us. This was one of the few times when I was angry with Keith. I sulked for days. I wanted nothing to do with him, and his teasing could not dislodge my anger.

Keith must have mentioned to Jim and Mary that he goofed by taking the house without asking me first and that I was upset. Years later, when Mary photographed my wedding, she gave me a copy of her cookbook, *Aspen Potpourri*. She signed the inside fly page and added a note saying, "Many thanks always for your playhouse."

The other time I remember being mad at Keith was when I was somewhat younger. Keith was milking the cows in the barn. Ingrid and I were playing in the hayloft. Keith warned me to be quiet, so I would not upset the cows. We were moving around, and I accidentally dropped something. A chain reaction occurred with the cow kicking over the nearly full milk bucket and splashing Keith. Keith was furious. I knew I was in trouble.

I jumped down from the outside loft door and ran up to the house, followed closely by Ingrid. There were two openings in the new wood fence that did not yet have permanent gates. I knew Keith would be close on my heels, and I needed to slow him down. I ran and got a hose and a sprinkler and set one in the granary gate and one at the end of the garden bridge.

That did not slow him much. He caught up with me and spanked me. I was humiliated and angry. Even when he laughed about it later and complimented me for my ingenuity, I was still angry. That was one of only two spankings I ever remember, and it seemed like a betrayal coming from Keith.

Playing in the Yard and with Nipper

When Ingrid visited, we spent time wading and tubing on the ditch or playing in the playhouses. We played croquet in the yard. Our version was not to set up the regulation set on the south lawn but to put the wickets in various locations around the house and play "miniature golf" with the croquet balls and mallets. One year we set up a Slip-N-Slide, and Ingrid, Gary, Barney, and I wore a groove in the lawn. I ended up with the worst sunburn I ever had on my back and the back of my thighs. There was no such thing as sunblock.

Ingrid and I planned several overnights in the yard. We brought out all the sleeping bags and zipped them together. Put them on top of tarps and put more blankets on top of the sleeping bags. We brought out our pillows and had a snack or two and a flashlight. We set up our camp under the willow tree. It was west of the kitchen window. The light coming from the window provided light for a while.

We crawled into our nests and told stories. Nipper joined us and slept on our bed, snuggled between us. Most of the time, we fell asleep for an hour, but then we woke up. By that time, the kitchen light was off, and it was very dark. There were all kinds of strange sounds – the sounds of leaves rustling or the scurrying of small animals or the sound of crickets. We never heard coyotes, although we suspected they were lurking nearby. During this time, there were no bears and no mountain lions this near to town.

Around midnight, we were both awake.

"Ing, are you awake?"

"Yeah."

"Okay." Neither of us said anything for a while.

"Are you cold?"

"Yeah." Then there were a few more minutes of quiet. A few minutes later,

"Do you want to go inside for a while?"

"Yeah."

We picked up our pillows and went through the unlocked back door, made our way down the dark hall to my bedroom, and crawled into the twin beds.

In all the years we tried to sleep in the yard, I don't think Ingrid and I ever made it till morning. Every time we abandoned our campsite, I felt terrible for Nipper, who, once again, was left alone outside in the dark. At least he had the sleeping bags and blankets. Although, with our warm bodies gone, he would be much warmer in the bale shed. Our only outdoor sleeping was on the enclosed porch in front of Ingrid's room. The sound there was the sound of cars on Main Street.

With the large yard, in addition to camping, we could set up all kinds of yard games. We had a concrete sidewalk from the driveway to the back door big enough for drawing a hopscotch grid with chalk. I played it by myself, but it was not as much fun as when I played at school. We had a large enough flat space on the south side of the yard for a badminton court or regulation croquet. The problem with playing either game was Nipper.

He was not like other dogs. He did not enjoy chasing balls and bringing them back. He liked chasing balls and keeping them. It was nearly impossible to get a ball out of his mouth. That was true whether it was a soft squishy rubber ball, which he often chewed and swallowed, a tennis ball, or a wooden croquet ball. He particularly liked shuttlecocks – especially the ones with real feathers. Keith, who was over six feet tall, used to hold a ball over his head, and Nipper could jump high enough to snatch it and run. With Nipper around, trying to play either badminton or croquet was challenging.

Nearly every late afternoon in the summer, Billy stopped by on his way home from work to play a game or two of badminton. At the time, he was working for Sepp Kessler doing landscaping. To get to Bill and Celia's house, he took a shortcut by our house and through the field.

For either game, we put Nipper in the house. He stood at the back door, looking longingly through the screen. He whined. It was not fair. He was outside most of the time and whined about not being inside, and then, when we were outside, he was inside wanting to get out. If he escaped, he ruined our fun.

Another thing he did was to try to catch my cotton jump ropes. Sometimes, I let him have one end. He ran away, and I ran after him, holding the other end of the rope. We went around and around the house this way. It was great exercise. Eventually, I gave up and let him have the rope. Unlike the balls he hid, I could find my jump ropes in the middle of the yard.

Another problem involved Nipper's animal encounters. At least twice a summer, he tangled with a skunk. He came up to the house in the morning for his breakfast and, not only did he smell like a skunk, but he also found a fresh pile of horse manure to roll in. He now smelled like skunk mixed with horse manure. To him, horse manure smelled better than a skunk. I guess I agreed. On those mornings, he did not get to come into the house for breakfast. We fed him on the steps to the back porch.

To get him clean, we threw branches and dandelions into the ditch. He loved to jump into the water and catch them. He was compulsive. After a day or two of enticing Nipper into the ditch, the manure skunk smell dissipated.

Besides skunks, Nipper had trouble with porcupines. A couple times a year, he came up in the morning with his snout full of quills. He looked sad and swatted his snout, which was usually swollen, with his paws. Surprisingly, he went to Dad and laid his head on Dad's knee and let him get rid of the quills. That was unusual. Nipper usually did not sit still for anything. Dad put Nipper's head under his arm and, holding Nipper's chin on his lap, stroked the top of his head. He patiently cut the ends off each quill and pulled them out one-by-one with a pair of pliers. Nipper winced a bit as each quill was pulled but did not snap or bite. Dad then opened Nipper's lip to make sure there were no quills inside his mouth. It was weird how Nipper understood Dad was there to help. When done, Dad washed Nipper's snout with warm water. Nipper shook it off and went back to be our not always user-friendly dog.

Construction Projects

Although I had two playhouses, another activity was building more stuff. Gary, Barney, and I built a fort out of bricks on what remained of the flue for the big chimney. We used mud from the ditch for mortar. We walked around the granary, avoiding the dreaded stinging nettles, went up to the ditch by the house, and each scooped a couple of lard buckets full of the soft mud. Then we carried it down to the building project. We made about ten trips each. Even at that, the walls did not rise as high as we envisioned, and we abandoned the project before its inevitable collapse.

One year we built a lean-to in one of the hollows on the upper part of the ditch below the small field. We got the ideas and "plans" from Barney or Gary's Boy Scout manuals. The big ditch ran the length of the little field a few feet below it. There were lots of willows along the ditch. We cut the willow branches and bent them over, burying the ends in the dirt. We bent more branches and wove them together with more branches – kind of like an upside-down basket. We used a little twine to hold them together. Then we added branches with leaves until there was a roof. We sat in the completed structure for about fifteen minutes and planned to return throughout the summer. We never did. All that remained the next spring was a pile of branches.

Once, we decided to build a treehouse. One would think in the mountains, this would be a relatively simple task. The problem is the area does not have big deciduous trees with large upper branches spreading apart that can support such a structure. Pine trees were prickly, and around the ranch were not close to each other. The apple tree by the ditch bank was too small. Aspen trees were too weak.

Eventually, we found a good spot in the sheep pasture. There was a group of several cottonwood trees on the north side of the ditch. We used discarded two-by-fours from Dad's lumber bin in the granary and formed a trapezoid between the trees, added boards to make a floor, and nailed rungs to one of the trees for a ladder. Most of the work was dragging lumber up from the granary and returning for tools and nails. The house was about six feet above the ground. We started a roof but never finished it. I went out there a couple of times after it was built and sat there reading or writing in my journal.

During one of the Cliftons' visits, Gary, Tim, George, and I built a playhouse on the north side of the driveway near the new wooden fence. It was from scraps of wood from their Elsie and George's cabin construction. It could not begin to compare with the two other playhouses, but it was fun to build. We crawled on the roof and had our pictures taken. It collapsed from its own weight shortly after they returned to California.

One summer, Ingrid and I decided to make a "playhouse' in the granary in the northeast corner of the shop where Dad stored some of the old cabinets and tables from the kitchen. It included the built-in ironing board cupboard leaning against the wall. It wasn't really a wall but the backside of an enclosure in the middle of the granary where relatives stored their old furniture and trunks filled with trinkets and photographs.

Ingrid and I cordoned off the area by draping irrigation canvases. We also defined the spot with the piece of linoleum. It was not that great of a playhouse, but it kept us busy for a day or two moving and arranging furniture and sweeping the floor.

The next morning after breakfast, I went down to work on the playhouse. As I was starting my labors, Judy came through the open granary door. She had been on her way to her summer job as a chambermaid at the Aspen Meadows, a hotel and conference center near the music tent. She and several of the local girls, including Peggy and Cherie, worked there in the summer. They worked in the mornings. They had fun but complained about their manager, Ruby Bandy. They thought she was taking the tips and was keeping the liquor bottles the guests left in the rooms.

When Judy came through the door, she was holding something in her hands. "Look at what I found."

She held out a tiny longhaired black, brown, and tan calico kitten with a white muzzle. I had never been this close to a kitten.

"Where did you get him?"

"I found him down by the cattle guard in some weeds. He was crying."

"Can I keep him?"

"I don't know. That's up to Mom and Dad. Keep him safe and feed him some milk until I get home."

She put the kitten in my hands. I could not believe what I was holding.

As she was leaving, she turned around and said, "I named him Jueves cause it's Thursday." Judy had just finished her first year of Spanish. For a long time, we assumed Jueves was a boy, but we later learned she was a girl.

I stuck her in the ironing-board cabinet and went up to the house for a jar of milk. I took her out of the cabinet, poured milk in the lid for her to drink. She was famished. I sat on the piece of linoleum and watched her. When the milk was gone, I picked her up. Her little belly was hard and full of milk. I held her and snuggled her under my chin and against my chest. I played with her and a piece of twine. This was one of the few times I had ever held a kitten. We had barn cats, but they were not friendly.

I did not know what to do with her. I wondered if Dad would allow me to keep her as a pet. Because I did not have the heart to leave her alone in the granary, I finally brought her up to the house. Nipper was interested and sniffed her. I took her to where Dad was working in the driveway.

"Daddy. Judy found this kitten by the cattle guard. Can I keep him?"

"Down by the cattle guard? Sounds like someone was trying to get rid of him." The cattle guard was near the Castle Creek bridge. Someone may have tossed over a bag of kittens. Dad looked at the kitten and at me.

"You are going to have to be the one who takes care of him. When he's older, he's going to need to be mostly an outdoor cat."

I was so excited. I hugged Dad. "Thank you, Daddy. I'll take care of him." As I ultimately learned, he was a she.

For several days, I kept her near me in my room, and she imprinted on me. I made an outdoor enclosure for her in the corner between the wall under Judy and Peggy's room and the front porch for when she went outside. For shelter, I used a wooden barn Keith made for a 4-H or Boy Scout project.

Because it was Keith's construction, he made it to scale. It had an opening and a little loft and a pulley and a hook for hauling miniature hay bales. It was the size of a rabbit cage. I enclosed it in a chicken wire "yard." It kept her confined until she was old enough to get by on her own. Eventually, I removed the chicken wire, and she used the barn for shelter when necessary. I assume she also spent time with Nipper in the bale shed, although she stayed in the house more than Dad noticed or anticipated.

Jueves became an important part of my life. She followed me around. She lounged in the sun on the back porch stoop. She climbed the willow tree and sat on one of the branches. I put her in Dad's fishing creel hanging from the clothesline pole. She seemed to like it. I could pick her up and carry her if I wanted. When I left the window in my bedroom open at night, she came in and out as she desired but slept most of the night with me.

She and Nipper shared their food. For breakfast, she had a bowl of milk while Nipper ate dried bread softened with milk. I don't know who thought of this, but Nipper liked it. I doubt if modern vets would approve. At dinner, I opened both ends of Nipper's Gaines dog food can and pushed it out about a half of an inch. I sliced it off with one of the sharp lids and gave it to Jueves in her bowl. Nipper got the rest. They ate in the kitchen side by side.

One spring, when she did not show for breakfast, I looked for her and found her in her shelter. I looked in and saw two tiny pink creatures that looked more like mice than cats. By the time I came back with Mom, there were three and a while later four. Jueves had kittens.

Talk about being in cat heaven. I spent hours playing with them. I named the two grays, Scotch and Soda, for the Kingston Trio song. The mostly white calico I named Alley, and the black and white, I believe, was named was Mystie. I wrote the name on the back of the photo but cannot read my handwriting. I guess Mrs. Goodrich was justified to give me a "U," meaning unsatisfactory, for penmanship in fifth grade.

When the kittens were older, Dad said it was time for me to find them homes. The caretaker at the golf course said he could use some mousers in Steve's old barn. It was toward the west end of the golf course and had an unobstructed view of Pyramid Peak. The barn had a vehicle or two, tools, and plant material. I brought the kittens, who were now about twelve weeks old. I was sad to let them go. I came back a week later to visit. They adjusted well. They were interested in me but not needy. That was the last time I saw them.

Toward the end of summer, a stray cat came by. I could not resist and tried to catch and hold it, but it wasn't the same as my "babies." It was a large orange tabby. I didn't think much about it until a couple of weeks later. At that time, I realized I had not seen Jueves lately. I went out and looked in her barn. She was curled in the back and did not want to come out. I realized she was sick.

Dad came out and looked at her and confirmed something was wrong. He called the vet, who told him to get something from the drug store. There were no vet offices, and they did not make house calls for cats. They only showed up for horses and cattle and then only bulls. If a cow was bloated, Dad put it in the squeeze shoot and "stuck it." That meant putting a device into the bloated stomach and releasing the pent-up gas. He had a veterinary bag with syringes and antibiotics for the cattle. I assume it had what he needed for a bloated cow.

Dad drove me to the drug store, and one of the pharmacists put a couple of tablets into a little envelope. I smashed up the tablet and mixed it with some dog food. I went out and tried to hand feed her. I gave her water. She was not interested in either the food or water, but I convinced myself she was taking the medicine and I was sure she was showing some more energy.

The next morning, I got up and went outside early. I looked in the shelter. Jueves was gone. "Wow, that is a good sign," I thought. Then I looked toward the ditch. In an alcove in the willow bushes, I saw her lying on her side. I came over. She was soaking wet. I wondered if she had come over to drink and fallen in the ditch and climbed out. I also wondered if it was sweat. I came over to pet her. She did not move.

I ran, screaming into the house. "Jueves is not moving."

Dad came outside and looked at her. He confirmed what I feared – she was dead. He got an old towel to cover her. We went down to the granary, and Dad made a small wooden box for her. We put her inside, wrapped in the towel, and dug a hole to the west of the garden. Mom, Dad, and I, and whichever other siblings and relatives were there that morning, said prayers. I sobbed as we covered the grave. Later, Dad helped me make a concrete headstone for her. We poured concrete in a box, and while still damp, I scored her name and the date on it. A few days later, I put it on the grave with a bouquet of sweet peas.

Dad told me I would not be able to get another cat. The vet said Jueves had distemper. He said the virus was now in the soil, and if we brought in other cats, they would get sick and die. The vet thought that the orange cat I tried to befriend was the culprit. I do not remember if the vet offered an option of vaccination against distemper for a new kitten. I'm not sure if it was even possible at the time. Dad took away the miniature barn and burned it in the incinerator.

Although I slept with twenty stuffed animals, it was not the same. Jueves no longer came through my window at night.

Playing in the Ranch Buildings and the Scrub Triangle

There were several small buildings on the ranch scattered mostly in the scrub triangle. They offered a myriad of opportunities for fun. When there were more than a few kids at the ranch, we played our version of cowboys and Indians. Our game was lawmen and outlaws, inspired by *The Life and Legend of Wyatt Earp* television show. We improvised a version of try-to-get-into-the-granary and gray wolf. We armed ourselves with cap guns in holsters and wooden rifles.

The center of this game was a building to the northwest of the barn across the fence from the corral and below the bank from the house. Dad used the building for tack for a while, and he put in a small gate for direct access from the corral. We called it the saddle shed. It was about the size of a single-car garage and had a loft. It was an original lixiviation building and can be seen in photographs. It, like the other original building in our driveway, collapsed under heaving snow.

We used the saddle shed as the sheriff's office and jail. The point of the game was for the lawmen to capture and jail outlaws and for the other outlaws to break them free. The second floor of the building was a jail. The outlaws had many hideouts – a secret compartment in the thresher behind the red barn, the corrugated pipes in the scrub triangle, the bale shed, the playhouses, and the horse trailer. The other barns and the granary were off-limits.

Lixiviation Works Ruins

Besides playing around the granary or making forts and tree houses and lean-tos, when Gary, Barney, or Ingrid came out, or Rod was in town, we explored around the ranch. One such place was over the hill behind the granary. We didn't spend much time in the immediate area behind it because it was covered with stinging nettles. Behind the granary, there were several terraces upon which the main buildings of the Lixiviation Works once stood.

What remained was a large footprint and some artifacts. The first level was a terrace about 20 feet below the granary and a hill with sagebrush, cactus, and broken or crushed bricks.

The terrace was flat and mostly covered with concrete as if it were a paved parking lot. For years I thought it was the parking lot for the lixiviation works. Obviously, that did not make sense to have a concrete parking lot in the 1890s.

As it turns out, the concrete was the cooling floor in one section of the main building. It was where a super-heated ore mixture was spread on the ground and cooled before it went through several chemical treatments as it progressed down the levels of the mill. Although chipped here and there, the concrete floor was mostly intact.

Dad talked about the main "lexavator" building. "If you think the granary is big, you should have seen the main building. You could fit twenty granaries in it and still have room left over. It's too bad. It was mostly gone by the time I bought the ranch. I just wish there were more photographs." He added, "I played there as a kid."

I saw one musty, water-stained sepia photo stored in one of the trunks in the granary. I can imagine how delighted Dad would be to see the many clear photographs available today. Along with Velcro and Zip

Ties, these photographs are one of the things that would have amazed Dad. I was sorry the building was gone. If I thought the granary was fun, the main building of lixiviation works would have been twenty times as much fun.

The edge was the "cliff" I jumped off one winter. It was a wall made of large, squared stones, each at least a foot thick, and some were several feet long. They were a pumpkin-colored peachblow sandstone. Most of the buildings in town, such as the Wheeler Opera House, the Community Church, the Courthouse, and the Hotel Jerome, used peachblow sandstone. I believe these stones came from a quarry up the Frying Pan River near Basalt. The wall was in perfect condition below and adjacent to the cooling floor. It was damaged near where the little chimney once stood. It had been a retaining wall and foundation for the largest mill building.

At one time, Dad let someone park a small house trailer on the flat. They lived there for a while. It was over the hill from the red barn, and electric wires draped from a light pole near the barn and extended to the trailer. In my mind, I remember the resident was Jack Ray, who used to help shoe horses and kept some of his horses in the river bottom. Jack had a stable near the Jerome.

The cooling floor area was strewn with rusting iron cables and round rusting metal rings. The rings were 8-10 inches in diameter and an eighth- to a quarter-inch thick. They were thick enough not to bend. The edges of the rings were about an inch to an inch and a half wide. As I remember them, I believe the outside of the edge was smooth and perfectly round, and the inside edge had gear-like teeth. I have searched in vain to confirm this. It may have been that the outside had the teeth, and the inside was smooth – more like a gear cog.

It appeared these rings were stacked together as part of some sort of gigantic gear mechanism in an electric generator, or maybe they were washers on some giant bolts. Whatever their function, there were hundreds of them strewn around the area. Apparently, they had not been worth salvaging when the building was cannibalized.

We threw the disks off this level to see how far we could fling them. We tossed them side-arm with some wrist action like skipping a stone. We did not know we were throwing an early version of the Frisbee. But we never caught them. They would have hurt, especially if the teeth were on the outside edge. The rings fell and rested in the vegetation on the lower levels. Years later, when I went down to the ruins, many adolescent trees had rusting disks hanging high in their upper branches.

Below the big wall was another terrace with another smaller, eight-foot wall to the east. Unlike the upper wall, it was crumbling and looked more like a rock-covered slope than a wall.

This terrace held five or six huge wooden footers made of vertical two-by-sixes nailed together, so they were about four or five feet square and rose at least six feet above the ground. They were high enough, so I could not climb on top without a boost. What looked like giant, rusting iron bolts stuck out vertically above the top surface of the footer. The wood was covered with creosote, and the footers were beginning to show signs of deterioration.

At the bottom of the ruins was a flat elbow of Castle Creek overgrown with aspen trees, pine trees, and brush. It was at least 50 feet below the granary level. When we were on that level and looked up, there was only a little sky visible. You could not see Aspen Mountain. We could only see the walls of the lixiviation foundations, vegetation, a glimpse of the river, and a steep bank on the other side. It was in the bottom of a noisy canyon

To get to the lowest level, we usually went down a brick-strewn path above Castle Creek. We could go the long way by using the Jeep path, which split from the granary road and led to the cooling floor. About half the way to the cooling floor, a steeper Jeep path split off and descended to the river bottom. We used this route to get to the bottom on horseback.

Jake Lewis built a small cabin in the bottom area nestled in the trees. He was the brother of the town's doctor, Robert Lewis. Dad allowed Jake to build a cabin in return for his help in dismantling the big chimney.

When Mom and Dad bought the property, both chimneys were standing. The big chimney, which was about 20 feet southeast of the granary, was 165 feet tall. It had embedded iron rungs on the outside, allowing someone to climb to the top. I'm not sure why Dad decided to get rid of them. The little chimney, which was on the cooling floor level, was crumbling and a hazard. We called it the little chimney, although it was fifty feet tall. The big chimney was in good condition, but its iron hand and foot rungs to the top would have been an attractive nuisance to kids wanting the thrill of climbing to the top. Dad wanted it dismantled.

Dad thought he could set a little dynamite, blow down the chimneys, and salvage the bricks. He tried it first with the little chimney. Judy remembered the day Dad blew it down. When it was time to set off the charge, everyone went up the hill and crouched down below the ditch bank. Judy hid in the ditch, covering her head until the explosion was over. When the dust settled, all that remained was the mound of red sand and gravel. Not a single brick survived.

Therefore, to salvage any of the bricks from the big chimney, he would have to take it down the way it went up – brick-by-brick. That's when he enlisted Jake Lewis to do the job. Not only was his brother our doctor, his wife, Connie, was one of Mom's best friends. Jake was a reclusive bachelor and a perfect candidate to do the job. Dad let him build a cabin in the river bottom, and Jake sold the salvaged bricks as a source of income.

Jake climbed the iron rungs to the top and removed the bricks. At first, he dropped them onto sawdust at the base of the chimney. Dropping them resulted in damage, just like with the dynamite. He eventually came up with a system that allowed him to dismantle most of the chimney and clean the bricks. It probably involved putting them in some sort of basket and lowering it to the ground.

Jake left before he completed the job, so Keith took over. Keith used the money he earned from selling the bricks to pay for college. The bricks were used in the fireplaces in Bill, Steve, and Ted's houses, in Steve's cabin, and Elsie's vacation home. They also made it into several buildings and restaurants around town as "used bricks."

I am ashamed to say it, but one time we went into Jake's cabin to snoop when he was gone. It had a working potbelly stove and an icebox. Not a refrigerator but a real icebox with space for a block of ice, and it was in good condition. There were a metal bed and a small table. The most interesting part was that he had a collection of "girlie" magazines. We pawed through the magazines while someone stood guard.

We did not stay long because we were afraid someone would catch us. Before we learned Jake was supposed to be there, we thought he might be a real outlaw, and for a while, we collected clues to prove our theory. We also thought whoever was using the trailer on the flat might have been part of the same gang, so we spent time hiding and spying on both the trailer and the cabin. We kept our investigatory notes in a spiral notebook. We never saw anything suspicious before we got bored and went on to something else.

After Jake left the property, we talked about going and getting the icebox from the cabin. We thought about using the cabin as a playhouse. The next spring, when we went down to the cabin, the roof had collapsed from the snow. The bedsprings had rusted, and the icebox was warped and ruined beyond repair. We knew we were never going to use this as a playhouse because, quite frankly, the river bottom was kind of creepy.

This lowest level in the elbow of Castle Creek was filled with vegetation that reminded me of the forests in Vancouver when we visited the Cliftons there. Deep in the vegetation, as if out of nowhere, was an imposing triangular timber structure. It was probably twenty to twenty-five feet high and not visible from any other location within the ruins, on the ranch, or from the terrace below Jimmy and Cherie's house. It reminded me of part of a gallows. It was disturbing how it loomed in the shadows.

For years, I thought it was remains of from the Midland trestle. That is what Dad and others thought it was. It never occurred to us that it was too far to the north to be the trestle. I now know it was a derrick used to hoist the electric cables to the lixiviation works from the Castle Creek power plant. It is visible in photographs and copies of the lixiviation architectural plans.

Although the lower area was like a rain forest, unlike a rain forest, it was not quiet. The steep walls amplified the roar of Castle Creek. It was almost impossible to hear someone talk. I cannot imagine living there.

The Tanks and the Flume

Besides exploring below the house, we hiked to the tanks and the flume. This adventure took several hours. This was probably my favorite hike or walk – ever.

We packed Gary and Barney's Boy Scout rucksacks with sandwiches, cookies, and fruit. Unless we planned and got bologna or salami from Beck & Bishop, the sandwich was usually Underwood Deviled Ham with Hellmann's Sandwich Spread.

Barney and Gary also brought their Army surplus canteens. They were stainless steel and fit into khaki canvas pouches with straps. I believe if the canvas was wet when it evaporated, the liquid inside got cooler. I wanted one, but I figured I couldn't because they were boys, and only boys could get Army or Navy surplus items. They shared their water with me and allowed me to use a collapsible Army surplus cup.

Across the Castle Creek Road south of our house was a large hill. In some places, it would be considered a mountain. It was a spur from Highland Mountain that became the Highlands Ski Area. It was across from the site of Celia and Bill's new house.

About halfway up the hill were a reservoir and two large water tanks holding Aspen's water supply. A wooden trough from the nearby reservoir filled the tanks. The tanks were large structures made from Michigan pine. Strips of iron girdled the tanks and were tightened as the water evaporated. Once the wood became saturated, it barely leaked. The tanks had roofs, but the reservoir was open. We owned the land around the tanks. When Lenny Thomas bought this part of the ranch, he donated that land to the City of Aspen, and hence it was named the Thomas Reservoir.

Two flumes filled the reservoir. One flume came from Castle Creek and the other from Maroon Creek. The intake for the flumes started miles up each of the rivers. The Maroon Creek inlet was near the T-Lazy-7 Ranch.

The flumes were like big ditches but were covered with wood to prevent debris and snow from falling into the water and blocking their flow. Part of the Castle Creek flume was built entirely of wood, and a portion near the tanks was cantilevered above the Castle Creek Road.

To get to the flumes, we walked to the far end of the little field and climbed the hill through the bushes and sagebrush to the Castle Creek Road at the future location of Bill and Celia's house. On the other side of the road was a wire gate and a small building over a run-off stream. The building was padlocked and had warning signs posted, including skull and crossbones. We walked up the steep two-track road to the tanks.

My sisters and other Aspen teenagers claimed they swam in the tanks. If they swam in anything, it was probably the reservoir. In any case, it was no wonder Aspen was noted for the Aspen Two-Step. It was an affliction that plagued people new to Aspen. New people in town often developed severe intestinal distress and dysentery until they acclimated to Aspen water. I later learned the water often had its share of giardia. I did not realize when I was growing up, the City of Aspen did not treat the water.

Portions of the flumes were above ground near the reservoir and the tanks. The land under the elevated flumes was damp from the drip of water coming from between the boards. The ground below was soggy, bright green, and mossy.

Once we got to the tanks, we walked west more or less under the dripping flumes until the flume was mostly in the ground. It was covered in wood and was like a wooden sidewalk through aspen trees.

I'm not sure how long it was, but we could walk for what seemed like miles as if strolling through our own private park. The trees formed a canopy over the walk, and the sky was barely visible through the leaves. It was quiet except for the sound of slowly flowing, gurgling water, a twig breaking, and the occasional sound of a bird. When I saw the movie *Stand by Me*, the scene of the boys walking through the woods on the railroad tracks reminded me of flume walking.

From time to time, there was a space in the trees where we could get a peek of the old ranch. The old ranch was mostly open, rolling fields and buildings clustered on a hilly area between the Castle Creek and Maroon Creek roads. There was a new log house next to the barn my grandfather built. A little below was the original small two-story house and the buildings where the Marolt boys lived when they were kids.

The only drawback to flume walking was Mom's fear. She worried we would get killed. When she thought of a flume, she thought of the flume on the other side of Castle Creek. That flume came from the tank area, crossed Castle Creek, and followed its east bank of the river down toward Seventh Street. It may have become the Hoaglund Ditch that supplied the water in the small ditches bordering Main Street. Unlike the new flumes, it fell into disrepair but still carried some water for a time. It was in that dilapidated condition when the doomed children walked on it. When she was little, at least one child drowned in that flume.

The new flumes were in good condition. Someone in the City had the job of walking them monthly, if not weekly. They repaired missing boards. Although I was pretty sure the flume was safe, I heeded Mom's warnings, and frequently I looked down as I walked.

Transition Year

Transition Year – Family and Town

The summer of 1960 was the last summer Mom and Dad, and all the kids were together on the ranch. Two of us were starting lives away from home.

Keith originally left home in 1954 for the University of Colorado. He came back frequently and was always there during the summers. His first stint at college did not go well. He was with a couple of Aspen High School friends, including Jim Blanning. They did not take school too seriously, and eventually, Keith dropped out. Jim Blanning was expelled. He allegedly sent an explosive device down a moat next to or under one of the sorority houses just for the hell of it.

Keith joined the Army Reserves in 1957 and went into basic training at Fort Leonard Wood, Missouri. His basic training was worse than the Army intended. Keith became ill with pneumonia requiring hospitalization. Fortunately, his stay at the military base was only for six weeks.

He worked for Jim Hayes while he fulfilled his commitment to the Army. He was required to attend weekly meetings in Glenwood Springs and extended time on the base in the summer. There were many tense nighttime trips to those meetings – especially in the winter. Glenwood was forty miles away. The two-lane road was prone to head-on collisions, was icy in winter, and next to the Roaring Fork River. That stretch of highway was known as "Killer 82." We were relieved when he came in the door late at night. Now that he was out of the Army Reserves, Keith was returning to the University of Colorado that fall.

Judy began her time at college in 1959. She went to Loretta Heights College in Denver. At the time, it was a prestigious private Catholic girls' school. She lived in a room with 15 other girls. They each had a desk, a chair, a bed, and a closet in which to change clothes. It was more like a prison or an army barracks than a dorm. She was miserable with homesickness.

The other girls were mean or, as Mom would say, "catty." They judged her the moment Keith dropped her off in our pickup. They thought of her as a hick from the sticks and treated her that way. Judy's only respite was visiting Elmer and his wife, Noreen, who lived nearby. She spent most weekends with them. She decided to transfer to the

University of Colorado in Boulder the next fall and would be there with Keith.

The fall Judy started at Loretta Heights, Dad traded in our 1956 yellow-and-black Chevrolet for a Dodge Matador station wagon. No one ever explained how that happened. Dad was a dedicated General Motors person. Maybe he bought some stock in the Chrysler Corporation and wanted to spread around his business. Perhaps someone at the Glenwood dealership talked him into it. Perhaps it was too good of a deal to pass up. Someone suggested Buck Parsons may have talked Dad into buying it. Regardless of Dad's reasons, it was a horrible decision and an awful car. First, it was peach-colored inside and out – the same shade as the "flesh" crayon in my Crayon box. That was about the time Crayola renamed the color "peach" – for obvious reasons. Besides the unappealing color, the car had fins. Even at the time, I thought they looked stupid. It featured a push-button transmission and lots of other buttons, but no power windows or air conditioning.

On the first planned trip to Denver to see Judy during the teacher's convention, it broke down as we were leaving Aspen. We took it to the Texaco station on Cooper Street. After about an hour, Dad came back with the news that the repair required parts that had to come on the bus, so we could not go to Denver. Judy was disappointed. She had been counting the days and hours until our visit. I had the impression she thought we did not want to see her and thought we broke down on purpose.

We broke down again on another trip to Denver the following spring. This time it was on the other side of Independence Pass, where the road straightens out after the big turns. It was something like a fan belt, and Dad was able to get a ride back to town to get the part. We sat for hours on the bank overlooking the north fork of Lake Creek while waiting for Dad. He returned with the part, and we finally made it to Denver.

When Judy came home for the summer of 1960, Mom, Dad, Judy, Peggy, and I took a family road trip throughout the western states. Keith stayed home to take care of the ranch and animals. After the first hay cutting, we loaded up the Dodge and set out on our journey. The plan was to head north through Wyoming and stop at the Grand Tetons and Yellowstone National Park. Then go into Montana and Glacier

National Park. From there, we were going to Banff, Lake Louise, and Calgary. We also wanted to stop at the Grand Coolie Dam and stop off to visit the Cliftons in Vancouver, British Columbia.

We planned to drive down the coast to visit relatives along the way. There were Dad's cousins, Art, and Ag Kelleher, in Crockett, California and Bev, Bob, and Rod in nearby Tormey Village. From there, it was down the coast to Los Angeles and to visit Dad's sisters Dorothy and Elsie and their families. For me, the main goal was Disneyland. From there, we would head home through Las Vegas and get back in time for Judy's long-scheduled dentist appointment.

For the most part, the trip went as planned. I collected felt pennants from all of the tourist attractions. They were shaped like college pennants with painted images of the main attraction. If they were available, I bought the slides from each attraction for my ViewMaster 3D viewer. The goal of the day was to stop at a Best Western Motel with a swimming pool. We were impressed with their quality and consistency, and Mom liked that there were coffee makers in each room.

Our first stop was Jackson Hole, Wyoming, where we saw the Grand Tetons and spent two days in Yellowstone. We saw Old Faithful, walked through one of the hot spring areas, and stayed in cabins next to the main lodge. Bears wandered around on the grass in front of our cabin.

By the time we hit Glacier National Park, it was getting cold and rainy. Low clouds and fog obscured most of the park. When we crossed the border into Canada, we learned there was snow at Banff and Lake Louise. Mom and Dad decided to cancel that part of the trip. Instead, we stopped at a tourist store north of the border, bought a few Canadian trinkets, and crossed back to the United States. Mom was disappointed; Lake Louise was the destination she chose for her part of the vacation.

Instead, we went west through Idaho and went to the Grand Coulee Dam. Dad was fascinated by the engineering. We went down to the turbines and watched some sort of register telling us the amount of electricity in terms of dollars being generated. We also found a funny sign, "Watch for falling objects. Restrooms on top of the Dam."

The next stop was Vancouver, where I got my first glimpse of an ocean. On our way north, we traveled on a freeway near Seattle and passed a fatal car crash. It was eerie – bodies lying on the pavement covered with sheets. The sky was misty and rainy, and the police car lights reflected off the highway. The scene reminded me of those horrible assemblies we had at school to warn us of the dangers of driving. They exhibited several enlarged photos of twisted vehicles and twisted bodies lying around on the ground. The bodies had black banners over their faces to hide their identity.

When we got to Vancouver, I remember coming over a hill, and down below us was a bridge crossing a large body of water. We spent three days with the Cliftons. They lived in a house on the Indian Arm Bay.

They were near rain forests. We made a short drive to one. It was fun walking through the ferns and the deadfall. We looked for Indian artifacts. I don't think we found any, but the cousins showed me arrowheads they found on earlier adventures.

The best thing we did was crabbing. The Cliftons had a floating dock about thirty feet offshore. We took a rowboat to the dock and put fish pieces in wire traps that we dropped over the edge. The water was so clear you could see the crabs going into the traps. We spent several hours catching crabs. Then we brought them up to the house. I was not at all prepared for the idea of putting them into boiling water. It was horrifying. And, for me, it was a waste. I did not try the meal Dorothy prepared because the crabs reminded me of giant spiders. I pretended to eat the food and spit it into a paper napkin.

We left Vancouver and took an auto ferry to Victoria Island for a day trip. I did okay on this leg of the trip. As with our entire Canadian vacation, the weather was damp and cloudy. We went to Bouchard Gardens. It was a fairyland. The flowers, trees, and walkways looked like varying sized bouquets among shades of green. We had lunch in a restaurant at a hotel with white linen tablecloths. I do not remember what we ate for lunch, but I remember I had the blackberry shortcake for dessert.

Then we boarded another auto ferry back to Olympia, Washington. That trip was rough, and I got seasick.

From there, we wound our way down the coast and finally got a look at the Pacific Ocean with sand and rock beaches. The highlight was going through the redwood forests and seeing the huge trees. We even drove through one of them – a well-known tourist destination with a matching pennant.

We stopped at a redwood lumber mill in Eureka. It was another one of Dad's planned stops. I liked the machine that sprayed the bark off the trees and the huge saws that cut them into boards. I wondered if this is where we got the wood for our fence. I brought home a box of redwood pencils. And a pennant.

Our next stop was to visit Dad's cousin, Ag Kelleher, the daughter of Dad's mother's sister Rose Smaker. Ag and her husband, Art, lived in Crockett, north of San Francisco. Art worked at the C&H Pure Cane Sugar factory. Ag's brothers and Dad's cousins, Tony and Steve Smaker, also lived in the area and joined us at Art and Ag's house.

Art and Ag lived only a few miles from Bev, Bob, and Rod Barnes. The Barnes lived in Tormey Village, a company town for the Selby smelter. Crockett was where Elsie, Frank, Jr., and later, Bill, lived when they left Aspen. Elsie stayed in California. Frank Jr. and Bill returned.

I played with Rod. He and I explored near his house. The area was industrial. They lived a few blocks from the smelter. There were train tracks and black and gray gravel; the Carquinez Strait and San Pablo Bay near the smelter seemed dark and murky. We caught small lizards and skipped stones in the bay. Rod showed me poison oak, which I successfully avoided.

We stayed in a motel in Vallejo but spent three days visiting Art and Ag and Bev and Bob. Art and Ag were generous people who loved to eat and cook. For our short trip, Art baked three or four cakes. He served cake as dessert even after a hearty breakfast.

That is where we first tasted the chocolate cake from the Nut Tree restaurant. The Nut Tree Cake became our favorite cake ever. Art also made a mashed-potato chocolate cake that I liked. It was moist and tasty. It had cream cheese icing.

Art took us to the C&H Sugar factory, where he worked for decades. We got a private tour, from the barge loaded with the sugar cane from Hawaii to filling powdered sugar packages like the packages we had at home. There was the strong smell of molasses from steaming vats. The inside of the building was hot and humid. At the end of the tour, we got sugar packages, a piece of sugar cane. But no pennant.

On our way back, we stopped at a big store. It may have been a forerunner of what would become Kmart. Art bought everyone a giant soft-serve, Frostee Freeze ice cream cone. Never mind that we had just finished lunch and were full. The soft-serve cones were huge. I loved soft serve, but not when I was full. I could only get about halfway down the ice cream swirl and never got close to the cone. Rod and I hid our uneaten cones behind a shelving unit so we would not offend Art.

Art and Ag and Bev and Bob took us out for separate dinners in San Francisco. We went with the Barnes family for dinner in Fisherman's Warf. I liked the deep-fried shrimp, a meatless Friday favorite.

The next day, on our way to their planned dinner, Art and Ag drove us through Berkeley, over the two bridges, to the Cliff House, down Lombard Street, to Coit Tower, where we viewed Alcatraz through binoculars, and walking around Fisherman's Warf. I got pennants and ViewMaster cards from every location.

The tour ended at an amazing Italian restaurant with white tablecloths and waiters dressed in tuxedos. We had seven or eight courses, antipasto, followed by minestrone, followed by salad, followed by a couple of kinds of pasta, followed by the main course of chicken or fish, and then dessert – Angela Pia, a whipped-cream pudding or mousse. The meal lasted for at least two hours. We talked about it for years. We had never heard of, let alone, experienced such a meal. Until that time, the standard restaurant meal was a steak dinner at the Red Onion or sauerbraten at Guido's.

We left the Bay Area early the next morning for Encino, where Dad's sister, Elsie, and her family lived. We were behind schedule and decided to take the direct route down the valley and skip Highway One next to the ocean.

Southern California was my ultimate destination. All I could think of was going to Disneyland. Before this trip, Judy went to Disneyland with Cherie when they drove to Southern California with Chuck Clifton after he finished Elsie and George's cabin. Cherie and Judy flew home.

Judy brought me a Golden Book about Disneyland and the adventures of Donald Duck, Huey, Dewey, and Louie visiting the park. In the book, Donald had trouble keeping the kids together and found them in various parts of the park just out of reach. Judy also brought me a Disneyland board game and a big map of the park. I was so excited to visit those places.

We made it to Elsie's house in the early afternoon. Elsie and her husband, George, lived in a sizeable new ranch style house in Encino.

George built high-end, custom homes. Their back yard was part of an old walnut orchard.

The day we arrived, we went to our cousin, Mary Elizabeth's house, a quintessential 1950s southern California house. There was lots of glass and turquoise blue. She and her doctor husband had a kidney-shaped swimming pool outside of the sliding glass doors. Mary Elizabeth, who I met for the first time, was attractive. She was wearing pedal pushers, wedge sandals, and her reddish hair was up in a pastel scarf. It was a treat to swim in a private pool, although it was quite small.

Shortly after arriving at Elsie's house, we realized there was a problem between Elsie and Dad's other sister, Dorothy. Dorothy wanted us to come to dinner one night, but there was no more time on the schedule if we went to Disneyland. Dad was caught in the middle. We expected Dorothy and her husband would meet us at Elsie's house. Dorothy insisted we go to her house. The two sisters each planned dinner the next day in different locations.

Dad's compromise was to cut Disneyland short. He agreed to leave Disneyland earlier in the afternoon and go to Dorothy's for an early dinner and then go back to Elsie's for a late dinner. This compromise made everyone unhappy – especially me.

We got up early the next morning and left Elsie's house. Her house was shielded from the Los Angeles basin. As we wound through the hills, the air changed. A sea of gray was before us. The sky was gray. The freeways were gray. The buildings we passed were gray. Wavy light radiated off the freeway. Silhouettes of gray palm trees were barely visible through the thick air. My eyes burned. My nose tingled. I doubted Disneyland existed in this mess.

However, when we got through the gate of Disneyland, everything was as good or better than I hoped. Going through the entrance into Main Street was truly "magical." The sky was still gray, but the inside of the park was an oasis in the gray, smoggy Los Angeles stew.

We bought our booklets of A to E tickets. The A rides were simple vehicles such as a fire truck on Main Street or a tour of Sleeping Beauty's Castle. We toured the Monsanto house of the future – a C ticket. The raft trip over to Tom Sawyer's Island was a D ticket. I was reminded of the raft at Steve's pasture with the same dark water. Although we spent fifteen minutes on the island, I suspected Ingrid, and I could kill an entire day there.

The new rides – the submarine and the Matterhorn were E tickets. We tried to even out the tickets. We went on the Jungle Cruise and the Submarine. I was too short for the Matterhorn and to drive in the Autopia. I was annoyed because I had been driving the Jeep for a while. Instead, I rode with Peggy while she drove. It was still cool to be on a miniature freeway with miniature stoplights.

We rode in the Teacups, which, not surprisingly, made me sick. We did not go on the train because it was not that special and would take too long. We skipped the Skyway because it was like a chairlift. Similarly, we did not ride the mules in Frontierland. While we explored, Mom and Dad went to a show in a Frontierland "saloon." We did not have enough time to shop on Main Street except for me to get my pennants and ViewMaster slides.

Given the short amount of time allotted to the adventure, we got a remarkable amount done. As it turns out, we went to the park the day after Labor Day. Because most schools in the Los Angeles area and around the country opened on that day, it was one of the least busy days of the year. But for that inadvertent day selection, we would have made it on two rides at best.

On the way out of the park, we stopped and bought a snack to save room for our late lunch at Dorothy's and left. I was disappointed. There was so much more I wanted to do, to see, and to explore. I would not come back again until I was in college. At the time of the family trip, I never imagined a future in which my kids and I would have Disneyland passes and visit the park seven or eight times a year – sometimes for a single ride down Splash Mountain or for Christmas shopping on Main Street.

After leaving Disneyland, we drove again through the smog to Dorothy's house in Hacienda Heights. The smog seemed even worse here. She had a small house, and it was especially hot because she had been cooking. Their lot was big enough to raise chickens.

Dorothy, her husband, Will, and daughter, Bernadette, came to Aspen to visit over the years. Bernadette was a couple of years older than Judy, so she was not my playmate. Will King was a tall skinny man with white hair that used to be blond. He had a long beak-shaped nose and pale skin. He gave me the creeps; when I was little, and he visited Aspen, I refused to sit on his lap or hug him. Nothing changed on this trip.

Dorothy had sad droopy eyes and seemed depressed. Even as I kid, I could see that. She was close to Ted. She had been like his mother when he was a baby. She was nine years older than him. The two older sisters, Pauline and Mary, had been the ones raising Ted, but that changed after they died in the flu pandemic. Pauline's baby, Julia, needed care. Dorothy took over Julia and Ted's care. I have since learned that Dorothy's drooping eyes may have resulted from Bell's Palsy.

I don't remember Dorothy's meal, but I'm sure it was a traditional Aspen meal similar to what her family ate when she was growing up. There wasn't much for me to do that long afternoon except look at my ViewMaster and wish I was still in Disneyland. Later, we went back to Elsie's for yet another dinner. This time, it was food on the grill in the back yard. At least at Elsie's, the sky was clearer.

We left late the next morning and drove to Las Vegas. We followed George out of town on a shortcut through the hills. We did not have air conditioning, so it was a long hot drive. I doubt if many people had air conditioning in their cars at that time. At most, they may have had a window-mounted swamp cooler.

Once in Las Vegas, we found a motel on Main Street, but not on the "strip." Mom and Dad left us alone and went to the Sands Hotel to do some gambling. As they were walking into the casino, Sammy Davis, Jr., and his entourage blew past Mom. She was so excited to see such an iconic performer that close.

Despite Mom and Dad staying out late, we got up early the next morning. The plan was to drive straight through to home. Judy had a dentist appointment the next afternoon. She and Peggy drove some of the time to compensate for Mom and Dad's hangovers. At one point, Peggy slammed on the breaks to avoid hitting a bird on the highway. There was lots of yelling and screaming. We all survived, including the bird.

This was the longest day of the trip. It was hot, and there was little to see. Our previous routine was to turn out at each historic site to look at the wagon tracks and the sites of Indian massacres, but now we wanted to get home.

We made it to Grand Junction late in the afternoon and were too hot and tired to go the extra distance. We stayed one last night in a motel. I did not care if it was a Best Western or if it had a pool. If it had an air-conditioning unit in the window, that is all I wanted.

We got up early and struck out for home. I could hardly wait to be back to see Keith and Patty and Nipper and sleep in my bed and look out on beautiful blue skies, the last of which we had seen in Wyoming.

As we started into the De Beque canyon along the Colorado River, we heard a thumping sound, and the car swerved. Dad drove off to the side of the road. We made it all these thousands of miles in this horrible car, and it chose this final moment to break down. It turns out it was a blown tire. Changing the tire required unloading the back of the car to get the spare. Dad was able to change the tire. We debated whether we should stop and get a new spare but decided to take a chance and see if we could make it home.

We got home without further incident, but Judy missed her appointment. The dentist was mad and unforgiving. I believe his name was Dr. Markle. He was the dentist that pulled all of Mom's teeth and made her false teeth. He claimed she had pyorrhea. He had a dental office in his house on the corner of Main and Seventh Street. I never had any pleasant experiences in his office. After his temper tantrum, we never went to him again. Thankfully, about that time, the town got a new dentist – Dr. William Comcowich.

We kept that horrible peach-colored car for several more years. Dad then got the Buick he always wanted. It was a 1964 Buick Wildcat. This time he didn't go to a showroom and take whatever they had on the floor – like that yellow-and-black 1956 Chevrolet or the peach-colored Dodge. This time, he ordered what he wanted.

At that time, it was not uncommon to go to a dealer and place a specific order with the automobile manufacturer. Dad picked the color – maroon with a white top and saddle-brown leather upholstery. He got air conditioning and electric everything – doors, windows, and seats. He stewed over the order for weeks before placing it but ended up forgetting one item – an automatic windshield washer. Retrofitting the washer was prohibitive, so, despite getting the almost perfect car, having that one flaw dogged him. At least the Buick was handsome and reliable.

I found it sad that, at the time Dad got his car, a new girl from Texas came to high school. She drove the same car, except hers was a convertible with a white leather interior. Dad saved and worked for years for his car, and she got her car as a gift for her sixteenth birthday. I never mentioned it to Dad. This incident portended significant changes to Aspen.

When we returned from our trip, it was every bit as good to be home as I hoped. It was now early September getting cool with patches of yellow on the hillsides. It was so nice to see Patty. Nipper was happy to see us. Ingrid came out, and we hung my pennants on the wall above my bed. There were at least 20 of them. She viewed all the ViewMaster slides. She filled me in on everything that happened while we were gone, with our friends and the current gossip.

Within a day or two, Judy and Keith packed and left for Boulder. Peggy was a senior. I was in sixth grade. By this time, it was noticeable that Aspen was growing and changing at a rapid pace. Many of the ranch kids were gone. Their ranching operations experienced the same problems Dad and Steve had with range rights. For instance, the Rene Duroux's, who shared the range with Dad, moved further down the valley. That meant LeRoy Duroux left my class. The same happened to some of the Skiffs.

Doctor Lewis and his family left for Glenwood Springs. Connie Lewis was one of Mom's best friends, and I played with Julie. Visiting them in Glenwood was not the same. Earlier, George and Pepper Tekoucich moved to Glenwood. Each year when school started, we were curious to see who was new and who was gone.

The red brick school could no longer hold all twelve grades. The county decided to build a new elementary school kitty-corner to the old school on the other side of Hallam and Center. It was the site of the skating rink. The new school was modern and made from yellowish bricks. It was supposed to open when we started school that fall, but it was not completed at the beginning of the year. At the first of the year, some students went to school in the morning and others in the afternoon. If they split my class, I was in the morning session. I would have remembered if I had to wait to start school late. I was never good at waiting. I wanted to get school and church and piano lessons over, so I did not have to ruin my day, dreading the impending loss of freedom.

That year we had a new teacher, John Kuehlman. He was the first male elementary teacher in Aspen. I liked him, although it was clear he had a favorite student – Nick DeVore. He got Nick's attention by kiddingly hurling chalkboard erasers at him. Mr. Kuehlman taught us the bones in the body. I still remember them.

I finally got a bicycle. Dad and Mom got me a girl's Raleigh English Racer with three-speeds, narrow tires, and hand brakes. Dad got it from Bert Bidwell at the Mountain Shop. It cost nearly $100.00. Because it was a girl's bike, I could ride it to school wearing a dress or a skirt. Girls were still not allowed to wear pants to school except ski pants on activities days. I wore pettipants – shorts made from slip material – under my skirts.

I got a cute wicker basket for the front of the bike as a gift. When I loaded it with schoolbooks, it was too heavy and pressed on the front fender, and the fender rubbed the tire. Dad built a device he attached to the hub of the wheel to support the basket. I rode the bicycle to school every day when the weather permitted. Upon Mom's orders, I walked my bike on the elevated sidewalk across the old narrow Castle Creek Bridge. She did not want me riding along with cars, and I didn't argue. The State of Colorado replaced the bridge the next summer.

By late fall, the school building was completed. One afternoon we got a tour. It was going to be so cool to have a new school. It had that new school smell. We went back to our old classrooms in the red brick building and picked up our desks and carried them across the street to our new room.

Our classroom was toward the front of the school, and the windows faced north. Each of the rooms had an outside door as an emergency exit. There was now a music room in the school, and this is where I had my piano lessons with Mona Frost. She was now the principal. My sixth-grade class made a mosaic mural of construction paper tiles of the new school that covered the back wall of our room.

The school had an all-purpose room, which was half the size of a gymnasium. We used it for physical education. We tumbled and did calisthenics. There may have been a couple of basketball hoops, and we played badminton and volleyball. We also played a variety of other games.

One game was steal-the-bacon. In that game, we lined up on opposite sides of the gym, and each side counted off. The teacher put a bean bag in the center of the room, and if they called your number, you, and the person with the same number on the other side ran to grab the "bacon." If you could run back with the bacon without getting tagged, your team got two points. If the other person tagged you, his team got one point.

One day my number was called, and because I always took competitions seriously, I ran full speed to the center of the room and ran headfirst into Robert Troyer. Robert was about a head taller than me and twenty pounds heavier. I smashed my nose on his head. I suspect I broke it, although it was not dislodged. It knocked me on my back, and the pain was intense. I ended up with a swollen nose and black eyes.

Beneath the all-purpose room was a lunchroom. It had some high windows on the south side. Eventually, this was the room used for high-school dances. It was easier to decorate than the old school gym and a much better size for our school population.

It was in this lunchroom where I committed my second serious crime. I had previously stolen a set of sewing needles from the Kalmes' store. In this cafeteria, I purposefully stole a carton of milk. I did not need or want milk any more than needles, but for some reason, I was overcome by a desire to steal. What made this instance so memorable was that I was more aware of the sin of stealing at this time than I was previously, and I knew I was not going to confess it. I knew that if I admitted the theft, Father Bosch would condition my forgiveness on telling Mom or Dad. They would make me go to school and confess. This was not going to happen, so I did not confess. Instead, I went around with a blotch on my soul.

I pictured my soul as an oval white flat pillow in the chest area. I'm guessing that is how someone drew a soul in a catechism class. If one was free from sin, the soul was bright white. Venial sins were gray and were of different sizes depending on the severity – how big a lie, how badly we disobeyed, or how bad was the thought. Mortal sins, on the other hand, left a black mark. Stealing was a black mark. However, the size of the theft seemed to matter in my mind, so my milk theft left a relatively small black spot. It was probably smaller than if I committed the mortal sin of missing Mass or eating meat on Fridays or inappropriately touching myself. I'm guessing murder made the soul totally black.

During the first Christmas vacation in the new school, Keith married Joyce Olson. She was from Boston but was living in Aspen and working as a lab technician at the hospital. She met Keith through

Betty Beck. Betty was a nurse at the hospital. She met Max when she tended to him because of a severe back problem. Earlier that year, Max married Betty. Both were attractive. Betty was tall and blond with her long hair in a French roll, and Joyce had short black hair. Joyce had a Boston accent.

At that time, the hospital was still the old creepy looking brick building where I was born. The nurses and technicians who worked there lived in the building. They were not paid much but got a lot of perks. They had free rent while living upstairs in the hospital and got free lift tickets and discounts on everything imaginable, including meals at restaurants.

Keith and Joyce married right after Christmas. Joyce made Christmas miserable that year because she was always late. She was not a few minutes late; she was really late. That Christmas, Keith wanted us to wait for Joyce before we opened presents. That was something we usually did about 6:00 am. I reluctantly agreed we could wait until 7:00. Joyce and Keith did not get to our house until after 9:00. I had been sitting waiting for hours, and then we rushed through our presents as we rushed through Disneyland earlier that year. I felt like there was some sort of conspiracy to ruin my most anticipated experiences.

Keith and Joyce got married at the Catholic Church, although she was not Catholic. Joyce was wearing a walking cast because she broke her leg skiing earlier that fall. She wore a white satin toe sock. They left the church in a horse-drawn sleigh and had a reception at the Golden Horn. Joyce's parents, her sister, and her brother came from Massachusetts for the wedding. Instead of a white cake, she had a brownish and dense cake, but it had cream-cheese icing. That was my second experience with that delectable treat.

They moved to Boulder until Keith finished school. Joyce worked at Wardenburg, the medical center at the University of Colorado.

That same vacation, Judy got engaged to Chuck Tesitor. She and Chuck first met when they were in grade school, but Chuck left town when his family moved to Grand Junction. He was related to Buck Parsons and Buck's sister, Marjorie Jenkinson. She was now running the movie theatre. Chuck was handsome with dark hair and blue eyes. He was an exceptional tennis player and worked as a tennis instructor at the Meadows. Chuck was also going to engineering school at the

University of Colorado and had been Keith's roommate the fall before Keith married Joyce.

In the spring of sixth grade, besides getting a new bike, a new school, and a soon to be new bridge, I got a new horse. Although Patty was still a good saddle horse for short distances, she had asthma. We needed another horse for work around the ranch. Dad and I went to the T-Lazy-7 to trade hay for a couple of horses. Had Deane, along with his wife, Lou, owned the ranch. The Deanes had many horses for their ranch operations and for guests of their dude ranch. They grew their own hay; however, Had liked Dad's hay for some of his horses because it did not have any dust.

Dad and I met with Had. He culled out a couple of horses he thought would meet our needs. They were a bit too spirited for dude ranch guests but were suitable for more experienced riders and herding cattle.

The two light gray and tan, medium-sized appaloosas – who were probably siblings – were in one of their corrals near the barn. They were about four years old, were broken, and would meet our ranching needs and long trail rides. They were nice looking but not fancy. I'm not sure if they were mares or geldings.

Then I saw Ringo. I do not think that was his name at the time. He was shiny black with four white socks. He was tall and regal, and his mane waived as he trotted back and forth at the back end of the corral. He was every little girl's dream of the horse – just like Black Beauty. Someone said he was a thoroughbred. Once I saw Ringo, I had to have him, and I begged and begged and begged.

Dad, too, was getting emotional over the available horses. He saw a white horse. He commented, "That horse looks just like Snake." Remember, as far as the Marolts were concerned, there never was a horse like Snake. He asked if the two horses were available for trade and Had said they were. I bet Had thought Dad had lost his mind because these were not the types of horses typically used for ranch work.

While both horses were broken, neither was trained as a cow pony. Had said he knew a couple of guys down the valley who were available to train them if we wanted. Against his better judgment, Dad decided to forgo the appaloosas and for our emotional choices.

Had delivered the horses a couple of days later, and the two of them pranced back and forth in the corral next to the granary and the barn. I bet Steve looked at them and drawled, "That ain't Snake." I bet he did not think much of the black horse because he was too tall for a cattle horse. That being said, they were a beautiful pair

Dad named the black horse Ringo after *Johnny Ringo* – the song and the outlaw. He named the white horse Rowdy for Rowdy Yates on *Rawhide*. Although Dad and Steve had done their share of breaking horses, Dad hired a wrangler from Carbondale to work with them. That decision did not work out well. Dad said the wrangler made Ringo skittish because he waived a coat or cloth of some sort before his eyes and around his ears. After that, Ringo seemed to look out of the corner of his eye, ready to jump sideways if something even slightly surprised him. I do not remember riding Rowdy.

Within a year or two after we got them, Rowdy developed some sort of illness. Dad worked with the vet to heal him. I do not recall what was wrong. One morning, Dad found Rowdy dead in a lower pasture near the highway. Dad buried him there. That left us with Patty and Ringo.

Ringo was too big and powerful for me. He was easy to catch and friendly when no one was riding him. I rode him rarely because he was prone to jump to the side if I moved my arm too quickly, or he heard the snapping of a twig. He was tall, and it was a long fall to the ground. Even with a saddle, it was a reach for me to put my foot in the stirrup. I never rode him bareback.

He was hard for me to control. I fantasized about riding him into town where everyone would turn their head and be jealous of my beautiful horse. I did not trust riding him to town or on the trail rides to places like Willow Lake or American Lake. Instead, I admired the beautiful horse but continued to ride Patty when I wanted a short ride. I knew I made a mistake based on what I thought others would think of me because I had a beautiful horse.

A couple of years after we traded for Ringo and Rowdy, I stopped by the old ranch after walking on the Maroon Creek flume by myself. Although Ted sold the ranch to Elizabeth and Walter Paepcke in the early fifties, it remained a ranch for years. Mrs. Paepcke built a modern log house, fixed up the big barn, and hired Danny Barry, an Irishman, to run the ranch for her. He raised hay and horses. He lived in the house.

I stopped to watch Danny working with his horses in a riding ring. The ranch had many horses, and Danny taught English riding and jumping. Every year at the time of the Kentucky Derby, he came to our house to watch the race on our TV. He brought along beer – Guinness Stout, I presume.

The day I stopped at the old ranch Danny showed me a sorrel mare named Lady. He suspected Dad was not happy with the new horses. "Are you riding that big black horse of yours?"

"A little."

"I think he's too big for you. Would you like to ride Lady for a couple of days? She's a nice horse."

"Really? That will be fun."

He saddled her with an English saddle. I never learned how to post, which seemed like an integral part of English riding, so my use of an English saddle was wasted. I adjusted the stirrups as if it was a western saddle without the horn. I took her home and thoroughly enjoyed riding her. She had a pleasant gait. She was easy to control.

Danny thought Lady was a good horse for me. She was a bit taller than Patty, but younger and healthy and easy going. Dad agreed she was a good horse but said we already had Ringo and Danny wanted $300. He said I could not keep her.

I believed at least part of the reason for Dad's decision was he didn't want to bring in another new horse and take flak from Steve for choosing Ringo and Rowdy in the first place. Dad pretended they were what we wanted. If we got a new horse, Dad was admitting he made a mistake. Steve would gloat, "I told you so," – so, no new horse for me. I continued to ride Patty, and from time to time, I tried to ride Ringo.

The summer after I got Ringo, we focused on Judy's wedding. She and Chuck chose Mom's birthday, August 19, for the ceremony. One would think Mom would be honored to have her daughter choose her birthday as a wedding date, but Mom was miffed. Mom loved her birthday, and Judy stepped on her special day.

Several years earlier, Dad arranged for a surprise birthday party for Mom. I do not think it was a special year because I was about nine or ten at the time. Mom turned 40 when I was four and 50 when I was 14. The party was somewhere in between.

Dad planned the event and wanted it in the back of the house. He brought in chairs and tables he borrowed from the Catholic Church. The guests brought potluck dishes, much like picnic food. Judy or Peggy made Mom's favorite yellow cake with seven-minute icing sprinkled with flaked coconut and ringed with orange and yellow nasturtiums. They picked the flowers in advance to assure the little black bugs that often lived in the plants would be out of the flowers and not crawl all over the cake.

Dad's biggest concern was making sure it was a surprise. He made it clear that everyone was to park at the granary and walk up the trail to the back of the house. He was most concerned that Celia and Albina did not get there late.

The ruse to get mom out of the house was a shopping trip in Glenwood. That gave us the time to set everything up behind the house. Albina and Celia were early. Unfortunately, Celia walked around the house and was in the kitchen, getting a drink of water when Mom and Dad walked in. Mom did not seem to think it strange that Celia was in the kitchen without her car parked in the driveway. She probably thought Celia had walked down from her house if she thought anything at all. Despite that one glitch, the party was a surprise and a lot of fun. Dad installed a floodlight on the back of the house so they could party late at night. There was polka music for dancing.

When Judy got married, she had her reception in the front part of the lawn. Judy prided herself on being conservative and practical, so she bought a knee-length dress with a short veil at a department store. She made the yellow bridesmaid dresses for Peggy and Cherie. I was too young to be a bridesmaid and too old to be a flower girl. I just got to wear a new dress and a new lace chapel veil. LeRoy Thompson, a caterer in town, baked the cake and catered the reception. Mom took cooking classes from him in later years, and I still use many of his recipes, including "Chicken LeRoy." It was his version of chicken tetrazzini. Franz Berko took the wedding photographs.

There was plenty to drink. For the main reception, there was a champagne punch with an orange-juice and tea base. Mom bought a glass punchbowl from one of the discount catalogs. There were ice rings with either fruit or flowers inside. After the bride and groom left on their honeymoon, Max brought out Wild Turkey.

Max got toasted. He drove Edmund down to the end of the road to where the State of Colorado was just completing a new Castle Creek Bridge. It was due to open in a day or two. The State blocked access to the bridge with heavy road equipment. That did not stop Max. He got on one of the vehicles, managed to start it, and moved it out of the way. Then he and Edmund drove across the bridge and claimed the distinction of being the first to cross it. I do not know if anyone knew what they had done, but knowing Max, I doubt if he went out of his way to keep it a secret.

Part IV

The Next Six Years

Only Child

Only Child

In the fall of 1961, I started junior high, and for this and many other reasons, my life changed. That fall, Peggy left home for the University of Colorado at Boulder. When I was growing up, there had always been a brother and sisters in the house.

As Peggy prepared to leave for college, she had tons of clothes to pack because, as a junior, she lost a lot of weight. When in grade school, she and a girlfriend were riding bicycles in town and were hit by a car. Although not seriously injured, she started gaining weight. Junior high and early high school were awkward because of the extra weight, glasses, and a short pageboy haircut.

After the weight loss, Peggy was petite and pretty. She had a tiny waist, a brilliant smile, and sparkling eyes. Dad was so proud of her and her accomplishment that he took her on a daughter-father trip and bought her new clothes at Bullocks in Glenwood Springs. Among other items, she got a yellow blazer with black piping and a matching yellow-and-black plaid skirt. It was the outfit featured on the cover of *Seventeen Magazine*.

When she left for college, I went with Mom and Dad to drop Peggy at her dorm. She was in Farrand Hall. I was jealous. I thought it looked like fun to be in college – especially in this college in this dorm that looked like a castle. Peggy flourished in college – especially in her social life. She was active in the Newman Club and had lots of friends. She was the University's Harvest Queen. That fall, Keith, Judy, and Peggy were all going to the University of Colorado at the same time.

When we got home, I started seventh grade, and it was like I was an only child. The house seemed big, empty, and quiet. I was used to Keith's room being vacant most of the time. I liked his room. It was next to my room, but with two windows. It was very light. A few of his artifacts remained, including his baseball-playing monks. They were three porcelain monks about eight inches tall in their brown robes with rope belts. One was a catcher, one was a batter, and the other was an outfielder.

Most of his childhood books were in the bookcase he built in shop class. That is where I was first introduced to Jack London and read other books and stories Keith collected. With Peggy gone, the room across from the bathroom was also empty. That was the one with the connecting, single beds, and the corner desk unit. It, too, had some of Peggy and Judy's knick-knacks.

I went back to school in the red-brick building. It now housed junior high and high school. Junior high was seventh and eighth grades. In junior high, we went from class to class, like the high school students. The teachers stayed in their rooms. Each teacher taught two subjects. Being in junior high, we had lockers. Unfortunately, the new junior high lockers, shared by two students, had only one shelf. Therefore, I commandeered Dad to help me make a second shelf above the space for our snow boots.

Thinking about my locker, I realize that I went through both junior high and high school without the benefit of backpacks. I do not remember backpacks when I went to undergraduate school, either.

In junior high, one of my friends had a plaid satchel, but it could carry only one or two thin books and a few spiral notebooks. For the most part, we brought our books to and from home in our arms.

In high school, the "cool" guys carried their books with their arms down and pressed slightly next to their hips. I carried mine in my arms, hugged to my chest. Every day I brought home at least four books and my loose-leaf binder. The binder had a tab for each class and a pencil pouch, and a ruler.

One time at catechism class, I brought in my stack of books. That year we had our class in the kitchen of the church. I hoisted my books onto the counter, separating the kitchen from the big all-purpose room.

Mrs. Fitzpatrick, the teacher, asked, "Do you really need to carry around all those books?"

"Yes. I have an assignment in each of the books. It's like this most days."

While carrying our books, we were vulnerable to other students coming up and knocking them out of our arms as a joke. Many times, on my way to Pearl's house, the books shifted in every direction and fell into the snow. It was because of the heavy books that Dad needed to make a brace on my bicycle for the wicker basket.

Besides having lockers and changing classes, junior high brought other changes. One Monday late in September, Ingrid was not at school.

I saw her the weekend before. While the teacher took roll, she stopped at Ingrid's name.

"I need to tell you children that Ingrid will be out for a while. I am sorry to report that her father passed away last night."

"Passed away," I thought. "What does that mean?" I knew the answer, but the words did not register.

I was sitting in one of the rooms on the west side of the building. I looked up through the school's windows with the ski hill blurred in the background and felt confused. Parents are not supposed to die. I never heard of this before. Was this what the nun was warning me about back in sister school?

Before that day, while I had been around for Grandma and Grandpa's death, I was young and did not understand the importance or the finality of their passing. I did not know what I would do if it were me, and I had to live without Mom or Dad. For the first time in my life, I realized losing a parent was a possibility.

When Mom picked me up at school that day, I went with her to Ingrid's house to drop off food Mom prepared for the relatives and friends gathering at their house. Ingrid's eyes were red and puffy. I had no idea what to say.

I am not sure if we went to the rosary, but I know we went to the funeral Mass. I do not remember going to Red Butte Cemetery. I wished Ingrid could get her father back.

It is not surprising that I started to notice Dad's health. His health issues were not constant but affected him from time to time. There was talk about his need to change his diet because of cholesterol. He was supposed to stop eating butter. We began using Fleishman Margarine. We broiled chicken instead of frying it. There was talk Dad should consider moving to a lower altitude. Most importantly, Dad was supposed to quit smoking. Quitting smoking was a long process for him. Although we thought Dad stopped smoking, I found hidden cigarette packages in the granary and an occasional butt floating in the basement toilet.

As far as I was concerned, Dad's biggest issue was his breathing. From time to time, I noticed he had shortness of breath when he was exerting. Often, his color changed. I gauged how he was feeling by the color of the tops of his ears. If they were bluish to purple, it was bad. If they were pink, it was good. In the late fifties, the Asian flu exacerbated the breathing issues he had from the time he was a child and had a bad case of pneumonia. A doctor told his parents Dad had permanent lung damage, and if he ever got pneumonia again, it would kill him.

Other than the breathing, Dad complained, "Arthur has got me." That meant he was experiencing arthritis pain in his knees. He also had bouts of gout. Like other members of his family, Dad was prone to depression. It often occurred when he said good-bye to his children. When that time came, he got quiet and was glum for a day or two. I tried to cheer him up, but it did not work. Instead, I got blue too.

For the most part, these health issues did not dominate our life. Dad did about everything he had always done around the ranch and in the house. The health issues were now in the background of our daily life.

Besides being like an only child, the change in my life was coming at an awkward time. I was in seventh grade. Because I was a little slow to mature, I was probably more like a sixth grader, so I was still a kid.

In 1962, the summer after Seventh Grade, we had a large family reunion at Bill and Celia's house. Judy and Chuck were in town for the summer. Chuck was teaching tennis at the Meadows, and Judy was pregnant. Her baby was due in July. Relatives came from out of town – Keith and Joyce, Bud and Jeanine and their children, Jamie and Ted, Rose, Joe, and Julia Strauss and two of their daughters, Cindy and Mardi, and their son Ronnie, and Elsie and George Rinker. Peggy and Billy were both home from the University of Colorado. Max and Betty were there with their two children, Marlis and Roger. Of course, Steve, Polly, and Ted were there as always. The only missing family members were Bev, Bob, and Rod, who arrived later that month.

It was a fun event. The best part of the get together was Billy's trampoline was in the back yard before he moved it into the pit over the hill. We jumped on it late into the night, where the only light was from the kitchen window.

A few weeks after the family reunion, Judy gave birth to the first grandchild, Karen. Late one afternoon, there was some commotion and some hushed conversation. Judy and Chuck left the house and said they were on the way to the hospital. Chuck came back later that evening because he was having a bout of hay fever or a cold. Judy gave birth before he got back to the hospital. We went to see Karen over the next several days, and then Judy brought her home. It was odd knowing Judy was a mother. I liked holding Karen – she was small. Billy and I were her godparents.

Sometime after giving birth, Judy experienced postpartum depression to such an extent that she had to be sedated. Of course, they did not know what it was or what caused it. She blamed Mom, who she said was making her feel guilty for not helping entertain out of town guests. I do not remember the particulars, but it would not surprise me if Mom were neither aware nor considerate of Judy's condition. Mom was probably subconsciously extracting servitude in exchange for the room and board. Mom had a streak where she started feeling people were overstaying their welcome.

Later that summer, Judy, Chuck, and Karen returned to Boulder. They lived in the barracks near the Quonset huts used by the University as married-student housing. It was off Water Street. The site later became Canyon Boulevard. On one of our trips that fall, Dad made and installed kitchen cabinets from some of the Masonite from Camp Hale. A football game was also part of this trip. Dad loved Colorado football.

By late summer, before entering eighth grade, adolescent awkwardness started hitting me. I gained some weight. I noticed it first around my waist. I sat on a bench in the big room on the church's first floor and looked down. I saw fat rolls on my midsection, and the shirtwaist dress was gaping at the buttons. It was getting uncomfortable.

Late that summer, Ingrid got her hair cut short at Amelia's Hair Salon. Until that time, Ingrid and I both wore a long braid down our backs. If cutting her hair short was not enough of a shock, she also got a perm and curled it into a perfectly round bubble haircut. It looked like the hair on my Barbie.

I immediately followed suit. Instead of Amelia's, I went to the Klip & Kurl. Jean Frye, the owner, put in a rubber band at the nape of my neck, braided my hair straight down my back instead of first putting it into a high ponytail. My braid went almost down to my waist. Then with one clip, she cut it off and handed it to me. I had that sick feeling like I had in the movie the *Nun's Story* when they cut off Audrey Hepburn's hair. The haircutting scene convinced me I would never be a nun.

I am not sure if this is accurate, but I have an image of Jean with a lit cigarette between her lips as she cut my hair. Jean tended to look masculine with short hair and slacks. Years later, I learned that she and another female hairdresser in her shop were a couple.

As I looked in the mirror, she snipped at my hair here and there. Then she curled it on small pink and blue rollers and poured on a foul-smelling liquid. This was the perm. After she rinsed out the chemicals, she put slightly larger rollers in my hair and put me under the hairdryer. After the hair was dry, she brushed it out, teased it, and sprayed it with hair spray. My hair looked like a carved-out brown ball on my head. I would have described it as an Afro, but the curls were too big. Perhaps it was a bit more like Little Orphan Annie's hair. Because I was now getting chubby, this haircut looked worse on me than it did on Ingrid.

When I came home, I pretended I liked it. Everyone was polite, but I knew, and they knew this was a huge mistake. I went into my room and took out the braid, which I tucked in a box in my hutch drawer and wished I could reattach it. I tried wetting the hair and hoping the perm would go away – it did not. It smelled for a long time, and I had to endure growing it out. Most of the time, I tied a bandana on my head. I had a triangular madras scarf with ties, which came with a matching dress, and I wore it all the time. Once I got the pattern, I drug out the sewing machine and made several scarves to match my clothes. By ninth grade, my hair was straight in a blunt cut below my chin. It stayed that way throughout high school. I finally got my long hair back when I went to college and became a hippie.

To top off my adolescence, I was getting acne and dandruff. I was sitting in civics class while Mr. McEachern droned on about the senate and the house of representatives. I scratched my scalp and watched dandruff snow building up on my dark-blue canvass-covered binder. I liked seeing how much dandruff snow I could make in one sitting.

My acne problem was centered on my forehead. At that time, no matter how many times I washed my face, it always seemed greasy. In that same civics class, a few days later, I felt a huge pimple on my forehead. Mom warned me about popping pimples. Once again, doing so could kill you. She said she knew of a girl who popped a pimple or a blackhead on her upper lip, pinched a nerve, and died of a brain "rupture."

I questioned the story, but just to be safe, I made sure the pimples were ripe enough that it took little effort to extract them. As I sat there that day, I could almost feel the skin pulling across this large pimple. I reached up to my forehead, barely touched it, and it erupted, shooting all over my desk. I am not sure if anyone saw it. It was sort of embarrassing, but yet so satisfying. That was my most memorable pimple ever.

Ironically, as awkward and bad as I felt about my changing body, I became a junior high cheerleader. Can you imagine? Our sports mascot was a skier, and our colors were – hold on – red and black. As junior high cheerleaders, we took the color theme to an extreme. We had black circle felt skirts, black turtlenecks, red sweater vests, red tights, and black tennis shoes with red pom-poms. Looking like that, we swaggered down the hall on pep-rally days. Ingrid was also one of the five cheerleaders, and she, like me, was sporting her matching bubble haircut. At least her hair was blond. The sophisticated high school cheerleaders had white sweaters and skirts, red pleat inserts, and a black letter "A" on their chests.

Besides being a cheerleader, the fall of eighth grade was not going well with my haircut and changing body. It got even worse when Dad and I went to a movie together. I watched many movies at that time: *Village of the Damned*, *Journey to the Center of the Earth*, *Psycho*, and *The Birds*.

Dad, on the other hand, rarely went to movies. That fall, he learned the theater was going to show the movie *Mein Kampf*, which was a documentary about the rise and fall of Nazi Germany and how Hitler was able to hoodwink an entire nation and the world. I was not particularly interested in world or military history but jumped at the chance to go to a movie with Dad. That night, I was conflicted because it was Sunday night, and I wanted to stay home and watch TV. The best television was on Sunday evening.

As we sat waiting for the movie to start, I wished I had a wristwatch with a tiny TV screen so I could see my programs anywhere. My fantasized TV was an upgrade from the *Dick Tracy* two-way radio watch. I would never have believed such a thing would exist in my lifetime.

That night, I also realized it was time for me to start using deodorant. Wow – that came on suddenly!

I cannot say how profoundly the movie affected me. It showed the rise of Nazi Germany, but there was a part of the movie focused on the treatment of the Jewish people in Poland. This was the first time I had heard anything about the Holocaust. There were photographs and films of the concentration and death camps. There were photos of piles of skeletal bodies, piles of eyeglasses, and piles of human teeth. There were photos of the naked women and children holding bars of soap as they headed into showers.

The motion pictures in a Polish ghetto particularly horrified me. One of the scenes was on the sidewalk, where German soldiers taunted children and made them dance for a limp carrot. These particular scenes may have come from Joseph Goebbels' files, and the monster may have filmed them himself. The children, who were about my age, were starving skeletons covered with skin. I was horrified. I could not sleep for weeks, haunted by the images.

When we left the theater, Dad did not say much. I think he, too, was disturbed and regretted going himself, let alone taking me. I do not believe he had any idea of the focus on the Holocaust. Until that night, most of what I knew about Hitler and World War II was in movies in the theater about famous battles and American heroics – the John Wayne type movies. I do not know if Dad understood the scope and horror of what happened to the Jewish people before that movie. I doubt if he had ever seen pictures like those we saw that night. I know he would not have taken me had he known.

I later learned one of Dad's cousins, Maria Rupert, who remained in Austria during the war, spent time in a concentration camp. She was a Catholic doctor who was helping Jewish families. She survived and came to the United States in the late forties. We never met her even though she ended up in Denver. She was now a "crazy" recluse who had many dogs. Dad may have realized this was some of what she experienced. No wonder she was the way she was.

At Christmas that year, Dad, and I again got next to a bit of history. We went to late Mass one Sunday during the holidays. Going to late Mass was rare. There are few absolutes in this world, but Dad had two.

One was we must always go to early Mass, and the other is Miracle Whip is not mayonnaise.

As to mayonnaise, there was only one, and it had to be Hellman's (now Best Foods). Dad detested Miracle Whip and forbade it in our house. He looked down scornfully on people who liked it. He claimed it tasted like the spider webs clinging to chokecherry clusters. I may have tasted the remnants of chokecherry spider webs, but they tasted kind of dusty and old and not at all like Miracle Whip. Regardless, I did not like Miracle Whip because Dad did not like Miracle Whip.

Dad's other absolute was early Mass. As far as he was concerned, there was something wrong with those who went to the high Mass at 9:00 a.m. We barely knew or associated with those people. We were all Catholics, but it was as if we were in different sects. Maybe it all came down to pragmatism. I guess he thought we sacrificed more than the late Mass crowd because we got up early on a Sunday morning to trudge to church, often while it was still dark.

Now I realize we may have done it for purely selfish reasons. Mass was shorter, with none of that time-consuming singing. During high Mass, each one of the hymns was at least three to five minutes long. The priest even sang portions of the Mass in Latin. At early Mass, the sermon was short because the audience was small. Usually, we made through an entire Mass in 35 minutes. I knew because I timed it.

The 9:00 a.m. Mass often lasted a full hour. Also, those of us going to early Mass did not have to spend too much time missing our coffee and breakfast while we fasted for communion. We got it over soon. By the time we got home before 8:00 a.m., we were done, and the rest of the people were getting ready to start. So as far as I was concerned, Dad was right about early Mass.

He did not always care about regularly attending Mass. Before I went to school, Dad went to church only on Christmas and Easter. Perhaps the event that triggered Dad's more regular attendance was the day he was crossing the street near the church when a large black Cadillac came speeding down the street. Dad jumped quickly to the edge of the road to get out of the way. The car screeched to a halt and backed up. The window rolled down, and Father Bosch stuck his head out and laughed, "Don't worry, Mike, I wouldn't hit you. I need you too much at Christmas and Easter." He was referring to the offering checks Dad wrote for those occasions.

In reality, Dad's attendance had more to do with Peggy and Judy leaving home. Dad had to take me to church, so he might as well attend. He continued to go even when those siblings were home on vacation. We were happy that his soul was saved.

On one of the rare Sundays when Dad and I went to late Mass, we were too late to sit in our usual pew on the church's east side. We ended up in the back row of the left middle section. A family crowded in the pew in front of us was bookended by a man on the isle and a woman on the inside edge, and stairstep children in between. The woman wore a large scarf decorated with horse heads and bridles. She was hunched over and appeared to be in pain when she tried to sit and kneel. Shortly into Mass, I realized it was Ethel and Bobby Kennedy and several of their children. When I went to communion, I stood next to them in line.

After Mass, I could hardly wait to talk about it, but Dad beat me to the punch.

"Did you see those people in front of us?" he said. "Did you see how sick that poor woman was? She was in a lot of pain."

"Dad. That was not some poor woman – that was Ethel Kennedy!"

"Well, I wouldn't want to be her if I felt like that."

Either that year or a year later, Bobby Kennedy and his family spent time at the Hotel Jerome. Ingrid's brother, Don, was now managing it, and she had the opportunity to meet the family one afternoon when they were in the Pink Parrot. The Pink Parrot was an ice cream parlor in the hotel. I was jealous Ingrid got to meet people like that. But on the other hand, I had Dad. I bet she would rather have her dad back.

During eighth grade, Ingrid got braces for a small space between her upper front teeth. The closest place for orthodontia was Grand Junction. That meant many trips down the valley. I went with her for her Saturday appointments. I spent the night at her house so we could leave at 6:00 a.m. for the two-and-a-half-hour trip.

At that time, Svea had a new type of Volkswagen – a dark green Type 3. It was more like a sedan than the traditional VW bug. I don't think it had any seat belts because we snuggled in the back seat and napped as Svea drove down the valley in the dark. Most of the time, the roads were dry, but sometimes they were snowy, at least as far as

Carbondale. I do not remember being afraid of the roads. I bet Svea was nervous.

When we got to Glenwood, the sky got lighter. After Glenwood, the route was canyons and gravel hillsides dotted with sparse vegetation rising above the mostly brownish-gray, and the scary-looking Colorado River. Once we got into Grand Junction, it seemed open and devoid of vegetation. In the summer, it was hot.

Ingrid's appointments were in an office over what I remember as a bank building. Svea and I sat and read in the waiting room while Ingrid got her adjustments. The waiting room had high ceilings and tall double sashed windows, and light green walls. It was a typical two-story turn of the century building.

After Ingrid's appointment, we got our reward. We ate an early lunch – usually at a soda fountain or diner – and then did some shopping. We went to J. C. Penney or Hested's. J. C. Penney had an escalator that made it feel like we were in a big city. For each trip, I brought a couple of dollars. My income sources were selling chokecherries, babysitting, and found dimes I kept in a dime bank. It held 50 dimes and did not open until there was $5. I spent one or two dollars on these shopping trips on mostly frivolous stuff such as hot-pink nail polish, headbands, or bubble bath.

The best shopping trip was on one of our last trips in 1964. By that time, Ingrid was wearing a retainer, and her appointments were coming to an end. At the same time, Grand Junction was undergoing a facelift. They built a "mall" downtown by turning Main Street into two lanes that meandered around brick or concrete planters and offset parking to make it pedestrian-friendly to encourage shopping. It was an innovative idea to revamp a deteriorating downtown. Although I doubt anyone from snobby old Aspen admitted it, the Grand Junction mall probably inspired the Aspen Mall.

This final trip to Grand Junction was when I was a freshman and after the Beatles appeared on the Ed Sullivan show. That night, after the Ed Sullivan Show, the catechism classes scheduled a Mardi Gras dance in the big room on the first floor of Saint Mary's Catholic Church. Someone had a copy of either the newly released Meet the Beatles album or one of their earlier, less-known albums. I think it was one of the earlier ones because I did not remember hearing "I Want to

Hold Your Hand" until I had my own *Meet the Beatles* album. The song I remember hearing over and over was "I Saw Her Standing There."

At the dance, we played the album over and over, swooning at the record player. I could hardly wait to get my own album. I had never heard anything like this before, and before this, rock and roll didn't interest me. I liked folk music and pretended not to like Elvis because Dad thought Elvis looked smart-alecky. Then one day, he heard Elvis singing a ballad and admitted, "That guy can sing." By that time, I was beyond Elvis and into the Beatles.

On this last Grand Junction trip, we parked near a record store. It had just received one of the first shipments of *Meet the Beatles*. There were cartons of albums that sold as fast as they were opened. I may have known that the album would be on sale because I brought enough money to buy it for $5.

Ingrid and I returned to her house and played it over and over and over again on the record player in her brother's bedroom. I felt a thrill listening to "I Want to Hold your Hand." Then I brought it home and played it on the Hi-Fi and sat on the floor looking at the lads from London, wondering if they were too old for me. Paul sure was cute.

In the spring of my last year in junior high, Mom, Dad, and I visited Keith in California. The previous summer, he moved there after he got a job working for the California Department of Transportation, Caltrans, as a civil engineer in Marysville, California. That was convenient. The California Zephyr went directly from Glenwood Springs through Marysville. Therefore, we took the train for a week-long vacation. We were not prepared for this trip.

We boarded the train in the afternoon dressed in our finery. At that time, travel by train or airplane required our Sunday best. Dad was in his suit and tie, and Mom wore her best dress, a fancy beaded necklace, and heels. We either could not afford it or did not think it was necessary to have a sleeper car and decided to spend the night in the cab car.

The trip started okay. It was fun to go into the Vista car above our cab and view the scenery and the Colorado River from up high. It was fun to have an unobstructed view of the canyon on the way to Grand Junction. Sometime after Grand Junction, we went into the dining car for dinner. It was so fancy – white tablecloths, a bud vase with a rose next to the window, silver looking coffee pots and water pitchers, and black men in white jackets. We enjoyed our dinner as we headed into the sunset somewhere in the Utah desert.

Then we went back to the car. Mom and Dad read for a while, and then we tried to sleep. Although the cars had reclining seats, they did not go back more than a couple of inches. I did not have someone sitting next to me so I could sleep curled up on the seats. It was chilly, so we threw our jackets or coats over our shoulders.

As the evening went on, the train made stops in Utah and Nevada late at night. It was spring, and as the doors opened to let passengers on and off, the cold swooped in. The car remained cold for the night. Dad complained he got a chill. I got about two hours of sleep. I was jealous of the people who were in their sleeping cars nestled under warm blankets. We were miserable, and even breakfast in the fancy dining car did not help.

We got to Marysville late in the morning. Keith and Joyce were resident managers of the Sutter Arms Apartments – four two-story buildings around a central swimming pool. I tried to swim, but it was too cold, and it rained. We used one of the empty furnished apartments for the week.

We had a nice vacation. We went to Sacramento and Sutter Fort. Dad got his "dam" fix by going up the Feather River to where they were constructing the Oroville Dam. Dad was impressed with the bucolic image of the live oaks, the green hills, and grazing cattle.

On the return trip, we brought blankets and a bag of food. We dressed warmly and forgot the fancy clothes. We were so glad when the train pulled into Glenwood Springs, and we could go home.

During the summer of 1963, Dad built the garage. He and Mom always intended to have a garage, and it seemed odd not to have one in the snow country. But then, again, not too many people had garages in Aspen. Only the new houses such as Ted's and Celia and Bill's had garages. I am not sure what finally prompted him to build it. Perhaps the timing was right because of the collection of creosote boards Dad salvaged from the Castle Creek Bridge.

When the State of Colorado replaced the Castle Creek Bridge in 1961, Dad obtained many of the creosoted planks making up the roadbed. They were 12-foot-long two-by-fours about five boards wide, nailed together, and covered with creosote. Dad put the supply of planks by the bale shed, and when he had time, he used a crowbar and pulled them apart. He used the boards for repairs, for what he intended to be a temporary corral behind the granary, and a stud wall separating his shop from the rest of the granary.

In the early fifties, Dad started building a garage. He made a foundation in the northeast corner of the driveway in front of the house. He abandoned the plan when he realized it was over the water main going into town. The winter after Dad built the foundation, the water main broke, and we had an ice sculpture at least 15-feet high coming out of the ditch next to the garage foundation. Dad never completed this garage, and the foundation eventually disappeared. For a while, it worked as a platform for mounting Patty when riding bareback.

This time the garage was on the opposite side of the driveway on the southeast corner. It was parallel to the front fence about three feet away. The two-car garage had a pitched roof, the garage door on the north, an outside door on the east, and a window on the west side. Dad did not bother to put in insulation or finish the inside, and the room perpetually smelled of creosote. I am guessing it might not have been all that healthy if we spent any significant time there. Dad finished the outside with the aluminum siding he saved when he put the siding on the house.

Dad had a cement company pour the floor. He wanted to imbed a silver dollar or a fifty-cent piece in the floor to indicate the construction date. Because he could not find such a coin, he made a ring of 1963 quarters in the threshold. Although we did not have an automatic garage door and there was no heat, it was nice not to have to get up early to scrape off the cars. Besides, it made a convenient spot for our skis, my bicycle, the lawnmower, the wheelbarrow, and the barbeque.

We were not the only ones becoming more modern. At that time, the town was changing. The post office was moved from the Elks Building to Spring Street – across from where the Frank Marolt Bar had been. Instead of the old building with wooden floors and clanking radiators, it was a modern building with stone walls, a pitched roof, and a large east-facing window. The floors were vinyl tile. The public interior was L-shaped. The post office boxes were on the long side, running east and west, and the counters were on the right-facing Spring Street. Our box was still No. 423.

I remember sitting in our peach-colored Dodge waiting for Mom to bring out boxes of what I hoped were Christmas presents. As far as I was concerned, the modern building was not as good as the old one. The diagonal parking spaces in front were its only improvement. Another change was the City paved all the downtown streets and added curbs and gutters. Thereafter, the changes were constant and accelerating.

High School

The Start – Freshman Year

For the most part, I enjoyed high school. I enjoyed it despite losing cheerleading trials. I enjoyed it despite never being chosen as a "favorite" or a "queen." I enjoyed it despite having only one real date. After all, I lived in Aspen. I lived on a ranch. I had Mom and Dad. I had visits from my sisters and brother. I had Nipper, Patty, and Ringo. I had friends. I had aunts, uncles, and cousins. I enjoyed what I had.

By the time I started high school in 1963, the family consisting of Mom, Dad, and me and seemed normal. My hair had grown to the point that I wore it as a chin-length bob. As I look back on pictures in the yearbooks, I look normal and modern even after all these decades. No one could tell the year of my school photographs based on my hairstyle.

My weight regulated, and I was no longer plump. Now, I was a typical teenager wearing a size 8 to 12 depending on the brand. The chubby fat rolls were gone.

School was important. I continued to take piano lessons. I rode my bike to school, weather permitting. I preferred being home on the ranch riding Patty and spending time with Dad at the granary than being in town. I helped with ranch chores – feeding the horses and cattle and helping move cattle from one pasture to the next.

I liked going with Mom to visit Pearl, Celia, Albina, and Polly. I enjoyed doing art projects. I taught myself how to paint with acrylics. Perhaps it was an extension of John Gnagy's *Learn to Draw* television programs Ingrid and I watched. I did mostly still lifes and landscapes. I have a painting of the view from the living room window looking west with the orb of the sun descending behind the hill between the cottonwoods in the field. I wrote stories and kept journals. I never had a problem amusing myself at home or around the ranch.

I spent less time on the ranch with my cousins and Ingrid. Gary and Barney no longer came to "play." Now they were into hiking and camping with their friends. We continued to ski together, and sometimes we went to the movies with groups of our friends. Barney was into photography, and I went with him when he took photographs and watched him develop the photos in the darkroom he set up in their basement. Sometimes I was his model playing my guitar or looking dreamily through a barn window. Gary and I played chess. I was not that good – I didn't have the patience to plan my moves. Gary was more serious and a much better player.

Ingrid still came out to the house, and I went to hers. We did teen things – talking, listening to music, watching TV, and sunbathing. There was no more playing in the pickup or in the granary. Now, however, she was equally interested in spending time with new people in town.

Accelerating Changes

By the time I started high school, some of my old friends were leaving for boarding schools or the Colorado Rocky Mountain School in Carbondale. New people from out of state replaced them. The new people came from Illinois, Texas, and California. They quickly rose to the top of the social strata and became the popular people. They were my direct competition and interfered with my waning possibilities of being "popular." I ended up on friendly terms with most of them: "If you can't beat them, join them."

In 1963, it was Diane Pierce who came from California with cool new clothes. She cooked frozen tacos for lunch. I never heard of tacos before that time. She had two Siamese cats. She wore skirts that could be unzipped on the sides to reveal matching shorts underneath. She was attractive, thin, and blond. She immediately became a cheerleader.

In my sophomore year, the new arrivals included Ron and Gail Stebner from Illinois. They had a younger sister – Sue Sue. Their mother, Susie, had a ski-clothing shop in a new building at the base of Little Nell. I think their father was a contractor or a developer and may have built that building. He built the family an ultra-modern house on McClain Flats overlooking the airport.

Most of the south-facing side of their living area had two-story windows. Gail's bedroom was in a loft above the kitchen overlooking the living room. The other bedrooms were along a hall on the west end of the house. After they sold the house, it did not last even a decade and was replaced by something more grandiose. Gail became a cheerleader. Her GPA, which she transferred, put her ahead of me at the top of the class.

In my junior year, Mallory Alexander arrived from Houston, Texas, and she knew the Stebners. She had a freckled face and blond hair. She also had a younger sister, Susan. The year before moving to town, Ron Stebner brought her to a school basketball game. I thought she was conceited.

Mallory's mother, Barbara, was a beautiful brunette who was a former model. Mallory's mother was widowed from Mallory's father and was now married to a wealthy playboy-type man from Houston – David Seville. David should not be confused with the music director for Alvin and the Chipmunks.

Mallory's mother and David rented a duplex off Smuggler or Francis in the west end. One Christmas, Rock Hudson and Robert Wagner rented the adjoining unit. Mallory wondered if they were "homos," which was the term at the time.

Mallory turned out to be fun and funny. She managed to date the most desirable of the old and new Aspen crowd. The first time we did something together was after school with Melissa Jenkins and me in Mallory's VW bug. We went up the hill next to or just below Lift No. 1 on South Aspen Street. Mallory drove fast down the hill while we stood up in the opening of the sunroof. When the car hit a bump, we flew up and held on for dear life. We wanted to see how high we could go without getting thrown out. After riding down it a couple of times, I realized Mallory was not going to do it, and I had no interest in getting killed.

Ingrid remained popular, even with the new people. She was Homecoming Queen and some other sort of queen or favorite and had several boyfriends. She spent much of her summers at the Hotel Jerome swimming pool with some of the summer people. One of the summer people was Mary Janss, whose father was developing the future Snowmass Ski Area. Others of note were the Hardy brothers Gordon "Gordie" and Johnny, later known in his successful music career as "Jack." Their father was head of the Aspen Music Festival and School. They, like Mary Janss, did not go to school in Aspen.

The Hardys lived in a big house across Hallam from the yellow-brick school and across Center Street from the red-brick school. It is the house that belonged to Mrs. Brand when Mom worked for her after Keith was born. I begged Mom and Dad for a Jerome pool summer membership. It cost $40.00. I thought I could mingle with the new "high-class" people like Ingrid. Mom and Dad said, "No." They meant it.

I had another bad experience with some of the new people. I continued to help Dad on the ranch, and we still fattened cattle in the summer. I helped move them from pasture to pasture. One of the pastures we used belonged to Jimmy Moore. It was west of the old ranch at the location of the current Aspen schools. One day Danny Barry, who was still running the Paepcke Ranch, noticed a group of horseback riders chasing our cattle in the pasture. Dad was furious.

He and I jumped in the Jeep and headed into the pasture. Dad went through the gate and tore up the hill and drove into the middle of the group. He was angry. He was shaking. His face was darker than usual. He yelled at them. I noticed they were a group of popular younger kids – mostly new people. They were using horses from the Heatherbed Lodge a few miles up Maroon Creek.

The kids were making faces, rolling their eyes, and snickering at Dad. I was embarrassed and was concerned they would make fun of me too. I was ashamed my first thoughts were about these new people I barely knew thought of me. They were never going to be my friends, regardless of what Dad said or did. The incident left me feeling sad and disappointed that my initial reaction was to be embarrassed by Dad instead of being angry at the trespassers. I was beginning to resent the new people.

I did not spend any time in the local hangouts where old and new teens congregated. The main spot was the Sweet & Snack. It was near the corner of Cooper and Galena next to the Sinclair gas station. Town kids spent hours hanging out with each other, eating hamburgers and soft-serve ice cream, listening to music, and playing pinball or pool – a few smoked cigarettes in the alley. I went there a few times, but it was not particularly memorable.

I did, however, enjoy going with friends to a new restaurant, Pinocchio's. It was a pizza place that sold 3.2 beer. In Colorado, kids over 18 could drink it. It is one of the reasons some considered the University of Colorado, a party school. Pinocchio's was across Cooper Street from the Sweet & Snack. I never drank beer here in high school because I would be 17 until after I graduated.

Pinocchio's was in a new shopping area, the Aspen Grove, next to the Independence Building. The shopping area also had an Austrian restaurant, the Wienerstube, which would become one of my favorite local restaurants, and a cute gift shop called the Golconda. Betty Straud, who owned the Golconda, offered free Bavarian Mints to customers as they came in the door. They were the most awesome smooth and creamy chocolate mint from a single layer oblong candy box. The sugar cube-sized chocolates had the texture of butter.

My friends and I usually went to Pinocchio's on Fridays. That was unfortunate because I could not eat meat on Friday, and I had to eat plain cheese pizza while everyone else was eating pepperoni pizza or burgers. I felt guilty if I ate a piece after I took off the pepperoni. I worried that some meat grease remained on the slice, thereby sentencing me to Hell or an extended stay in Purgatory. At least I could drink Coke. Tom and John Marsing were Mormons and could never drink Coke or, for that matter, anything with caffeine, ever. The Catholic Church discontinued meatless Fridays in December of my senior year.

As a supporter of my school, I attended football and basketball games. Our teams were bad, and we rarely won. Occasionally, I went to out of town games on the pep club bus. Sometimes, the pep club bus trips were fun. Once, Svea met us before we got on the bus to Battle Mountain and brought us Hershey sandwiches. It was a meatless Friday. Hershey sandwiches were made like a toasted cheese except a Hershey Bar replaced the cheese, and there was no pickle on the side.

I went to movies several times a month. The ISIS Theater had first-run movies on Fridays and Saturdays and a variety of movies during the week. The ISIS schedule came out the first of the month and was posted by the door. I particularly liked *The Longest Day*, *Tom Jones*, *Lawrence of Arabia*, and the *Pink Panther*. Most of my movie companions left about an hour into the *Longest Day*. I made it through the entire movie by myself. I saw *Tom Jones* five times and went to Glenwood with Cherie to see *Lawrence of Arabia* at the drive-in. It was the fourth time for that movie.

Around this time, I went to see *The Lord of the Flies* at a special showing at the Aspen Institute. Although it was in black and white, it was a good movie. I loved the *Kyrie Eleison* sung by the boys' choir. The young angelic voices were antithetical to what the boys did on that island. I wished the movie played in a regular theater. I would have seen it multiple times.

Academics

A large part of high school was about academics. I was in the advanced classes. I took four years of math – two years of algebra, geometry, trigonometry, and math analysis that included a little calculus. I had all the history and social sciences and three years of French. I took the college-bound science classes – biology I and II, chemistry, and physics. I was not a physics fan. One day studying at the kitchen table, I was reading about strobe lights and not getting it. I read and reread the section and got so flustered and angry that I took out a pen and scribbled angrily in the book until I tore through the page.

Despite my tribulations with physics, I loved the science room in the red brick school. It was on the northeast corner of the old part of the building. The room appeared to have high windows on the eastern wall, which I now realize they were the same windows as all the other rooms but partially obscured by lab stations.

Inside the glass-paned entry door on the right was a storage area. It was dark with shelves on all sides and extending from floor to a few feet below the ceiling to store supplies. It smelled like formaldehyde because there were specimens preserved in jars. There were reptiles and fetal animals. I swear one jar contained a human fetus.

The room was crammed with scientific paraphernalia. Around the rest of the room were lab tables, shelves of chemicals, and high shelves with animal skeletons and other artifacts. There were planets and models of molecules hanging from the ceiling. The celestial bodies could be raised and lowered on pulleys. There was a model of the moon that was five feet in diameter. It sat for most of the time on top of the storage area.

Periodic tables and diagrams of evolution and topographical relief maps of the Aspen area filed any available wall space. There were cabinets with drawers filled with rocks and minerals and a refrigerator with a medicinal smell. Our teacher was Bob Marsh, but most of the science room furnishings and equipment were from the long tenure of Bob Lewis, who taught there for years.

In biology, we dissected frogs that we had to pith and a preserved cat with different colored organs. We sprouted beans and grew mold.

We set up wave tables and had strobe lights and model cars for physics. In chemistry, we made smoky concoctions under the chemical fume hood. We made crystals. Although the new school's science rooms were modern and had the latest equipment, the new rooms did not compare to the character of the old science room.

The two classes that had the most enduring relevance for me were English and typing. In my freshman year, I had English with Margaret Heath. She was new to the school. She previously taught college English at the University of Colorado. She was rigid and made sure we acquired writing skills before we began "creative" writing. While my friends in Mr. Lum's class were having fun writing poetry, we were diagraming sentences and making outlines for our essays – topic paragraphs, topic sentences, transition sentences, transition words between paragraphs, and conclusions following the same pattern. When I stopped resisting, I learned to appreciate the skills I acquired. As an attorney, I rely on these fundamental skills for legal writing.

Typing was the other skill I still use daily, and which supported me for years. Don Alexander, who also taught Spanish, was the teacher, and the class was in one of the new rooms on the south side of the building. We each had a standard Remington commercial typewriter and exercise books. The exercise books had the spine on the top so we could open them next to the typewriters. Employing all the letters of the alphabet, we learned to type, "the quick brown fox jumps over the lazy dog." Being proficient at touch-typing was an asset when writing essays and a skill that led to clerical jobs. Now, I use it every day. I am using it as I type this memoir.

On the other hand, Home Economics was fun but worthless. The room was next to the science lab, had four stoves, a large refrigerator, a couple of sinks, and sewing stations. Compared to what I learned at home and in 4-H, it was uninspiring. The most memorable experiences were making a mediocre tuna-and-cheese roll and gagging as we cleaned silverfish and their carcasses from under the cabinets.

I had a fair amount of homework in high school. I studied mostly at the dining room table. I set up a desk in the basement, inspired by a design I saw in *Seventeen Magazine*, but I rarely used the space. It was too isolated, and the main room was not completely finished.

One winter, Keith came home for a couple of weeks to help Dad complete the basement. They put in acoustic tile on the ceiling, dark paneling on the walls, and encased the steel beams to look like solid wood. They removed one foot of each piece of the paneling to fit with the seven-foot ceiling. Dad finished and tiled the enlarged windows and windowsills.

The basement looked better and had fewer spiders. It was a place for overnight guests using the old living room furniture. Mom later added furniture from moving sales and decorated it with artifacts she collected from her later travels to Mexico and the southwest.

Instead of using the basement desk, sometimes I sat on the living room floor and did math problems while Dad watched TV. Dad loved TV. He liked the westerns and *The Fugitive* and comedians like Red Skelton and Myron Cohn. Sometimes he laughed so hard he blew snot out of his nose.

I was getting too old now to snuggle next to him on the couch. Instead, I sat on the floor leaning against the couch next to him. In the evening, I took a shower in the basement, got ready for bed, and again sat on the floor and put rollers in my hair.

I used those giant magnetic rollers. They were the size of juice cans. Dad made an insert in my hutch drawer so I could bring out my curling supplies to sit cross-legged on the floor in front of the TV, rolling my hair.

Sleeping was difficult in these rollers. I had to sleep on my stomach and rest my forehead on my fist. During the night, I ended up lying on the rollers, and the weight of my head flattened them into oblongs that resulted in bent curls. Life would have been so much easier if I could have gotten up in the morning and used a blow drier. No one used a blow dryer, even if they existed at the time.

Hair driers at the time looked like small suitcases or plastic hatboxes with plastic tubes connected to a plastic bonnet. We even had a hair dryer attachment for the canister vacuum cleaner. It attached to the exhaust end! Ah, nothing says beautiful hair like air through a vacuum. In later years, "portable hair dryers" could be slung over the shoulder like a big purse.

Kennedy - 1963

My seemingly ordinary high school experience changed forever on November 22, 1963. It was a typical fall day - chilly with slightly gray skies and dead vegetation with remnants of an earlier snowstorm. I was in social studies on the south side of the west end of the school. It was near lunch when Wava Turner, who was acting as an assistant principal, came in. She whispered something to Mr. Mueller, and then she came to the front of the class wearing her usual moss green shirtwaist dress.

"Children, I have some awful news to relay." Her voice was low and cracking slightly. She had a Texas drawl. She continued, "President Kennedy has been shot in Dallas, Texas. It does not look good. It appears he may die." Everyone gasped. She continued, "We are going to dismiss school so you can go home and be with your families and turn on the TV if you have one." There were no TVs in the school and probably only one radio in the office.

No one knew what to do. I went outside with people from the class. We stood on the sidewalk. Vickie Goodhard, who lived across the street from the school, told us to come to her house. They had a TV.

I was praying hard, "Oh God. Oh, God. Please don't let him die." About ten of us crowded into her small living room to look at the black and white screen. It was mostly commentators talking, and then the word came over the TV. John F. Kennedy was dead. They were starting to talk about swearing in Lyndon Johnson. I said to myself, "I don't want Johnson. I want Kennedy."

I made it home. I probably went to Pearl's or Ingrid's and called Mom. For the next several days, when we were not going to Church for special masses or rosaries, we stayed glued to the TV watching the grainy images and listening to Walter Cronkite.

I cried watching the funeral parade and the riderless horse with the backward facing boots or John John saluting the flag-draped casket. Mom collected copies of newspapers and the Life Magazine with the black-bordered photograph of Kennedy. Inside were the time-lapse black and white scenes of the shooting, including the one of Jacqueline Kennedy climbing toward the back of the limousine.

Thanksgiving a week later was not as fun as it had been in the past. Albert was quiet about Kennedy. When Kennedy ran for president, he was adamantly against him, and I was concerned his and Dad's divergent opinions would lead to an argument. Dad thought Albert's support for Nixon was because Kennedy was Catholic, and Albert, a Freemason, was not fond of Catholics.

Other than this Thanksgiving, all the Thanksgivings and Christmases were as they had been in the past. One difference was Peggy came home from college, and Judy and her growing family alternated holidays between our family and Chuck's family in Grand Junction.

Keith and Joyce, who now lived in Marysville, California, rarely came for the holidays opting for longer trips in the spring or summer. It was fun to have them visit, but it was hard when they left. I no longer got toys at Christmas. Instead, I got clothes, art supplies, books, cosmetics, a portable typewriter, a bonnet hair dryer, and ski equipment. Santa no longer visited.

Aspen Sports

Another difference was that I worked at Aspen Sports for the week before Christmas. For the first couple of years, I was in the basement wrapping presents. I am not sure how I got the job. Before that, I regularly babysat for Gale and Ellie Spence.

They were nice people. They lived in the Castle Creek subdivision on the east side of Cemetery Lane – less than a mile from our house on property Dad sold in the early 1950s. Their house seemed like it was always under construction. They had many hyperactive kids and no TV. The worst part of babysitting for them was they came home later than promised. I bet that had more to do with Gale than Ellie. Before accepting the job, I told Ellie I needed to be home by 10:00 p.m. She promised to be home by then, and instead, they come home at 2:00 a.m. I tried to nap in their living room, but it was chilly. That was a problem when I had school or Mass the next morning. It finally got to the point that I had a list of excuses by the telephone if I got a babysitting call for a night I did not want to work. I had a made-up reason at the ready. "Oh, sorry, I have a school newspaper meeting."

"Oh, I have a slumber party that night." This new strategy applied to anyone calling for babysitting. I hated babysitting.

I gladly went to work for Gale at Aspen Sports. Aspen Sports was the premier ski shop in town with a large equipment rental section. Originally it was between the Golden Horn and the Red Onion. When the Red Onion abandoned the high-end gourmet section west of the main bar, Aspen Sports took over that space.

Aspen Sports focused on ski equipment and good-quality ski clothes. The leading clothing brand was Roffe. Bogner, the expensive, high-fashion ski clothes, were in stores like Sabatini Sports, Ellie's, or the Country Store. Aspen Sports and the Mountain Shop had similar ski brands, but the Mountain Shop was open in summer selling summer sports equipment. Aspen Sports was exclusively for skiing and only open during the winter.

For the first couple of years, I wrapped Christmas presents in the basement – robin egg blue slick paper and navy blue bows with the same color scheme from the store's shopping bags – light blue bags with a dark blue snowflake.

In later years, I worked in the main store selling merchandise. Nearly every Christmas vacation throughout high school and college, I worked for one or two weeks. It was a fun place to work. I walked across the alley for lunch and got a sandwich or soup and a pastry at the Delice Bakery.

Gale and his partner John Oakes were good employers. Gale was flamboyant and out in public. John was quiet and in the background. I got to wait on or see numerous celebrities – Robert McNamara, Robert Conrad, Cher, and Eva Marie Saint are a few I remember. Gale and John paid generous bonuses, which I mostly redeemed for ski boots, sweaters, and gloves. One of the years I wrapped presents, they gave me a $50 bonus. That was more than I made doing my job!

The fall of 1963 was a difficult time because of the assassination, but in the first part of 1964, I was looking forward to Billy being on the United States Olympic Team headed to Innsbruck, Austria. There were no live televised events, so we either read about the results or caught an intermittent radio broadcast. Billy placed reasonably high, but not enough to warrant a medal. Billy's friends, Jimmie Heuga and

Billy Kidd, placed second and third in the slalom. Those may have been the first Alpine ski medals in the Olympics for the United States.

Headlines marred the event. After they were no longer competing, Billy and a couple of members of the United States bobsled team went out on the town. Local police stopped them after they drove in the wrong direction in a borrowed car. The boys got into an argument with the police and were arrested, fined, and given suspended sentences. I felt terrible and wondered if Billy's skiing career was over.

California Trip

The summer after my freshman year, I returned to Marysville, California, on the train by myself. This time, I had one of the small sleeper rooms – what a difference. I had a small room with a reclining seat next to the window, a washbasin, and a toilet. The bed folded down over everything, and to use the toilet in the middle of the night required folding up the bed. I was lonely. As we passed houses with lights on, I knew the people were home with their families. I wanted to be home with Mom and Dad.

I stayed with Keith and Joyce for a couple of weeks, and, this time, I could swim in the pool. Unlike my earlier trip where my hair was still in a bubble, my hair was longer and straighter. I had a crush on a boy who lived there but never talked to him. I helped Joyce clean apartments – mainly, I stripped wax from kitchen and bathroom floors.

Joyce was a clean freak, and she was obsessed with making sure the apartments were pristine. She took me to an ice-cream store with many flavors. I fell in love with the coffee flavor and got a single-scoop cone daily. The scoop was the size of a baseball. Keith had friends from Caltrans who came over to the apartment for burgers, and we played Monopoly and Scrabble until late at night. Keith played a lot of cribbage, bridge, and pinochle at work during lunch. Mom, Keith, and Judy were Scrabble nuts.

Keith took me to San Francisco. After shopping at Macy's, where I bought a navy-blue light wool jumper with a flippy skirt and a striped knit top, I wore it to a Giant's game at Candlestick Park. I fought it inflating in the breeze at "The Stick." Fortunately, I always wore pettipants with skirts. After the game, we went to dinner at an Italian multi-course restaurant named Panelli's. Keith and Joyce knew how to entertain.

Joyce took me to see *Oliver* at a theater in the round in Sacramento and another trip to Fisherman's Warf. We stopped at Cost Plus, which I thought was incredible, such a large space filled with so much cool, colorful, and cheap stuff. I bought brightly colored enameled, divided picnic plates for Mom.

We looked forward to a stop at the Nut Tree on the way back to Marysville. That was the restaurant where Art Kelleher got the recipe for what had become our favorite chocolate cake. The restaurant was originally a roadside fruit stand, much like Knott's Berry Farm, and was next to a walnut orchard. It had a small train meandering through the trees and an "airport" with planes for the kids. I was too old for the train, but I thought a little train around the ranch might be fun. I wished the ore-car spur near the granary was still there.

The Nut Tree restaurant was a large 1950s contemporary building. It had an area near the entrance with items like those in Cost Plus but with higher prices and baked goods, fancy fruits, nuts, and candy. The restaurant featured an exotic fruit salad, a vegetable salad, or a platter of cold cuts and cheese. Each meal included a miniature loaf of nut bread. I bought some of the tiny loaf pans to bring home. This time, I had the meat platter. Although the exotic fruit was unique, I preferred something salty. When not sightseeing, I read *Gone with the Wind*. When we drove back to Aspen, I remarked that the trip was many miles as my book was pages long.

The Pinnacle - Sophomore Year

The fall of 1964 was the beginning of my sophomore year. Besides the Stebners, we had many other new students. The most exciting were three brothers from Fort Worth – Rusty, Randy, and Riley Haws. They were in town while their father completed building the Shadow Mountain condominiums.

They had southern drawls. Rusty, the oldest, had red hair, freckles, and black horn-rimmed glasses. He was nice looking. Randy was cute and in my class. They were both on the football team, and I'm guessing they were a lot better at the game than the local boys. That particular year we had a huge football team – probably fifty players in all. Despite the size, we still lost all but one game. At that time, Carbondale was the best football school in our league.

I admired Randy from afar. He first talked to me after one of our English classes. We were giving short speeches to break the ice with the new students. At the time, there was a series of television advertisements for a new powdered whipped topping mix. I believe it was Dream Whip. The gist of the commercials was it was so easy to make, you could make it practically anywhere. I decided to do a parody of the ad. I rode my bicycle into the room and stopped at a stop sign pinned to the blackboard. I narrated as I prepared a package of the Dream Whip in my bicycle basket and rode on. It was funny. Everyone laughed.

When I left the classroom and wheeled my bike down the hall, Randy caught up with me. He said, "I loved your speech." He then held out his hand and said, "I'm Randy Haws."

Of course, I knew his name. I had been snatching glances of him since the start of school. I shook his hand and blushed,

"I'm Vicki Marolt." As if he didn't know.

I could tell people were curious why he was talking to me one-on-one and laughing and smiling. They passed us like water in a stream, moving around a boulder. He continued.

"So, I was wondering if y'all would be interested in going to the homecoming dance with me?"

I was in shock. No one had ever asked me to a movie or on a date, let alone the school year's premier social event. Without attempting to be coy or pretending I had to check some social calendar, I said, "Yes."

"Great. I'll talk to y'all after history." He turned and walked in the other direction. As I walked my bike the rest of the way down the hall, I could not believe this was happening. I would have skipped or jumped up and clicked my heels if not for the bike. Of all the girls in school, I would never guess I would be the girl who caught his eye. I knew there were other girls much more popular than me that he would have asked if he had known better.

In an ordinary world, not one inhabited by teenagers, it was not out of the question for a new person in school to find me interesting or attractive. By that time, I was looking good. My brunette hair was shoulder length and straight. I had a bridge of freckles on my slightly turned-up nose. My eyes were green. I was as trim. I had a cute wardrobe from Cherie's hand-me-downs. I was smart because I was in advanced English, Math, and biology, and he was in these classes as well. I had friends and was generally well-liked. The only box I did not check on the popularity grid was cheerleader, princess, queen, or favorite.

For three glorious weeks, he was my "boyfriend." I made a point of going to Wagner Park and watching football practices if I was not committed to one of my activities or Church. We talked at school and met up with a group of people and went to Pinocchio's or the movies. Romantically, the most we ever did was hold hands in a movie. For me, that was exciting.

I could hardly wait for the dance. Mom was excited too. We went to town to look for a dress. We went to Elli of Aspen, thinking she might have something cute. Elli Iselin was the wife of Fred Iselin, one of the skiing pioneers from Switzerland who was one of the founders of the Aspen Ski School. Her shop was across Main Street from the Hotel Jerome and was light blue with flower boxes and Tyrolean decorations.

Elli's had the high-end, ladies' Bogner ski pants and parkas. She also sold cute turtlenecks with hearts and flowers, cute sweaters, corduroy skirts, and slacks. The primary summer items were dirndls made by Lanz of Salzburg. She did not have anything that looked right for the occasion but suggested we go to Terese David's down the street.

Terese David came to Aspen sometime in the 50s, and I believe she was from the east coast – probably New York. She had a boutique in one of two houses she owned on Main Street near the Sardy house and mortuary. I had never spent much time in the boutique. Before that, I thought she sold children's clothes. Later, she sold clothes for adults.

Her boutique was not like the clothing stores with the racks of similar clothes of various sizes. She displayed only one item, and she kept the extra sizes in the back. It never occurred to me until years later that this is where I would find two of my favorite dresses ever. The homecoming dress remained stylish, and I wore it for years when I needed to dress up for an occasion. The other was a simple yet elegant, long white prom dress when I was a senior in high school. I wore it to a few fancy parties in college and thought it might work as a wedding dress. Both dresses were classic and remained stylish for years.

The homecoming dress happened to be a Lanz, but not a dirndl. It was a dark green and blue muted paisley pattern in a slightly textured fabric. It had a round neck, a fitted waist with a slightly belled skirt. It had tight sleeves with tiny fabric-covered buttons that went through loops at the cuff and halfway up the sleeve. These were the type of buttons and loops found on the back of wedding dresses. I looked good in it. I believe it was the most expensive piece of clothing I owned up to this point. I could hardly wait – only a few more days until homecoming.

In the meantime, I was busy with school and activities. On one of those crisp, clear fall days with bright blue skies and long shadows, I was at Wagner Park playing soccer. I was a member of the women's soccer team, although I was only a sophomore in high school. Girls in Colorado were not allowed to have organized sports teams in high school, so we needed a town team composed of mostly adult women. Being at the park away from the school made it seem as though we were not part of the system. Our team could not be related to the school.

Soccer was new. None of us were great at it. I was a forward – mostly because I knew I did not want to be a goalie or a defender. I wanted to be out front.

About halfway through the practice, we lined up facing north toward the Wheeler opera house and the doctors' offices on the edge of the field. Someone started the ball moving, and those of us toward the front began dribbling the ball downfield. It took a while to get into the rhythm of moving the ball back and forth. Finally, the ball came toward me, and I started moving it a few yards a time. For a moment, I thought I might have a shot at the goal.

Then out of nowhere, Merry Cox came toward me looking like she would take the ball away. Merry was a year older than me and had fiery red hair and freckles. She was the best player, an exceptional all-around athlete, and the top girl on the ski team.

Instead of getting into a foot fight, I instinctively held out my left arm in front of me to ward off her advance. Of course, this was a foul – straight-arming. Before anyone could yell foul, my extended arm met Merry's shoulder.

In that slow-motion encounter, I could feel my arm bending not at the elbow but in the space between my elbow and my wrist. It was like someone slowly bending a willow stick. Then it suddenly snapped backward. At the same time, an electric sensation of pain shot down my arm.

Everything began getting shadowy as if my eyelids were closing slowly. I found myself falling backward and meeting the ground. As I sat on the hard surface, the pain was now engulfing more than my arm. My stomach was queasy, and I had a gagging sensation.

In the next minutes, as I sat on the ground, my vision began to clear. I was sitting in a circle of the other players looking down on me. My left arm was slack and lying on my lap.

Someone asked, "Are you okay?"

I looked up and slowly shook my head from side to side. "No. I think I hurt my arm." A couple of the adult women helped me to my feet, and I cradled my arm against my stomach. It was now throbbing. I did not look because I was afraid of how it might look. I suspected it was broken. I remembered Billy's arm when he fell from the rafters in the granary. It looked like he had stair-steps on his arm.

We walked to the edge of the field and the doctor's offices. How fortunate to have doctors so close.

After waiting a while in the examining room, I glanced at my arm and noticed it did not look like Billy's arm. It seemed normal. I had a glimmer of hope that it was not broken.

Dr. Robert Oden, who was the orthopedic doctor in town, had an office in the building. He had a thriving business. Sure enough, it was broken – greenstick fracture. I got a cast. I was worried about wearing the dress with the tight sleeves. Mom said she could carefully slit the seams on the dress to get it over the cast and close it with matching grosgrain ribbons. It would not be as cute, but it would be okay.

The next day was the night before homecoming, and there was a bonfire in an empty block near Little Nell. It was the lot used for skating and later became the Alpine Market after Albert sold Beck & Bishop in 1967, and later became City Market. For days before the bonfire, high school students piled lumber into a pyre.

I was in charge of the float for our class, so I could not go to the bonfire. Instead, the float committee worked on our float – built on our hay wagon – in Ingrid's carriage house. Our float was typical of the time – chicken wire and Kleenex and crepe paper.

The theme that year was famous quotes. Our float was a tall football player in a uniform in the team's colors. He was digging into a Kleenex snowbank and shoveling Kleenex snow. The quote was, "We will bury you." I wonder why we thought using a Communist slogan was a good idea. Regardless, we won the float competition.

As I worked on the float, I was disappointed I could not be with Randy that evening. The bonfire night was the time for a pep rally with the cheerleaders to motivate the football team to win the next day. There was not much for me to do during the float preparation because of my broken arm. It still hurt like a dull toothache and was not mobile because it was still in a sling.

Shortly after what should have been the end of the bonfire, several people showed up to help on the float. I heard some of them talking. Randy and Susan Bielefeldt, one of the cheerleaders, had been at the bonfire holding hands. Susan was the most popular girl in school. I pretended I did not hear them. I did not want to be humiliated.

I stayed with Ingrid that night. She knew I knew what had happened. We were in her guest room with the twin beds, and I sobbed most of the night.

The next day Randy called. "I guess y'all know I'm seeing Susan. I'd still like to go to the dance with you if you want."

I responded with a flat, "Sure."

I guess a person with principles would have said, "no." I guess I still held out hope that I could turn it around. I had that beautiful dress. It was not the event I hoped it would be. When we were dancing, I rested my left arm on his shoulder, and he complained about the weight of the cast. Maybe he was teasing, but it added to the hurt.

After the dance, Susan and Randy started openly dating. That status continued until his family left Aspen after Christmas and returned to Fort Worth. All the while, I hoped he would dump Susan for me. In order not to burn any bridges, we remained cordial.

There was a time when we went to movies in the same group when Susan was not available. He and I drove to Carbondale together for an academic competition. For months, I prayed every night that he would be my boyfriend again and that he would write or call and tell me how sorry he was. I wrote his name thousands of times, thinking that might be the magic to make it happen. It never worked.

Ski Equipment

When Christmas rolled around, I got metal skis. By that time, black, metal Head skis were becoming popular. There were also red metal Hart skis, but in my circles, they were not a status symbol. Both Head and Hart skis were expensive and too new for me to get as hand-me-downs.

I was becoming a good skier, and I needed better skis. Fortunately, Max was in the ski business. He worked for Iselin Imports, a European company that specialized in ski clothing. This company was not related to Elli and Fred Iselin.

By that time, Max and Betty rented Elsie's house after their twins, Mike and Steve, were born. Max called his daughter Marlis "Boo Boo," after the Yogi Bear's sidekick, and he called his other son Roger "Beaver" after the namesake on *Leave it to Beaver*. Max and Betty slept on a sofa bed in the living room. As Dad predicted, the house was cold and drafty in the winter. Elsie's house was across the road from Ted's house, and Max used Ted's lower-level garage to store his ski clothing and equipment samples.

Every year, I went over to Ted's when Max was ready to sell his samples at extreme discounts. I preferred name brands such as Roffe and Bogner, but the clothes Max sold looked good. The ski pants had double side zippers and made my stomach look flat. I was impressed as I admired my slim profile in the big mirror over the credenza in our living room.

I had black pants as the go-to pair, but I also had other pants and outfits. I had a pumpkin-colored pant, a matching long pumpkin mohair sweater, and a pumpkin and white checked shell jacket. I had a maroon ski outfit that looked like a Bogner. It had stretch pants and a jacket, with a high knit collar, made of the same stretch material. It looked nice, but it was cold. I even got a pair of pastel-pink pants – what was I thinking. I think Max gave them to me. Burgundy and pink were color pairings then, as were olive green and light blue. At that time, down parkas were not widely used. Having one would have made skiing so much more enjoyable.

I also got several Tyrolean sweaters and the Iselin version of a maroon "Loden" cape. Ingrid borrowed one of the Tyrolean sweaters for a photoshoot by *Seventeen* magazine at a club called Galena Street East. It was a new 3.2 beer dance club open to teens for Coke night once a week. It was in the basement of the Elks Building across from Aspen Drug. When the club opened, it was the first time I realized the street had a name. Don Fleisher, who owned Pinocchio's, started the club to draw the 18-year-olds to drink beer away from Pinocchio's, thus freeing the restaurant for families and tourists.

Ingrid and other model-worthy high school girls were selected to be part of an article on "where teens go and what they're wearing" in the magazine's December 1965 issue. That left me out. Ingrid's photographs did not make the final cut, but the cuff of my sweater did.

Besides clothes, Iselin Imports sold ski equipment. They carried Sohler skis, which were a combination of metal and epoxy. Max said they were better than Head, and he was probably right. When it came time for me to get new skis, Dad went to Max. The only pair he had on hand even close to being short enough for me were 200-centimeter blue Sohlers. They were a stiffer version of the green Sohlers. Using the traditional measures at the time, cupping an extended hand over the ski's tip – I should have had a pair of 190-centimeter skis. I was 5'5" tall. Regardless, Max told Dad the length was good for me. Learning to control them would help my skiing, and besides, they would be fast.

Also, Max convinced Dad I should try their new release bindings. He called them Messerschmitt bindings. I believe someone who worked for the Messerschmitt Aircraft Company designed them. I am not aware of the commercial name for the binding or if they ever made it into commerce. The bindings were modern and much easier to put on than the traditional bear traps or long-thongs with a rigid heel. To get into the Messerschmitt binding, I stepped on a plate in the back, and a metal lip came down to hold in the back of the boot. The heel was designed to pop up with a forward fall.

The toe was put in place by a lever that pushed the toe piece forward and locked it in place. The toe had rollers that released with side-to-side pressure, and the lever was designed to absorb the normal pressure from skiing. They had a short strap that hooked on the back of the binding and went around the ankle. They were a forerunner of modern step-in bindings.

Mom and Dad gave me the skis and bindings for Christmas. I had already discovered them in the back of Judy and Peggy's closet. Mom wrapped the heavy box holding the bindings. According to Max, if I wanted to get new boots, I needed to get them before attaching the bindings. Therefore, I went to Aspen Sports. I tried to talk Gale into giving me a new pair of Nordica buckle boots at a discount. He said he could not because he had a lot of kids to feed. I was embarrassed for asking. I believe he gave me a small discount anyway. I paid for them with my Christmas bonus. I was one of the first among my skiing friends to have buckle boots. As the ad said, I was "racing while others were lacing."

I liked the new equipment. I especially loved the boots. I felt smug when we stopped for lunch, and I could quickly unbuckle my boots and stretch and warm my feet, knowing it would only take a few seconds to get back in them. As for the skis, even with the extra length, they were much better than previous hand-me-down wooden varieties. I liked the bindings for a while, although they did not have the cool factor of long thongs used by the ski team and the ski patrol.

The first problem I experienced with the bindings was on a cold day when our breath hung in clouds in the air. We had been in the Sundeck waiting out the day because it was so cold. Eventually, we had to go down the mountain. I put on the skis and was ready to head to Silver Bell. As I started down the slight incline, I walked right out of my right ski. I tried to put it back on, but even with the lever pushed all the way forward, the toe did not engage. I walked back up the hill with one ski on and carrying the other to the Ski Patrol shack. I thought I might have to ride down on the lift. The ski patrolmen were unfamiliar with the binding but concluded it was frozen. They thawed it with a small propane torch, and I was able to put it back on and ski to the bottom with no problems.

For the next several days, the bindings worked, and I forgot about the other incident. Then, on another cold day, I was near the bottom of Copper Bowl when I made a reasonably easy turn and walked out of the same binding. Again, I tried to re-engage it, but it did not work. This time I had to ski-walk to the bottom of Little Nell. While holding one ski, I slid across the slope on the left ski, walked the turn, and repeated. It was a long cold trip to the bottom.

I talked to Dad about the problem, and he looked at the binding. He reluctantly agreed there was some sort of flaw, and I needed to replace them. The concept was good, but it got on the market before they worked out the bugs. To this day, I cannot find a photograph of that binding.

I did not want to mention it to Max and hurt his feelings, so I went directly to Aspen Sports. I got a Marker binding with toe and heel releases with long thongs. This time, Gale gave me a discount. I paid the balance with my money from working for the store. I kept these skis and the bindings for years. Although I skied with Max numerous times after the binding exchange, he never questioned the replacement.

Highlands Lift Accident

My sophomore year was a time for unique ski experiences. In January, around the time I replaced my bindings, I went skiing at Highlands with a group of friends. These ski days were a lot less about getting the most out of the sport and more about socializing. If I was serious about skiing, I went with Gary or Barney and later with Max and always to Aspen Mountain – the Big Mountain. I never skied at Highlands unless I was with friends who set the agenda. I didn't like it. I thought the trails were too straight, and Thunderbowl was too wide and open.

This day, the group included Ron Stebner, Diane Pierce, Mike, and Dee Dee Whitcomb, Dr. Whitcomb's children, and me. Other people joined us from time to time. For the most part, we watched high school racing on Thunderbowl. Because a full-day ticket cost $6.00, I did not want to waste money to stand up on the hill and watch others ski. However, for the sake of being social, I went along.

After lunch and after watching our hometown favorites race, we ate lunch in the lodge at the bottom and decided to make a few runs on the mountain. We rode up the first part of the Exposition Lift and then on the next part, now known as Exposition Lift II. It was a bright clear day, and not too cold for January. Diane and Mike got on the lift in front of Ron and me. Dee Dee and the rest of the group were somewhere behind us.

We were in the trees a couple of towers above the loading station and about twenty feet above the ground. We were over deep snow and had not yet gone over any ski runs. Suddenly, the lift came to an abrupt stop. Then the chair started going backward, which was normal following an abrupt stop. A chair would go back four or five feet and then bounce and stabilize. In this case, it did not stop. Instead, it seemed to be gaining speed. Within a few minutes, both Ron and I realized this was not normal.

Ron said, "Get your skis off. We need to jump." We wrapped our arms around the center bar. There was no safety bar. We started unwrapping our bindings and dropping our skis. Diane and Mike were doing the same. By this time, we were going past a lower tower.

I could hear people yelling below us at the loading station. I was about half the way finished unwrapping the second 200-centimeter thong when the lift shuddered, made a loud crunching sound, and made a sudden stop. Then it erratically bounced up and down. I had long since dropped my poles, and I hugged the center pole and closed my eyes. I was sure the chair would break off, and I was going to plummet to the ground.

After several minutes, the bouncing slowed. We swayed a little from side to side and then stopped. We were about twenty feet below the tower we just passed, and it looked to me like the cable was on the inside one of the wheels. It seemed as if we were at least 30 feet above the ground, but probably more like twenty. It was too far to jump. After I settled down and stopped shaking, I finished unwrapping the second long-thong and dropped the ski. We checked with Mike and Diane, and everyone was okay. Skis and poles littered in the deep snow under the lift.

I looked back, and there was chaos at the loading station with skiers' bodies flung to the side. Later, we heard there had been some injuries. I believe Dee Dee had been pulled off the lift and am unsure whether she was one of the people who broke an arm.

Somehow, we learned that we were to stay put until the ski patrol removed us from the lift. Ron was still talking about jumping, but then he magnanimously agreed to stay to keep me company.

As we sat on the chair waiting, the sun started to recede behind the trees, and it was getting cold. After an hour, the ski patrol came into view from above. They were bringing down discarded equipment and placing it under each of the occupied chairs. They had a canvas basket with a long rope. They got to Mike and Diane before us. They each got into the basket and were lowered to the ground. Finally, the patrolmen got to us. Ron was able to catch the rope and throw it over the cable. He let me go first. As I got into the basket, my parka scrunched up and exposed my stomach. I thought at the time that this always happens to me in lift mishaps.

After we were down, we put on our skis and made it to the bottom of the hill. It was late, and the sun was gone. It was past the usual closing time. We were some of the last people removed from the lift.

After this experience, every time a lift stopped, I panicked, and my face blanched. My pulse raced, and I grasped whatever bar I could and held tight and closed my eyes. After this incident, I avoided skiing at the Highlands.

Elk Herd

The lift accident was the first of a series of remarkable events in the winter of 1965. In early February, Dad came up from the barns and was concerned. He saw evidence of Elk around the bale shed. Although there were fences to keep out livestock, the fences were not a sufficient barrier for elk. They could seemingly leap from a standstill over high fences. If they got over the fence, the bale shed was open on four sides.

Near the bale shed, Dad found some clumps of hair, footprints, and droppings. The Forest Service Ranger alerted Dad that many starving animals were headed to lower elevations because of weather in the high country. The ranger was concerned they would find our bale shed, which would become a problem because we were so near to town.

The ranger gave Dad enough orange drift fence to enclose the entire bale shed structure. With help from the ranger, Ted, Steve, and Dad completed the project in a couple of days. While the work on the bale shed was progressing, Dad sent me up Castle Creek in the Jeep to search for the herd's leading edge and let him know where they were. That way, he could gauge how soon the herd would arrive. At the time, I was fifteen. I was not a legal driver, but that did not make any difference for ranch work. I did not see any elk from the road.

The elk arrived a few nights later in the moonlight. Mom, Dad, and I stood in the living room, with the lights out, looking across the big field in the direction of what is now the Prince of Peace Church. There was nearly a full moon. The elk funneled into the field through the gate off the Castle Creek Road and fanned out. It was beautiful but scary to see the huge animals filling the field. It was like watching the individual segments of time-lapse photography as they moved closer and closer and got bigger and bigger. I estimate there were at least 200 elk.

Some of them came into our yard. In the middle of the night, I looked out my window, and an elk's head was a couple of feet from my window. It was startling. He was nibbling on the exposed grass under the eaves of the house.

The next morning, we surveyed the situation. There were lots of hoofprints in the yard but no significant damage. There was evidence they surrounded the barns and tried to get into the bale shed. None remained. I do not know where they went.

Snowstorm

In March, around the spring vacation, we were experiencing a heatwave. This was unexpected because we had just had a slow trip home from vacation in Boulder fighting snow on the passes. I was excited about the warmth because, although ski season was coming to an end, it meant we were going to get to summer and shorten the ugly spring. Besides, despite the fact I was a teenager, I still amused myself for hours on end playing river on our road as I amused myself building with American Bricks. I weighed too much for crust walking.

Then one day, it started snowing. At first, on the Monday after spring vacation, it was like a regular snowstorm. The second day it was steady but nothing abnormal. I thought, "So much for an early spring!" Then on Wednesday, March 24, the snow started to pick up to the point that it was like downpouring snow.

After school, Ingrid and I walked to Pearl's house through the noticeably deepening snow. Pearl said Mom could not get out of our driveway to pick me up, and I would need to stay in town. After dinner at Pearl's, Ingrid, Barney, and I walked to the ISIS for a movie.

As was always the case when I went to school, I was wearing a skirt with knee socks or tights. I had some mid-calf faux leather fleece boots I could use either straight or folded like Cossack boots to show a band of fleece. I wore a wool winter coat with a knit headband and a pair of mittens tucked in the pocket. We were still not allowed to wear pants to school. Seriously – 20 degrees below zero and girls had to wear dresses or skirts! Before Ingrid, Barney, and I waded out into the night in the pouring snow, I borrowed a pair of Gary or Barney's jeans and long underwear.

After the movie, we walked down Hopkins with Barney. Ingrid and I walked down the middle of Main Street to her house. By this time, there were over two feet of new snow from that day alone. The fresh snow was on top of the foot and a half that fell in the previous days. Ingrid's mother said she heard they might call off school the next day. That would be a first. In all the years living in snow country, they had never canceled school because of snow.

Early the next morning, while it was still dark, Svea came upstairs and told us KSNO said there was no school. We went back to sleep for a while. When we awoke, the sky was bright blue. We looked out on Main Street in front of Ingrid's house at what I called the Elisha Hill. No one was traveling down it. The hill was notorious when there was a small amount of snow, and it was icy. Those coming east on Main Street could easily lose control of their vehicle on the hill if they were not paying attention. It was not unusual to see cars spinning down the hill and ending up in or near the Smart's yard below Ingrid's house. On this day, there was a small lane plowed on Main Street weaving in and out of huge lumps that hid abandoned vehicles under three feet of snow. No vehicles were moving on the street.

Ingrid and I thought we should go skiing, but then we realized that would be impossible, and I did not have my stuff. As it turns out, if the lifts opened at all, it was late in the day because it was nearly impossible to get the loading and unloading areas cleared, and there was no place to put the snow that gathered on the chairs.

Instead, Ingrid and I ate breakfast and walked out to my house. Dad wanted me to come home as soon as possible. He wanted me to put on my skis so I could go down to the corral and feed the horses. The snow was so deep Dad could not get down to the barn on foot. Albert was going to bring out his Jeep with a plow and see if he could take off a layer of snow so Dad could take our Jeep to get to the Cat or the John Deere. Our Jeep did not have a plow.

Ingrid and I walked up the semi-plowed lane in the middle of Main Street. We did not meet any vehicles. We walked down the middle of the Castle Creek Bridge. At our road, we walked up the track made by a Jeep late the day before, but it was still deep. Dad eventually got the main road and the driveway open that day using the John Deere to scoop a layer off the top.

When I fed the horses, I wished I had cross country skis or snowshoes. Long downhill skis kept me from sinking too far into the snow but were hard to maneuver. Once I got to the corral, I was able to walk in the area the horses trampled to get to the barn for hay. There was plenty of hay in the barn. Dragging a bale from the bale shed would have been nearly impossible.

After I fed the horses, Ingrid and I spent the rest of the day working on my model house for a school project. We had a long-term project every year for one of our classes. This year I decided to build a scale-model house. The year before, I painted acrylic landscapes, including the view from the front of the house of a sunset over the future site of the Prince of Peace Church.

I designed a contemporary three-story house with the front two stories above ground and the garage level below the back's grade. It was a typical style at the time and not very exciting. I made landscaping with a lawn, trees, sidewalks, and a driveway in the space around the house. The house was about two and a half feet square and about two and a half feet tall.

Come to think of it; it was a lot like Ted's house with an extra story. I even included his idea of a spiral staircase going up through the back decks. I framed the rooms with miniature two-by-fours and covering them with poster board "drywall."

I spent the better part of a day with Dad ripping the small pieces of wood for the framing, miniature redwood siding for the outside, and "shake shingles" for the roof. Each story was separate and could be stacked on each other. When assembled, the stairwells matched, and the siding lapped, making the house look like it was one piece. I made the windows with wood casings and clear plastic. I bought model brick material for the fireplaces and the chimneys from the architectural supply section at the University of Colorado Bookstore.

I set up shop in Keith's room and used the small tabletop bandsaw Keith used for his models and woodworking hobbies. I spent hours on the house. Often, I preferred to stay home and work on it rather than ski. I liked being at home.

Later that day, I drove Ingrid home. I went to school the next day, but then it started snowing again. By Saturday morning, Dad was concerned the barns could not hold any more weight, so for the next two days, he and I shoveled snow. I worried about him. He was breathing hard, and he frequently stopped and rested leaning against the shovel. For the last year, he seemed to have gained a lot of weight and seemed puffy. His face color was dark.

The first building to shovel was the red barn. It was critical to the cattle operation and had a big open expanse. Unlike the bale shed and the cattle shed in the little field with corrugated metal roofs, the red barn had wooden shingles, and snow did not slide from it when it warmed. We started in the center and fanned out and "plowed" the roof with shovels. Because the snow was so deep, we did not use the flimsy snow shovels but instead used the big scooped shovels like the ones used for shoveling coal. We started at the edge and pushed the snow over the edge. Then we cut back for another layer and continued until the weight on the roof was relieved. By the time we finished, the snowbank behind the barn was even with the roof. That year, it took until the middle of June before it completely melted.

After we finished the red barn, we moved on to the bale shed and the cattle shed. By that time, Dad was exhausted, so Barney and

Gary helped. The snow on these roofs slid easily. The cattle shed had a snowbank on the north side well into summer.

By the time that week's snowstorms ended, Aspen had received over six feet of snow. We did not lose any structures. However, the snowstorm caused the collapse of Tomkins Hardware. I remember seeing it and lamenting the loss of the old building. I was starting to dread the accelerating changes to the town I loved – some natural, some not.

Talent Show

My sophomore year culminated in a talent show and student-council elections for the following year. In the spring, the school had a talent show. Some of Mona Frost's students decided to play piano pieces. Kris Hemann, who also took lessons from Mona, and I decided to play Ferrante and Teicher's *Exodus* four-hand duet. Kris was a much better pianist than me. First, she probably had more talent and, second, she practiced. Somehow, I convinced her to play the lower part (Secondo) of the duet, and I took the upper – melody (Primo). We practiced for weeks with and without Mona's help.

Our first rehearsal did not go that well, but we practiced more and were now ready for the show. There were typical talent-show acts. Gary Sanderson did magic tricks. Melissa Jenkins sang and played guitar. She had a high clear voice and sang "Lullaby of Birdland." Others sang and played guitars. Barney and his friends Tim Willoughby, Phil Hemann, and Ron Long had a group called the Katydids. They were a comedy group, kind of like the Smothers Brothers, and did covers of folk and country songs using broomsticks and washtubs. They were funny.

Kris and I played our duet. We decided to have matching outfits. Oh, my God. My knit dress was baby-blue, and I had matching baby blue tights. Kris had a knit pastel-pink dress, and she had matching pink tights. We looked like Teletubbies before their time. The only way it could have been worse is if we still had bubble hairdos.

Before our turn, I sat nervously waiting on the bleachers with my baby-blue knee involuntarily bouncing up and down. We did a good job with only a few unnoticeable glitches and were well received. The Katydids won.

School Politics

Later that spring, I did another untypical thing for me. I decided to run for student-body president. I knew I was not going to win if it was a popularity contest. Earlier, I tried out for cheerleader and was one of two or maybe three who didn't make it. I was not an outcast; I just was not at the top of the list. Ingrid was my friend, and she was a queen for several events, and I was friendly with most of the cheerleaders such as Diane Pierce and Gail Stebner.

I would not be student body president if I ran against anyone popular or anyone truly bookish. Therefore, I decided the only way I would win was to get someone unique as my campaign manager.

I did something so radical that, to this day, I cannot believe I did it; I asked Gary Boyce to be my manager. Gary was a senior. He was a handsome bad-boy type who won most of the football awards, specialized in downhill ski racing and raced motorcycles. He wore leather jackets and motorcycle boots. At the time, I do not think I had ever even talked to him.

So, one day, I saw him alone and walked up to him and said, "Hi. I'm Vicki Marolt, and I'm running for student body president. I was wondering if you would be my campaign manager."

He looked at me and said, "Sure. I hope it's not a lot of work. What do I have to do?"

"Mostly give a short speech."

"Ok."

I was shocked; he talked to me, let alone accepted the position. His main job was to endorse me in a speech before the student body. A few of my friends and I made the campaign signs. I do not remember my opponent. At the election assembly, Gary gave a good speech wearing his leather jacket over a shirt and tie. I gave my speech in a light blue linen two-piece dress – not the baby blue knit. When the results were posted later that day, I won.

I was going to be Aspen High School Student Body President for the next year. I may have been the first girl in that position. Barney was the president the year before. Talk about a political dynasty!

Peggy's Wedding

That summer, Peggy graduated from the University of Colorado. We went to Boulder for her graduation. I loved the campus and looked forward to going there in a couple of years. Unfortunately, it rained for the ceremony, so we went to a small theater ceremony – no big event in Folsom Stadium.

Later that summer, Peggy married Tom Eckenrode, a graduate student from Pennsylvania she met at the University of Colorado. He was older than her, slightly taller, and wore glasses. Tom had a terrific sense of humor and was a great storyteller.

Peggy and Tom met and the Newman Club, a Catholic group at the University of Colorado. Tom and Peggy had many friends. Because of the Newman Club, Peggy became the Harvest Queen at the University. She looked pretty in a cocktail-length dress with a black velvet top and white brocade skirt. She wore a "diamond" tiara.

She and Tom had their wedding rehearsal dinner in an upstairs room in a new prime rib restaurant, the Abbey. It was on Galena Street across from the Elks. The bar and the back bar in the restaurant were from our grandfather's saloon. Although the restaurant did not last long, Jake's Abbey, a bar and nightclub in the basement, lasted longer. I don't know what happened to my grandfather's bar.

Tom and his family were devout Catholics from Pennsylvania. Tom was in a Jesuit seminary for a while. He was able to get a dispensation from the bishop so we could all eat meat that Friday night. I think that was the only time in my life to that point where I ate meat on a Friday. Six months later, the rule changed, and Catholics could eat meat whenever they wanted.

Julia's daughter, Bonnie Strauss, Judy, and I were bridesmaids. We wore peach-colored dresses with big flat bows on our heads. Judy made the dresses. Karen was the flower girl, and a photograph of her, taken by Franz Berko, was in his studio's window. Peggy convinced Dad to wear a white dinner jacket.

Peggy looked pretty. She was tiny. She was wearing a long silken dress with a tight bodice that Judy made. It had small buttons with looped enclosures down the back. A few minutes before the wedding, Jack O'Brien, one of their Newman Club friends and one of the ushers, showed up. She reached up and hugged him, popping four or five buttons. It was tense for a while until Judy was able to fix them. Like Judy's wedding, the reception was in the yard.

After the wedding, the relatives left, and again it was an only-child summer. After their honeymoon, Peggy and Tom moved to Rocky Ford, Colorado, where they both had teaching jobs. Keith, who had been out for the wedding, went back to California. Cherie rode back to California with him. She had a job working for a jewelry company in Palo Alto. Other than the wedding, the summer was typical of ranch summers – attending picnics, writing in my journals, and riding Patty.

During the summer, I learned Randy Haws was coming to town for a couple of weeks. I spent practically every day since we "broke up," mourning his loss. I kept a cedar box with the mementos from our relationship – a photo signed by him and the corsage I wore to the homecoming dance. When he was in Texas, I received one or two notes from him. I heard about him through Steve Bainbridge and overhearing Susan talk about him even though she had now moved on to a new boyfriend.

Randy's family was staying at the Shadow Mountains condominiums, which his father built. I did not want to contact him directly, so I decided to "run into him." The only place I knew where I could find him was at the condominium. Therefore, for probably three or four days in a row, I went on a "hike" past their condo.

That meant I hiked up the Shadow Mountain portion of Aspen Mountain. I started climbing by the mine dumps across from the old Midland railroad bed behind Riley's house. I angled up through trees and brush and past some abandoned mine shafts bearing slightly to the left until I reached the top of the Straw Pile on Aspen Mountain. My path was not a designated hiking trail, and at the most, it was a game trail. Once I reached the Straw Pile, I casually strolled down the slope below the condominiums. The hike took at least two hours with less than two minutes to run into him.

I never thought about what I would say if I saw him. "Oh, Randy! What a surprise to see you. I didn't know you were in town. Yes, I go on a daily hike on Aspen Mountain. Been doing it for years." One time, I thought I might have caught a glimpse of him, but otherwise, our paths never crossed at the condo. I was a teenage stalker.

I ran into him with friends in town, and we went out as a group for dinner and a movie. That summer, most of the kids in town were going to Galena Street East for Coke night. I liked going there to dance. I think that was the only time I ever enjoyed dancing. I liked dancing with Terry Drew. He was a little older than me and did "real" dances like the jitterbug. He could really twist. He seemed to enjoy teaching people, like me, how to dance.

That summer was the last I heard from Randy Haws until about ten years later. I worked for a pharmaceutical company in Boulder, Colorado, as an administrative assistant for the research and development department. Because I was cuter than the real chemists, all of whom were male, they dressed me up in a lab coat, and, with the two male department heads, I posed for a photograph in front of a stock market ticker in Denver. The photo appeared in an ad for our company on the back of a trade publication, *Chemical Weekly*.

A while later, I got a note from Randy, who was a chemical engineer in Fort Worth. He saw me looking up at him from the back of the magazine. We exchanged a few letters. I pretended I was a happy big shot. So, who got the last laugh, Susan? It was one of those moments I fantasized about after feeling snubbed, "Just you wait until I'm famous. You'll be sorry." In this case, it was, "Just you wait until I am a pretend scientist on the back of a trade journal chemists have to read."

Upper Classman

Compared to my sophomore year, my junior year was difficult. It started okay. I was student-body president. The new Principal, Gerald DeFries, presented me with a reddish-pink, heart-shaped wooden gavel to open the first day of school. He must have been impressed with a girl as student-body president. He then got mad at me a few weeks later when he caught me laughing and being disruptive with a group of people in the library.

In September, I got my driver's license. It was not that big a deal because I had been driving for years. It did, however, make driving legal. For the event, Dad picked me up at school. I was wearing an orange jumper with a yellow, poor boy shirt. Poor boys were slightly form-fitting, crew-necked, and short-sleeved, ribbed-knit shirts. Yellow-and-orange, maroon-and-pink, and olive-green-and-light blue were stylish color combinations at the time. I had several colors of the poor boys, including a maroon one that went with a pair of gingham bell-bottom pants. For my driver's license photo, my hair was in a headband because I was growing out bangs, and I had a noticeable zit on my forehead – not great for the photograph I used for years.

Dad took me county clerk's office and paid for the license. I stood at a high counter to take the written test. In the meantime, Dad talked with Lorain Herwick, who was the sheriff. He was a large jovial man with glasses and a bolo tie who wore a cowboy hat as part of his uniform. A clerk graded the test and took my picture. Lorain asked, "So, Mike, does she know how to drive?" When Dad answered in the affirmative, Lorain said, "Okay. That's good enough for me. She can now officially drive." He handed me a temporary license.

I did not have to take the behind-the-wheel test or show my proficiency with parallel parking. I had been practicing that for months between two oil barrels at the granary. Lorain signed the temporary permit and handed it to me. I drove the Buick home that day.

About a month later, I got my license, with the photograph, from the Department of Motor Vehicles in Denver.

The rest of the year was unremarkable. On April 3, 1966, life as I knew it took a huge turn. It was Palm Sunday. I was home after Mass, and I was in the basement, which Keith and Dad recently finished paneling. I was working on a school project. It was late morning when the phone rang. I answered the basement phone extension expecting a friend. It was Celia.

"I need to talk to your mom or dad." Her voice was tense.

I called upstairs. "Mom, Celia needs to talk to you."

Something was wrong. After I heard Mom pick up the extension, I went upstairs. Stella and Riley were visiting. Mom was standing by the recliner, holding the phone to her ear. I heard her ask a few questions and hung up the phone. She looked up. Her face was white.

"Albina is dead."

We saw Albina a few days earlier when she and Cherie stayed over for dinner after skiing. Cherie was back from California and planned to stay in Aspen to substitute teach. Mom made chili. Albina mentioned she had been having some indigestion problems. As always, we had a fun evening after a fun day of skiing.

On Palm Sunday morning, she complained again about indigestion. This time she mixed a teaspoon of baking soda in a glass of water and drank it to relieve the pressure. A short time later, Edmund found her dead on the floor of the bathroom. She had a heart attack. She was fifty.

Mom, Dad, and I drove to the Gerbaz house. I noticed the baking soda box was on the counter. Cherie, Jimmy, Edmund, Celia, Bill, Ed Tekoucich, and Max were there. Albina's brother, George, and his wife Pepper and their family were on their way from Glenwood. Another sister, Josephine, was coming from Denver. I knew Josephine because she visited often, and her daughter Sherrion, who we called Presh, spent a lot of time at Albina's house. Josephine was a louder version of Celia. Another sister, Edith, was coming from Arvada, where her family operated a large dairy farm. I had never met her. When Edith and her family arrived, I was shocked. She could have been Albina's twin. I secretly wished it had been her, instead of Albina, who died. For the next four days, we were at what I called Bina's house most of the days and evenings.

At the rosary in the mortuary, Albina's body was in an open casket in the dress she wore to Peggy's wedding. The funeral Mass was at St. Mary's. The pallbearers had the difficult task of bringing the casket up the stairs with their many tight turns. The elevator would be decades away. Her burial was in the Red Butte Cemetery. It was dreary, and I felt terrible leaving her alone. After the burial, we attended a get-together at her house. As usual for our family get-togethers, there was a lot of food and booze but no spaghetti and meatballs.

This was my first experience with anyone this close to me dying when I was old enough to understand, and the first time going to a burial at the cemetery. It was like a dream. I was frustrated, knowing there was nothing I could do to change the situation. There was no way to roll back the clock to get a do-over. There was a large empty spot in my chest. I knew there would be no more skiing with her, no more picnics with her pots of spaghetti, no more flowers from her garden, no more bologna and yellow-mustard sandwiches, no more long evenings listening to her stories, and no more cursing because she was late. The summer was not quite the same. The picnics seemed empty without Albina. Cherie, Jimmy, and Edmund were there, but Edmund was quiet and distant.

Peggy and Tom were in Rocky Ford. Peggy was pregnant, and in July, John was born. He was the third grandchild this year. Keith and Joyce had Mark the previous December, and Judy had Stephanie in February.

Mom, Dad, and I drove to Rocky Ford to visit Peggy and Tom and meet John. Rocky Ford is in the southeastern part of Colorado. It was hot, and it smelled like stockyards. Their apartment was dark, hot, and stagnant. John had a nasty diaper rash. Peggy and Tom came back to Aspen for a few weeks before heading to St. Louis, where Tom was going into a Ph.D. program in medieval history at St. Louis University.

That summer, I noticed Dad was feeling worse. He was quiet and had gained weight and had swollen ankles. During the previous year, I started noticing some weight gain. Now it was apparent. His breathing seemed heavy, even without exertion. He had a hard time getting the energy to do any work. When I got up in the morning, the first thing I did was look at him as he sat at the kitchen table, hoping his ears looked pink. Usually, his ears were purple, even tending toward black. That meant he was not getting enough oxygen. Sometimes, he went down to the basement to his work area and took a hit or two off a small oxygen bottle he used for an acetylene torch.

Senior Year – Another New School

That is the setting in which I started my senior year. Being a senior was okay, but I missed Barney and Gary, who were now both away at college. Barney was a freshman at the Northern Colorado University in Greeley, and Gary was a sophomore at the University of Colorado in Boulder. One long weekend Mom, Dad, Pearl, Albert, and I went to Boulder to see Gary and attend a football game where CU beat Oklahoma. I looked forward to going to college.

That year, we were in a new high school near the Highlands. It was across from the old dump that was now behind Shale Bluffs. The new high school was on a property that belonged for a short time to my Grandfather. Jimmy Moore donated the property for the school, and Sam Caudill, the architect who now owned Steve's river-bottom property, designed the building. The year before, we took many trips out to visit the site while it was under construction.

The building made from old bricks had six circular pods. The commons pod had theater-type seats that faced a view of Thunderbowl on Aspen Highlands through two-story windows. There was an administration pod, an academic pod surrounding an open library, a pod for the science classes, one for the gym, and another for music and art. Locker rooms and a space for a cafeteria were under the gym. When we started school, there was no landscaping, and the parking lot on the backside of the building was dirt. It was exciting to be in the new school, but I missed being in town.

That fall, I ran again for student body president and lost. My heart was not in it, and I didn't have a ringer for a campaign manager. This time the ringer was the winner, Gordon Forbes. He was a smart, funny non-conformist who refused to cut his Beatle bangs. Gordon dated Mallory, borrowed my *Revolver* album, and refused to return it.

That year, my birthday was sad. It reminded me of Albina, who celebrated it with us the year before. A few days later, Tom left for St. Louis. Peggy and John were to join him later. Dad and Mom drove Peggy and John to Denver so they could fly. Dad and Mom did not want to have them going across the country on a long trip. I dreaded Peggy living so far away from home. She did not plan to return before the summer.

When Mom and Dad went to Denver, I stayed with Celia and Bill. I came home after school, fed Nipper, fed the horses, and studied. Then I drove the Jeep up to their house for dinner and stayed the night. I returned in the morning to feed Nipper, shower, and get ready for school.

It was fun staying there. Billy was home part of the time. Like Peggy, he graduated from the University of Colorado but was returning as an assistant ski coach. Jimmie Heuga, a friend of Billy's from the 1964 Olympics, was staying at the house. One of the nights I was there, Bob Beattie, the current United States Ski Team coach, came by to visit with Billy and Jimmie.

Jimmie stayed there often. On an earlier visit, his Irish setter ate a hole through the garage door. This time there was no dog. During my stay, I hung out with Celia in the kitchen, drinking tea and listening to her describe the latest additions to her bottle collection.

Later, I watched TV in the living room with Bill. I sat on one end of the couch, and he on the other. It was kind of like watching TV with Dad. Only Bill, unlike Dad, provided frozen candy bars. We watched the same programs. I am not sure it was because we liked the same things, or because there was only one channel. It felt odd looking out their living room window across the field and seeing our house and knowing no one was home, and Nipper was alone.

During that fall, the school was trying out new sports and activities for physical education. We had scuba diving at the Hotel Jerome in late September. It was fun but cold. I ended up getting a sinus infection, for which I received many penicillin shots. Also, we went mountain climbing and learned to repel. Finally, we had ski training, including a lot of wall sitting and hiking through snow. We learned curling at the Brown Ice Palace. Curling was fun, and we spent most of the time laughing. That fall, I frequently babysat for Max and Betty, who were still in Elsie's house across from Albina's house. I couldn't lie about my availability to a family member who would know better.

Cherie, who was teaching in the elementary school, came to our house frequently. She was worried about Edmund. He did not seem to be snapping out of his depression following Albina's death. Cherie brought him to our house to visit with Dad and celebrate Dad's birthday on October 3. Edmund and Dad always had a good relationship. The day after Dad's birthday, Cherie thought Edmund was doing better. She was optimistic.

On October 5, when I came home from school, there were several cars in the driveway. It was not a good sign. I walked into the kitchen. Mom, Dad, Cherie, Jimmy, and Kevin Cassidy, Cherie's best college friend's brother, were sitting around the kitchen table. They were quiet. Mom said I have bad news, "Edmund has taken his life." When Cherie and Jimmy left for the day, Edmund went to sawmill near his house and shot himself.

Later that afternoon, Edmund's brothers and their families came to our house. There was a rosary, a wake at Albina and Edmund's house, a Catholic funeral, and a burial next to Albina in the Elks part of the Red Butte Cemetery.

In the days following Edmund's death, Cherie and Jimmy were overwhelmed and had to get away from their house. They stayed with us for several weeks. They could not be home with all the memories. By this time, Cherie had a boyfriend – Lennie Oates. He was a young attorney she met while in graduate school at the University of Colorado. Sometimes I went with them to Pinocchio's for pizza, to Tico's, which later became Toro's, for Mexican food, and to the Pink Parrott in the Jerome for breakfast.

By fall, it was clear Dad had serious health problems. He was swollen, and his color was dark. He split the sides of his slippers to fit them on his feet. He labored to breathe. He was feeling so bad we could not go to Golden, Colorado, for Billy's wedding. Celia was disappointed. After the first snow, Steve came out and plowed the main road and the driveway for Dad.

I was worried but busy with school and social issues. It was during the time we were preparing for the SAT scheduled in early December in Glenwood Springs. My preparation was minimal, taking one or two sample tests. I spent the night before the test at Mallory's house in Snowbunny. We stayed up too late and had to get up around five a.m. for the drive. It was snowing, and the roads were icy. It was unfair for kids from the valley to have the added stress of the hour's long drive in inclement weather. No one thought about getting a motel in Glenwood the night before.

We made it to the test on time. I was tired and did not feel like I did very well. As it turns out, I did okay. My math score was reasonably high, and I had an adequate English score – 673 in math and 559 in English. It was clearly enough to be accepted at the University of Colorado. I applied to the University of San Francisco as well and was accepted. I thought it might be kind of fun to be near Keith. It was a nice idea, but I only ever intended to go to the University of Colorado. Everyone in our family went there.

After the test, I took over Christmas preparation. Dad could not help with the tree. Albert brought us one, and with Dad's guidance, Mom and I added some extra branches. I did most of the baking. Judy and her family were coming. I was sad Peggy would not be there. She and Tom were going to his home in Pennsylvania. Keith was staying in California.

Before Christmas, Max showed up at the house with a friend, Dr. Albert Kukral, from Denver, who was in town for a skiing vacation. Betty worked as his nurse years before. Max was concerned about Dad's health. Dr. Kukral came into the living room and examined Dad, who was sitting in one of the wing-backed chairs next to the fireplace. He had his feet up on a footstool and was wearing his slashed slippers to ease the swelling on his feet. Dr. Kukral was alarmed. He wanted Dad to immediately go to Denver and check into St. Joseph Hospital to get rid of the swelling and monitor his kidneys and electrolytes. Dad did not want to leave before Christmas but agreed to go to Denver and check in after the holidays.

Dad had another concern – money. He had no health insurance. Because he was a rancher, Dad did not qualify for health insurance through an employer. He applied for insurance through another source, but they excluded coverage for "circulation problems." About everything wrong with Dad involved circulation, so he would have no real coverage.

Money was an ongoing theme. Both my parents were products of the depression. They talked about how they borrowed the money to buy the ranch and then borrowed money to pay the interest on the money they borrowed. I did not know how much my parents had or their income after selling pieces of property to Wally Mills and Lenny Thomas. I understood they got most of their income from the stock market. Mom kept the stock certificates in the metal breadbox in her closet.

The stock market was the main topic of the daily kitchen meetings. Dad subscribed to the *Wall Street Journal* and later to *Barron's*. Steve was usually pessimistic about the market. Steve criticized Mom and Dad for spending too much money on us kids and the furniture after the Thomas sale. Steve and Polly had no children, lived in a lovely home Polly freely and tastefully decorated, and she had fine china, silver serving dishes, crystal, and silver flatware. Steve was on his third new Jeep. He did not criticize Dad for getting a Jeep.

For the most part, my siblings were not privy to these types of financial discussions. I was the one who heard them because I was home when they happened. My siblings were in school or long gone. When we later got a television, I watched the five o'clock news with Walter Cronkite. I knew it would make Dad happy if I came out and reported the Dow Jones was up. I never reported when it was down.

There were things I wanted that they said we could not afford. We never had to tighten our belts from our everyday routine. Regardless, I worried we were one expense or one ruined hay crop away from falling into our own "family depression."

One time, the family went to eat in the new, gourmet side of the Red Onion. I was aware it was expensive, and it was a special treat. As we were getting ready to order, Buck Parsons showed up. Buck frequented the Red Onion and the Golden Horn to listen to jazz. Dad invited him to sit with us, ordered him a drink, and asked Buck to stay for dinner. I was worried. Was this the event that was going to send us into financial ruin?

Dad and money worries were in the background of our Christmas that year. It was not joyful and was more of a chore than a celebration. Judy and her family were there. We gave Dad lame presents. I gave him gifts from a new shop called the Wildweed. I gave him cute a cartoon mouse head drawn on an enameled disk and a set of colored cordials from the same store. The set included six small barrel-shaped glasses in different shades of clear glass – blue, green, pink, white, gold, and light gray – with etching on the side. Judy gave him a brass holder for firewood. Others gave him pajamas, a robe, and new slippers for his hospital stay. Dad was disappointed. Out of the blue, he said, "Next year, get me tools."

Lonely Winter

Mom and I spent New Year's Day putting away the decorations. That was a day earlier than usual. As I put the decorations in the boxes and sealed them, I wondered what changes there would be when I opened it next year.

On Monday, Mom and Dad planned to leave. It was snowing. Dad was nervous. He wanted to back out but finally decided to go. They left at 10:30. I stayed home. It was so lonely. Judy and her family were gone and now so were Mom and Dad. Celia stopped by for a while, and so did Barney. That evening, I went to Cherie's for dinner. We decided that I should spend the nights there instead of being home alone. I took care of the animals in the morning and came home for a while after school. I expected Mom and Dad home within a week or ten days.

That first night after dinner, I sat in the back bedroom at Cherie's house that had initially been Jimmy and Cherie's room. Cherie was now using her parent's room, and Jimmy had his room in front of the house.

It was cold back there. I was wearing the new bathrobe I got for Christmas. It was in quilted cherry red material with white line-drawn flowers. It zipped up the front, and it was sort of form-fitting. It was cute. I sat cross-legged on the bed and took out the Peanuts appointment calendar I got for Christmas. In the squares for each date, I wrote a short diary of events of the day. It was not so much about angst. It was mostly reporting. I would keep up this calendar tradition daily for over 20 years.

The next morning, I got up early. Cherie set the table set blue checked placemats, a glass of orange juice, a slice of homemade cranberry bread, and a cup of coffee. I went home and fed Nipper. He was confused. I hated leaving him alone to wander back down to the bale shed.

I changed and drove the Jeep to school. After school, I came home and fed the horses and let Nipper stay in the house with me until I left for Cherie's house. Sometimes, one of my friends might stop by, or I went to Ingrid's or Mallory's for a while. I babysat for Betty and Max. I usually went back to Cherie's to sleep. I expected this to be my basic routine for the next week or so while Dad received treatment.

One night, Ingrid and I drove the Jeep in a snowstorm to Basalt. That was not a good idea. First, there was only one electric wiper on the driver's side, which was worthless. Ingrid had to operate the wiper on her side manually. With the short wheelbase and heavy top, it was not at all stable on the icy roads. When we were at Shale Bluffs on our way home, we spun out and ended up on the bluff side of the road. Had we gone one more half-turn, we would have hit the guardrail and possibly gone over the edge. If we went over the edge, I have no doubt we would be dead. Although we were in some deep snow, I was able to put the Jeep in four-wheel drive, get out, and go home. I never took the Jeep beyond school and the house during a snowstorm after that night. It was years before I told anyone of our near mishap.

On the weekend, Mom and Dad were still gone, but reports seemed good. Dad was shedding water weight and was looking forward to watching the upcoming first Super Bowl. He was disappointed his favorite team, the Baltimore Colts, and his favorite quarterback, Johnny Unitas, would not be playing. He hoped to be out of the hospital and watch it at Judy's house in Boulder.

I ended up visiting with Pearl and coming home to study. When I did my English essays, I missed my spell checker – Mom. I used to call to her in the next room, "How do you spell …?" I would get annoyed if she did not answer right away. At this time, though, I had a lot of chemistry and math analysis homework. I wanted to make sure I was at least the Salutatorian of my class. Besides, I was never wild about skiing in early January.

On Friday of that second week, I was sick and stayed home from school. I had another sinus infection and was alternating chills and fever. Later that evening, I called Judy to see how Dad was doing. She was upset. He had pneumonia because of the hospital stay. That was terrible news. We were warned if Dad ever got pneumonia again, his lungs could not handle it, and he would probably not survive. Before I went to bed that night, I knelt and prayed he would be okay.

At 4:30 a.m. on January 14, I heard the phone ring in a distant room in Cherie's house. A few minutes later, she came in and told me it was Judy. Dad was in bad shape, in intensive care, and may not make it. Peggy and Keith were flying to Denver.

Cherie said she and Lennie would drive me to Denver, hoping I could see Dad before he was gone. It was snowing. I went home and packed, called Steve, and asked him to take care of the animals. Steve was tense. I could hear the tightness in his voice as if he were fighting back tears.

Cherie and Lennie picked me up. I did not know if Dad was alive. When we got over Vail Pass, we learned that Loveland Pass was closed, so we diverted over Berthoud Pass. The trip took much longer than the usual five hours. I went to a payphone when we got gas in Georgetown, but I could not reach anyone to get information. Finally, late that afternoon, we made it to Denver and St. Joseph Hospital. Cherie and I went inside. I crossed my fingers when I inquired at the desk. I was terrified to hear Dad's status.

"I'm here to check on the status of Michael Marolt."

She looked through some papers. "He's in intensive care. Tenth Floor. You need clearance to see him. Check with the nurse."

He was alive. Thank God! We went up to the intensive care floor and was told I could find my family in the waiting room.

That night I was together with my entire family. I only got a glimpse of Dad. He was not awake and was hooked to breathing equipment. We started taking turns staying with him twenty-four hours a day. At first, Mom and I stayed with Rose, a nurse at the hospital. I eventually stayed at Judy's house at night, and during the day at the hospital, I put together jigsaw puzzles, prayed in the chapel, and snacked in the cafeteria.

During the week, Dad improved, and finally, a week later, he was released from intensive care. I needed to return to Aspen and school and planned to fly home on Sunday. I had never flown before and was terrified about the prospect. I looked out the window at Rose's apartment near Stapleton Airport and saw the planes coming and going. I did not want to get in one. I did not want to be alone.

I never said anything to anyone about my fears because they had enough worries. After seeing Dad and saying good-bye, Keith and I went to the airport. There were flurries in Denver, and it was snowing in the mountains. The flights to Aspen were canceled, and there was no bus. Like other people from the flight, a couple near us decided to get a rental car and drive. Keith asked if I could ride with them, and he gave them some money. It was a long, lonely ride. They were tense. So was I. They did not know how to drive in the snow.

Miraculously, we got to Aspen late that afternoon. As we neared the main road to the house, I could see the drive was unplowed. So, I had them drop me at Pearl's. There was no way their car could make it up the main road.

Albert brought me home in his Jeep and made sure I could start the Blue Goose. I got home, saw Nipper, and went back to Cherie's. I was back to the old routine – home in the morning, shower and feed Nipper, drive to school, do the cool high school senior fun stuff, home in the afternoon, feed the horses, an hour or two with friends, close the house, and send Nipper to the bale shed.

I drove in the dark to Cherie's house, wishing I were home in a lighted house with Mom, Dad, and Nipper. If it were today, Nipper would be used to getting in and out of vehicles and could go with me to Cherie's. Instead, he was a farm dog who had only one place to stay.

Not even a week after I got home from my week hanging out in the waiting room at St. Joseph's, I got another call. Dad was back in intensive care. This time, they told me to stay home and wait. One afternoon, I came home from school and sat in the kitchen chair Dad used this time of day, put my head on the table, and cried. I was so lonely. All I wanted was to be home with my family.

Everyone tried to make it okay. Cherie, Pearl, and Celia were always available. I babysat for Max and Betty. I went skiing with Betty, Marlis, and Beaver. Steve and Ted started coming out to the ranch on Saturdays and Sundays to carry on their conversations in the kitchen. They may have been coming out during the week when I was in school. I sat at the kitchen table and listened and occasionally commented. I was a little annoyed I was not getting my schoolwork done, but then again, I knew how much they missed Dad and Mom and their routine. I was glad they cared.

I started to stay home at night. It was lonely and a bit scary, but it was home. I let Nipper remain with me in the kitchen or the porch. One Saturday mornings, I heard a loud rapping. In my semi-dream state, I put on my robe and went to the door. Max was standing there in his ski gear.

"Hey, Slick, let's go skiing."

"I was going to sleep in."

"You're up. Let's go.

How could I refuse? I grumbled and dug through my drawers to find my stuff. A few minutes later, I was ready. Max and I went to Buttermilk. We rode to the top of the mountain, and Max said,

"I'll race you to the bottom."

Even though I was no competition, I did my best not to be a chicken. We started at the top and schussed. While I was in my best tuck, Max was ahead casually skating. At the bottom, he waited, and we tied. Later, we ran into Dr. Kukral and some friends and skied with them for a while. Then Max looked at me and said,

"Aren't you tired of this up-hill skiing?" We took off and schussed to the bottom.

Max came out several more times, and we skied at Buttermilk and Aspen Mountain. I do not remember Max skiing at Highlands. Skiing with Max was a bright light in an otherwise dark year.

Several days later, I rode with Gary, who was home for semester break, to Boulder. I went to Denver for long enough to stop at the hospital and say "hi" and turn around and get on the train to come home.

Finally, eight weeks after Dad and Mom drove down the road for Denver, they were coming home! I spent the better part of a week making sure the house was clean and in order.

It was so nice to have them back. Although he was a little weak, Dad looked good. He had lost so much weight – probably 50 to 60 pounds. His color was good. Steve and Ted were glad to have him back. They hugged each other in that stiff sort of brotherly way. Pearl and Celia were happy to see Mom. The house was filled with friends and family and bubbling pots of soup.

Although Dad and Mom were glad to be home, they had to deal with a $10,000 hospital bill. That was as much as Mom and Dad paid for the ranch. When he got the bill, Dad marveled, "Can you believe it? Each one of those big old potassium pills cost ten dollars." They were able to pay the bill from savings but feared another illness or an accident without insurance would deplete their assets.

Spring

In March, Mom, Dad, and I went to Denver during spring vacation for Dad's check-up. Dr. Kukral thought it might be a good idea for Dad to see how he felt at a lower altitude. Keith talked Mom and Dad into coming out to Marysville, California, for a couple of weeks. It was March, and there was nothing much going on at home. I decided to go with them for the rest of my spring vacation plus another week. I arranged with the school to do my classwork on my own.

We flew out of Denver later that night. It was the first airplane ride for all of us, and I was not worried because I was with Mom and Dad. I sat by the window. Mom was in the middle, and Dad on the aisle. We were impressed being above the clouds with the sun setting and the pink puffy clouds below us. I was fascinated at the lights below as we came over Stockton. Dad thought he could get used to this kind of traveling. Keith and Joyce met us at the airport. We stopped at Bev and Bob's house to pick up their son, Mark, and headed to Marysville.

This was not a trip to visit tourist attractions. Instead, Dad played with Mark and walked. I studied – chemistry, math, history, and English. Ten days after we arrived, Keith, Dad, and Mom drove me to San Francisco to fly home by myself. They were going to stay a couple of weeks longer.

Everyone went to the gate. This was during a time where there were no gate restrictions. It was early evening and getting dark outside. I did not want to be separated again. I did not want to say good-bye. I did not want to fly alone. I was scared. Dad reached into his pocket and took out a pill bottle and handed me a pill.

"This is a Milltown. They are tranquilizers to keep you from getting too nervous. Take half of one now. Don't take the other half unless you need it. They can knock you for a loop."

I took the half before I got on the plane and folded the other half in a Kleenex and put it in my purse. I sat in a window seat facing toward the airport concourse. Mom, Dad, and Keith were standing at the windows waving and me. I wanted them to come home. I hated seeing them recede out of sight as the plane pulled away.

The tranquilizer calmed me down, and I had an uneventful trip to Denver. Judy and Chuck picked me up, and the next day I returned to Aspen on the train. Cherie and Jimmy met me up in Glenwood.

On Sunday after Mass, I spent most of the day at home. I was so lonely. It was getting to me. I continued to do homework and worried about whether I was too far behind and was ruining my chances of being at least Salutatorian. Late that Sunday afternoon, to control my nerves, I searched through my purse and found the last half of the Milltown.

I took it and, sure enough, I was feeling better. In fact, I was feeling pretty good. I thought maybe I should have a little something extra to take off more of the edge. I looked under the sink. Most of the liquor was gone. Steve had a shot or two of whiskey when he came to visit or take care of Nipper, and it was gone. We only had gin or tequila in the summer. There was, however, about a half of a bottle of sweet vermouth Dad used to make Manhattans. Unlike martinis, which he liked, he decided he did not like Manhattans.

Somewhere in the back of my mind, I thought vermouth was wine, so I poured some in one of the cut-glass the decanter glasses we reserved for Christmas port.

I poured another. Pretty soon, I was feeling good. I danced around the kitchen doing high kicks and looking at my reflection in the kitchen window. I did some somersaults and splits on the floor.

The next thing I remember, it was dark, and a flashlight was shining in on me through a window. I was disoriented. I realized I was lying on Mom and Dad's bed in a pile of vomit. I got up and stumbled to the front door. It was Cherie and Lennie and someone from the sheriff's office. It was late, and they were worried. I was supposed to stay with Cherie that night. I told them I took half a tranquilizer and drank alcohol. Because of the drug, they took me to the hospital to make sure I was okay. I went back to Cherie's. I felt sleazy and embarrassed.

I managed to make it to school the next day but felt terrible. However, I found that my worrying about being behind academically was unnecessary. With my concentrated studying in California, I was far ahead in my classes. A week later, I learned that I was indeed second in the class and would be Salutatorian.

The next week, I interviewed for a summer job at the T-Lazy-7 dude ranch working in the day camp. Mimi Deane, an attractive woman with long coal-black hair, interviewed me. She was married to Buck Deane, who was running the ranch along with his mother and brother. She hired me on the spot to start in late June.

Finally, in April, Mom and Dad came home for good. I made homemade soup for the occasion. Cherie came for dinner and stayed the night because Jimmy was gone.

A couple of weeks later, Mallory said David, her soon to be ex-stepfather, wanted to take Mallory and a friend with him for a trip back to his home to Fort Lauderdale, Florida. From there, Mallory and her guest would travel on his 65-foot yacht for a couple of weeks in the Bahamas. It sounded like the grand prize on *The Price is Right*. Mallory asked me to go, but I was worried about leaving Mom and Dad.

I mentioned the idea to Mom. She did not like it. She did not know David and was worried I would get hurt. On the other hand, Dad said it was a fantastic opportunity – kind of like his trip to La Jolla when he was young. He said he would be fine. He looked good and was no longer having trouble breathing.

Mom and Dad said they would give me some spending money as a graduation present. I deserved to have some fun after everything I had been through that winter. I needed to be home by the end of June to start my job. I did not have to worry about Dad and Mom being lonely because Peggy, Tom, and John were coming home in late May to spend the summer. I decided to go. To work with my schedule, we planned on leaving two days after graduation.

Peggy and Tom got there for my graduation, as were Judy and her family. It was the first graduation in the new school. I was Salutatorian and gave a speech about Tom Dooley. Dad and Mom were proud of me. I remember looking out in the audience and seeing their faces.

Summer of 1967

Summer of 1967

Two days after graduation David, Mallory, and I left on our trip. We drove to David's mother's summer home in Hunt, Texas, for two nights. She was wealthy and had servants. We swung from ropes and dropped into the Guadalupe River, dodging snakes and giant spiders. We spent a couple of nights in Houston visiting Mallory's friends, including dinner with Dee Dee Mosbacher. Her father was Robert Mosbacher of yachting and political fame. In Houston, David rented us a yellow Mustang so we could drive around town. He failed to get a car with air conditioning, but we pretended we had it by keeping our windows closed. We left Houston and stopped for a night in New Orleans at the Monte Leon, where Mallory and I had a few too many hurricanes. The drinking age was 18, and we were close. Then we went on to Florida.

We stayed in Fort Lauderdale for several days getting supplies for our trip and waiting for heavy rains to clear. I bought a birthday present for Peggy – a papier-machete bottle cover – and I bought Dad a copy of George Plimpton's book *Paper Lion* for Father's Day. I managed to find a church for Mass and borrowed David's station wagon to get there.

Then we left for West End in the Bahamas. It was a long trip. The refrigerator door flew open in the galley. I stood there, holding it closed, and yelling. At one point, while leftover chicken-noodle soup sloshed over my feet, Mallory found me. I was green with seasickness. I went up on deck and stayed the day. There was no sunblock in those days. I barely noticed I was getting sunburned because of the sea breeze.

I got over the burn and the seasickness. We spent a little over a week going from one small island to the next. One Sunday, we were anchored in an alcove in an uninhabited island with no church. That day we water skied behind the Boston Whaler, a squared-off dinghy David towed behind the yacht and the vehicle we used to go on shore. Despite having a lot of fun, I worried I would be in trouble for missing Mass.

A few days later, in Hope Town on Elbow Cay, we ran into Mead and Joan Metcalf from the Crystal Palace in Aspen. We spent the day at the beach with them. It was nice to see someone from home. We ended our trip in Nassau. We went to Café Martinique, which was recently in the James Bond film, *Thunderball*. We had frozen daiquiris – no drinking age in the Bahamas. On Sunday, I walked to a small Catholic Church for Mass.

We flew to Miami and on to Chicago for a couple of days with Mallory's grandparents – her deceased father's parents. We flew back to Denver and rode home in a private plane flown by Mallory's mother's current boyfriend. It was a little too much flying for me. I was so glad when we landed in Aspen. Dad looked good. Finally, I was home. Everything seemed normal. Peggy and Tom had arrived. My cousin, Gary Clifton, was in town for the summer working for the ski corporation. I would have another movie and hiking companion. I started my job at the T-Lazy-7 dude ranch.

The T-Lazy-7 job was as much fun as I expected. I caught a ride to the ranch with a woman who worked for Mimi Deane and helped with the day camp. Before the kids arrived, we made sandwiches in the cabin between the corral and the Maroon Creek Road. The sandwiches were for a daily picnic.

We spent most of the day on the ranch or in the Maroon Creek area. There were between six and ten day-campers. We swam at the pool and took saunas near the cabins used by overnight guests. We spent time across the road in a wooded area near the river, where there were picnic tables used for chuckwagon dinners. We did art, archery, and played horseshoes there. I made a design with pebbles from Maroon Creek and twigs on an old shingle. It still hangs in an alcove dedicated to Aspen memorabilia in my house.

Once a day, we went to the corral, where the wranglers saddled horses for a horseback ride. The rides went up Maroon Creek or Willow Creek and lasted at least an hour. Several times a week, we went on field trips. We had picnics at Weller Lake and Maroon Lake. We hiked around the grottos. We drove down the valley to the fish hatchery in Carbondale or St. Benedict's Monastery in Old Snowmass.

In mid-July, we had an overnight with a breakfast ride. I went to work late and planned to return by noon the next day. It was fun. The breakfast was yummy – bacon, eggs, and pancakes. We returned to the ranch, and the parents picked up their kids early. I went home.

I did not know that shortly after I left for work the day before, Riley walked out to our house. No one was home. Riley had started drinking again. He convinced himself he could have a beer now and again. This day he was drunk.

When Mom returned, she found Riley lying face down under the willow tree on a collapsed lawn chair. When she got near, she realized he was covered with blood. His nose was nearly severed. Somehow, she got him to the emergency room.

He cut his nose on the lawn chair. The lawn chair was a gift of patio furniture and equipment from Bud's boss, Floyd Biegert. One year, he gave Dad a cast aluminum barbeque known as a Portable Kitchen. It was made in Arkansas and was a revolutionary product at the time. It had an oval tub cast-aluminum lid and was big enough to roast a large turkey. We roasted a turkey once. It tasted good, but everyone agreed we preferred our turkey with dressing and mashed potatoes. It was probably the best charcoal cooker we ever had. My nephew still uses it.

When Mr. Biegert gave Dad the barbeque, he also gave him a set of patio furniture from a high-end patio display from his Cherry Creek store in Denver. It included two folding chairs and a chaise lounge. They had thin aluminum slats for the seats and back that rotated slightly to adapt to the contours of whoever was sitting on them. They had upholstered, yellow and orange, striped cushions tied on the frames – the same color combination as in my driver's license photo. The chairs sat on the lawn under the willow.

On the day of the accident, when Riley discovered no one was home, he decided to sit and wait for someone to return. He stumbled and fell onto one of the chairs, and an aluminum slat sliced into his nose. These slats were thin – like dull knife blades. It was only a matter of time until a small child stood on one of the chairs or slipped under the cushion and severely cut one of their limbs. When she got back from the hospital, Mom packed up the furniture and threw it in the trash. Riley never drank again.

When I arrived home at noon the next day, there was activity at the house and many cars. As I came through the gate, Tom, Peggy's husband, greeted me.

"Hey, Vick, I have some bad news." He looked grim.

"Oh, God. Not Dad?"

"No. It's Bill."

"Bill? Is he okay?"

"No. Sometime during the night, he died. Celia found him. It was probably a heart attack."

This was not registering. Then Tom continued, "If that's not bad enough, Riley had a bad accident here yesterday, and he is in the hospital."

"God. What happened to him?"

"Fell into one of the lawn chairs and badly cut his nose. He may lose it."

I wondered how much stuff could go wrong. I sat on the stone stoop and put my head in my hands. I could not comprehend the magnitude of the loss. Bill was one of those people I assumed would always be around. I had spent a good part of the fall with him while Dad and Mom were gone. Unlike Dad, Bill had no bad habits and always looked good. I had no idea he had health issues.

The day before he died, he was feeling ill. Rod, who was staying with Bill and Celia, took him to Dr. "Bugsy" Barnard. Although Bill was experiencing breathing problems and should have been in the hospital, he went home. In the middle of the night, he complained of pain and breathing issues. It is unclear when he died or whether Celia was with him at the time. All I knew, out of nowhere, Bill was dead. I was getting tired of funerals.

Over the next several days, all of Bill's children came to town – Billy and his new wife, Connie, Bev and Bob, Bud, Jeanine, Jamie, and Ted. All of Dad and Bill's living siblings came to town – Rose and the Strauss family from Denver, Elsie, and George from Encino, California, and Dorothy, Will, and Bernadette from Hacienda Heights, California. Max and his family were living in town, as were Steve and Ted. Peggy and her family were here. We gathered at Celia and Bill's house before and after the funeral. There was another rosary, funeral Mass, and burial at Red Butte Cemetery. Bill's grave was next to the Marolt family plot because Bud was able to buy the adjacent plots.

Over the next few weeks, I finished working at the T-Lazy-7. Dad looked good and was doing well. He finished putting up the second cutting of hay. Tom, Gary, Barney, and Gary Clifton, and some of their friends hauled it.

In late August, Cherie and Lennie were married in Taos, New Mexico. Dad, Mom, Celia, and I drove to Taos for the wedding. It was a small event at a nice resort hotel – The Sagebrush Inn. It included Jimmy, Lennie's parents, our family, a few of Cherie's college friends, including Ann Cassidy and her parents. It was bittersweet because neither Albina nor Edmund were alive. Albina would have loved planning a wedding. We had a good dinner the night before at Frenchie's, a well-known restaurant.

Cherie wore a sleeveless street length classy white dress with white beading on the bodice. After the civil ceremony, we had champagne and a delicious fruit-type cake with cream-cheese icing. We missed Albina, Edmund, and Bill.

When we got home, Peggy and Tom were preparing to leave for St. Louis. Gary Clifton was going back to California. I was going to the University of Colorado in Boulder.

In late August, Ted, Peggy, Tom, John, Gary Clifton, and I took a trip to check out the new ski area Gary had been working on that summer in Snowmass. At the new ski area, I realized this was another of the accumulating and escalating Aspen changes. I was losing family, and my familiar hometown was changing exponentially. The ski area was huge. It was so much bigger than any of the other mountains. It was like Vail, except it was at the end of a road and not next to a major highway. Gary Clifton left a few days later.

On August 29, Peggy and Tom packed their car. Unlike the year before, Peggy and John were driving with Tom to St. Louis. They planned to stop in Rocky Ford, Colorado, to return borrowed baby furniture on their way to Missouri.

I hated days like this when family members left home. I felt empty. Worse, I dreaded the effect it had on Dad. He never said he hated it. Instead, he receded quietly into himself. For hours or sometimes days, it was hard to get him to break into even the faintest smile. This goodbye was worse than usual because in a little over a week, I would be the one leaving. I was leaving for college. What was going to happen to Dad then?

While Peggy finished collecting things inside the house, Tom put John in the car. John was excited about a car trip. He bounced up and down in the front seat, holding onto the steering wheel. Dad, Billy, and Ted leaned against the Buick while Tom leaned against his car, all chatting with each other. Knowing Tom, he was probably telling a joke. I snapped a few pictures of John mugging for the camera. Boy, I was going to miss him.

As I returned to the house, I had an overwhelming sense I needed to take a picture of the men leaning against the cars. My inner voice said, "They will never be together again." Before I put my hand on the doorknob, I turned and took their picture. I felt a chill.

A few minutes later, after handshakes and hugs, Peggy, Tom, and John got in their car and drove over the culvert and down the road. Ted and Billy stayed a few minutes and left. Everyone was still reeling from Bill's death a few weeks earlier.

I went into the house and down the hall to Peggy, Tom, and John's now-vacant room – Keith's old room. There were reminders of family members who were now in their car, moving away from us. There was a Q-tip here; a receipt there, and some miscellaneous trash that, for a moment, gained sentimental significance.

Mom and I got busy cleaning the rooms and changing the linens. We took down the crib, folded it, and put it away in the "doghouse" behind the fireplace. We swept the floors and emptied the waste cans. Soon the evidence of a summer of mixed reviews would be gone.

Later that afternoon, Dad did what he often did on these departure days; he busied himself around the ranch. Today, he said he needed to work on a gate by the barn – the gate leading to the culvert over the ditch and the field beyond. That was where there was a little hidden meadow, where Keith built his village, south of the culvert where I liked to go and daydream. It was below the spot where I planned to build my house.

After I hung sheets on the clothesline, I walked out on the granary bridge. I saw Dad standing with his right foot on the lowest rung of the gate, his hands on the top, and looking toward Aspen Mountain over Castle Creek. The top of the gate was about shoulder height. He did not look like he was having any physical problems, but I wondered if he was thinking about leaving Aspen. For his health, the doctors thought it might be best if he moved to a lower altitude. That was another one of those things we understood, but no one wanted to discuss. I was going to miss this place when I was at college.

After we hung out the laundry, Mom and I went to Cherie's to pick out and try on some used clothes. Cherie was an excellent seamstress and made most of her clothes. If she found a pattern she liked, she made four or five garments in different colors or fabrics. When she got tired of any of these outfits, she gave them to me. Most of my high school dresses came from her. She had all kinds of dresses, jumpers, and skirts that would work for me in college. The orange jumper in my driver's license picture was from her. The clothes only needed a few alterations here and there.

When we got home that afternoon, Pearl called. She invited us to come to their house that evening to watch the final episode of *The Fugitive*. All of us, and especially Dad, were big fans of the show. It was rumored Kimball would finally find the one-armed man and be exonerated.

Pearl and Albert had one of the few color TVs in town. The color was not great – tinted a bit heavy with pinks – as if it was one of those old black and white photographs colored with transparent paints. It was a Sylvania "Halolight," which meant it had a fluorescent light around the screen. Despite its now primitive nature, it was much more interesting than our black and white TV. Besides, it was an excuse to get away from the empty, depressing house.

Pearl had cookies and coffee. Gary and Barney were still home from college. Gary was going to be a junior at the University of Colorado, and Barney would be a sophomore at the University of Northern Colorado in Greeley.

After Albert selected his lounge chair, pulled up his ashtray stand, we each found spots on the sofa or the carpet in front of the TV. I sat on the floor with my back on the couch between Mom and Dad. The final episode was worth the wait. We were relieved when Kimball got the one-armed man and was no longer a fugitive. We didn't stay long after the program ended at 10:00 p.m.

When we got home, Mom went to bed. I was in the kitchen. Dad reached under the kitchen sink and brought out a bottle of sherry. He picked out a couple of the colored cordial glasses I gave him for Christmas.

"What do you say we have a glass of sherry?"

I was surprised. That was not something we normally did. "Sure."

We sat at the kitchen table. I sat by the window where he sat in the morning. He sat in the chair by the door to the dining room.

"So, are you excited to go to CU?"

"Yeah." And then I added, "I'm worried I'll be homesick."

"You'll be okay. Everyone has a little of that. I did. I was homesick – especially for my mother. But I liked going to school there. Wish I could have stayed longer."

He seemed to linger on those thoughts and said, in a teasing voice, "You'll forget about being homesick when you start drinking beer at The Sink."

The Sink had once been a fancy restaurant, "The Sunken Garden," where Dad waited tables when he was in college. It was now one of the favorite beer joints on the Hill in Boulder. The Hill was the college hangout near campus. The Sink was now for drinking beer, eating Sink burgers, and devouring greasy, skinny fries heaped on paper plates. Graffiti adorned the walls and ceiling. At the time, the drinking age for 3.2 beer was eighteen. I was two weeks away from that milestone.

"I worry about you and Mom."

"Mother and I will be fine. You'll be home all the time. Gary comes home a lot. You can come with him. We'll come over for a football game. Believe me; it will go fast. Maybe too fast."

Then he added, "All four of my kids graduating from CU. That's something." We clicked our glasses.

I think Dad was putting up a good front. Knowing how much he hated having his children leave, I guarantee he was dreading the day he and Mom dropped me off in Boulder and were the ones returning to Aspen without me. I appreciated his efforts to assuage my fear of leaving them. It made a good end to a long day. At 11:00 p.m., we put our glasses on the counter, turned out the lights, and went to bed.

After putting on my pajamas and kneeling to say my rosary, I crawled into bed. Tomorrow I would start getting ready for school. I had the clothes from Cherie to hem and needed to start making piles of things to take with me. I decided I would go through sorority "rush." No one in our family had done it before. Cherie had been a Kappa Kappa

Gamma at Fort Collins, and Billy's new wife, Connie, was a Pi Phi. Both Cherie and Connie said I should give it a try.

As I lay in bed, I thought about boys. I especially thought about my recent crushes, including one of Peggy's friends from college. Too old for me, but still crush-worthy. I did not want to admit it, but I was excited to go to college and maybe get a boyfriend. There were no boyfriends for me in Aspen after Randy Haws. Soon, I was asleep.

Suddenly, I woke up to Dad screaming. I sat up. The overhead light went on in Mom and Dad's room. I ran to their door. Dad was sitting on the edge of his bed in his underwear. He was rubbing his leg. Mom was walking around near the door.

"I got this really bad Charlie horse," Dad said.

A few minutes later, he said, "I need some oxygen. Get me my oxygen. It's on my bench in the furnace room."

As I ran to the basement, I turned on the overhead light in the hall, the overhead light in the dining room, the overhead light in the kitchen, the light in the back porch, and the light in the basement. On the way, I glanced at the kitchen clock above the sink. It was 2:30 a.m.

I found the blue oxygen tank on the white metal counter in the furnace room, generally used for acetylene torches. From time to time, when Dad was having breathing troubles, he would "take a hit" off it and had rigged up a mask of sorts.

I made it back to their room. Mom was now in her pink housecoat. Dad was in the black watch plaid robe and slippers he got last Christmas. They were walking down the hall. He was leaning on Mom.

Mom said, "We need to get Daddy to the hospital."

I went to my room. I put on the cherry-red quilted robe I got for Christmas only nine months before. I slipped on my loafers without socks. I did not own slippers.

Mom went ahead to get the car out of the garage. I helped Dad down the hall and out the door, onto the stoop where I stood that morning compelled to take a photograph. I helped Dad into the back seat of the car. As Mom drove, I tried to help Dad with the oxygen.

Mom went straight down Hallam, thinking it would be faster than Main Street. She forgot about the stop signs.

In a panicked, plaintive voice, Dad said, "Mother, please hurry."

She started running stop signs. There was no traffic. She turned sharply by Reinhard Elder's house behind the Jerome and immediately turned left again to head up Red Mountain on Hospital Road. She gunned the engine as she headed up the hill. The trip took maybe ten minutes.

We got to the hospital, and Mom pulled up in front of the emergency room. I jumped out and went inside. In a few minutes, nurses and orderlies loaded Dad on a gurney and wheeled him inside. I followed. There was a flurry of activity, and I heard someone on the phone calling Dr. Gould to come to the hospital.

They rolled Dad into an area, pushed the curtain back, and hooked him up to oxygen and other gadgets. While Mom parked the car, I followed Dad on the gurney. I held onto his arm. He looked up at me with his dark eyes. He was scared. He slowly shook his head from side to side and said, "This is it."

Dr. Gould arrived and went into the room. I left him with Dad. I asked at the desk if I should call Father Bosch. Without speaking, someone dialed a number and handed me the phone.

After it rang for a while, there was an answer. "Father. This is Vicki Marolt. I'm at the hospital. I don't think Daddy is going to make it."

"I'm on my way," he said.

Father Bosch arrived within minutes, wearing mostly civilian clothes, a plaid shirt over his black shirt and collar, and black slacks. He was carrying a black satchel. I waited in the emergency room with Mom. I paced. Father Bosch stopped briefly at the desk and went to Dad. After a while, he came out and gave Mom and me a hug. That was so unlike Father Bosch. He was usually gruff and standoffish. He did not say anything. I knew Dad was gone. Someone took Mom into Dad's room.

I stood there in my red quilted robe with the white flowers. It felt like the room was swirling. The greenish fluorescent lights seemed to be flickering. What was I to do? This could not possibly be happening. I could not do this on my own.

I borrowed the phone and made a call. After several rings, Steve answered. His voice was groggy.

"This is Vicki."

"Vick. What's wrong?"
"Daddy." I choked. "We're at the hospital. Daddy is gone."
"What do you mean?"
"Daddy is dead."
"Ah, shit."
There was a moment of silence.
"I'll get Ted. I'm on my way."

I would have called Ted, but he did not have a phone because of his hearing loss.

Then I sat in the waiting area, washed with that iridescent green light, and waited. Eventually, Mom came out of the room with Doctor Gould and went to a desk and signed some papers. I heard blood clot, lung, and drowned. When Mom was done, we hugged for a long time. Then there was nothing else we could do.

We walked silently to the car, which was near the entrance. It was probably 4:30 a.m. Mom gave me the keys and sat in the passenger seat. She did not say anything. I started the car, turned on the headlights, and backed out. The oxygen tank rocked back and forth on the back seat. I turned out of the parking lot and down the hill from the hospital.

As we reached a turn, I saw headlights coming up the hill. It was a Jeep. It started to pass and then came to a screeching halt and backed up. I stopped. The Jeep's doors flew open. It was Steve and Ted. They jumped out of the Jeep.

I got out of the car and ran across the road. Steve put his arms around me. I could tell he had been crying. Then I hugged Ted; he was crying. My life experiences up until then were this threesome – Dad, Steve, and Ted. It was lopsided with only the two of them.

They came to the passenger side of the car. Mom put down the window, and they spoke briefly. Then they got back in the Jeep, made a U-turn, and followed our car. We turned onto Main Street by the Hotel Jerome. There was no longer any need to hurry on the back streets.

As we came up the main road and crossed the culvert, the house was brightly lit. The basement windows were aglow. The overhead lights were on in the back porch, the kitchen, the dining room, the hall, and two bedrooms. It was rare to have even one overhead light on in the house. Now it was as if none of them were off.

We went inside. I put the keys on the hook on the inside of the first upper cabinet in the kitchen. I looked down and noticed the sherry glasses next to the sink.

Steve and Ted came in and took up their usual spots in the kitchen. Steve hunkered in the space between the door and the refrigerator, and Ted leaned in the corner between the door and the cabinet. Mom leaned against the kitchen counter in a daze. They asked questions in hushed tones, and she responded as she and Steve chain-smoked.

I walked down the hall and looked into Mom and Dad's bedroom, hoping I was wrong. I hoped Dad would be in bed, propped up against the headboard, with his glasses on, and reading the book I gave him for Father's Day. Instead, there was an empty rumpled bed. I could see the spot on the side of the bed where Dad was sitting a few hours earlier. His boots were by the door, his jeans and shirt over the arm of an easy chair, and his Stetson on the chest of drawers. His silver rosary was on the bedside table.

I picked up the hat, climbed on top of the bed, sat cross-legged in the middle, and buried my face in Dad's hat. I rocked back and forth and soaked in the scent of my father. As I was sitting, hugging his hat with tears streaming down my face, the sky began to lighten out of the eastern window of Mom and Dad's bedroom.

I finally crawled off the bed and put the hat on the chest of drawers and turned off the bedroom lights. I turned off the light in my room. I turned off the hall light and the light in the dining room.

I asked Mom if we should call Judy, Keith, and Peggy. She said, "Yes." I called Judy. She was confused. Once she finally understood what had happened, she said they would leave as soon as she packed.

I called Keith. He was stunned but said, "I'm on my way." It took a little while to find a phone number for Peggy and Tom's friend in Rocky Ford, where they planned to spend their first night on the way to St. Louis. The woman answered the phone. I said who I was and told her I had terrible news. She handed the phone to Tom. Tom said they were turning around and headed back to Aspen.

Then, I called Cherie. She took up the task of calling local relatives and friends. Steve called his sisters. In the year and a half since Albina died, this was the fourth time we had gone through this drill.

By the time the sun came up, Max was at the house along with Billy and Cherie and the other new widow, Celia. Pearl and Albert arrived. Riley came out and still had a substantial bandage on his nose.

Throughout the day, others arrived. Judy and her family got in early in the afternoon. Peggy, Tom, and John got in a little later. Keith was the last to arrive. Dad's Denver relatives would be there by the next day. Most of Dad's out of state relatives could not come back because they had just been here for Bill's funeral. Elmer and Noreen came from Denver.

Tom Sardy called later in the day and asked Mom to pick out some clothing for Dad for the viewing. The next day, she took out the suit and shoes he wore a little over a week before at Cherie's wedding. Somehow, she delivered them to the mortuary and picked out a modest mahogany casket. I did not go there with her and Keith.

Before the funeral, there was a rosary in the mortuary. I found Dad's silver rosary in the milk-glass lamp base on the bedside table. His mother gave it to him as a gift. He said it every night. I took it to the morgue. I asked Mom if I could keep it. She said, "Daddy would like that." Since that day, I have had it with me every day, whether in my purse or under my pillow. Even when I was not an active Catholic, I kept it with me and often said a rosary. I rub the beads when I am on a bouncing flight. I still hold it often when I sleep at night.

The rosary featured an open casket like Albina's and Bill's rosaries. I looked, but not for long. It looked like Dad and not like him. I have since declined to look at anyone in an open casket.

I don't remember much about the funeral Mass, except there were several beautiful floral displays. One huge display was from Lenny Thomas and another from Art and Betty Pfister. I do not recall the pallbearers – perhaps Ed Tekoucich, Buck Parsons, and Frank Loushin. There were many town people, down valley ranchers, and Church members. We were getting much too practiced at this funeral stuff.

Unlike Bill, Dad was not buried adjacent to or in the Marolt Family plot. The family plots were gone except the ones allocated to Ted and Rose. Instead, Dad was buried in the Elks plot one section away. There was a space next to him for Mom. Several days before and after the funeral, friends and family filled the house. Most of it was a blur.

I remember being upset because some of my nieces and nephews, and cousins were playing with my toys stored in the basement closet. The toys were spread around on the floor of the main room. Before I put my toys away, I carefully cleaned, sorted, and boxed them for preservation. Someone told the kids it was okay. It wasn't okay with me.

When I saw my toys all over the floor, I broke down and sobbed as I sat on the basement stairs. It was not so much about the toys. It was about the time they represented. I was afraid if they ruined my toys, it would desecrate or destroy my memories of a time that was now gone.

Part V

Home and Away

The Aftermath

As I dealt with losing Dad, I had another issue. I was scheduled to go to the University of Colorado at Boulder within a week. I was registered for sorority rush.

There was talk among my siblings, aunts, and uncles that I ought to put off college for a year and stay with Mom. Part of me thought that was a good idea. Mom, who I expected to agree, was adamantly against the idea – she wanted me to go to school as planned. During the funeral preparation, she took time to have Keith drive us to Glenwood to take money out of her savings account for my college. It would be a while before she could access the joint bank and stock accounts. With that money, I opened a checking account at the First National Bank in Glenwood to cover my expenses for the first semester.

On the day after Labor Day, five days after Dad died, Keith, Mom, and I drove to Boulder. The afternoon the day before we left, I went to the cemetery and said good-bye to Dad. There were a few flowers on his grave that the caretaker sorted and rearranged. There was a rectangle of dirt and a metal cardholder with Dad's name. I sat on the ground and patted it as if Dad could feel my hand. I cried. I thought briefly of how many days and years Dad farmed and ranched a few feet from this spot. For years, I visited Dad once or twice on each return trip. God, I missed him. I still do.

When we got to Boulder, Mom and Keith helped me haul my belongings to my Kittredge Complex dorm room. My dorm, Buckingham Hall, was only a year old. I had a surprise when I arrived. Although my room was smaller than most rooms, it had a small balcony overlooking a stream. There were only a couple of small balcony rooms in the entire complex. The large balcony rooms were reserved for resident advisors.

Before I could look around, Mom said they had to leave and get back home. They were not going to stay and visit with Judy. Mom had business to take care of with Dad's estate, and she wanted Keith's help for as long as possible.

I have an image of looking down an enclosed stairwell to an open door and watching Mom and Keith get smaller and smaller and disappear. In reality, I went down that stairwell with them and out that door to the parking lot. I hugged them and said, "Goodbye." I watched as the maroon Wildcat disappeared out of the parking lot. I sat on those stairs. I cried. I do not think I ever felt or will ever feel so lost and alone.

I was luckier than some because Judy and her family lived in Boulder. Gary was a junior, and Billy was a University of Colorado ski coach. My roommate was pleasant. She was from Lakewood, Colorado, and the daughter of a successful physician. Because she had a boyfriend and was a Kappa Kappa Gamma legacy, I saw little of her. If she was not with her boyfriend, she was at the sorority. She liked Motown and, in particular, The Four Tops. I had never heard much of their music before and was not sure whether I liked them or not. She and I went together to K-Mart and bought matching bedspreads. The first check I ever wrote was for that purchase.

I met other people going through rush, including Angie, a girl from Winter Park, Florida, who was raised by a single mom. She was petite, with a freckled face, and smart. We ended up spending much of the first year together.

My heart was not into rush. I was never good at social functions, but it had been less than a week since Dad died, and the loss was pressing on my mind. Although I was distracted and teary, I made it for several days and got several return invitations. None were from what I thought were the top-tier sororities. In retrospect, they were from the sororities that would have been a good fit for me.

I decided to drop out. Angie did too.

School kept me busy. Gary took me out for my first legal beer on my eighteenth birthday. We went to the Sink – the spot where Dad teased that I would be spending a lot of time in college. The back room was dark and crowded with low ceilings and graffiti purposefully placed on the walls, ceilings, and pipes. Someone shouted to move our feet as they wheeled through a dolly with a keg of beer. It sure did not look like the Sunken Garden of Dad's youth. Dad was right; I would come here often with friends. Another popular spot on the Hill was Tulagi with its dance floor, strobe light, and popular bands.

I talked to Mom from time to time, but mostly we wrote letters. Long distance phone calls were costly. A three-minute call could cost $5. Because of the expense, we restricted calls to only a couple of minutes and only when critical. I now marvel that I talk long distance to my sisters for hours at a time for free.

I was homesick not only for Mom and Dad, but for my house, my bedroom, the view of Aspen Mountain, Nipper, Patty, and my extended family in Aspen. I was homesick for the ranch.

In October, Gary, Phil Hemann, one of Barney's high school friends, and I drove back for homecoming. We came home over Independence Pass and dropped Phil at his house. His family had a house and gravel operation up the Pass. Then we went through town. As Gary drove me home, the road to the house was so familiar yet so alien. That day the hills and trees were golden fall colors, with about half of the leaves gone. It was chilly. I wanted to be back when I lived there with Mom and Dad – before they left me alone.

When we got to the house, Mom was nervously waiting for me by busying herself in the kitchen. She had changed bedrooms. She said, "I was lonely at that end of the house." She moved her furniture into Peggy and Judy's room. It was next to the living room and directly across from the bathroom. She got a long phone cord and could keep the phone by her bed at night. She added nightlights in the hall and bathroom. She put Peggy and Judy's furniture in hers and Dad's room. Because of the extra window in that room, the configuration did not work as well, but it still looked nice.

She said, "I just couldn't sleep in our bedroom without Daddy. It's scary at the end of the hall when I'm the only one here. At least, I feel better now that Nipper sleeps on the porch." Celia often stayed in Keith's old room because she did not like being alone either.

My room looked like it did when I left. As I went to bed that night, I pretended none of this had happened. That it was another night like most of the 18 years of nights, but that feeling did not last.

Several months after Dad died, Mom got a job. Although Ted and Steve still stopped by to chat, the house was lonely when they left at noon. Before Dad died, Mom went to the Klip & Kurl to get her hair done every week. She continued that tradition after he was gone. After a while, they asked her if she wanted to work as a receptionist. She jumped at the chance to dress up and be out among people all day long.

Later Doris Willoughby, the Klip & Kurl's bookkeeper, taught Mom how to do its books while sitting at the reception desk. Mom had no experience with bookkeeping but caught on quickly. Doris brought Mom books from other businesses, and Mom set up an electric adding machine at the end of the kitchen table and worked on the books at home in addition to the receptionist job.

A few years later, Mom began working full-time in the office of Sabatini Sports as their bookkeeper. She loved working for Dexter and Stephanie, the new owners, and they liked her. The employees loved the trays of Mom's over-the-top Christmas cookies.

As for the homecoming event, I went to the game and saw some people. Ingrid was there, as was Barney. They were both going to school in Greeley. I saw them from time to time when they came to Boulder and visited with Gary and me. I do not remember ever visiting them in Greeley, although we met up with them in Fort Collins for a Simon & Garfunkel concert.

Surprisingly, Aspen won the homecoming game. I did not care. I was far more interested in seeing Cherie, Pearl, Ted, Steve, Celia, Max, and others. I felt grounded when I went to Sunday Mass. The church was a constant comfort. I felt the same calm going to church in Boulder at St. Thomas Aquinas, the Catholic Church near campus. Gary and I returned to Boulder late that afternoon. I ached in the pit of my stomach when we crossed the cattle guard and turned to go up the Pass.

I came home for Thanksgiving and Christmas. Thanksgiving was as always at Pearl's house. I got home before Christmas in time to decorate the tree. Mom bought a tree from the Elks, and she did her best to insert a few extra branches using Dad's tools.

Opening the Christmas decorations was difficult. When I put them away the year before, Dad was so sick. At the time, I looked forward to the next Christmas when he was well, and we gave him tools.

This was the beginning of the memory triggers – each of the holidays, each of the birthdays, each family picnic, and each of the seasonal changes with the way the light came through the window brought back a flood of memories. Every time I got in the Jeep, I remembered our trips into the field together.

Peggy, Tom, and John came from St. Louis for Christmas. We shared this Christmas with Celia's family because we were all missing our fathers. Celia, Billy, and Connie came down for present opening.

Christmas had been a Peterson event, including Ted. This year it was a combined Marolt and Peterson affair.

The problem with Christmas break in my first year was that it came before classes ended and before finals. I did not work at Aspen Sports that year. I spent most of the vacation worrying about returning for finals. The good part was I got to return home for about a week during semester break in late January.

I purposefully planned some of my classes based on the final schedule to get the most days for the break. I did that even if it meant I had to have eight a.m. classes two days a week across campus. At the time of the semester break, skiing was better, and there were no crowds. I had ten days in January for the break and skied with Gary, Cherie, Betty, and Max. For the remainder of the year, I came home with Gary every month or so for a weekend.

One Friday, I got home late in the afternoon. It was spitting snow. Mom was not home. I got the key hidden in the clothesline pole – that was the hiding place for the entire time I lived in the house – and went inside. Nipper greeted me inside the back porch. Mom made a cozy permanent bed for him in the space between the dryer and the door.

As I stood in the kitchen near the sink, I saw car lights come into the driveway and stop at the gate. The back door opened, and Mom and Cherie came in. Mom had lost weight, and her hair had gone from light brown to silvery white. She had it in a new, sophisticated hairstyle. Although neither the weight loss nor the hair color was intentional, Mom looked good. She was wearing a pair of stylish high boots with heels, a turtleneck with hearts, and a long black wool coat. She was now a beneficiary of Cherie's hand-me-downs.

During spring vacation, Mom and I took a trip to St. Louis to see Peggy, Tom, and John. We visited many attractions – Anheuser-Busch and the Spirit of St. Louis. We went to some of the locations in Mark Twain's books. I tasted Kentucky Fried Chicken for the first time and liked it. That is what we were eating the night Lyndon Johnson announced he was not going to seek reelection. By that time, the Vietnam War was raging and a concern for me and my classmates.

I returned home in May for the summer. No one "brushed the meadows" this year, although Mom tried irrigating. When irrigating in the little field, she cut oxalis daises, which was one of Dad's favorite flowers, dried the bouquets, and collected seeds. Year after year, she spread the seeds on the eastern side of the trail leading to the picnic grounds. Years later, "Mike's flowers" covered the bank. I have since learned oxalis daises are a noxious weed. Oh well. They were still pretty, and, besides, Dad liked them.

The first year after Dad died, there was a small hay crop thanks to Mom's irrigating. She hired a rancher from down valley to put up the hay. That was the last year for hay on our ranch. We still had plenty of hay for Patty and Ringo from the previous years stored in the bale shed.

I stopped riding Ringo a couple of years earlier. One day, I was invited to ride with a group of popular kids, all of whom had horses. None of them were my regular friends. They wanted to go up to a bridle path Danny Barry made along the Maroon Creek flume. It was a dirt trail with optional horse jumps made of aspen logs. One access to the trail was through our field and pasture, so they needed to invite me to join them. I could not ride Patty because she could no longer keep up with other horses. The fact Patty had health issues was the reason I wanted Ringo, and besides, I wanted to show off to the new people. I was wearing sneakers and using one of the western saddles.

Riding along the flume was miserable. Yes, it was still beautiful, but Ringo was causing problems, and I was tense. Before the T-Lazy-7 acquired him, Ringo was trained for English riding and jumping. The jumps triggered a latent desire to jump. I imagine he could think of nothing better than cantering along the trail and jumping each of the jumps. I had no experience jumping, so I fought hard to keep him under control. Fortunately, no one else was jumping.

At the end of our ride, we crossed the Castle Creek Road and started down the incline to the big field. Ringo was either startled or decided he was tired of being controlled. He straightened his neck and pulled out the reins. I did not have the strength to pull them back. Before I knew it, he was in a dead run. He jumped the lateral ditch in the middle of the big field south of the railroad bed.

I held on for dear life, and although I still had the ends of the reins in my hands, I could not do anything to stop him. My left foot slipped into the stirrup, and I was only moments from falling off or being dragged. One of the boys was able to get near Ringo, head him off, and stop him. I was terrified and embarrassed. I never rode Ringo again.

At the end of the first summer without Dad, I sold Ringo to Jim Griffin, a well-known local cowboy, for $250 in cash. He said he always admired this beautiful horse and was glad to have him. I watched from the granary steps while Jim loaded Ringo into his horse trailer. I cried a little for what might have been and felt sad for Patty. She was now alone.

At that time, it was unclear what would happen to the big field and the other property Dad sold to Lenny Thomas. Lenny died in a fire in his home earlier that summer. Later, we were relieved to learn he or his estate donated the big field to the City of Aspen as open space.

Once the City of Aspen owned the property, it no longer raised hay. It did a little irrigating, but the big field returned to a more natural state. Near the original cattle shed site north of the Midland railroad bed, they created a community garden. The big field became the landing area for hang gliders coming from Aspen Mountain. Mom continued to irrigate the little field to provide pasture for the horses.

That first summer I was home from college, Mimi Deane no longer had her day camp at the T-Lazy-7. She and Buck separated, and she moved her day camp to Snowmass. I worked for her for about a week, but it was not the same. There were no horses and no swimming pool. It was not worth the drive to Snowmass for a group babysitting job.

That summer, Gary Clifton returned but had not cleared living arrangements before his visit. A day or two after he arrived, he was gone. The previous summer, Gary stayed with Ted. Ted did not want him to stay for another summer. However, he did not want Gary's mother, Dorothy, to know it was his decision, so he asked Steve to tell Gary he was not welcome.

For the rest of the summer, I earned money helping Celia. She was a housekeeper for Edgar and Polly Stern at their Starwood Ranch house. Celia brought me large laundry bags one or two times a week, and I learned how to iron lots and lots of shirts.

I still rode Patty, although she was getting slower, and her asthma was worse. I rode across the Castle Creek Road to that favorite spot with the babbling stream hidden in the jack oaks. It would remain untouched for a little while longer. Once again, I tried to pretend nothing had changed.

A year later, the Thomas Estate donated a small piece of property at the tip of this parcel for the Prince of Peace Church (now the Aspen Chapel.) The rest of the property across Castle Creek stayed untouched until 1977 when the hospital association built a new hospital. Its parking lot was smack dab in the middle of my meadow.

The first summer after Dad died, Steve and Ted put a new roof on the barn. For a while, they continued their daily visits to the ranch even when Mom was working. They visited in the kitchen and read Mom's *Barron's* stock market magazine. They also used the barns and the granary and borrowed Dad's tools.

When called upon, Steve, Ted, and Max helped Mom. Steve came over in the middle of the night when the pilot light went out on the furnace. He eventually showed her how to light it, and after that, she handled it herself. One of those winter nights, she was running up the steps and caught her slipper, tripped, and hit her head on the concrete stairs. She was okay but had a nasty black eye. I often wondered if that lead to a detached retina, she experienced years later.

Mom began leasing space in the barns and granary in what she called her barter system. When the hay was mostly gone, she let Neil Beck store his plowing and earthmoving equipment in the bale shed in return for guaranteeing she was the first person plowed after a snowstorm. She leased two sections of the granary to a construction company for storage. She left Dad's shop section alone for a while. Over the next several years, Keith selected a few of Dad's woodworking tools and took them back to California. She leased the red barn to Terry Morse for his woodworking shop.

The year after Dad died, Mom allowed Mimi Deane and a friend to pasture their horses in the little field along with Patty. It was a relief to know Patty had company. She was getting old. We no longer rode her except to lead her with a toddler on her back. She also now had cataracts. Mimi kept her horses at the ranch for several years.

Mimi was at the ranch with her horses near the small cattle and horse shed in October of 1969 when she saw Nipper chasing a bird. She said he collapsed mid-stride and died. She buried him near the shed.

A year or two later, Mimi was engaged to a man who had a ranch down the valley. She no longer needed our pasture and offered to take Patty with her so Patty could live out the rest of her life with Mimi's horses. I had mixed feelings. Patty was part of the family, but she also needed other horses. We no longer had an unlimited hay supply, nor could Mom feed her in the winter. I knew Mimi was good with animals, and Patty would be okay.

I comforted myself by saying I would visit Patty when I came home. I never did. Mimi called Mom a couple of years later and told her Patty died of natural causes. Curiously, close to the day Patty died, Stephanie, one of Judy's daughters, said to Judy, out of the blue, "Patty is dead."

After Dad died, Steve invited us to the pasture frequently. As it turns out, he asked us more frequently than when Dad was alive. I think he was acting as a surrogate grandfather to all the grandkids. Sometimes, I squinted my eyes, and pretended Steve was Dad.

We continued having picnics at the picnic grounds with the changing group. Betty, Max, and Celia kept up Bill's tradition. A new generation of picnic-goers was forming with the additions of Max, Peggy, and Judy's children.

Peggy, Tom, and John were back for the first summer, and us girls redecorated the dining room. The upright piano and the table, chairs, and sideboard were dark. We started to refinish the table and found it was a laminate. Therefore, we "antiqued" it in white with a dark brown top with white chairs. We did the same white for the piano and made the sideboard blue. It turned out better than expected. The blue sideboard looks good to this day in the foyer of my house. Mom's china cupboard with the curved glass front remained untouched in the corner.

Peggy learned decoupage and other techniques while in St. Louis and arranged her artwork above the sideboard. Judy upholstered the chair seats and laminated the shades with matching fabric. It is not clear whether it was related to working on the furniture, but Peggy miscarried that summer.

For the next several years, I continued the school routine. I returned home frequently during the year. In my second year, finals were before Christmas, so I returned to working at Aspen Sports during Christmas and skiing after New Year's. I spent summers at home. In the summer of 1969, I went to work for Sport Obermeyer in their accounting department. The office and the warehouse were over the hill from the courthouse.

Max was now one of Sport Obermeyer's national reps. Working there was a great way to make money and get ski clothing and equipment at a discount. One day after staying up late, I came to work with a hangover. As I leaned against a file cabinet, Klaus Obermeyer teased, "A little too much dancing last night, eh?"

When I came home for visits, Mom went out of her way to make it fun. We often shared the fun with Celia and Cherie. Whenever I came home, it seemed like there was a new restaurant to try or a new shop to visit. We had breakfast at the Wienerstube after Mass, where I had a cheese Danish and a half of cantaloupe if it was in season. Mom, who was not Catholic, started going to Mass every Sunday after Dad died.

She was expanding her horizons elsewhere. She was active in the Literary Club, which was a group of local women and had been in town for decades. She had surgery to repair the hernia that developed after I was born. Her hernia had been severe, and she had to wear a restrictive girdle, which she called a "girdle belt" to prevent it from becoming strangulated. Because of the girdle, she was uncomfortable wearing pants or slacks. That kept her from participating in activities like hiking. Once she had the hernia repair, she rarely wore a dress. She and a group of her women friends became avid mushroom hunters and hiked all over the mountains. They packed their lunches just as she and Rose had done when she was a teen.

Although she knew what she was doing with the mushrooms, I never voluntarily ate any of them. The mushroom hunters went on many hikes connected with their hunting. She bought hiking boots like us "hippies." She got cross-country skiing equipment from Sabatini Sports so she could hike around the ranch in the winter. She even went cross-country skiing in Ashcroft a few times with her friends.

She started going on Jeep trips with them to ghost towns on the other side of the mountains. She and Celia went to Mexico with Don Alexander, the high school Spanish and typing teacher, and some of his students. She took gourmet-cooking classes from LeRoy Thompson. He had a catering business and made Judy's wedding cake. I still make many of the dishes Mom learned from him and taught me,

Two years after Dad died, I returned to Boulder for my junior year. Gary had graduated, and I no longer had a ride home. Catching rides with friends and the buses were inconsistent, and I did not want to fly. Therefore, at Christmas, Mom and I went to Glenwood to look for a car. We were going to get one of those new Mavericks that looked like a miniature Mustang.

For once, an honest car salesman talked us out of it. He said we would be much better off with a used Mustang. He said the Mustang was a substantial car with much better resale value. He showed us a used turquoise 1967 Mustang with a standard shift. That was not a color I would typically choose. I always thought I would have a red car. The Mustang was not a great snow car because of the short backend, but it became one of my favorite cars ever. Many years later, I sold it for twice what Mom paid for it.

It was during the summer of 1969 I met my first husband, John Paulson. He was working with Mallory at the Meadows. He was from California, extremely handsome with dark wavy hair, bright blue eyes, and a square jaw. Best of all, he was a veteran. John completed his stint with the Marines in Vietnam. All he said about the experience was to describe some Vietnamese foods he liked and that he drove a truck between Da Nang and the front.

That winter, he worked in public relations at Aspen Highlands, planning picnics and social events on the mountain. He was typical of the twenty-somethings whose goal was to hang out and do enough work to ski and eat. Sometimes he slept on couches or in his Volkswagen bus. With him in Aspen, I was even more motivated to come home.

I was relieved I would not end up dating someone only to end up with them killed in that awful war. I did not learn until 30 years later that his truck-driving job was transporting bodies of the fallen from the front so the government could send them home. I did not realize the war experience could cause hidden psychological problems that manifested later in a lack of focus and depression.

I graduated from the University of Colorado in 1971 with an education degree. That summer, John and I married. I had a 70s wedding with Simon & Garfunkel and *Jesus Christ Superstar* music. I came into the church with "Bridge over Troubled Water" and walked out with "I Don't Know How to Love Him."

Judy made a long linen dress, I wore ribbons in my long brown hair instead of a veil, and I carried a bouquet of sweet peas. Mary Hayes took the photos. She used a photo of John and me leaving St. Mary's for the *Aspen Times* cover that week. Ingrid and Mallory were my bridesmaids and wore flowered linen dresses. The flowers on their dresses looked like sweet peas. Gary, and John's friend Dave, who had hair down to his shoulders, were the ushers. Keith gave me away. We had the reception on the lawn like the ones Judy and Peggy had. John and I drove to Lake Tahoe for our honeymoon.

Now the town was changing even more quickly. The invasion of "hippie" types was at its apex. I was not sure about the direction the changes were taking. They seemed like they were swarming all over town. I went to a few of their fairs and a couple of parties and attended rugby games where John's roommate was one of the star players.

For the most part, I was neutral on most of the new people, and there were a few I disliked for their anti-establishment arrogance. They chastised Guido Meyer and Burt Bidwell for their dislike of the "hippies." While their generalization of all the young people was unfair, many did not respect property or boundaries. There were crowds of twenty-year-olds partying everywhere from downtown parks to Conundrum Hot Springs, the Punch Bowl, and the Grottos. For the most part, they did not leave the areas the way they found them.

When I was home, I went out frequently and checked to make sure people were not camping in the river bottom or at the picnic grounds. We were concerned they would leave trash and smoldering fires. When we asked them not to cross our property, they flipped us off. For the first time, we locked the granary and the barns.

I suspect it was one such person who was responsible for the loss of the red barn. Mom rented the barn to Terry Morse to use as a woodworking shop. In May 1973, the barn caught fire and burned to the ground. I was upset. It was a part of the ranch that held many memories. I remembered the light coming through the upper windows in the enclosed area we used for storage. I remembered the smell of old hay and old wood. We stored the thresher behind it. The thresher was not only a hiding place while playing hide-and-go-seek, but it also gave ready access to the roof. I liked playing in the cattle shoot to the side of the building. It was one of the buildings Dad built himself. It was always the first building he saved in a snowstorm. After the fire, the concrete floor from the storage and milking side and the concrete footers supporting the shed side remained, as did part of the fence near the granary and the water trough.

At first, we believed there might have been an electrical fire in a junction box, or Terry left oil-soaked rags that spontaneously combusted. An investigation did not substantiate an electrical issue. Terry had it rewired before he began working there to meet current standards and to provide 220-volt service for his woodworking equipment. He had Ken Broughton, who was an experienced, licensed electrician, do the rewiring.

Terry has since told me he blamed the fire on an arsonist. He believes someone set fire to the building to conceal a burglary. After the fire, Terry discovered no remnants of several expensive items he stored in his shop, including some heirloom treasures and an expensive bicycle. It may have been one of the people we frequently saw trying to set up camp on the property. One of their favorite locations was below the red barn in the lixiviation ruins. Because the ranch was no longer active, days could go by before anyone happened to go down by the barns.

Unlike other people our age having fun in Aspen, John and I returned to Boulder after our wedding. John got a job in a lumber company in Denver. We planned that John would apply to Colorado University and attend school using his G.I. Bill benefits.

I worked as a teacher's aide with Connie Marolt in a new elementary school in Boulder. I took over as a sixth-grade teacher when the male teacher, Jim Walker, died of a heart attack during a volleyball game. I was too young and inexperienced to deal with hard-to-handle kids assigned to him. I could no more control those kids than I could control Ringo. The school was going to get a more experienced teacher the next year. They said I would get a job in a lower grade or be guaranteed a slot when one opened, but I could return as a teacher's aide in the meantime. I felt humiliated. The University of Colorado rejected John because he needed better grades or higher SAT scores.

Rather than stay in Boulder with what I considered a demotion, John and I decided to move back to Aspen. If things had worked out differently, I might be living there today.

We planned to stay with Mom long enough for each of us to find work. I hoped to get a teaching job. I expected John could find something. He had mechanical skills and drove a truck in the Marines; he seemed perfect for a job at the iron mine run by Morrison-Knudson up Castle Creek.

There were no teaching-job openings that fall, and John's job hunting was sporadic. He seemed more content to do fix-it projects around the ranch, such as building an elaborate bridge to replace the broken garden bridge. He also spent his time on an invention for a ski carrier that could fit in a pocket. If I wanted, I could have worked for Sport Obermeyer or Aspen Sports. I probably could have worked as a secretary for Lennie Oates. If John had wanted to, Red Rowland would have hired him to work for the Aspen Skiing Corporation.

Even if we found interim jobs, the living situation was difficult. Because of the influx of young people, there were few places to live. There were a few "apartments," and small houses were used for large groups of people. Therefore, I thought of fixing up the barn for a small house. I figured out a way to turn it into a two-bedroom home. At that time, it would have been possible to make such a renovation without any significant planning and zoning hurdles. Mom agreed that it might work if we found a way to pay for it.

After being there for well over two months with no job prospects and no serious job hunting, Mom was losing patience. Over the years, relatives came and stayed, and she felt they were "taking advantage of her." We had no money to pay for expenses but helped with chores to attempt to alleviate her concerns. That was not enough. She was getting anxious for us to find our own place. That was unrealistic. It would take a couple of months to get completely out of the house, even doing our best.

For a while, I believe if Mom had given us a set deadline, such as three months, we would have found solutions to both housing and employment. I would eventually get a teaching job. I think Mom saw John was not motivated to look for work, and she did not see that changing regardless of how much time elapsed. Because John had a happy-go-lucky personality, no one realized he was severely depressed and suffered from what we now know as PTSD.

When it seemed like Mom did not want to continue facilitating our stay in Aspen, I looked for teaching jobs in the Durango area, but there were too many teachers and not enough jobs like the rest of the State. I did not look for jobs in Glenwood, Basalt, or Carbondale because I was still too much of an Aspen snob.

Instead, John and I decided to return to Denver, where he could attend Red Rocks Community College and reapply to the University of Colorado. We found a one-bedroom apartment in a new complex in Arvada. We had a view of Interstate 70 behind a scraggly cottonwood tree that tended to collect highway debris. The air to the west below the foothills had a yellow haze. The complex was so new it had no phone service and would not have any for months.

John was lucky and worked in an apprentice program at IBM, allowing veterans to work while they went to school. He was a typewriter installer. Wearing a conservative business suit, a white button-down shirt, a rep necktie, and wing-tipped shoes, he delivered electric typewriters to businesses. His job was to bring in the carton with the machine, set it up, and instruct the secretaries. The next year the introduction of the IBM Correcting Selectric kept him busy.

I worked as a substitute teacher in the Jefferson County schools. Each morning I got up at six and went to the payphone downstairs by the elevator to call to see if there were any work assignments. There were always assignments on snow days when the roads were treacherous. I hated the experience. The kids were difficult, and the teachers were unhelpful and unfriendly. It was hard to find the schools at a moment's notice early in the morning – no GPS at that time. I hated Arvada because it seemed lifeless and polluted. I was depressed and gained 30 pounds.

John made it through the two-year program and was accepted at the University of Colorado in Boulder. We moved back to Boulder. By that time, I lost the weight mostly by chain-smoking and eating carrots. I was so relieved to be back near the mountains.

I got a job working for Arapahoe Chemicals as an administrative assistant in the R&D department. Taking chemistry and advanced math courses in college were significant in my selection. John continued at IBM. We had a nice apartment in north Boulder. It was a townhouse with skylights, a brick fireplace, an enclosed patio, and an upstairs balcony. We returned to Aspen often, and Mom looked forward to our "short" visits.

Happy times didn't last. In early 1976, I learned John had been pretending to go to school. He pretended to study – in front of the TV. Unbeknownst to me, he flunked out a semester earlier, and for a few weeks, he pretended to work. IBM terminated his employment when they learned he was no longer going to school. I figured it out when the paychecks stopped. John had no explanation.

Our marriage did not last. We separated in the summer and divorced in the fall of 1976. He sold his belongings and hiked around South America. I continued working and had a burgeoning social life with the twenty-somethings in Boulder. We were doing in the Boulder and Gold Hill what the other twenty-somethings were doing in Aspen – a lot of partying at bars and elsewhere.

I still longed to move home and returned as much as possible. It was the bicentennial. There was a big celebration in town – lots and lots of young adults. That year we had what would be the last big picnic at the picnic grounds. We had our party and celebration with old-timers. This was one of the first Fourth of July celebrations, not at Steve's pasture.

Mom decorated the lean-to with patriotic bunting and had bouquets of red paintbrush, blue lupine, and white daisies. Every relative who was alive and lived in Aspen and who frequented the Aspen picnics were there with their kids and grandkids. Judy, Peggy, and Gary Bishop and their families were there. Loren Clifton and Rod Barnes happened to be in town. This picnic included many old-time town people – Popishes, Maddalones, Jenkinsons, Loushins, and Cassidys. Red Rowland stopped by after riding one of the horses he boarded at our ranch in the parade in town. The next generation of children looked ready to carry on the tradition.

In the spirit of earlier picnics, we had horseshoes and other games. After lunch, we had a tug-of-war over the ditch. I was on the winning team. As I fell backward when our side won, my right leg brushed past the top of the horseshoe stake, and the ragged edge sliced open my thigh. At first, Mom tried to treat it with Bactine. It soon became apparent I had sliced my leg to such an extent that the yellow fat layer in my thigh was hanging out. Lennie realized I needed to go to the emergency room and get it stitched. I spent a couple of hours in the emergency room, got some stitches, and returned to the picnic. I failed to take care of my stitches, and they spread apart, leaving a noticeable bicentennial scar on the inside of my thigh just above my knee.

Gone But Not Forgotten

Dad's estate settled ten years after he died. Throughout those years, Mom worked to clear the title to the property and increase its value. As Dad anticipated, Mom had a legal fight with Dorothy Shaw over the Midland Railway right-of-way near our house and across the river near the Gerbaz house.

While Mom would have prevailed in the adverse-possession case Dad anticipated, worried over, and prepared for, she wanted to avoid protracted litigation. She settled by transferring a lot across the river at the old sawmill site to Dorothy in exchange for the residual rights in the Midland right-of-way through our property.

Mom traded easements to the City of Aspen for water, gas, and sewer. In exchange, the City of Aspen upgraded all our utilities. With the water upgrade, we had sufficient fire hydrants or, as Mom called them, "fire plugs" to protect the house and barns. Natural gas replaced oil as a source of heat. We were finally connected to the sewer system, so our sewage no longer dripped into Castle Creek.

There was an issue over dividing the property. It was after Dad died that I first learned Keith was not Dad's son. Because Dad did not adopt Keith, he did not share in the intestate succession mandated under Colorado law. The property would go one half to Mom and Judy, Peggy, and I each got a sixth. We wanted to figure out a way for Mom to keep the property, or at least for Keith to get a share equal to his sisters' shares.

It was disappointing Dad did not prepare a will or an estate plan after his hospital stint. I imagine the denial of his mortality was a factor, but I cannot imagine Dad would want to leave us with these problems. If he had an estate plan, Dad would have made sure Mom got the property less four lots on the edge of the little field above Castle Creek.

Instead, after several years of legal wrangling and family disagreements, we settled Dad's estate. Mom ended up with a half interest in the real estate, and each kid had an eighth. Some of us wanted to quitclaim our shares to Mom, but there was no point without unanimous agreement among the children. I received $1,800 as my share of Dad's separately owned stocks and bonds. It's interesting that even though the kids each owned an eighth, none of us helped or even offered to pay our share of upkeep and taxes. We left that to Mom.

Mom resented the division. She did not say much, but if she could not have all of the ranch in her name, she wanted her own property. With the help of one of Billy's friends, she bought a new condominium in Boulder. It was near the intersection of Iris and Folsom, next to a creek. Mom had a hunch that things might not work out for her in Aspen, and she needed a place of her own. She agreed to rent the condominium to me. I got to pick out the finishes and do the decorating. By this time, I was ensconced in Boulder, working as a commercial real estate manager for Boulder's only high-rise building – The Colorado Building.

By then, Aspen had radically changed, and the political climate did not favor the old-time landowners. We learned that lesson shortly after the estate settled. My sisters, Keith, and I were together in Boulder and were looking at some maps. Instead of lots in the small field above the Castle Creek River, we decided to keep the Holden Tract. Mom would keep the house. We would make three small condominiums in the granary, and I would convert the barn into a small house. We would sell some of the small field to pay for taxes and improvements.

However, our solution was no longer possible. While we were finalizing Dad's estate, the county changed the rules. The newly elected Pitkin County Commissioners – several young attorneys who recently moved to town –worried the area was growing too fast, and the beautiful open spaces, which happened to be private ranches and farms, might be lost to development. The commissioners were concerned the owners might allow someone to build an unsightly tract-type home or allow a child to live in a doublewide trailer on their property. They argued allowing ranchers and farmers to manage their own property would be like a gateway "drug" leading to tacky developments, strip malls, and burger joints from Basalt to Aspen. The commissioners looked at old-timer landowners as ignorant, tasteless hicks.

Instead of working with farmers and ranchers to restrict development through tax incentives or conservation easements, the new commissioners restricted growth by making it impossible for ranchers and farmers to split off parts of their property for their children or to pay for ever-increasing property taxes.

Therefore, they enacted rules making it impossible for people like us to keep our property. The rising real estate values meant increased real estate taxes. People living on a fixed income and a small stock portfolio could not keep up. The only solution was to sell all of their property.

The new rules allowed the sale of 40 acres "lots" without approval. Coincidentally, our remaining property was slightly under 40 acres. We could no longer have building lots on our own property. Lennie Oates told us to do what Dad anticipated would now require subdivision approval, which would be difficult and expensive.

We were disappointed that we could not immediately proceed with our plan, but we put it out of our minds. We still had the ranch. Mom was keeping it up with the taxes and upkeep for the time being. It was a wonderful place to visit. I always hoped to move back home someday.

The summer Dad's estate settled, Ted Bundy escaped from the Pitkin County Jail and was on the run for several days. The night before they caught him, Celia was alone in her house off the Castle Creek Road below the water tanks. She was sitting on the stairs of her split-level house talking on the phone when she heard someone jiggle the back door. A few minutes later, someone tried to turn the front door handle. In a loud voice, she told the person on the other end of the phone, "Call the sheriff. Someone is trying to break into my house."

The sheriff arrived a few minutes later. Knowing that whoever was at her house would probably head through the little field, another sheriff's car came by our house and into the field. The sheriff's officers did not mention who they thought it might be but told Celia she should stay with Mom. They should have told Mom and Celia to stay in town. Whoever tried to get into Celia's house was probably hiding near our house.

The next day, Ted Bundy stole a car near Snowbunny, across Highway 82 and about a half a mile from our house. No one confirmed that Bundy tried to break into Celia's house, but it seems likely because he had been staying in a cabin further up Castle Creek. It was lucky Celia locked her doors and windows that night. The incident scared her, and she started thinking of leaving her house. Rising property values made selling her property increasingly attractive.

In 1978, both Celia and Riley purchased new tract homes in El Jebel. Riley sold his house in Aspen. Once Riley sold his house – Grandmother's original, unaltered Victorian – was immediately razed and replaced with a Victorian-looking duplex. So much for historic preservation. Celia rented her house for a while. She sold it in the early 80s to an investment group. It, too, was razed. Eventually, the City of Aspen purchased the lot and built 20 housing units where her home sat.

The same year Riley and Celia moved, Max or Celia found Ted dead at the bottom of his basement stairs. He had been sweeping the floor when he had a heart attack. Ted was 64, and, like Dad and Bill, he suffered from heart issues.

I saw Ted two weeks earlier when I came home from Boulder to take photos with a new camera. I spent most of Sunday morning after Mass talking to him in the kitchen. As always, he was interested in what I was doing, and we discussed current events. Unlike Dad, Ted was slightly built and did not look ill. At first, when I heard Ted died, I was in shock. It did not register. As the realization dawned, I was distraught and awash with sorrow.

I regretted having taken Ted for granted. I expected him to be a part of my life forever. Ted was at our house daily. On weekday mornings, he was there with Steve and often came by himself on weekends, especially after Mass. He came to our house to spend time with us when we came home to visit and was there to say good-bye when we left. He had tears in his eyes when he gave us one of his stiff, awkward hugs. He was at every picnic and every Marolt event with a case of beer. He was the first to volunteer to take friends and relatives on Jeep tours of the mountains. He brought an envelope with new bills for our birthdays and Christmas and did the same for his great-nieces and nephews.

Ted had no will, so his living heirs split the estate. He had two undesignated life insurance policies valued at less than $5,000. Steve, who handled the estate, asked Ted's three surviving sisters if they would agree to give the proceeds of the policies to Mom because she had done so much for Ted over the years. Steve believed Ted intended the policies for Mom or Dad because he bought the policies when he lived in our house. The sisters refused Steve's request. That day, Elsie, Dorothy, and Rose were sitting in Mom's living room eating food she prepared.

So, Steve gave Mom a rocking chair Ted recently purchased. Referring to his sisters, Steve told Mom, "Don't tell them I gave it to you. It's none of their goddam business."

Although she was deeply hurt, Mom never said anything to the sisters. After that, her attitude toward them changed – even with

Rose, who had been one of her best friends. In later years, there were a couple frosty encounters between Mom and the sisters' daughters. They may not have understood the reason for the chill or the depth of her anger. Her anger was not about the money; it was about not being acknowledged for the important part she played in their brother's life.

As was apparent by the sisters' attitude about the life insurance policies, there was no chance the sisters would agree to keep Ted's house for the family. Because keeping the house was not possible, Steve sold it. With the sale of the house and Ted's stock portfolio, each share of Ted's estate was about $50,000. Accordingly, my three siblings and I split our share. I got a little over $12,000. This time, no one questioned whether Keith was an heir, and he received a full share.

Shortly after Ted's house sold, Mom took a walk in the field toward the picnic grounds to admire Mike's daisies that were now thriving along the bank. She looked across the river and froze. Ted's house was gone. She said that, upon seeing the gaping wound from Ted's razed house, grief overwhelmed her. She sat on a rock with a sick feeling in the pit of her stomach, trying to catch her breath. Mom and Ted were classmates. He lived in our house for 15 years, and she saw him almost every day for most of her adult life. Ted was like a brother.

When she came home, she wrote to me and lamented, "Everything that belonged to Ted and everything he worked for all these years is gone in one swipe of a bulldozer." She was not completely right. Mom had his rocking chair. I had a small octagonal wooden plant stand Ted made in his high school woodworking class and a wooden lamp made by either him or Dad. Besides those small items, we have memories, a few photographs, and what I can preserve of his life in this memoir.

About the time Ted's house was razed, Mom got an offer for the ranch. It was for $1,000,000, contingent on the purchaser getting development approval. The price seemed low. Lennie agreed and suggested we list it with a reputable broker. We talked to a few realtors, but they did not have wealthy gentleman farmers interested in the property. Potential buyers knew development was the end game, and the value reflected the need for development approvals.

We were not interested in selling outright. We wanted to keep the house and some of the remaining property. Cary Clark, a financial planner, who presented the offer to Mom, arranged a family meeting with an estate-planning attorney, Jim Buchanan, in Denver to advise us on how best to pursue our goals with the ranch.

Jim Buchanan set up a meeting with Cary Clark and a real estate development attorney, Jim Mulligan. After a few meetings with Jim Buchanan, Jim Mulligan, and Cary Clark, we decided to develop the property ourselves. They said, "Why wait for on a contingency for someone else to develop your property when you could do that yourselves, keep the profits, and, best yet each keep a piece of property in Aspen." It sounded good, and although the advisors were young and inexperienced, they talked a good game. Those meetings set into motion a series of disastrous events leading to the loss of the ranch.

We borrowed money against the ranch when interest rates were the highest they had ever sbeen. Interest rates were at 18%, and our rate was two points higher. The development-approval process was lengthy. We hired financial advisors, attorneys, developers, planners, and architects. They billed plenty and paid themselves generously from the line of credit. There was high anxiety for several years of approvals, delays, and setbacks. The bills were horrendous, but then, we were each looking to make millions and keep a piece of property in Aspen.

We had to be annexed to the City of Aspen to avoid the county zoning. When we submitted our final annexation papers, the final development was a disappointment. Over several years of prodding, the advisors finally convinced us we needed to tear down the house, the granary, and the barn to optimize the development's value. It was clear any developer hoping to make a buck would have done the same thing. Thus, the final plan included 25 free-market units on the old Holden Tract and 75 employee-housing units at the picnic grounds. The employee-housing units were the price the City extracted for annexation and development approval.

The carrot the advisors dangled for us to agree to tear down the house, the granary, and the barns was we would each get one of the new condominiums. The three-story stone condominiums were stylish at the time but may not have aged well. We would also each receive several million dollars. Shortly after the approvals went through the City of Aspen, we had a celebration at the house with the team of advisors.

Within days, some recent transplants formed the Aspen Growth Management Group and sued to stop the development. Jim Mulligan told us the way to stop the injunction was to start building some of the development's infrastructure. We hired the developer Jim Mulligan recommended to divert the Holden Ditch into large pipes as part of the proposed employee-housing site, destroying the picnic grounds,

As I would soon learn in law school, spending money does not create the irreparable harm necessary to prevent an injunction. Accordingly, it did nothing to stop the growth management injunction. Instead, the developer filed a mechanics lien for over $300,000 for the infrastructure folly.

In the meantime, we hired yet another attorney to represent us in the Growth Management lawsuit. As the growth management lawsuit lingered, we could not afford the delay with interest eating away thousands of dollars daily. Interest rates exceeded 20 percent, nearing the point where we would lose the property to the lender. It was desperate.

We fired Jim Mulligan and Cary Clark and asked Bob Joyce, another attorney who briefly worked on the project, to take over. He negotiated a sale/donation to the City of Aspen rather than wait out the growth management lawsuit because it was not looking good. Jim Mulligan failed to file a proper notice for a crucial hearing, thus possibly voiding the annexation.

We sold the little field to the City of Aspen for $2,100,000 and donated what remained of the Holden Tract to the City at a value of $1,900,000. The money we received went mostly to pay off the bank loan, attorney fees in the growth management suit, and the developer's mechanics lien. We netted $400,000. Out of that money, we still had to pay fees to defend collection actions brought by Jim Mulligan and Cary Clark in Denver.

We filed a countersuit, which we lost. The case was complicated, and the jury had no sympathy for women and a man living in California trying to develop their own property. Besides, they, too, were charmed by Jim Mulligan and Cary Clark. I eventually received about $25,000 for my share of the ranch.

Bob Joyce asked the City of Aspen to allow Mom to keep a life estate in her house. The City refused. It claimed it needed it for employee housing, but they agreed to allow her to stay in the house for three years. The city leased the granary and the barn to the Aspen

Historical Society. The city built the employee housing over the picnic grounds on our proposed development footprint.

In 1990, the Lixiviation complex ruins, including the granary and the barn, were listed on the National Registry of Historic Places. The registry did not include the house because of the changes made to convert it from an assay office to a home. Those changes were made in the 1930s.

Before the development project went south, I married Mark Buchanan, Jim's brother. I began law school at the University of Denver a week later. We lived in Denver. By the time the ranch sold in 1983, I was working as a clerk in a litigation law firm in Cherry Creek. On the day I went to Bob Joyce's office to sign the deeds to the City of Aspen. I sat in my office's parking structure, in my burnt orange suit, and cried. I never expected something like this would happen. I always thought I could go home forever.

I finished law school at the end of that year. I continued to go to Aspen over the next several years to see Mom and the remaining relatives and friends. It was hard, knowing our time there was limited, and it was no longer our property. The spirit of the house was gone. Mom had no interest in the house and did the minimum lawn and house maintenance. She stopped planting flowers and painting the fence.

Mom was to vacate the house by early August 1986. On January 3, 1986, Celia died in a car accident. She was coming to Aspen from El Jebel in the morning and had a late Christmas present for Mom in her car. She lost control of her car on ice and plunged into the Roaring Fork River.

I came to Aspen for her funeral. This time Max and Betty were in charge of the family gathering at their house, and they had a public reception at the Elks Club. Celia had just sent me a note saying how excited she was that I was expecting a baby. Like Ted, I assumed she would be around for a long time. I would miss her.

I returned one final time to the house at the end of March. Mom asked me to go through my belongings and decide what, if any, furniture I wanted to be delivered to me in Denver. Mom decided what she would take to her condominium in Boulder. She could not figure out a way to keep the hutch in the kitchen Dad built for her.

I wanted the cabinet Dad built for my room, the dining room set, the headboard from Peggy and Judy's bedroom, and my dresser. I also said I would take the stove and side-by-side refrigerator Mom recently purchased. I remodeled my little kitchen in Denver around them.

Regrettably, I forgot to mention I wanted the Blue Goose. Mom sold the Jeep a couple of weeks later. I understand it ended up in Florida, hauling boats in and out of the water. They took off Dad's hardtop.

I got rid of all but a few of my toys and special mementos. The toys I carefully packed and stored in the basement had succumbed to visits from children over the 20 years since Dad died. They were now damaged and had missing parts. I had stopped asking the parents not to let the little kids play with my stuff. I was tired of being told I was selfish.

Although she did not need them, Mom took the blinds from the living room. They were custom made two-inch wooden blinds stained to match the reddish-brown woodwork. She took them to Boulder and gave them to Goodwill. She took the blinds and the appliances as an "f-you" to the city for refusing to let her stay in her home.

After 72 years in Aspen, she was leaving. She would miss seeing Pearl every day. She would miss Steve and Polly and Cherie and Max and their families. Although she saw them less, now that they moved out of Grandma's house, she would miss seeing Riley and Stella. She would miss her friends at the literary club and her surviving mushroom hunting and hiking buddies.

On my last trip, the snow had recently melted near the house. I walked through the yard to the granary bridge and looked over at the granary and the barn. They looked sad with stacks of unrecognizable items at or near them. The Aspen Historical Society was renovating the granary. Someone filled the bale shed with plows and trucks. The red barn remains were a scar on the ground punctuated by a section of dilapidated fence. I did not go down to any of the buildings.

As I walked across the lawn, it was still yellowish-brown and trampled from the snow. Some flies or gnats were buzzing near the surface. If we were still engaged in the house, someone would have raked the yard to get it ready to add fertilizer. The ditch was empty. There were no leaves on the trees.

Before I returned to Denver, I took a long look at each of the rooms. I sat on my bed and looked out of my window toward Aspen

Mountain. I did not take any pictures. At the time, I felt like I would be photographing a corpse. Although I have strong, specific memories of every room and nook and cranny in the house, I now regret not doing so for later reference.

Before I left Aspen that last time, I went to see Steve and Polly. I expected to see Pearl and Albert because they came to Denver to visit Gary and his family and Elmer and Noreen. Cherie also visited Denver and Boulder frequently. I was not sure I would see Steve and Polly again because they no longer traveled. They both looked good. Steve was getting older and walked slower and stooped more. He was 79 and mostly blind because cataracts clouded his good eye. Polly, who was in her mid-80s, looked pretty much the same. She always seemed to have wrinkles and gray hair.

Steve was sad. I know he did not want Mom to leave and was mad that the ranch was gone. He probably blamed Mom for the loss, although he did not have any ideas on how she could have saved it in the face of the unrelenting changes and escalating taxes.

The next day, a day I never contemplated, happened. I drove away from the house. I refused to look back. A couple of months later, in August 1986, Mom did the same. She said, "When I closed the door, I got in the car, drove out of the driveway, and I did not look back." It took me almost twenty-five years to look back.

Epilog

Epilogue

After the sale of our property, Mom resigned to move on. She started the process of disengagement over the next three years. After I drove away from the house on March 26, 1986, and Mom left in August, I returned to Aspen a few times for funerals and a class reunion. For some of the funerals, Mom and I stayed with Pearl. Being in Aspen was not the same. It was torture. I refused to look toward the ranch on those trips. I shielded it from my view.

I came back once for a dedication event at the granary sometime in 1992. The children, William and Adrienne, and I walked on the bike path into the little field past the culvert near one of my daydreaming spots and where I thought I would build my forever home. I refused to look at the house. I was sad my children would never come there to visit Grandma and Grandpa. I regretted I could not take them to or let them discover all the special spots on the ranch. I regretted they could not walk on the fence. I guess this book is a substitute.

Mom moved into her new condominium in Boulder and enjoyed being closer to Elmer, Noreen, Peggy, who was now living in Boulder, and me. Ironically, by that time, Judy was divorced and was in law school in California. Later that fall, Riley died from cancer. After he died, Stella, who had lupus, moved back east to be with her brother and died a few years later.

Mom liked Boulder and her condominium. I designed a remodel of the unfinished garden level basement to accommodate much of the Aspen house's living room furniture and give her a laundry room and a full bathroom. Peggy did the decorating and selected the finishes. They were classy.

Mom made friends with the people she met in the neighborhood. She was always good at making friends and staying active. She walked in the parks and greenbelts in the summer and the Crossroad Mall in the winter. I lived in Denver and visited often and brought her new grandson, William, with me. From time to time, Mom drove to Denver and stayed with us for a couple of days.

The Aspen changes continued. Steve and Polly sold their pasture in 1987, the year after Mom left. Although the new owners built a house, they did not develop the property, and the lake is still there. It appears on Google Earth as the Marolt Reservoir. I am not sure if the cabin still exists. One of my cousins thinks it does, but I cannot find it on Google Earth.

Steve died of natural causes in the hospital in 1990. His sisters Elsie and Dorothy predeceased him. The last Marolt of Dad's generation, Rose, died in 1994. Polly, who adamantly refused to be shuffled off to a nursing home, died in her home in 1998. After Steve and Polly's estate sold their house, the house became the "foyer" of a mega-mansion.

Albert died in 1999 in his home of a heart attack. A few years later, Pearl moved to the assisted living facility near the hospital on what had been part of the ranch near my favorite meadow. Pearl could see our house and the granary from her balcony.

Later, the original old ranch house and barns, where Dad and his family moved in 1917, were plowed down for an even newer and bigger hospital and parking lot – so much for the town's feigned interest in historic preservation. The house and one of the barns were some of the oldest buildings in Aspen – period.

In the meantime, Gary fought the city against its attempt to preserve Pearl's house as a historical Victorian and reduce its value. Unlike Grandmother's original Victorian house, which was razed after Riley sold it, Pearl's house had none of the original Victorian features. Gary was finally able to get a waiver to sell the house. Soon after it sold, Pearl moved to a nursing home in Salida, Colorado, to be near Gary, who had moved there from Denver. In the meantime, Barney settled in Kentucky near where he served in the Army.

In 1995 after Mark and I divorced, my children and I left Colorado so I could open a branch office for my law firm in Newport Beach, California. It took me all of one phone call to convince Mom to join me in California. She sold her Boulder condominium and moved into a two-bedroom apartment.

The apartment was across the open space and a nature park from my subdivision. Her patio overlooked an Olympic sized swimming pool. To the east, she could see the snow-covered mountains near Big Bear through palm trees. To the west, she saw palm trees above the ocean. Mom enjoyed coming to my house and sitting under the Canary Island pines on my side patio and reading. She liked doing dishes in my kitchen. The kitchen window overlooked a small swimming pool, a group of palm trees, and tropical flowers. It reminded her of being home and doing dishes with a view.

Mom drove for a while, but she mostly walked to her hairdresser and the grocery store across from her apartment complex. Although my children, William and Adrienne, did not visit Grandma's house in Aspen, they got to visit Grandma's house in Newport Beach. They rode their bikes across the green belt and the nature park and climbed up an ivy-covered hill to her apartment.

Adrienne loved the writing desk Mom had in her living room in Aspen. Like me, she hid things in the "secret compartments." Except for Swedish cookies, Mom rarely made homemade Christmas cookies. Instead, she kept a supply of Pepperidge Farm cookies in the cupboard.

Pearl, Albert, Elmer, and Noreen came to visit, as did Cherie. Mom was proud of where she lived. She enjoyed taking them sightseeing, to Los Brisas, her favorite restaurant overlooking the Pacific Ocean in Laguna Beach, and brunch on a Hornblower Cruise ship. Albert and Elmer were impressed with the meatloaf and mashed potatoes at the Yankee Tavern.

In 2002, Mom fell and broke her hip. After a while in the hospital and rehabilitation, she moved to an assisted living facility in Irvine, a few miles from my house. My sisters and I divided most of her remaining Aspen furniture. As of this writing, all the furniture she brought from Aspen is still in the family. We could refurnish our Aspen house as it was when Mom left.

Mom had another fall in May 2004 in her apartment. A few days after she was admitted to the hospital, she died from sepsis. Until that hospitalization, her mind was sound. She read a book a week and did several word puzzles daily. The last time I saw her conscious and awake, she sat up in her hospital bed, reading a new paperback novel with her magnifying glass. I thought she was doing so well I left to buy a washer and dryer. When I returned, she no longer knew me.

On the night before she died, and before she completely stopped communicating, Mom talked to me as if I was her friend Rachel who lived across Main Street when she was a little girl. Then she talked about Alexander Hamilton. I have a picture of Mom from when she was in high school in a costume playing him in a school play.

When Mom died, I saw her spirit leave when she was on the phone with Cherie. Cherie told her it was time to be with her guardian angel. Mom vehemently believed in guardian angels. A half a minute later, Mom's body went still, the pink faded from her face, she became waxy, and I knew she was gone. I left her room and went to a small elevator lobby and sat. I sensed her spirit swirl around me and rise to the ceiling, hover for a minute, and depart. It was similar to the spirit I saw in my bedroom when I was a child.

A couple of months after Mom died, we had a service and Mass at the St. Mary's Catholic Church in Aspen, and we buried her ashes with Dad at Red Butte Cemetery. Mom was not a Catholic, and we did not bother to enlighten the new priest of that fact.

We had a reception at the granary. I walked up to the house with William and Adrienne, some of my nieces and nephews, and my sisters. That was the first time I went near the house since I left in 1986. No one was home, so we peered through the windows and were pleased to see the kitchen had not changed.

The summer before Mom died, Max died suddenly from a massive heart attack while skiing in Argentina. In 2010, Keith died in Reno, Nevada, of heart failure. Until Mom died, he was in daily contact with her. I spoke to him frequently, and we talked a few days before he died. Because of health issues, he did not travel much in later years. His ashes are on the ranch in a special place. His name is on the family headstone, where I want mine to be.

Pearl died of natural causes in 2011. Elmer followed in 2015 and his wife, Noreen, in 2017. They were the last of Mom and Dad's generation. Jimmy died in 2022

Cherie and her family, Jimmy until his recent death, and Max's family still live in Aspen. It is ironic. They were land poor when I was growing up, and yet they were the ones who were able to stay. Property taxes strangled us – too much of a good thing, I guess.

The process that ended with us losing the ranch was extremely painful. What happened is why I denied ever living in Aspen or caring about it. It was something for a long time I purposefully forgot.

Several years ago, I detailed what happened in the development process as part of a memoir related to my legal career. The Aspen project occurred during law school and my first legal job. The development project led to me becoming an attorney hoping I could stop what was happening. The memoir was primarily about my law practice, two large cases I handled in California and Texas, and my law firm's dissolution.

The details of the Aspen project are unnecessary here. Suffice it to say, we were not prepared nor equipped to become real estate developers. We were advised to borrow money against the ranch when interest rates were the highest in history. We had family disagreements. We got terrible legal advice and had a conflicted attorney.

After decades of angst, I have come to terms with the fact that there was probably no way we were ever going to be able to stay in our home in Aspen after the county changed the zoning. We were going to have to sell it at some point to keep up with taxes. A buyer would probably have developed it into something as trendy or trendier than what we eventually planned. The house, the granary, and the barn would be gone.

In retrospect, I am grateful the buildings are still there, and my family played a huge part in keeping it that way. The granary and the barn will stay intact because of their historic designation. I hope the City of Aspen leaves the house alone. It did not qualify for the historic designation because of the remodeling by my uncles and Dad. It should still be eligible as historical for the bygone era of the 1950s.

I am glad the Marolt Ditch and the Marolt Open Space surround our home, granary, and barn. I am glad the granary bridge still exists, behind Mom's lilac bushes, in the shadow of Aspen Mountain.

...

One final note – why the title? It took me almost twenty-five years for a postcard to open the floodgates of memories of my life on the ranch and of Aspen. However, a small crack opened a few years earlier.

I attended a seminar on a ranch in Northern California near the wine country in the late nineties. It was one of those team-building retreats. Besides seminars and meditations, much of the program featured ropes courses and physical challenges, including the high ropes, the high "V," telephone pole to trapeze jumping, and leaning face forward over the edge of a cliff. One of the days was a low-ropes course. There were rope webs to climb, logs strung on chains to cross, and platforms from which to plummet backward into the arms of strangers,

Our group moved to a station with a cable stretched about three feet above the ground between two live oaks. Two ropes dangled from a cable above. The object was for one person to start at one tree and the other person at the other tree, walk on the cable, pass each other like Robin Hood and Little John and get to the other tree as fast as possible without falling.

My partner and I watched the other teams. We did not discuss how we would get to the cross over point. Like everyone before us, we assumed it would be by standing sideways, sliding feet along the cable holding tightly to the dangling overhead ropes. We worked out a plan for the cross over. Since my partner was taller, once we met, she would step around me, we would exchange ropes and go to the other end.

The male team in front using the sidestep technique almost made it, but one of the men lost his balance at the end. Now the leader asked me, "Do you choose to do this event?"

"Yes, I choose to do this event."

Someone gave me a boost up, and I stood with my feet perpendicular to the cable and one arm around the tree trunk. Someone handed me the overhead rope. It felt awkward rocking back and forth, so I shifted. Now I faced forward with my back leaning against the tree. I stood with my feet like the third ballet position, one foot in front of the other, and took the rope and held it horizontally between my outstretched hands at chest height. It felt natural.

Someone said, "Begin?"

I walked face forward, one foot in front of the other, to the middle, and waited for my partner. She made it by employing the sidestep technique. Our cross over was a little awkward, but it worked. I took her rope, stretched it out, and I walked effortlessly to the other tree in record time. At the end, I jumped off.

"Where did you learn that?" the instructor asked.

"What?"

"The way you were walking. You looked like a professional tightrope walker."

I thought for a second. A warm feeling washed over me. I smiled, "It was from walking on fences."

A few days later, after I returned to Southern California, a manila envelope arrived. It was from Betty, Max's wife. "Just ran across this the other day. Thought you might get a kick out of it."

Inside was the cover photograph of me walking on the fence at Steve's cabin.

Acknowledgments and Sources

Editing:

Mark Buchanan

Genealogy:

Judy Marolt's extensive genealogy on Ancestry.com. It was invaluable for research and in writing the family history.

Continuing Contributors:

The following were a constant source of information and reviewed and commented on and edited sections of this work while in progress:

    Judy Marolt
    Peggy Marolt
    Cherie Gerbaz Oates
    Gary Bishop
    Barney Bishop
    Bud Marolt
    Ingrid Elisha Stuebner

Interviews and Questions:

The following answered questions along the way:

> Elmer Peterson
> Noreen Peterson
> Bill Marolt
> Betty Marolt
> Marlis Marolt
> Roger Marolt
> Mike Marolt
> Steve Marolt
> Nejc Marolt
> Lennie Oates
> Karen Tesitor
> Michele Tesitor
> Rodney Barnes
> Gary Clifton
> Mallory Alexander Ronaldson
> Jim Markalunas
> Terry Morse
> Tim Willoughby
> Laura Bishop
> Debbie Overeynder
> Phil Overeynder
> Aspen Historical Society

Oral Histories

> Steve and Polly Marolt – recorded by Ellen Feinsinger (4 hours)
> Opal Marolt - AHS
> Peggy Marolt - AHS
> Keith Marolt - AHS
> Polly Marolt - AHS

Other Family Sources

Vicki Marolt Diaries –1964 to 1984
Vicki Marolt Journals
Vicki Marolt Mementoes and Scrapbooks
Family Travel Journals

Letters

Among Marolt sisters – Mary, Pauline, Elsie, and Dorothy
From Frank Marolt, Jr. while serving in the army in WWI
To Frank Marolt, Sr. regarding business
From Francis Marolt to daughters
From Elmer Peterson to Opal Marolt during WWII
Among Opal Marolt's family members
From Ted Marolt
From Celia Marolt
From Opal Marolt

Financial Ledgers

Frank Marolt, Sr. business ledgers
Alma Peterson home financial ledgers

Photos and Photo Albums

Opal and Mike Marolt Family Photo Albums and loose photos.
Vicki Marolt Photo Album – 1967 - 1971
Alma Peterson Family Album
Polly Marolt Loose Photos
Judy Marolt Family Photo Album
Elsie Marolt Rinker Photo Albums – Provided by Gary Clifton

Charles Clifton Photographs

> 1946 Ashcroft Picnic
> 1946 Marolt Ranch Operations
> 1957-1958 Vacation Photos – Aspen
> Loose Photos

Vicki Marolt Wedding Album – Mary Hayes photographer
Judy Marolt Wedding Album – Franz Berko photographer
Peggy Marolt Wedding Photos – Franz Berko photographer
Tim Willoughby –Frank Willoughby photographer

Purchased Photos

> Aerial Ranch Photos
> Vintage Post Cards including RC Bishop postcards
> Aspen Historical Society
> Denver Public Library

Other Sources

> The History of the Holden-Marolt Site, Lysa Wegman–French, Aspen Historical Society, October 1990
>
> Aspen Historical Society Photos and Archives
> Aspen High School Yearbooks
> Colorado Historical Newspapers
> Maps including original Aspen Ranch Map
> Deeds
> Aspen Before 1960 – Facebook
> Friends of Aspen 1960s to 1970 – Facebook

Memoir Writing Courses:

> University of California at Irvine
> Writing Salon – San Francisco

www.ingramcontent.com/pod-product-compliance
Lightning Source LLC
Chambersburg PA
CBHW060830190426
43197CB00039B/2535